TO-DAY AND YESTERDAY:
THE HISTORY OF MANKIND

General Editors

J. M. PARRISH, M.A. (Oxon.)

JOHN R. CROSSLAND, F.R.G.S.

TO-DAY AND YESTERDAY: THE HISTORY OF MANKIND

ANCIENT AND MEDIEVAL HISTORY
MODERN, CONTEMPORARY AND SOCIAL HISTORY

Advisory Editor
PROF. ERNEST BARKER, Litt. D., D. Litt.
LL.D., *Professor of Political Science*
University of Cambridge

Edited by
R. J. WOODWARD, M.A. (Oxon.)
Headmaster of Tetbury Grammar School, Gloucester

ODHAMS PRESS LIMITED
LONG ACRE, LONDON, W.C.2

INTRODUCTION

DAY by day, hour by hour, and minute by minute, history is being made. The happenings of the moment are continuously shifting—falling back into what we call the past, shaping what we call the future. For convenience' sake we say that history is a record of man's past, the tracing back of the path that he has travelled. The description is good so long as we remember that this path leads through the present into the future, that it is the same path ; as long as we remember that history is not a collection of dry facts : dates, names, conquests, dynasties that have had their day and ceased to count. This sort of history can interest only the antiquarian and the kind of school examiner who is, fortunately, becoming rarer. We do not now regard history as something to be studied in spare moments with idle curiosity and mild amazement at the quaint customs and outmoded manners of our ancestors. For the past lives in the present. The political scene of the present moment branches out from the stem that is rooted deep in the centuries.

For this reason we cannot rightly estimate what is happening now, the events which we personally, in however small a measure, are helping to bring about, without understanding the relation which these events bear to others that have gone before—gone before, but are not therefore dead. To-day a dictator sets out on a colonial conquest. Few would be so ignorant as to suppose the idea entered his head in an idle moment, or that he mobilised his people to satisfy an idle whim, yet how many persons could connect such a momentous move in world history with even six of the major events, during only the last fifty years, of which it is the direct outcome ?

It is the same with another aspect of life—of greater importance than wars and conquests—the social betterment of mankind : the reforms in living conditions, the fight for political liberty, amelioration of working conditions. These struggles in the past, with their slow gains and sudden setbacks, were the same struggles that occupy the political arena to-day ; remote as the origins are, they supply the key to the present situation, and teach their lesson to modern man. There is no theory of reform put forward to-day that has not been striven for in the past ; and if no cause of wide-reaching reform ever succeeded as splendidly as its champion hoped, if Alexander's or King Asoka's dreams of a world state failed through the unpreparedness of the people for their acceptance, still they mark a forward step, enter into the present, and form an essential part of modern aspirations.

HOW THIS BOOK HAS BEEN PLANNED

This history of the world has been planned to provide the non-specialist with that historical perspective that alone can make the events of the day understandable ; that alone can make any judgment upon them valuable, any action in connection with them justified. It will be noticed that the narrative progressively broadens as it proceeds from remote times to the present day. The editors have mapped the part dealing with post-war events to a larger scale, since it is to the events immediately preceding the present that we must turn for a detailed interpretation of the news. How necessary this arrangement is may be seen by calculating the length this book would have assumed had it all been written in the same detail as its second half, dealing with the history of the last twenty years. Then the part from the birth of Christ to the present day would have been as long as two thousand novels, and this would only have been a small chapter in the whole history of mankind.

The first part ends with the Armistice, and the remainder of the book is about what has happened in the world since then. This second half is divided into sections dealing with the different fields of activities : economics, politics, social reform, the fight for peace at Geneva. It affords an immediate background to the present-day scene.

The first part must necessarily be read as a consecutive narrative, and the post-war history should then be tackled as a sequel. The second half may also be used for reference purposes, since, though the sections are in a sense/interdependent, they have each their allotted sphere, and will be found useful to trace the origins of day-to-day events.

CONTENTS

IN THE MORNING OF THE TIMES

*by L. CORNEY, B.A.(Oxon), formerly Scholar of
St. John's College, Oxford*

MODERN science tells us that the earth is but a tiny fragment of the sun, broken off from it countless ages ago,
and that the sun itself is but one of innumerable stars
scattered here and there through space. When we consider
that the volume of the sun is over a million times greater
than that of the earth, we realise how tiny is the stage on
which human history has been worked out.

At first the earth was nothing but molten matter, and
countless ages passed before its surface cooled, and the first
rocks could form. These rocks, produced by the heat of
the inside of the earth, are called igneous (fiery) rocks. Then
the steam-clouds condensed into rain, and the water began
to deposit the various kinds of matter it carried with it. The
deposits, in time, formed another group of rocks, which
are called stratified, because they follow one on top of another
in regular layers or strata. The arrangement of these layers
has, however, been complicated bewilderingly by upheavals
and sinkings of the earth's crust. For the interior, eight
thousand miles deep, on which this crust rests, is still cooling
and contracting, hence volcanoes and earthquakes.

All the igneous rocks and half of the stratified rocks preserve no trace of life and are therefore called Azoic (lifeless).
Then the greatest of miracles happens, and life appears where
there was none before. Preserved in the rocks are found
shells and worm-tracks of creatures that arose in shallow tidal
waters. These were followed by a higher organism, the
fishes, whose backbones (vertebræ) gave them a stronger
structure than their invertebrate predecessors.

The next step was the invasion of the land by plants and
animals, which, by developing new organs to deal with the
new conditions of breathing, could live partly on sea and
partly on the land. A continuous succession then leads us
to the Mesozoic (middle life) age, with its terrifying dinosaurs,
huge animals up to one hundred feet in length, bulky but
comparatively brainless. But the race was not to the

physically strong, and they were replaced by the mammals, who are the leading type of the next Cainozoic (new life) age. The mammals suckle and tend their young, and from this connection of child and parent arises mutual under-standing. The brain grows because of the interplay with another brain, and becomes more able to meet changing conditions.

MAN APPEARS UPON THE EARTH

OUR grandfathers were very angry with Darwin when he, in effect, reminded them that man was an animal who, by developing enormously the front part of his brain, had outstripped his kinsmen, the monkeys and the apes. To-day we accept the relationship. Our only wonder is at the length of time which must have elapsed during man's develop-ment, so infinitely delicate were the alterations of bodily structure necessary before man could move on two legs instead of on four, or before he could transform his brute cries into articulate speech. There have been discovered recently in Africa remains which suggest that even a million years ago man had already developed a brain approximating in size to that of his modern descendant.

Man started on his career with two great advantages ; he had a brain which enabled him to " look before and after," and he had freed his hands for the service of that brain, but the struggle for existence in the tropical jungle which then covered the whole of Europe must have made life " solitary, poor, nasty, brutish, and short." The two greatest discoveries which have enabled man to hold his place in nature are language and fire. The first enables him to exchange information and ideas with his fellow-men, and to secure that the inventions of the present become the legacy of the future. By means of the second, he was able to withstand the changes of climate, to frighten away the great beasts, and, when he had invented pottery, to gain a more varied and nutritious diet.

Europe has four times undergone severe changes of climate, resulting in four ice ages with milder intervals. The last of these ice ages covered England with a sheet of ice as far south as the Thames. The tropical beasts could not endure the cold and either died or fled, but man sought refuge in natural caves in the hills. There he left the remains which reveal to us his way of life. By chipping flint stones in various ways he had invented edged and pointed tools. With his primitive chisels and drills he made new weapons, such as daggers, and arrows for his newly-invented bow. The bone needles he left behind prove that he had found further protection against the cold. The bison and the wild horse not only provided him with food, but their skins when stitched together now helped to keep him warm.

Most surprising of all, he had reached a high level of artistic creation. His carvings in ivory and limestone, and his paintings and drawings on the cavern walls, are full of vigour and show close observation. The drawings of bisons in the cave at Altamira in Spain give a most realistic effect of savage defiance. Nor was he merely a creature of use and wont, living only for the day. The fact that he had his tools and ornaments buried with him shows that he hoped to use them in the life hereafter.

NATURE BECOMES THE SERVANT TO MAN

As yet the early savage had been living in a world not realised. It was not until the ice retreated, and Europe was left with a temperate climate, that he could begin methodically to adapt nature to his own ends. His tools were now no more made by chipping, but by pressure or by grinding, and were wonderfully effective. He had made them still more so by fitting handles to them. He could build wooden houses, and enjoy such luxuries as wooden furniture and wooden articles for table use. The discovery of pottery made it possible for him to try new foods, and to make them more appetising by cooking.

The old hunting life gave way to the more settled life of the herdsman or shepherd, tending his sheep and cattle for the food and milk they could give him. By domesticating wheat and barley, he in turn became an agriculturist, who must wait for his crops to ripen in due season. He had to work harder, but his labours were more profitable, and in order to lighten the work, he invented the plough and taught the ox to draw it, instead of himself having " to groan over the heavy hoe."

This advance had other results. Already in the past men had probably banded themselves together for the purposes of hunting. Now stronger motives for union appeared. Increasing herds and food supplies had to be protected against the greed of neighbours. The best way to do this was by forming a permanent settlement and surrounding it with a ring-fence of earth and stone, or by building lake-villages on piles. In Switzerland there has been discovered a village where fifty thousand piles had been driven into water eight feet deep. Such an achievement proves a high degree of social organisation. So, too, the gigantic columns of Stonehenge could not have been brought together and erected without skilled direction and co-operation.

Greater comfort led to specialisation. There arose the trades of the potter and the weaver, the farmer and the miner, who exchanged their products by barter. At Brandon in Suffolk the trade of flint mining and knapping is still carried on where Neolithic miners loosened their flint stones with a red-deer's antler for a pick.

THE CIVILISATION OF ANCIENT EGYPT

COMING naked into the world, man had gradually provided himself with the essentials of civilisation except the means of writing. He had an assured food supply, language in which to sing the praises of the heroes of his race, and the promise of a stable society in which he could grow to the full height of his powers. It is easy to take all this for granted and to forget by what ages of striving and by what genius of invention these results had been attained. The man who discovered how to chip a flint to the shape he wanted used as much fundamental brain-work as the man who invented the steam-engine, and the bow and arrow was as revolutionary in its effects as gunpowder and the cannon ball.

The peoples of Europe were still in a state of savagery when those of Egypt and Babylonia had long reached a high level of civilisation, and so we must now examine the contribution to human progress which came from these two lands.

Egypt was from early times divided into two parts—Upper Egypt, consisting of the river valley from the first cataract up to the Delta ; Lower Egypt, consisting of the lands watered by the Delta. Here all the conditions for a steady development occur together. The Nile floods the narrow alluvial plain every year and leaves a rich sediment, which fertilises abundant crops of wheat. On either side, about ten miles away, the desert protects the land from invasion. The climate is dry and healthy and permits an open-air life all the year round. Here men have cultivated the soil since the earliest times. The value of irrigation was soon recognised and led to co-operative action for bringing more land under cultivation. In each village some chief must have made himself responsible for seeing that every one did his fair share of the work.

Gradually these villages were united into the two kingdoms of Lower and Upper Egypt, which were joined together about 3000 B.C. under King Menes. An outburst of creative activity followed in every sphere of life for several centuries.

MAN MAKES AN ALPHABET OF PICTURES

IN early times knowledge was transmitted from generation to generation by word of mouth only, and no guarantee existed that it would be remembered. In Egypt and Babylonia men discovered the means of putting their knowledge on permanent record. Man's first step towards writing was by pictures representing the events he wished to recount. If he wanted to show that he had slain six men, he drew a picture of himself triumphantly treading on six very diminished heads. The next step was to make pictures of actual things, to represent mental ideas as if in English " I fly " were to be indicated by an eye and a fly painted next to each other. Then the pictures would become associated permanently each with one particular syllable, and when put next to each other, would form complete words, *e.g.* a name, such as the equivalent of Birdwood, could be indicated by the picture of a bird followed by that of a wood.

The Babylonians and Assyrians never got past this stage, and any one wishing to learn their language has to make himself acquainted with some five hundred different syllabic signs. The Egyptians did take the last step of making each sign stand for one consonant, but their conservatism kept them to their hieroglyphics, as their syllabic signs are described. It was left to the Phœnician, that trafficker in other people's inventions, to popularise the alphabetic system. The Egyptians, by sticking together thin strips of a reed called the papyrus, and reinforcing them by similar strips stuck on crosswise underneath, created a material both light and smooth which could retain the marks made by a pointed reed pen dipped in ink, a mixture of vegetable gum, soot and water, which was also an invention of theirs. This was a tremendous advance in convenience and speed on the old method of using a clay tablet in which impressions were made with a blunt reed or an engraved seal.

The indispensable convenience of being able to explain simply when an event took place or when it is going to take place, is another Egyptian contrivance. By observing the rising of the star Sirius at a certain time of the year, they had managed at least as early as 4241 B.C. to devise a calendar with the year divided into twelve months of thirty days each, plus five additional days.

The primitive instinct is to fix the year by the occurrence in it of some memorable event, just as we say " the year the Great War began." This the Egyptians replaced by a reference to the year of the King's reign. Even to-day we date our Acts of Parliament thus. An Act passed in the sixth year of the reign of George V. is dated not by the year of our era but as " 6 G.V."

EARLY ATTEMPTS AT EXPLAINING THE MYSTERIES OF LIFE AND DEATH

THE Egyptian religion was an undigested mixture of crude with sublime beliefs. There were local gods, often represented as half-beast and half-man, with a falcon's or a jackal's head on a human body, and national gods, chief of whom was Ra, the Sun God, giver of life and increase.

Of the same type as Ra were Osiris, the giver of immortality and judge of the dead, and Isis, his wife, who were eternally at war with Seth, the spirit of evil. The Egyptians believing that the soul of man lived on after death, and needed the pleasures and articles used in this life, tried to ensure the preservation of the body by embalming it, and built colossal tombs in which the dead could dwell at ease.

They deserve respect because they used the universal belief in a life after death to inculcate a higher morality, which taught that one's fate in the next world would be decided by one's actions in this. The soul would be put on trial and weighed in the balance against an ostrich feather, the symbol of truth and justice. If condemned it would be devoured by a savage beast, but if acquitted it would dwell with Osiris. Such a creed afforded a motive for righteous living on earth, and successfully fostered the virtues of truth, honesty, and charity. Unfortunately, it was perverted by routine and vulgarity. Magic and prayers came to be employed to force an acquittal, and a long list was prepared, to disarm judgment in advance, the so-called "negative confession" of offences which had not been committed.

One attempt was made to break through the stereotyped formalities into which religion had been degraded when Amenhotep IV. (about 1375 B.C.), the king of Egypt who changed his name to Ikhnaton ("the Sun God is satisfied"), banished the beast-gods and declared his faith in Aton alone,

THE ARTIST KING OF ANCIENT EGYPT

Ikhnaton with his queen and young children. The sun, symbol of the new spiritual values in religion and art introduced by this king, stretches its protecting rays towards humanity.

the Sun God, whose rays were so many hands reaching out to help mankind. It was a great step forward, but the age was unprepared for such a belief. Soon after Ikhnaton's death, the vested interests of the priests combined with the stolid materialism of the peasants to blot out all memory of this unwelcome enthusiast. The world had to wait until, with the rise of Israel, a really spiritual religion developed.

THE PYRAMIDS : RESTING-PLACES OF THE SOUL

THE Pharaohs, as the kings of Egypt were called, were gods in their own right, and kept divine state both in life and death. Early in the third millennium B.C., several of these kings built pyramids for the soul's last resting-place. These enormous structures are more remarkable to us as feats of engineering skill than as religious monuments. The Egyptians had no power-driven machinery, and no means of transport except sledges, yet they brought millions of tons of stone by boat from quarries far up the river, and dressed and fitted the blocks so accurately that their skill wins admiration from modern scientific observers.

The Pyramids were not the only religious structures of the Egyptians. The main feature of Egyptian architecture is an excessive reliance on the effectiveness of mere size. This is seen in the huge Sphinxes (human-headed lions), the granite obelisk shafts, and the seventy-foot columns of the great temple of Karnak. Subsequently Greece was to learn the elements of architecture from Egypt, but without imitating the extravagance of its originators.

The finest memorials of Egyptian art are a magnificent series of portrait statues, which show us, for example, the unimpassioned confidence of Chephren, or the full-blooded vigour of Amenemhet III. The head of Ikhnaton reveals the man himself, very æsthetic and very earnest, and very conscious of his own charm. A wooden figure grasping a staff of office reminds us irresistibly of Bumble, " dressed in a little brief authority." In a limestone figure of a scribe we see the eternal clerk, zealous and obsequious.

Society was divided into an aristocracy, consisting of the king and the great landowners, a middle class of professional men, such as architects and doctors, and the peasantry, whose toil in the fields ensured the national prosperity. Besides these there were the priests, whose increasing power in time deadened all the early spirit of progress. In the houses of the wealthy, which were full of the refinements of life, art penetrated to the kitchen, and made even the spoons and cups into things of beauty. The peasant, however, had to earn his bread by the sweat of his brow, clearing the irrigation channels, reclaiming the marshland, and attending to the labours of the farm. The song of the Volga boatmen must have had its predecessors among the thousands of labourers who toiled at the limestone blocks of the Pyramids.

WHY THE MIGHT OF ANCIENT EGYPT DECAYED

THE domestic history of Egypt relates the struggle between absolute monarchy and a rebellious feudal aristocracy. The first kings assembled their nobles at Court, and gave them positions of honour in the government. This made it easy to keep them under observation, and to check any plans for founding semi-independent dukedoms. Later kings were weaker and allowed the great landowners to remain on their estates and set up private courts. The strength of the country was dissipated, and about 1800 B.C. it was conquered by foreign invaders from Western Asia called Hyksos, who ruled the land for over two hundred years, and are said to have introduced the horse and war chariot into Egypt. A native dynasty then regained the throne, and extended Egyptian power into Palestine and Syria and as far as the Euphrates (1600 to 1200 B.C.).

Syria and Palestine were never securely held, and after 1400 B.C. various peoples from the north and east began to nibble away the frontiers. A collection of letters dating from this period has been preserved. They are chiefly from the kings of the Hittites, a growing power in Eastern Asia Minor, and from the Babylonian and Assyrian kings ; they present us with a vivid picture of secret diplomacy based on subsidies and dynastic marriages. The Hittites possessed iron mines, and were beginning to make iron weapons, which were much superior to those of copper and bronze, that had been used up till then. Their king, feeling confident in his new weapons, is very peremptory in his tone.

The decline was checked temporarily by a new line of kings, of whom Rameses II. (1292 to 1225 B.C.) is the best known, but the loss of Syria to the Hittites had to be accepted as permanent. The Egyptians had never been a conquering race, for they were very well satisfied with their own Nile Valley, and had a great contempt for foreigners. The kings had to resort to mercenaries, paid foreign soldiers, who finally seized the government.

Between the twelfth and eighth centuries B.C., the land suffered a long decline materially and spiritually under alternations of foreign or priestly rule. In the seventh century B.C. the Assyrians overran the country for a brief period, but soon withdrew. A short-lived revival kept Egypt independent with the aid of Greek mercenaries from 663 B.C. to 525 B.C., when the land was absorbed into the Persian Empire.

Egypt made great contributions to civilisation : in thought, the promise and the partial development of a higher morality ; in politics, the first united nation under a single government ; in the arts, statues and temples from which the Greeks borrowed suggestions for their own restrained and humane art. Above all, we should remember the Egyptians as the main authors of our modern alphabet and the discoverers of the paper on which man first wrote.

THE ANCIENT EMPIRES OF THE NEAR EAST

LONG before Egypt was united into a single kingdom, the southern portion of the plain, watered by the lower courses of the Euphrates and the Tigris, was the home of a settled people. Here, if the sun was more scorching than in Egypt, the soil could be made even more productive. The land near the ancient mouths of the rivers consisted of rich alluvial earth, which, under irrigation, yielded plentiful crops ; this was the site of the Biblical Garden of Eden. Of this land, the northern and less fruitful portion was called Akkad and the southern Sumer.

The district of Sumer must have been in settled occupation long before 5000 B.C. Excavations at Ur of the Chaldees in southern Mesopotamia (" the land between the rivers ") have uncovered a bank of clay eight feet deep, which could have been deposited only by a flood of very long duration. Underneath the clay were further remains of human habitation. Thus the Old Testament story of the Flood is based on more than an empty myth.

The Sumerians belonged originally to the Indo-European peoples, who from the earliest times had roamed on the grasslands which extend from the Danube far into Asia. These peoples, originally of one stock, called Aryan, divided early into various tribes, which developed different languages, and, with their horses and wheeled carts, roamed over the steppes, living a semi-agricultural life. One section invaded northern India in the second millennium B.C. and established its rule in Hindustan. The western section has, at different epochs, when a drought has dried the pastures, let hordes of invaders loose upon the more fertile land to the south. In

Italy and France, in Greece and Asia Minor, nomadic conquerors have thus, at various times, driven out or enslaved the aboriginal populations. But it is in Mesopotamia that an Indo-European people first encountered the Semites.

THE SUMERIAN EMPIRE GIVES PLACE TO BABYLON

THE tribes which wander from oasis to oasis in the Arabian desert have been called Semites. Like the northern nomads, they too, when starving from widespread droughts, have advanced in hordes upon the richer lands in the river valleys, or have filtered into them as wandering traders. Since 3000 B.C., at least, the Aryan and the Semite have more than once engaged in a tug-of-war, of which the Mediterranean lands and those of Western Asia have been the prize. The first encounter took place between the Sumerians in the south and the Semitic Akkadians in the northern part of the plain. The Sumerians had drained the swamps, built irrigation canals, and established flourishing little city-states. These city-states were always fighting against each other in boundary disputes. But about 2750 B.C. they had to combine, though too late, against a Semitic invasion from Akkad. These Semites had drifted into Akkad from the desert, and they now proceeded to invade and conquer the wealthy Sumerian cities. Under the first great Semitic conqueror, Sargon, they won an empire which extended from the Tigris to the coast of the Levant. The empire did not last long, but in Sumer the two races mingled together, and the Sumerian culture and religion were shared by both.

The next empire was that of Babylon. This city lying in the northern part of Akkad, just below the point where the Euphrates and the Tigris come nearest to each other, had been unimportant in early times. About 2200 B.C., however, a new dynasty arose and established a short-lived but brilliant empire. The city, which was the centre of roads from the desert, inherited the traditions of Sumer, and became the religious as well as the commercial centre of Western Asia.

The Sumerians had developed a bustling urban life long before the rise of Babylon. Writing was already familiar and clay tablets were used on which impressions were made with a blunt square-tipped reed. The wedge-shaped signs made by the reed in the clay are called cuneiform. Contracts were sealed by rolling over the clay tablet a cylinder seal on which signs or pictures were cut in relief. Some of these pictures are marvels of delicate craftsmanship. Printing on movable types is merely an extension of the principle of the cylinder seal. Schools existed in which boys learnt the four hundred signs of their alphabet and the calendar of twelve lunar months with one intercalary month. From this people we derive our week of seven days, with twenty-four hours to the day, and the division of the hour into sixty minutes.

WHAT THE BABYLONIANS BELIEVED

ANOTHER Biblical story finds its origin in the stepped temple-tower of the Sumerians, which was somewhat like an American skyscraper in appearance. The origin of this tower is rather curious. The Sumerians in their early highland homes had worshipped their gods on the hilltops. Babylonia, to which they had migrated, is a flat plain, and so, as a substitute, they invented these stepped towers with a spiral ascent running round the outside, and a roof garden (the Hanging Gardens of Babylon) on the top. Their religion was that of all early agriculturists who asked their gods for " earth's increase, foison plenty, barns and garners never empty." To symbolise their hopes, they brought the gods offerings of green date-palm branches (" the tree of life ") set in jars of water.

Each city had its own private god, though every one also worshipped the gods who typified natural powers—the Sun God and the Mother Goddess, Ishtar, the giver of life to all. The gods were like human beings, with very human qualities. They had their homes in the temples, where they enjoyed human meals and " married " mortal women. In return for the people's ministrations, they protected their city against its neighbours. The prayers to the gods are not exultant and joyful, but reflect the hard conditions of life, where violent extremes of heat and cold, and bloodthirsty insects plague the flesh. The " Garden of Eden " was very like a hothouse in summer and was swept by bitter winds in winter. British troops in Mesopotamia during the Great War learnt by bitter experience that life there must always be lived on the defensive.

OUR DEBT TO THE STAR-GAZERS OF BABYLON

THE Babylonians, believing that it was possible to fore-tell the future by observing the relative positions of the stars, mapped out the planets and fixed names and signs for the stars of the Zodiac. If to-day we scoff at this superstition, we can be grateful for the real advance in astronomy to which it gave rise.

The Babylonian religion, in spite of some wider views, remained confined to outward observances. The worshipper was like the king in *Hamlet* who wished to be pardoned and to retain his guilty gains. To attain this end he had resort to magic, whereby some other object was made the " whipping-boy," to be punished by the gods for the offences of which he himself was guilty. From this practice comes the idea of the scapegoat, to which later religions imparted a lofty allegorical meaning.

The greatest king of Babylon was Hammurabi (about 2100 B.C.) whose code of civil and criminal law provides for a complicated social and economic structure. It sounds very modern with its court of first instance and court of appeal. A dissatisfied litigant could even get a third trial by appealing to the king himself. The punishments appear needlessly severe by twentieth-century standards, but they probably represent maximum sentences, and in any case are not more savage than those of our own legal code down to the end of the eighteenth century. The death penalty is laid down not only for murder, but also for various forms of burglary and theft. The primitive method of retaliation in kind (" an eye for an eye ") still existed. A jerry-builder, whose house fell and killed the occupier, atoned for his scamped work by his own death.

Women were comparatively free, and could even set up in business on their own account, but it was very much a masculine world, which punished slovenly house-keeping with death by drowning. Marriage was a civil contract which favoured the husband. He was allowed one chief wife, but could take as many concubines for his harem as he could afford. If he wanted a divorce there were few difficulties in his way—he had paid for his wife and could do as he pleased with his own property. The Kingdom of Hammurabi, after lasting for several centuries, succumbed to a people called the Kassites, who were succeeded in turn by other dynasties until the rise of the Assyrians.

THE ASSYRIANS : THE "APACHES" OF ANTIQUITY

THE most bloodthirsty and savage nation who ever lived had their home in the highlands of the Upper Tigris. In the eighth century B.C. they overran the countries from the Tigris to the Nile. Their success was due to a combination of grim ferocity with supremacy in the art of war. They were the first nation to adopt iron weapons exclusively. The land was an armed camp, the nation a standing army of archers and heavy-armed infantry, supported by horsemen and charioteers. Few walls could withstand their battering-rams and siege towers. Their art matched their character. The animals in their hunting scenes snarl with tigerish ferocity, and the human-headed bulls glare intimidatingly from the glazed bricks of their palace walls. Grim bearded warriors, these people stand out from their reliefs, pitiless and unrelenting, as they flay or blind their victims, or carry off whole nations into captivity.

In repeated campaigns, the Assyrians devastated the fairest countries of Western Asia, and exhausted their own population. Some of their kings showed an interest in the learning of the Babylonians, and one of them collected a large library. But their chief literary interest was to write boastful chronicles of their terrorism. Towards the end of the seventh century they were caught between raiding tribes on the North and the rising powers of the Medes and the Chaldeans on the South, and in 612 B.C., Nineveh, their capital, was captured and destroyed. Nahum, the Hebrew prophet, voiced the universal delight when he cried, " Nineveh is laid waste. Who will bemoan her ? "

The Medes and Persians were kindred tribes on the eastern bank of the Tigris who had helped to destroy Assyria and had taken the largest share of the spoils. The Medes were the ruling tribe until overthrown by the Persians under Cyrus (558–529 B.C.) who founded the first great empire built on a firm basis. Crœsus, the wealthy ruler of Lydia, a kingdom of Western Asia Minor, tried in vain to resist Cyrus. A great believer in oracles, Crœsus had, on this occasion, consulted the famous oracle at Delphi in Greece. The ambiguous reply said that if he crossed the river Halys, which was the eastern boundary of his kingdom, he would destroy a mighty empire. Crœsus took this as an answer favourable to himself. He crossed the river, but the empire which he destroyed was his own, for he was defeated and slain by Cyrus in 546 B.C.

L.S.D. AND A.B.C.

To Lydia we owe the invention of coinage. The business of the world had previously been conducted either by barter or by bullion (gold bars of a certain weight). Every merchant had to carry a set of scales with him to see that he was not being cheated. Henceforth, as a guarantee of purity and weight, the state fixed its own stamp on pieces of metal, cut up into convenient sizes. This was a great help to commerce and was adopted everywhere.

To another people, the Phœnicians, who were absorbed in the Persian Empire, we owe our alphabet, which, unlike the four hundred signs of the Babylonians, contains a very small number of letters, and makes written speech easy. The device came originally from Egypt, but the Phœnicians, who lived on the coast of Syria, adopted it and taught it to the Greeks. They arranged twenty-two consonants in a fixed order, and gave them names by which they could easily be learned. When the Greeks borrowed this list in the ninth century B.C., they added vowels to it, to make the spelling of words more simple. The Romans borrowed this improved alphabet from the Greeks who settled in Italy, and handed it on to us. (The word " alphabet " is derived from the Greek words *alpha* and *beta*, which were themselves of Phœnician origin, and were used for the " A " sound and the " B " sound respectively.)

The Phœnicians, issuing from their seaports, Tyre and Sidon, won a monopoly of the carrying trade of the Mediterranean. At the centre of the north coast of Africa, they founded the great seaport of Carthage. They even passed through the straits of Gibraltar and founded a city at Gades (Cadiz) on the Atlantic coast of Spain. Cotton and spices from India, tin from Spain, and amber from the Baltic were distributed by them to all countries.

After the fall of Nineveh, Babylon flourished for a short time under Nebuchadnezzar (605-561 B.C.), who carried off the Jews into captivity. But the political vitality of the Semitic peoples had ebbed. The last king occupied himself with antiquarian research and religious quarrels, and was easily swept aside when the priests treacherously opened the gates to Cyrus in 538 B.C. The victories of Cyrus mark the first triumph of Aryan over Semite in the struggle for Western Asia, but though Cyrus laid the foundations, it was Darius (521-485 B.C.) who successfully organised the empire. Avoiding the Assyrian policy of oppression and extortion, he allowed the subject provinces a good deal of internal freedom. The empire was treated as a business proposition and carefully nursed so as to bring in good returns.

THE ENLIGHTENED RULE AND RELIGION OF THE PERSIANS

THIS empire, extending from Egypt to India, was divided into provinces, each under a *satrap* (Viceroy) with full military and civil powers. The administration of these satraps was liable to examination at any time by officials called " The King's Eyes." The national army, too, remained under the king's direct orders, as did the garrisons stationed at strategic points commanding the grand trunk roads leading from Susa, the capital, in Persia, to the farthest provinces.

The best security for the permanence of the empire was the loyalty of the ruling classes and the contentment of the subjects. The Persian was tolerant to other religions, as the Jews, who were restored to Jerusalem from Babylon, could testify ; and he also encouraged agriculture and trade. It was no wonder that, in spite of the feebleness of later rulers, the structure held firm until Alexander's coming in 331 B.C. Not until the golden age of the Roman Empire in the second century A.D. did the world enjoy a government as just and as gentle.

The kinder rule of the Persians was no accident, but arose partly from the teaching of their religion. A teacher, Zoroaster, had taught them that the world was the scene of an everlasting struggle between the forces of light and of darkness, between Ahura-Mazda, who manifested himself in fire, and Ahriman, creator of evil in the world and in the heart of man. It was each man's duty to take his stand with Mazda, and to help to make the world fruitful and his own heart clean. This sublime belief was later perverted by the Magians, the Persian priests, who insisted on the necessity of avoiding the pollution caused by contact with anything dead. It was considered wicked to burn or to bury the dead, and they were exposed on " Towers of Silence " for the vultures to devour, just as they are by the Parsees in India to-day. Later still, the people worshipped the impure gods of the Babylonians. Their practical code was summed up in the admonition, " To ride, to draw the bow, and to speak the truth."

THE PEOPLE OF PALESTINE

PALESTINE, lying on the road from the Nile to the Euphrates, was the Belgium of Western Asia, overrun by the opposing armies of Egypt and of Babylonia in turn. The

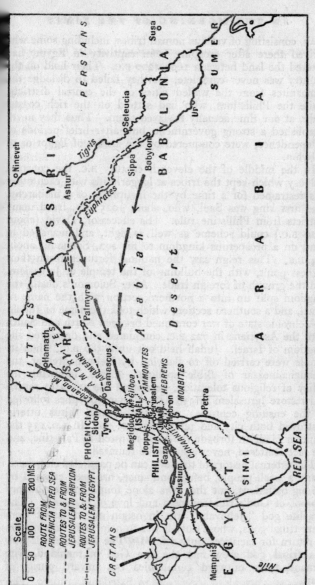

PALESTINE'S POSITION BETWEEN THE WARRING EASTERN EMPIRES

Jews, consisting of various nomad tribes, including some who arrived there after escaping from captivity in Egypt, had entered the land between 1600-1200 B.C. Their hold on the country was never complete, for they failed to dislodge the Canaanites from the walled cities of the central districts, while the Philistines, who had settled on the rich coastal plain, at one time actually enslaved them. Thus they never established a strong government, but, after brief periods of independence, were conquered by the armies of Egypt or of Babylon.

In the middle of the eleventh century B.C. the constant jealousy which kept the tribes at loggerheads with each other was restrained for a time by the institution of a monarchy. The first king was Saul, who, about 1025 B.C., freed many districts from Philistine rule. His successor, David (about 1010 B.C.) could scheme as well as fight, and managed to hand on a prosperous kingdom to his son, Solomon, about 974 B.C. This reign saw the national fortunes reach their highest point, with the building of the temple at Jerusalem, and the growth of foreign trade. After Solomon's death, the kingdom split up into a northern section with the name of Israel, and a southern section, which took the name of Judah.

A chronic state of war continued between North and South until the Assyrians in 722 B.C. conquered and destroyed the kingdom of Israel. Judah held out until 586 B.C., when its people were carried off to Babylon by Nebuchadrezzar, the Nebuchadnezzar of Bible spelling. Cyrus, following his policy of religious toleration, permitted the exiles to return and restore Jerusalem in 538 B.C. Varying fortunes followed in the ensuing centuries until the Roman Titus utterly destroyed both city and temple in A.D. 70. In A.D. 135 the emperor Hadrian forbade the Jews to dwell in Palestine, and the race scattered, never again to be reunited.

The external history of the Jews can be paralleled elsewhere. Many a small people, before and since, has been crushed by the big battalions, but the Jews alone found in their history a proof of God's righteousness and love of mankind. The Israelite god " Jehovah " was in origin not different from other tribal gods, whose duty it was to help their worshippers in return for sacrifices duly offered. The Bible reveals how this tribal god grew into the one God of mankind, who demanded no outward ceremonies but inward purity of heart.

THE HEBREW PROPHETS OF A GOD OF JUSTICE

THE prophets who brought about this transformation did not belong to any special class ; one was a shepherd, another a highly-born noble ; but all believed that God inspired them to speak. In the name of the Lord, they crusaded against luxury and vice, against bad government and the oppression of the poor by the rich. Their aim was not to provide any philosophical basis for religion, but to give advice here and now as to what a man and a people should do in order to be saved. They saw the downfall of great nations as God's punishment for sin, and recognised in Cyrus an instrument of God's will. The prophets vary greatly in their appeal, but we may mention Micah, whose definition of righteousness, " Do justice, love mercy, walk humbly with thy God," though brief, is not inadequate. Isaiah, the sublimest of all, taught that the Jews were to proclaim one universal God, whose omnipotence was equalled by his loving-kindness, and who would bring peace to the war-worn peoples.

The Old Testament is a medley of poetry and prose, of naïve stories and thrilling histories, of religious hymns and prophetic sublimity. The story of Abraham is one of simple grandeur, such as comes from people whose " thought is speech, and speech is truth." Later on, some of the chapters in Kings and Chronicles are breathless with drama, and have an intensity surpassing anything even in the Greek historians. A more conscious art is seen in the Psalms, where the method of parallelism, of reinforcing a statement by putting it from another point of view, attains some magnificent effects, as in Psalm 91. The majesty of the Book of Job is equalled only by Æschylus among Greek, and by Dante and Milton among modern writers. Throughout there is the characteristic quality of the Semite, a vivid imagination, abounding in parable and symbolism, and an intense emotionalism which falls at times into fantastic exaggeration, making " the mountains skip like rams."

CRETE: THE CLEARING-HOUSE OF EGYPTIAN CULTURE

BEFORE the Greeks settled in the land which bears their name, there had lived in Crete a people of high civilisation, of whom later Greeks knew little, except that their king, Minos, had possessed a large fleet with which he had put down piracy and had ruled the Ægean Islands. The

Athenians also had a vague tradition that Minos used to exact a tribute from them of maidens and boys to be sacrificed to the Minotaur (the sacred bull of Minos), until Theseus, their great hero, went to Crete, and, after finding his way through a winding maze called the Labyrinth, killed the Minotaur and rescued the captives.

In our own day, excavations at Cnossos, on the north coast, have disclosed a palace whose bewildering mass of buildings could easily have been the source of the story of the Labyrinth. Here were found beautiful fresco paintings, and ornaments and pottery of the highest artistic and technical merit. The national sport was acrobatics, with a bull as vaulting-horse. In one scene, a youth appears grasping by the horns a charging bull and somersaulting on to its back—a most dangerous feat, which, if imposed on unpractised captives, might easily give rise to the legend of the Minatour.

Crete, lying on the way from Egypt to Greece, was a clearing-house for Egyptian culture, which it developed in original and charming ways, and handed on to the mainland. The Cretan power, which was at its height between 1600 and 1400 B.C., was succeeded by the leadership of Mycenæ, " rich in gold," on the Grecian mainland. The Mycenæans belonged to the original Mediterranean race. The tribes had not yet developed any common name, but were often called " Achæans," after the largest section of them. Later on they called themselves " Hellenes," after Hellen, who was supposed to have led them into the land. The name " Greek " (Latin, *Græci*) was given to them by the Romans because the first Hellenes they met were a tribe called *Grai*. In the twelfth century B.C. the tribes were led by Agamemnon, king of Argos.

THE ISLES OF GREECE

WHEN Helen, the wife of Agamemnon's brother, Menelaus, was abducted by Paris, a Prince of Troy (or Ilium), the wealthy city at the southern entrance of the Dardanelles, Agamemnon led an expedition against Troy. The city fell after a siege of ten years. Such is the account given in the *Iliad* of the poet Homer. It has been suggested that the real cause of the war was the founding of Greek settlements in Æolis, on the north-west coast of Asia Minor, which Troy attempted to oppose. The war, as Homer's other immortal poem, the *Odyssey*, reveals, caused widespread unsettlement n Greece, with the result that, about a century later, the land succumbed to the invading Dorians.

Although a branch of the same race as the Achæans, the Dorians did not mix with them, but either expelled them completely or enslaved them. Attica alone escaped invasion, or its poor soil offered no attraction to the conquerors. The strongest Dorian state was that of the Spartans in the Southern Peloponnese, who, although far outnumbered by them, enslaved and oppressed the natives, called Helots. The wave of invasion extended to Crete and to Doris, the south-western coast of Asia Minor. The expelled Greeks colonised Ionia, the central division of the western coast of Asia Minor. This district, with Æolis and Doris, formed a fringe of Greek settlements from the Dardanelles to Rhodes.

These towns, taken over from native settlers, and situated at the terminal points of caravan routes from the East, prospered exceedingly. They first felt the fertilising influences of the older civilisations and showed their Motherland the way to scientific and intellectual progress.

Greek history is obscure after the Dorian conquest, until, in the seventh century B.C., we find the land divided among various city-states. There was Athens, which included the whole of Attica ; Sparta, ruling most of the South and West Peloponnese : Argos, strong in the North-East Peloponnese; and Bœotia, a confederation north of Attica, under the leadership of the city of Thebes. The struggle for mastery between these states lasted till they all fell to Philip of Macedon in 338 B.C.

THE SEAFARERS OF THE CITY-STATES

THE Greek spirit of adventure and independence was fostered by the geographical conditions. The east and south coasts are everywhere cut up by bays and inlets of the sea, and the Ægean Isles are so near to each other that one can cross to Asia Minor without losing sight of land. In such a land-locked region, men easily went down to the sea in ships. Seafaring was also encouraged because the mountains everywhere barred easy intercourse by their height and ruggedness.

" Little town by river or seashore, or mountain-built with peaceful citadel." These words of Keats well describe the sites on which the Greek city-states were built. These city-states were a great contrast to the large empires of the Assyrians and the Persians. Here were small communities,

entirely self-sufficient and not desirous of extending the
privileges to others. Even the largest of them was only about
the same size as an average English county, yet they had
their own systems of government and their political parties
debating home and foreign affairs. The result was an intense
interest in the problems of government. Every citizen took
an active part in the state and thought that a man who was
uninterested in politics was useless.

The original constitution of the Greeks, as revealed in the
Homeric poems about 900 B.C., consisted of a king, who was
leader in peace and war and religion, a council of chiefs whom
he consulted, and the assembly of the people, who were
summoned together to hear the decisions of the king and
council. Membership of the state was confined to those who
belonged to the tribes by birth. Already in Homer we see
the king largely controlled by the council of chiefs. The
people, however, are still unable to make themselves heard,
for Odysseus, one of the Homeric chiefs, tells the heckler,
Thersites, that " the rule of many is not good," and enforces
the lesson with a beating.

THE POLITICAL EXPERIENCES GAINED BY THE GREEKS

IN the eighth and seventh centuries B.C. the landed nobility
overthrew the kings or else kept the bare title and divided
the royal powers amongst themselves. The nobles called their
government " aristocracy," which means " the rule of the
best men." The common people suffered great oppression,
but were not yet strong enough to resist. During this period
numerous colonies were founded on the Mediterranean and
Black Sea coasts by discontented aristocrats or profit-seeking
merchants. This movement was encouraged by the nobles,
for the poor soil could not support a large population, and in
spite of infanticide there was not enough land to go round.

Ultimately these colonies reached the rich corn lands of
south Russia, which supplied the deficiency of home production. " The merry Grecian coaster " sailed into the
western Mediterranean also, encroaching on the preserves
of the Phœnician. In south Italy so many colonies were
founded that the district was called " Great Greece." They
also fringed the east and south coasts of Sicily, where they
found the Phœnician already before them. A Greek colony
was an independent state which owed no duty to its mother
city except that of religious respect. Sentiment, however

together with trade connections, usually kept them in close touch with each other.

The safety-valve of colonisation did not always work, and the general discontent often led to the seizure of the government by a single man, whom the Greeks called a Tyrant. This name originally meant an absolute sovereign who had obtained power irregularly. The power of these Tyrants rested on the goodwill of the people and on the circumstances of the time. The Tyrants satisfied the grievances of bankrupt peasant-farmers and of rich traders who were excluded from the government by the landed nobility, but instead of retiring after they had put things right, they clung to power and thus earned an evil reputation. Yet their services to Greece were invaluable, for they destroyed the prestige of the aristocrats, promoted prosperity, and fostered literature and the arts.

In many states a Tyranny was followed by a Democracy (Greek *democratia*—rule of the people), but often the rich men would seize the power for themselves and establish an Oligarchy (Greek *oligarchia*—rule of the few). We can trace most clearly in Athens the various stages from monarchy to democracy. In the prehistoric age there had been a kingship, but by the beginning of the seventh century B.C., the state was ruled by an aristocracy which provided the annual magistrates called *archons*, and a council (the Council of the Areopagus), which was also the chief criminal court of the state, and whose members held office for life.

Since the nobles alone knew the law, and often misused it for their own ends, the first reform which the people desired was to get to know what the law really said. This concession was made when Draco, in 621 B.C., wrote down the laws for all to see. Later ages thought them very severe, and said they were "written in blood" (whence comes the term "Draconic"), but at least the nobles had to keep within them.

STATESMEN AND REFORMERS IN ANCIENT ATHENS

As conditions did not improve, the Athenians empowered Solon, an enlightened noble, to make all political and social changes he thought fit (594 B.C.). He cancelled all loans made on the security of personal freedom and all mortgages of land. But it was his political reforms which earned him the title of founder of European democracy. The citizens were divided into four classes, graded according to their income. Only the first class was eligible for the chief magistracies, but—

and this was the great innovation—election was by the votes of all classes. Secondly, courts of justice were established in which the juries were taken by lot from all citizens. Thus the citizen was assured of justice against the noble, and could control the magistrates, who were made accountable before these courts for their actions while holding office.

The economic problem remained unsolved because the nobles held most of the land of the country. The tyranny of Pisistratus who seized the government in 560 B.C., and, with brief intervals, ruled Athens until 528 B.C., brought great prosperity. The people received small holdings from the lands of ejected nobles. Manufacture and commerce, art and architecture were encouraged. Even the Solonian constitution was left unchanged, except that Pisistratus took care to have magistrates devoted to his own interests.

On the fall of the tyranny, shortly before 500 B.C., a great democratic reformer, by the name of Cleisthenes, appeared. Attica was still divided up into local parties based on family connections. Cleisthenes created new tribes or wards which were based on territorial divisions but so arranged that no tribe contained sections from adjoining districts. He thus cut across the old local parties, so that henceforth political debate was concerned only with general measures and not with local patriotism.

Cleisthenes also established a law by which the people could meet and banish any citizen who might be thought dangerous to the state. At least 6000 votes had to be cast altogether, so that there was no danger of injustice. A vote was given by scratching the name of the citizen to be banished on a broken piece of pottery called an *ostracon*, whence the term ostracism is derived.

ATHENS AND SPARTA : A CONTRAST IN CULTURE

MEANWHILE at Sparta a very different kind of state had developed. It has well been said that the Spartans became " the slaves of their own conquests." They were a small military caste, holding down a mass of mutinous serfs, and all their institutions were designed for the training of soldiers. Male children were destroyed if they had the slightest physical blemish. At the age of seven the boys were taken from their parents and given a training rather like that of the English public schools in the early nineteenth century, when physical fitness and undemonstrative courage were cultivated at the expense of literature and the arts. The boys had their own officers, corresponding to the prefects at English schools, whose duty it was to set an example of hardy endurance and to ensure discipline by severe punishments.

The women matched the men in courage, and showed no emotion save pride if their children were killed in battle. A Spartan mother, when sending her son to war, would point to his shield and say, " With it or on it," implying that victory or death were his only alternatives. (The words " With it or on it " are a typical example of the " laconic "—from Greek *Lacon* — or *Lacedæmonian* style of speech on which the Spartans prided themselves). The people became invincible in war, but the cost was high, for they never developed any broad views of Greek patriotism, and took no part in the glorious march of Greek civilisation.

The testing time for Athens soon came. She had helped the Greek cities in Asia Minor which had been conquered by the Persians in 546 B.C. and had revolted just after 500 B.C. Darius, realising that he would have no peace while there were free Greeks on the west of the Aegean, sent a large fleet bearing an army which landed at Marathon, on the coast of Attica. The Athenians sought help from Sparta, but before it could come they had fought and won. The first attempt on Greek liberty had been repulsed (490 B.C.).

HOW ATHENS SAVED THE CIVILISATION OF THE WEST

THE effect on Athens was electric. The people were filled with pride and self-confidence, and they found in Themistocles a leader of genius. He realised that the Persians would return, and persuaded the Athenians to build a large fleet, which proved the salvation of Greece. In 480 B.C. the long expected invasion came. Xerxes, who had succeeded Darius, brought an immense army and many ships. Yet even at this crisis the Greeks refused to work together, and some states actually submitted to Xerxes. The Persian advance was checked momentarily at the pass of Thermopylæ, where Leonidas and his three hundred Spartans were slain, after performing prodigies of valour. This stand was commemorated by the famous epitaph :

Go tell the Spartans, thou that passest by,
That here, obedient to their laws, we lie.

The decisive battle took place off the west coast of Attica. The strategy of Themistocles lured the Persian fleet into the straits of Salamis, where the ships were crowded together and got in each other's way. Then the allied fleet, the greater part of which consisted of Athenian vessels, attacked and won a complete victory (480 B.C.). Xerxes hurried back to Asia, but left behind a large army which was beaten at Platæa in 479 B.C. by Spartan courage and Spartan leadership.

The final repulse of the Persians meant the victory of freedom ; not only of political freedom, but freedom of thought, for the Greek criticism was justified that " In the Persian Empire all are slaves except one." Henceforth Greece was to provide future ages with the example of a nation in which religion and privilege were no longer exempt from criticism. Reason would be free to " follow the argument whithersoever it leads."

" EYE OF GREECE AND MOTHER OF ARTS "

AFTER Platæa, Sparta retired into her shell, but Athens formed a league to make the Aegean safe for Greek freedom. In a series of campaigns her brilliant general, Cimon, swept the seas clear of Persian ships, and of piracy too. These successes enabled Athens to convert the league into an empire before it was thirty years old. She used the contributions which the cities paid to keep the seas clear to adorn herself with beautiful temples. Her specious excuse was that so long as she kept the Persians away, the allies had no right to complain. Athens even attempted to establish a land empire, but was checked by Sparta and Bœotia (445 B.C.).

Although Athens was so ready to interfere with Greek liberties, she was herself an example of the most complete liberty. In 461 B.C. the old council of Areopagus, the last stronghold of aristocratic privilege, was stripped of its political importance. Henceforth the popular council of five hundred members, who were appointed by lot from all citizens over the age of thirty, prepared all state business for the decision of the general assembly of all the citizens. The laws were administered by citizen-juries. There were six thousand jurymen from whom smaller juries were chosen by lot for the different cases. The courts were kept busy, for the Athenians insisted that all important cases from all cities of the empire should be brought to Athens.

Although the number of slaves equalled that of free citizens, yet with this proviso, it is true that nowhere has the rule of all by all in turn been so completely carried out. Practically every office was open to every one, and the system of appointment by lot, together with the prohibition of re-appointment to the same office, made political experience universally familiar. Even the poorest could serve the state, since a small payment, just enough to buy a bare minimum of food, was given to all jurors and officials. The passion for democracy did not go so far as to leave to chance the direction of state policy, for the ten Generals who managed not only military but also financial and foreign affairs were appointed by election. Re-appointment to this office was permitted, and thus continuity of policy was made possible. Usually, one of the Generals was recognised as commander-in-chief, and exercised power analogous to that of a modern Prime Minister.

HOW STATESMEN MANAGED TO HIDE THEIR MISTAKES

THE fatal flaw was the gap between the person who proposed a policy in the assembly and got it carried, and the General who had to execute it. At first this defect remained hidden, because the General came from the old ruling classes, and could usually both get his own policy accepted and execute it in person. Later on, however, irresponsible demagogues of a lower social class appeared, who deluded the people with reckless promises. If a policy failed, the General who had had to carry it out, even though he might have disapproved of it, became the victim of popular disappointment, while the proposer got off scot free. The contrast with modern governments is instructive. If our Cabinet decides on a policy, it accepts responsibility for it, and resigns if its policy is not accepted, or if it proves a failure.

Between 460 and 429 B.C., Athenian affairs were controlled so completely by Pericles, a member of one of the noblest Athenian families, that the state was described as " nominally a democracy, actually the rule of the foremost citizen." Pericles at first advised a forward policy on land and sea, but, finding that the population of Athens was being exhausted by the endless wars involved, he devoted himself to making the city " a liberal education for Greece." His confession of faith was, " We are lovers of beauty without extravagance and lovers of wisdom without effeminacy." Athens was filled with beautiful statues and stately temples. These years were, indeed, the golden age of Athens, when

drama and the arts flourished, and philosophy, the love o
wisdom, found in Socrates its greatest apostle.

The Greeks, unlike the Romans, never learned how t
establish an empire. The city-state was an exclusive club
from which all outsiders were barred. The Athenians allowed
strangers to settle and trade, but excluded them from citizenship. Their attitude to the subject cities of their empire was
similar. No attempt was made to give the subject cities any
voice in the government ; the allies were to be milch cows for
the benefit of the tyrant city.

COMMERCIAL JEALOUSY CAUSES A WAR

THE fears roused by the peaceful penetration of Athenian
commerce resulted in the Peloponnesian War (431-404
B.C.). The Corinthians, Athens' chief business rivals, became
jealous of her amazing activity. Their description of the
Athenians was, " They are born to have no rest themselves,
and to let no one else have any." Another reason for the war
was the autocratic Athenian control over the politics and legal
affairs of her allies, who did not consider generous financial
treatment and free trade to be any compensation for the loss
of freedom. Dissatisfied states appealed to Sparta for help,
and Sparta ultimately gave it. Athens could have ended the
war speedily and on favourable terms had not the evil genius
of Cleon, the leather tanner, a typical leader of the new type,
incited her to expect impossible gains.

It was not until Athens had dissipated her energies by a
disastrous attack on Sicily (415 B.C.) that Sparta, with the
help, be it added, of Persian gold, was at last victorious in
404 B.C. The end of the war brought no peace, for the
Spartan was more oppressive than the Athenian had been.
The Greeks of Asia Minor were betrayed and again became
subjects of Persia (387 B.C.), and oligarchies, supported by
Spartan governors, were established in the conquered cities
of Greece. There followed a short-lived Theban leadership (371–362 B.C.) under the brilliant statesmanship of
Epaminondas. The states then continued their futile bicker-
ings until 338 B.C., when Philip, King of Macedon, ended
Greek freedom on the battlefield of Chæronea, and united
the city-states, with the exception of Sparta, into a league
under his control.

The Greeks had no creed to which all had to subscribe,
no powerful priesthood or established Church, no sacred

book which all had to believe. There were priests, but a man could approach the gods himself. Besides the local gods dwelling in rivers and springs and woods, and attended by nymphs and fauns and satyrs, there were greater gods worshipped throughout the land. Chief of the great gods was Zeus, who lived on top of Olympus, the highest mountain in Greece. He wielded the thunderbolt, and protected the poor and helpless. Of the other gods, the most prominent were Apollo, God of Music and Art and Prophecy, and Athena, Goddess of Wisdom and Serene Courage. These gods were represented as human beings of surpassing beauty, and, on the whole, superior morality. The gods in Homer, though their own actions were often disgraceful, did set up conscience and public opinion as guides to conduct, while Zeus in the dramatists upholds justice and righteousness.

LIGHT-HEARTED WORSHIP OF MANY GODS

THE Greeks did not take their gods with the intense seriousness of the Hebrews, and they could joke about a god without being convicted of sin. The philosophers sneered at the many gods of the common people, but, besides inculcating morals, these gods inspired great compositions in music and drama and sculpture.

In honour of them, numerous festivals were established. The best known was that celebrated every four years in honour of Zeus at Olympia, in the Western Peloponnese. Here athletic competitions were held which attracted entrants from the whole of the Greek world. (The modern Olympic Games were instituted in 1896 in direct imitation of the old Greek festival.) At Athens the festival of the god Dionysus witnessed the rise and growth of Greek drama, which was originally an offering of worship to the god.

The Greek views of an after-life were not optimistic. There was, for select heroes, the paradise of the Elysian plain, but for the rest, " youth and bloom and this delightful world " were replaced by a dim world of shadows. Achilles, the great Greek legendary hero, spoke for all the Greeks when, in the *Odyssey* of Homer, he said that he would rather be a hired servant of a poor farmer than king of all the dead.

This people, which has left the world such an imperishable legacy in every branch of thought, had a standard of living which would be intolerable to even the poorest to-day. The towns had grown up haphazard, and consisted of narrow passages leading to the market-place. Their houses were little more than covered sheds, devoid of all sanitary conveniences.

The climate made these conditions less harmful, at least for the men, because they could spend most of their time in the open air. The position of women, on the other hand, was unworthy of the race. The Athenian woman was a prisoner at home, busy in bringing up the children and weaving the clothes of the family. It was considered disgraceful for her to appear outside unattended by her husband. The best praise of a woman was that there was no talk about her amongst men whether for good or evil. The result was widespread immorality. Even Pericles openly kept a mistress, Aspasia, who was famous for her beauty and her wit.

Although the material needs of life were few, there was still plenty of manual labour to be done; for this the Athenians depended, to a large extent, on slaves. We must never forget that these Greek states rested largely on a basis of slave labour. It is calculated that in Athens alone, the number of slaves was equal to that of the free citizens. But the slave did not have to suffer the hateful oppression which the Roman slave had to endure. He often worked side by side with his master in the pottery or the stonemason's yard, and was independent to the extent that a critic of Athenian democracy said the slaves were so impertinent that they would not get out of the way for one in the street.

THE IDEAL OF INTELLECTUAL BEAUTY

EARLY Greek education consisted of reading and writing and a little arithmetic. Boys learnt long passages of Homer by heart, not only for the literature, but for the religious and moral teaching. Skill in playing the flute and the harp was more than a social accomplishment, since it was believed that musical rhythms had a great effect on character and could make the soul harmonious and orderly. Athletics, chiefly wrestling and running and field events, were widely practised. Schools were private ventures, and teachers were despised. The state intervened only when the young men, at the age of eighteen, were compelled to do garrison service on the frontier for two years.

Although there was so little formal education, the citizen could easily obtain a wide and deep culture. In the temples he could see inspiring sculpture and architecture and, in the market-place, if he were a contemporary of Socrates, he could listen to the great teacher cross-examining some unwary victim who thought that he had knowledge which in fact he had not. The dramatic festivals, the law courts and the assembly all contributed to this education. In the evenings, dicing and drinking bouts and contests of wit provided diversion. The Athenian despised a man who was not adept in the give-and-take of conversation.

In the fifth century B.C., a class of teachers arose called Sophists (professors of wisdom) who taught grammar, mathematics, and astronomy. The most popular studies of all, however, were social virtue and the eloquence which could make a man successful in the assembly and the law courts. Such a training often subordinated plain honesty to the plausibility which could " make the worse appear the better reason." Some of the Sophists did a great service by insisting on the part played by education in developing character, but there were others who scoffed at traditional morality as the device of the weak to keep down the strong.

SOCRATES IN SEARCH OF FOUNDATIONS FOR VIRTUE

THE father of philosophy, Socrates of Athens (468–399 B.C.) sought to counter these lawless views by finding a basis for the virtues in the real needs of a man's best self. Philosophy before him had been busy with the study of the external world and the constitution of matter. Man had always wanted to know what the world is made of and how natural phenomena occur, but before Greek philosophy began he had been satisfied with a personal explanation—it was Zeus who sent the lightning. Thales, in the early sixth century B.C., brushed aside such explanations and said that the original substance was moisture. Other philosophers developed the idea of the four elements, earth, air, fire, and water. Pythagoras, a great geometrician and scientist, said that " things were numbers," that is, that the real essence of the world is to be found in proportion and mathematical relations. Democritus said that the world consisted of an infinite number of atoms moving about in infinite space.

Before Socrates man had given examples instead of definitions and had said that courage consisted of fighting bravely in battle. Socrates wanted to find a definition that would fit all the aspects of goodness. His own answer was that virtue was knowledge, that no one errs knowingly, but only because he thinks that he is benefiting himself. But this answer, which overlooked the element of will in deciding on an action, failed to solve the problem involved in the sentence " I see and approve the better course, but I follow the worse." The great achievement of Socrates was to concentrate inquiry, not on the world without, but on the soul within ; to ask " What is the good, and what are the relations of justice and courage and temperance and prudence to each other ? "

His dialectic, with its constant cross-examination, undermined the old beliefs without making shallow minds realise that devotion to truth should be the driving force of life. Some young men who had taken part in discussion with him attempted in 404 B.C. to overthrow the democracy. The attempt failed, but Socrates was accused of corrupting the youths and was condemned. Plato's description of his last hours is hardly inferior in pathos and majesty to the New Testament story of the death of Christ. The life of Socrates shows that the perfect identity between citizen and city which had made Athens so splendid was breaking down. Men were beginning to think that the individual could develop a life of his own apart from the state.

ATTEMPTS TO MAKE CERTAIN OF IMMORTALITY

BESIDES the worship of the Olympian gods, the Greeks had other cults more closely connected with their own lives. Orphism, named after a mythical bard, Orpheus, taught that man was a sinful creature who could be cured by receiving inspiration from the god Dionysus. The converted were promised eternal bliss. Another way of finding salvation was by initiation into the Mysteries. At these, the imagination of the worshipper was wrought to a high pitch of excitement by fasting and religious ecstasy, and the priests then acted a miracle play, an allegory from the annual death and resurrection of the corn, " the young green corn divinely springing." This produced a sort of conversion among the spectators, who became better men in this life and believed that they were certain of immortality.

Matthew Arnold has popularised the belief that the Greeks loved beauty, the Hebrews righteousness. The antithesis is too sharp. Nowhere is there more passion for righteousness than is shown in Plato (427–347 B.C.). He was not satisfied with the Orphic claim, " to save men by the barrel-load," but tried to give reasons for his views. He wrote many dialogues in which Socrates is supposed to be the chief speaker. In one of these, when told that the clever orator is so powerful that he can get the true statesman condemned to death, Socrates admits that this may be so, but does not give up his view that truth is best of all. The same spirit is shown in discussing punishment. If, he says, our aim in life is to make a man better, savage retribution will only make him worse. (Not until recent times did the English legal system show the same spirit of humane reasonableness.) Nor does this quality appear only in Plato. Once, when the Athenians had voted for the wholesale execution of rebellious subjects, a speaker pointed out that the death penalty was no deterrent if the motive for crime was strong enough, and suggested that generosity would be the truest wisdom.

Plato's greatest work is *The Republic*, a picture of a state governed by philosophers. In spite of its narrow outlook, based on the conditions of the city-state, *The Republic* surpasses all other books, except portions of the Bible, in the power to inspire a hunger and thirst after righteousness. Plato taught that there exist ideas, eternal and changeless, of which objects on earth are somehow copies. He said that the soul could learn to recognise these ideas and to guide its life on earth in accordance with them.

ARISTOTLE: "MASTER OF THOSE WHO KNOW"

THE permanence of the influence of Aristotle (384–322 B.C.) justifies Dante's description of him as " the Master of those who know." In every branch of learning, Aristotle based himself on close observation of fact. His pupils made a collection of a hundred and fifty different constitutions to form the basis of a theory of government. Alexander the Great, who had been his pupil, sent him specimens of animals and plants for his studies in biology and botany. In logic and philosophy, in ethics and politics and literature, he both summarised past learning and extended the bounds of human knowledge. His collected works form an encyclopædia of learning, so imposing that succeeding ages neglected to look beyond them and search out truth for themselves.

In the study of medicine, Greek lucidity of thought was revolutionary. Earlier peoples, believing that disease was sent by God, had tried to cure it by a mixture of magic and drugs. The new view was that all symptoms were equally divine, but that all obeyed natural law, which knew no exceptions. It was the doctor's duty to examine symptoms, and to decide on the result of that examination. It seems obvious enough now, but the Greeks pointed it out first.

THE GREATEST ACHIEVEMENT OF THE GREEKS

NEARLY every literary form used in Europe originated with the Greeks. Poetry, epic, lyric, elegy, drama, history, rhetoric, and comedy, are all names of Greek origin. In each of these a perfection was reached which has rarely been equalled.

Epic poetry starts with two poems by Homer, the *Iliad*, the story of Achilles' quarrel with Agamemnon and its consequences, and the *Odyssey*, the tale of Odysseus' wanderings on his return from Troy. Here, at the dawn of Greek and of European literature, we meet with all the qualities of the nation's genius perfectly united. An infinitely flexible metre and a rich vocabulary are handled with complete mastery. There is also that " simplicity, the greatest element in a noble character," which looks at things as they are and describes them easily and sympathetically. The Greeks do not " tear a passion to tatters." In the parting of Hector and Andromache, the meeting of Achilles and Priam, the death of Hector, we are made to feel the " pity of it all " with the utmost economy of means.

The *Odyssey* remains the world's greatest adventure story, with its gallant refrain, " so we sailed further, grieving for our friends, glad at our own escape from death." Greece never recaptured the freshness of that early world, when the eye saw all things new.

The new age, that of the lyric and elegiac poets, who sang of love and fighting, reached its climax in Pindar of Thebes (522–448 B.C.), the bard of the winners at the games. " The Theban eagle " soars in language of obscure splendour. His outlook on life is pessimistic. Life is short—darkness broken by gleams of light. The glory of victory at the Olympic games can lighten the darkness for the moment.

This view of life is reflected more deeply in the tragic drama. The drama grew out of the song of a chorus dancing at the festival of Dionysus. The addition of an actor in 534 B.C. turned this song into a dialogue. Later on, a second, and, finally, a third actor was added, thus making it possible to act a story instead of singing it. Within a century three composers of supreme genius developed the drama from a choric song to an action in which the problems of the universe are discussed. Æschylus (525–456 B.C.) tries to justify the ways of the old Greek gods to man in language of overpowering grandeur. Macbeth's " the multitudinous seas incarnadine " would have appealed to Æschylus. He taught that we learn by suffering, and tragedy, he said, came when men, " waxed fat and kicked " against the limits set by law or God, and a curse came upon the house where the " fathers had eaten sour grapes and the children's teeth were set on edge." The knot could only be cut by the intervention of the gods.

THE QUALITY SOPHOCLES AND SHAKESPEARE SHARED

SOPHOCLES (496–406 B.C.) exemplifies in his drama the Greek proverb, " Nothing in excess." He sees the gods as ordaining the rule of duty, " Stern daughter of the voice of God." His great heroine, Antigone, claims to be obeying divine law as against human. Full of natural piety and dignity, Sophocles is the typical classical writer. His style does not take the emotions by storm, but, with its subtle cadence, plucks at men's hearts. Shakespeare again provides an illustration. Othello, in his last speech, uses no metaphor or heightened expression, but merely " speaks straight on," yet his words are charged with an almost unbearable emotion. Sophocles could produce the same effect.

Euripides (480–406 B.C.) poured the new wine of fifth-century free-thinking into the old bottles of the divine myths. He was not an atheist ; the divine power, he felt, must exist, but why did it allow the sacking of cities and the brutal treatment of women ? He paints men as they are, not as they ought to be. Masculine self-satisfaction must have been shocked when the hero, Jason, is shown as a callous opportunist, impervious to Medea's attack on the fools who think that they are brave. " Why," she says, " I would rather stand in battle three times than bear a child once." His sympathy with human suffering made Euripides, in later ages, the best-loved of the dramatists. George Bernard Shaw has, likewise, tilted at tradition and attacked man's inhumanity to man, but with the weapon of comedy instead of that of tragedy.

THE UNCENSORED SATIRE OF ARISTOPHANES

WE must not fail to mention the unique genius of Aristo phanes, who, at the end of the fifth century, wrote comedies which mingle broad farce with lyrics of tender charm and bitter criticism of party opponents with exquisite pictures of life in Athens before the war took away " the margin of daily life." It is astounding to those of us who have experience of the close censorship exercised on speech and writing during the Great War, to see how freely Aristophanes could pillory the leading statesmen of Athens, even while she was fighting for her life.

In the writing of history, too, the Greeks were pioneers. Herodotus (484–425 B.C.) was a great advance on the chroniclers who had drily recorded events as they happened year by year. In order to write a history of the Persian wars, he engaged in an account of the whole world, and told some beguiling stories by the way. But he was more than a mere story-teller. His judgments were cool and fair, as when he showed that the Persians were not the cowardly slaves portrayed by Athenian patriotic dramatists, but brave, truthful, and able men. On the other hand, Thucydides (about 470–400 B.C.) described the Peloponnesian war on scientific principles. A subtle analyst of character and motive, he has drawn an unforgettable picture (every detail of which can be paralleled from contemporary Europe) of the baleful effect of civil war in corrupting normal decency. For massive concentration and political insight, Thucydides has no peer.

Free speech and political debate developed the art of oratory among the Greeks. Pericles owed his unique position to his masterly eloquence. After him there was a sequence of orators who spoke either in the courts or in the assembly. The greatest of them was Demosthenes (383–322 B.C.), who vainly attempted to arouse the Greeks against the rising power of Philip of Macedon. His last speech *On the Crown*, in which after Greek freedom had been destroyed, he justifies the policy he had advocated, is a marvellous vindication of the Greek city-state and the unrestricted liberty which it gave to all. It ranges from the bitterest invective to solemn panegyric of the heroic qualities of fifth-century Greece.

THE MAJESTIC BEAUTY OF GREEK ART

So deep was the Athenian love of sculpture that they did not abandon the policy of building temples to the gods even when the treasury was being exhausted by the war. Athene's temple, the Parthenon, begun in 447 B.C., with its processional approach, the Propylæa, was the greatest work

BURLESQUE BATTLE ON THE GREEK STAGE

Many scenes out of Greek comedy are represented on ancient ceramic vases. This incident, copied from a vase, shows two characters fighting before the goddess Juno.

of Greek architecture. Here the Athenians worshipped their goddess, not more in ritual forms than in marble. The emancipation from the stiffness of Egyptian statuary is complete, and the human form, naked and unashamed, lives and moves.

We still possess the frieze which ran round the outer upper part of the temple. The young Athenians are riding their horses in the Panathenaic procession, idealised human figures, for ever young and for ever new. We possess only descriptions of Phidias's great statue of Zeus at Olympia, but they can give us an idea of its profound majesty. The next age depicted the gods, not as the bearded councillors of Zeus, but as men of great beauty and grave serenity. There is no anguish on the brow of the Hermes of Praxiteles. His countenance is godlike in its unruffled contemplation. No greater mistake can be made than to suppose that Greek sculpture was one of cold perfection. The men and gods whom the Greeks sculptured were calm because they rested secure in their view of life, and believed that the gods approved "the depth and not the umult of the soul." Later sculptors could not breathe this rarefied Olympian air, and showed men in violent action, with their faces expressing every sort of emotion. A better taste will prefer the tombstones, which show us many examples of restrained sorrow. Emotion is there, but no hysteria, for " mortals must have mortal thoughts." Many of the

THE GLORY THAT WAS GREECE

Raised high above the city and the sea, the Parthenon has looked down on the passing of Athens' greatness.   But its columns remain, deep gold in the Ægean sunlight, undying, serene testimony to the ancient Greek genius.

statues were painted, but the colouring was done with restraint.

The design of the Greek temple has its limitations. Great spaces could be covered only by making the columns more ponderous, for the arch with which the Romans built their gigantic aqueducts and bridges was unknown to the Greeks. The Greek temple, particularly in the early Doric style, was simple and unadorned. Every part was designed to fulfil a special function, and was not loaded with superfluous ornament. Various optical corrections were introduced to give the impression of stability and straight lines. They even made the end column thicker because, being in the light, it would otherwise appear smaller than the columns against the background of the building.

FREEDOM: THE LEGACY OF GREECE

IT is doubtful whether the interior of the temples was as fine as the exterior. It seems that here the Athenians had not yet freed themselves from the Egyptian love of size for its own sake. The statue of Athene, which Phidias made to go inside the Parthenon, must, by its dimensions, have destroyed all the proportions of the interior. Yet the Parthenon, as seen on its hill above Athens, rests complete and whole and perfect. Compare the Gothic glories of Lincoln Cathedral, where the soaring columns appear to stretch on and on and lose themselves in the illimitable spaces of the vaulting.

Starting from Thales at the beginning of the sixth century, Greece had, in the years between, developed the most precious of human possessions, freedom of thought, and trusting steadily to the powers of reason, had opened up new worlds for the mind. This was the greatest period of mankind's history, when man threw off the age-long chains of servitude to priests in the spiritual life and to kings in political life, a free man who could " see life steadily and see it whole."

CULTURE IN THE WAKE OF GREEK CONQUEST

A CRUSADE of the united Greeks against decrepit Persia had been advocated, in the middle of the fourth century, by Isocrates, a political pamphleteer. Isocrates appealed to Philip of Macedon (359–336 B.C.), who accepted the suggestion and, after defeating the Greeks in 338 B.C., started to organise an expedition against Persia. In 336 B.C. he was assassinated and was succeeded by his twenty-year-old son, Alexander, who considered himself the destined missionary of Greek civilisation.

Alexander first quelled a rising of the Greek states, and then set out to conquer Persia. In 334 B.C. he landed in Asia Minor with a force of about forty thousand trained soldiers. It seems a small army with which to undertake the conquest of an empire, but it had been welded together by years of fighting, and was led by a supreme military genius. The Persian army, on the other hand, consisted chiefly of untrained levies differing in language and in equipment.

Alexander's first act on landing in Asia Minor was to visit Troy and, by sacrificing to the gods there, to invest himself with the halo of Homer's heroes. Then, in a series of great battles, he overthrew the Persian Empire, and by the year 331 B.C. was the acknowledged ruler of the Ancient East. The next five years were spent in establishing a chain of Greek settlements and garrison posts all the way from Persia, right across Asia, and over the Khyber Pass into India. When he reached the Punjab, his Macedonians refused to accompany him further, and so he sailed down the Indus to the Indian Ocean, and then marched back to Babylon along the coast, 325–324 B.C.

COSMOPOLITANISM AND THE CULT OF THE KING GOD

ALEXANDER planned a universal empire in which there was to be no distinction between Greek and barbarian. To further this end, he not only founded many colonies to serve as centres for the spread of Greek civilisation, but himself took a Persian wife and made his Macedonian and Greek officers follow his example. The great governorships were not restricted to Greece, but were shared with Persian nobles. By having himself proclaimed a god, he sought recognition for his universal empire overriding the loyalties due to each separate city-state. It must not be supposed, however, that either he or the Greeks really believed in his divine origin. His conquests widened his outlook spiritually as well as geographically and made him the first to dream of a " Parliament of Man and Federation of the world."

On Alexander's death in 323 B.C. the empire at once broke up into three sections, Egypt under Ptolemy, Asia under Seleucus, and Macedonia under Antigonus. Of these kingdoms, Macedonia had the worst fortune. She was continually struggling to hold down rebellious cities in Greece, and to repel invading Celtic tribes from the Danube. These tribes, called the Gauls, were in the fourth and third centuries

B.C. advancing upon the Mediterranean countries from Asia Minor to France.

Greece itself remained as disunited as ever. Athens, now unimportant politically, became the university of the Greek world. Sparta continued in unsociable isolation. The rest of Greece took some steps towards forming confederations. The Ætolians, to the north of the Gulf of Corinth, and the Achæans to the south of it, each established federal centres, to which people came from the outside districts to vote at the elections ; but there was no regular meeting of the assembly, and power was in the hands of the elected generals. These two confederacies continued to fight each other, and Sparta and Macedonia as well, until they were put down by the Romans in the second century B.C. They had been warned in 217 B.C. that Rome would swallow them up if they did not unite. They agreed that the advice was good, but continued to disregard it. It was little wonder that the Romans despised the unpractical Greeks.

THE GREEK IDEAL SPREADS THROUGH THE EAST

ALEXANDER succeeded in his main aim of spreading Greek civilisation, for the Seleucid kings of Syria built their palaces in Grecian style, filled their courts with Greek artists and philosophers, and founded Greek colonies. The passion for Greek culture and speech spread among the natives, who often forgot their own languages, and produced able writers and scholars. The Parthians, in the second century B.C., after taking Mesopotamia from the Seleucids, continued to delight in Greek drama. The Jews themselves, the most clannish and exclusive of peoples, had to translate their scriptures into Greek, because so many of them were ignorant of Hebrew. (This translation is called the Septuagint.)

Egypt, under the Ptolemies, flourished exceedingly. The capital, Alexandria, became the greatest commercial port of the Mediterranean. Here was founded the great university and library, whose professors, paid by the state, conducted researches into every branch of knowledge. This period from 300 to 100 B.C. is remarkable for the marvellous discoveries made in mathematics and astronomy, botany and zoology. Not until the great revival of learning in the fifteenth and sixteenth centuries A.D., was there any comparable advance in knowledge. Euclid wrote the text-book on geometry which is the basis of our school geometries to-day. His love of learning for its own sake is illustrated by his retort when a pupil asked him what he should gain by learning geometry. Turning to a servant, Euclid said, " Give him three pence, since he must needs make money by what he learns."

Archimedes, a great engineer, discovered the principle of the lever and invented the water-screw, which is still in use to-day. Aristarchus anticipated Copernicus by showing that the earth moves round the sun, and itself rotates on its own axis. This discovery was not accepted at the time, and it was left to later research to prove its truth. Eratosthenes measured the circumference of the earth fairly accurately, and Hipparchus invented trigonometry and discovered and estimated the precession of the equinoxes.

PHILOSOPHERS OF THE LATER GREEK WORLD

PRACTICAL studies can flourish even under a tyranny, but philosophy withers in the artificial atmosphere of a court. The ethical teachers of the new age settled not in Alexandria but in Athens. Man had dwindled in stature with the growth of the military empires and the degradation of city-states into country towns. The new kingdoms aroused no patriotic or national feeling. Men had to turn from the invigorating atmosphere of politics and submit passively to royal officials and tax collectors. The endless wars which devastated Greece and Asia Minor made the ordinary individual feel a helpless victim of blind chance. Menander (342–292 B.C.), the famous writer of comedy of this age, gives us an unlovely picture of the narrow and monotonous social life which men endured. The morality of his stock characters is as mean as that in a comedy of Congreve, but their conversation lacks Congreve's redeeming wit.

The new philosophies no longer sought absolute truth, but tried to offer men some prop to lean on in an unstable world. Thus Epicurus (341–270 B.C.) said that pleasure was the end of life, but by pleasure he meant the absence of pain, not sensual indulgence. He himself lived a retiring life, content with friendship and frugality. He held that though the gods existed, they took no interest in human affairs, and that when life ended there was nothing thereafter. Progress had come by a natural development, and not by any divine plan. This teaching was unpopular because of its attack on the old superstitions, and its disbelief in divine interest in human affairs. It also incurred odium because too many people

misunderstood its teaching and professed Epicureanism as an
excuse for their own debauchery.

On the other hand, Zeno (about 336–264 B.C.), the founder
of the Stoic school (Greek *stoa*, a covered porch, where his
students gathered at Athens), taught that virtue was the only
thing worth seeking, that actions were neither good nor bad
in themselves, but depended on the state of mind in which
they were performed. The road to happiness lay in disregarding all material considerations for the sake of personal
righteousness. Alexander's conquest may have suggested to
the Stoics their political theory that the universe was a single
city in which all men were brothers akin possessing freedom
and equality without distinction of colour or creed. Rousseau's
" Man is born free, but is everywhere in chains," reminds us
at once of this view so radical and revolutionary in its possibilities. The Stoic teaching, with its emphasis on duty and
conscience, appealed to the finer spirits among the stern,
unbending Romans whose history we are soon to examine.

THE CIVILISATIONS OF ASIA

THE Greeks and Romans were satisfied with their own
Mediterranean world and knew little of India and China
except as lands from which came spices and silks. It might
have surprised them to know that in these remote countries
dwelt peoples who enjoyed good government and a fine
civilisation. India had been invaded in the second millennium
B.C. by some Aryan tribes who belonged to the great group
of Indo-European peoples. The newcomers spread over
Northern India, subjugated the dark-skinned natives, and
imposed on them their language, and, finally, their religion.

In course of time, the population became divided into
separate classes, each with its own status and functions.
These *castes*, as they were called, were intended to keep the
fair-skinned conquerors apart from the dark-hued subjects, and
consisted of the priests, the nobles and warriors, the peasants
and traders, and, lastly, the lower labourers who belonged to
the native races. Below these came the " hewers of wood and
drawers of water," despised members of the native races who
were " outcasts." The separation between these classes was
rigid and permanent, for no intermarriage and no personal
contact was allowed between them.

These Aryan invaders spoke a language called Sanskrit,

which, though more primitive than Latin and Greek, is of the same type. We still have their religious books, called the Vedas, from which it appears that they first worshipped the powers of nature. Later on, they came under the control of their priests. These priests who were called Brahmins (from *Brahma*, which means the supreme God), did not insist on worship of one god only, but allowed the people to worship as many as they liked. The religion became a mixture of luke-warm belief in one spirit which pervades the universe, and fervent devotion to many local gods and spirits.

The outlook on life of these people was very different from that of Western races. They believed with us that life is full of pain and evil, but whereas we decide that our task is to improve the world, they drew the conclusion that the only remedy was to retire from the world and " to study being dead," because only thus could the soul be freed from the prison-house of the body and be reabsorbed in the all-pervading soul of the universe. It was not easy, according to the priests, to purify the soul completely. One had to be reborn on earth over and over again before the desires of the body were com-pletely purged. So arrogant were these priests that they excluded the lower labourers and the outcasts from sharing in this creed.

GREAT RELIGIOUS TEACHERS OF THE ORIENT

THEN arose a great teacher, Gautama (557–477 B.C.), to whom the name Buddha (the Enlightened) was given. He denied that the Brahmins had the monopoly of religious truth, and opened to all classes without exception the possibili-ties of reaching *Nirvana*, which means the removal of all base vices and the extinction of future existence and pain. Though he did not attack the caste system, he taught that Nirvana could be won, not by self-torture or by special rites, but by practising virtue, which consists above all else in loving others and injuring no living thing. Buddha's preaching was immediately popular, but was not widespread until the reign of Asoka (264–228 B.C.)

This king was the grandson of a Hindu who had met Alexander when he conquered India in 327 B.C., and had unfolded to him plans for further conquests. Alexander had been prevented by his soldiers from following these suggestions, but the Hindu had won himself a kingdom on his own account in the Ganges Valley (321–296 B.C.). Asoka was so convinced

(Left)
Kartikeya
(the War God)

(Right)
Surya
(the Sun God)

Ganesa
(God of
Prudence)

Krishna
(the Preserver)

CURIOUSLY FASHIONED HINDU DEITIES

These figures, typical of the mysticism of the East, are worshipped as symbols of the forces of destruction and preservation.

of the truth of Buddha's teaching that he sent missionaries to spread this gospel all over India, and even established a Ministry of Religion to see that the creed remained uncontaminated by false doctrines. His care extended to the body as well as to the soul. Under his encouragement wells were dug and trees planted, and medical treatment provided for men and animals. Later, however, when the Brahmins regained their old powers, Buddhism found a new home in China, where it became the most popular of all religions.

China had been occupied in the third millennium B.C. by a yellow race called the Mongols, but its history is obscure for thousands of years. The land was nominally under the rule of a central monarchy, but actually was split up into numerous independent states which were constantly at war with each other. The first great name we meet with is that of Confucius (551–478 B.C.), a sage who laid no claim to any divine inspiration, but tried to teach men how to live together in society. He taught the golden rule that one should do as one would be done by. His remedy for the troubles of the country was to find a model ruler who would guide the people according to the ancient ways.

CHINA: CONFUCIUS AND THE GREAT WALL

IN philosophic depth, Confucius cannot be compared with Buddha, and his practical teaching suffers from the universal fault of his countrymen, namely, the tendency to look backward instead of forward. His teachings were later expounded by Mencius (371–288 B.C.). The Chinese had yet another religion called Taoism which surpassed Confucianism in its attempt to explain the universe, but which was contaminated by superstitious practices. These religions were forced to take second place when Buddhism reached China in the first century B.C. The ordinary man, however, whatever his nominal creed, refused to give up his candles and his incense, and his prayers for help directed to his local deities.

The Chinese early attained a high degree of civilisation, and then developed no further. Their system of education demanded a knowledge of the sacred books edited by Confucius. As these books harp on the twin virtues of filial piety and respect for the past, the people's lack of originality is not surprising. Nor did their language help to counteract this conservatism, consisting, as it did, of thousands of symbols, each of them representing a word or part of a word. Not even Babylonian, with its four or five hundred syllables, could be more difficult than this. Yet the people were not lacking in energy. They built roads and canals and made the land fertile. One of their kings in the third century B.C. built the Great Wall of China, 1500 miles long, to protect the northern countries from the raids of the nomad Huns, another Mongol tribe. Those who are accustomed to marvel at the remains of Roman roads and walls cannot deny that they appear quite insignificant compared with this gigantic feat of construction.

THE WEST ENTERS WORLD HISTORY : ROME

IT was a fortunate event that geography placed Italy and Greece back to back. Italy with a rugged east coast has all its good harbours on the west. Greece, on the other hand, faces east towards the ancient civilisations, and presents its mountainous west coast to Italy. Thus Greece was enabled to learn the rudiments of civilisation from Egypt and Babylon, and to develop its own culture before being absorbed by the military power of Rome. Italy offered an opportunity for the growth of larger associations than the Greek city-states. Three groups of peoples inhabited the country. There were the warlike and uncultured Indo-European tribes who had entered Italy in the second millennium B.C. ; the Etruscans, who held the whole of the west coast down to the Tiber, and lay across the whole breadth of Italy to the north of Rome ; and the prosperous Greek colonies in the south.

The site of Rome lies fourteen miles from the mouth of the River Tiber, which flows into the Tuscan sea half way down the west coast of Italy. The advantages of this position were numerous. It was far enough from the sea to be safe from raiding pirates, and the hills on which the town was built rose up above the malarial swamps of the plain and kept away fevers and plagues. Here, moreover, the lowest practicable ford across the river made the city the centre of traffic routes from north to south.

Rome's first appearance on the stage of history was not brilliant. Together with a group of tribes in the district called Latium, south of the Tiber, she was conquered by the Etruscans. Her native kings were expelled and a line of Etruscan rulers laboured to make the city prosperous. Republican sentiment later branded them as tyrants, but they gave Rome her military training and her passion for building, her religious system and her faith in divination. In 509 B.C. these kings were expelled by a rising of the native Latins, led by the tribal chiefs.

WHEN ROME WAS RULED BY WEALTH ALONE

FOR the next two hundred years the internal history of Rome consisted of a struggle in which the Senate and the hereditary nobility of wealthy landowners, called Patricians (*Patricii*), tried to prevent the Plebeians (*Plebs*), the commoners, from acquiring equal status.

The assembly of the people started as a group on a combined family and local basis. This decayed, and was succeeded by an assembly based on wealth, as shown in the capacity to provide oneself with arms. The wealthy classes were ensured control because the votes were weighted in their favour. The Roman assembly was less effective than the assemblies of the Greek city-states because only magistrates had the right to address it. There was no debating between rival politicians, and all that the citizens could do was to answer " yes " or " no " to the questions put before them.

The chief magistracy was the consulship, an annual office, for which only Patricians were eligible, although the whole body of citizens voted at the elections. The Consuls, of whom there were two, each with power to veto the other's actions, were the embodiment of the authority (*imperium*) of the State. They were attended by officials, each carrying a bundle of rods (*fasces*), with an axe in the middle, to indicate that the Consuls had power to scourge and to execute. (The Fascisti of modern Italy derive their name from this Latin word.)

As the State grew larger, some of the duties of the Consuls were divided among subordinate officers. The *quæstors* attended to financial affairs, the *prætors* both administered and developed the law by their decisions, very much in the way that our judges do, the *censors* guarded the traditional decency and dignity, kept the roll of citizens, and assessed the taxes. In times of crisis, a dictator with absolute power was temporarily appointed. The restriction of office to one year, and the division of office between two magistrates who could veto each other's acts, was meant to prevent any attempt at monarchy. It was possible only because the Romans had a strong sense of what is right and proper (*gravitas*), and, believing strongly in precedent, altered their constitution to suit the needs of the time.

"A BODY OF KINGS": THE SENATE

THE "Council of Old Men," consisting of three hundred patricians, gradually usurped control of the government, not by any legal enactment, but by slowly extending custom. The Consuls always asked for their advice and always took it. The Senate made the laws, and the assembly's consent became a mere formality. This oligarchy contained the accumulated experience of the State, and kept its policy sane and consistent. It could sympathise with a defeated general, and did not make panic decisions as Greek democracies had been liable to do.

The first plebeian gain was the institution of "tribunes of the people," elected by the plebs in their own tribal assembly. These officers were the watch-dogs of the people. They could initiate legislation which should be binding on all plebeians, and could veto safely any act of any magistrate, because their persons were declared sacrosanct. The next step was the publication of the Twelve Tables of the Laws in 450 B.C. Henceforth a man knew the extent of his liabilities, instead of having the threat of unknown penalties hanging over him.

Gradually the plebeians obtained full equality, social and political, with the patricians, and by 280 B.C. decisions taken in the assembly of the people were binding on the State. This, however, did not help the common people, as the patricians absorbed the leading plebeians into their own ranks. The high offices of State became the preserve of a close oligarchy, and a Consul who was self-made, and had no ex-Consuls in his family, was a very rare phenomenon.

RIVALS BEAT IN VAIN AT THE DOORS OF ROME

THE young Republic survived with difficulty an Etruscan attempt to restore the expelled royal house (510 B.C.). Soon after this date, the Etruscan power began to decline under repeated Gallic raids. Rome herself was sacked by the Gauls in 390 B.C., but bought them off.

The city's chief enemies were the tribes on the foothills of the Apennines, and on the plain to the south. She fought them again and again and beat them one after the other. To hold them down, she started building military roads, and establishing colonies, detached portions of Rome, at strategic points. Her own allies in the Latin League of cities in the region south of Rome, feeling themselves overshadowed, tried conclusions with her in vain (338 B.C.). The conquered cities were not allowed to have direct relations with each other, either in politics or trade or marriage. This was the famous policy of " divide and conquer," which not only kept the cities apart but made Rome a centre of trade for them all.

By chance, in the fourth century B.C., Rome evolved a method of government which was new in world history—the method of gradual incorporation in the Roman State. The Italian communities were first given private rights of marriage and trade with Rome, combined with the duty of military service. Later on they might receive " Latin rights " which included the privilege of becoming full citizens by settling at Rome. The last stage was the grant of full citizenship. Athens had failed because she did not take her subjects into partnership. Rome made her citizenship a desirable privilege which loyalty could win. At first she imposed it by force and the victims objected to losing their national identity. Then, when the profits of success came to be distributed, the tribes clamoured for admission, and fought with her because it was denied. The Roman Empire succeeded by bringing its subjects under one universal rule. The British Empire, on the other hand, maintains itself by training its subjects for self-government, a more difficult, though a higher and more fruitful achievement.

By the year 280 B.C., Roman conquests had reached the hills overlooking the Po valley. Then after beating Pyrrhus, exponent of the highest military science of the Greeks, who had come to help the Greek cities of the South against her, she annexed the rest of Italy down to the Straits of Messina (266 B.C.)

THE MEN WHO MADE ROME

THE Roman family was based on *patria potestas* (the power of the father), which gave the father the power of life and death over wife, unmarried daughters, and sons with their wives and children. Even if the son were a Consul, the necessity to obey his father remained undiminished. The mother, though confined to housekeeping duties, was not, like the Greek wife, just an instrument for bearing legitimate children, but was revered as the guardian of pure morality. This close bond of authority on one side and obedience on the other produced men to whom duty and devotion to the State were all in all. They were very like the English in their respect for tradition and their dislike for logic. Unlike the Greek, who tried to plan the future, the conservative Roman preferred to "muddle through," and to solve each emergency as it came.

The Roman religion was one of purely external forms. Man's relation to the gods was one of give and take. The

BATTLE FORMATION OF THE ROMAN LEGIONARIES

After the front rank had thrown their spears, they ran on the enemy with their short swords, falling back, eventually, for the next rank to make a fresh onslaught. The men in the third rank were armed with 18-foot pikes.

gods received victims and incense and were expected to give their help in return. Set forms of worship were prescribed, and any flaw meant that the rite had to be started all over again. This was typical of the national insistence on the letter of the law. The god would get out of the bargain, if he found his worshipper making a mistake.

The Roman citizen was a peasant farmer. He loved to tell stories of how his heroes were called from the plough to battle, and returned to the plough as soon as the enemy had been beaten. The long wars, however, could not be carried on with occasional levies of untrained peasants, and early in the fourth century the institution of soldiers' pay enabled a trained army to develop.

Rome beat her enemies by superiority in the art of war. Military discipline gave her soldiers that " two o'clock in the morning courage " which no other nation of antiquity ever possessed. The phalanx, the body of spearmen who won by weight of numbers, was borrowed from Greece, but made more flexible by the arranging of the legions—the army divisions— in such a way that the front division was spaced out more, and left room for the second division to come forward without crowding the line.

THE "MACHINE-GUN FIRE" OF THE ROMAN LEGIONS

INSTEAD of the long spear of the Grecian heavy-armed warrior, the soldiers were equipped with short throwing-spears, which were used in a way analogous to modern machine-gun fire. As soon as the enemy came within range, these spears were aimed at their shields. The point penetrated deep into the shield, but the shaft, being of soft metal, bent so that it could not be pulled out and thrown back straight. The soldiers then advanced on the embarrassed enemy with the short and handy stabbing sword. So thorough was the discipline that after each day's march a mound of earth was dug round the camp. This was crowned with a palisade of stakes, and kept away surprise attacks. The Roman soldier, with his sword and spear, his entrenching tool and his stakes, and his rations for seventeen days, must have carried as heavy a kit as British soldiers did in the Great War. The legions were divided into units called centuries, each in command of a centurion, who combined the duties of a sergeant-major and a captain. The higher officers consisted of the Consul and his picked staff of young nobles. In the fourth century, the inconvenience of making a Consul leave the army at the end of his year of office led to the institution of the proconsulship, which enabled him to stay in command for another year.

The battle between the Indo-European and the Semite which had been fought in the Eastern Mediterranean, was now renewed in the West. Commerce and trade had developed with the growth of Empire, but the Roman merchants, anxious to extend their operations overseas, found the way barred by Carthage, which controlled the corn trade of North Africa, the silver mines of Southern Spain, and the carrying trade of the whole Mediterranean. She even had commercial posts on the Atlantic coast of Africa, and allowed no foreign ship to pass through the Straits of Gibraltar. Carthaginian colonies in Sardinia and Corsica and the west coast of Sicily had existed for centuries. Peaceful expansion for Rome seemed impossible. Therefore she turned to war, where the chances were good. The Carthaginian government was an oligarchy of wealthy traders, relying on a mercenary army and navy, not on land-owning citizen farmers, hardened by two centuries of war.

HOW A WEAK NAVY CONQUERED THE SEAS

IN the first Punic War (264–241 B.C.), Rome improvised a fleet, but her generals were far inferior in naval tactics to the experienced admirals of their opponents. This weakness was overcome by means of the *corvus*, a drawbridge with a large spike in the middle of the under side. When the ships had drawn up alongside, this was let down upon the enemy's deck, thus making it impossible for him to use the skill of his rowers. It was a crude device, but it turned a sea-battle into a land-battle, and gave victory to the Romans. They exacted a large indemnity and annexed Sicily, their first province.

In the following years, Rome seized Sardinia and Corsica, contrary to the terms of the treaty, and also extended her empire over the Po valley. Carthage sought compensation by the conquest of Spain, where she built up a powerful army. The second Punic War (218–202 B.C.) was started by her general, Hannibal, a great strategist, who crossed the Alps and invaded Italy from the North. He had only forty thousand soldiers against the seven hundred thousand of the Roman confederacy, yet, in a series of battles, he nearly overthrew the Republic. Army after army of the Romans was cut to pieces, but even after the fatal day of Cannae (216 B.C.) when seventy thousand soldiers were slaughtered, the Senate refused to despair. The Italian allies stood firm and very few of the Latin cities revolted. Southern Italy went over to Hannibal, but did not give him much real help. The policy of Fabius, nicknamed *Cunctator* (the Procrastinator), that of constantly harassing the enemy but always avoiding pitched battles, was adopted. The revolting cities

were won back, and the relieving force, which Hannibal'
brother Hasdrubal was bringing from Spain, was annihilate
in 207 B.C.   Meanwhile, Rome had herself found a genera
Scipio, who, after driving the Carthaginians out of Spai
carried the war across into Africa.   Hannibal was recalled
but was defeated at the battle of Zama in 202 B.C., and Carthag
surrendered.

Rome exacted an enormous indemnity and forbade Carthag
to build a navy or to make war without the consent of th
Romans.   Finally, when Carthaginian prosperity began t
revive, a pretext for war was found, the people wer
treacherously deprived of their arms, and their city razed t
the ground in 146 B.C.   In the next two generations Rom
annexed Macedonia and Greece, made Egypt a vassal state
and acquired a large province in Asia Minor (201–133 B.C.).

A CHANCE THE EMPIRE-BUILDERS MISSED

IN the struggle with Carthage, Rome, however uninten-
tionally, had been the champion of civilisation.   A Carthaginian victory would have choked the channels by which the
achievements of Greece were being conveyed to the West.
But the Roman Senate did not fully grasp its opportunity,
and never conceived the possibility of incorporating the
provinces in the Roman state.   Each province as it was
conquered received a Roman governor with unlimited civil
and military power.   The governor was not trained for his
position and his brief period of service gave him no chance
of acquiring experience.

There was no body of civil servants to establish any continuity of practice, but each governor took out with him his
own staff which was as inexperienced as himself.   The
provincials were permitted to retain local self-government
but were disarmed and not allowed to make war independently.
Taxes were imposed, but the collection of them was farmed
out to private capitalists, with the result that the helpless
provincials were fleeced by tax-gatherers as well as by governors.   Their only hope of redress lay in a direct appeal to
Rome.   In 149 B.C. a court was established to hear charges
of extortion against governors, but Rome was far away,
and the Senate, which should have been the agent of
justice, was composed of friends and relations of the
accused, and lavish bribery nearly always secured an
acquittal.

THE MINDS AND HOMES OF ROME ENRICHED

ROME was filled with the wealth of the world, and the old spirit of frugality gave way to extravagant luxury. Refinement in housing and manners led to attempted refinement in culture. Greece took her savage capturer captive. Even Cato, who had inveighed against the new-fangled learning, himself learnt Greek in his old age. Roman education had demanded little more from a boy than an elementary knowledge of the three R's. This was now supplemented by training in Greek literature; Greek tragedies and comedies were translated into Latin, and teachers of rhetoric found ready pupils. Two writers of comedy, Plautus and Terence, who flourished after the second Punic War, wrote fairly original plays based on Greek models. The Roman mob, however, preferred to watch the organised brutality of gladiators fighting to the death, and the breath-taking struggles of the chariot races.

Rome was crowded with an unemployed population, eking out a living on free corn distributed by the State, and bribes dispensed liberally by rival seekers for office. The second Punic War had laid waste large districts of Italy, and many soldiers who had found country life dull after the excitement of war sold their ancestral farms and drifted to Rome. Rich men bought up the small estates, and formed large sheep farms worked by gangs of slaves. Even if a man wanted to keep his farm, he could not compete with the cheap grain which poured in from Sicily, Africa, and Egypt. Large areas of the country went out of cultivation altogether. The slaves, made savage by their treatment, broke out in ferocious revolt, which was as ferociously repressed. In 73 B.C. a gladiator, Spartacus by name, rallied discontented gladiators and slaves and terrorised Southern Italy for two years. The roads of Italy were infested by bands of robbers. In the provinces things were even worse. It seemed as though revolution was imminent.

THE FIRST POLITICAL MURDER IN ROME

THERE were two main problems to be faced; the first was to get the city populace back to the land, the other to pacify the Italian allies who had fought Rome's battles for her without sharing the proceeds of victory, for the old policy of bestowing citizenship liberally upon conquered

3

tribes had been long ago abandoned, and there were large areas of Italy still unenfranchised. But nothing was done by the Senate, which had degenerated into an assembly of selfish plutocrats.

The initiative was taken by the tribune Tiberius Gracchus who, in 133 B.C., brought forward a law for resuming the state lands which had been appropriated by private individuals. This proposal, which interfered with vested interests, was passed only after a bitter struggle, and when Gracchus sought re-election he was murdered by a band of Senators. The introduction of an economic dispute into the struggle of parties had caused the first political murder in Rome.

Gaius Gracchus, the brother of Tiberius, renewed the struggle on a greater scale. He tried to organise an opposition class of capitalists who were outside the Senate. This class of rich men called *equites* (knights) received a virtual monopoly for collecting the taxes of the province of Asia, and from them was formed a court to try Senatorial Governors accused of extortion in the provinces. Gracchus also proposed to found colonies and to create employment by building roads. But he went too far, even for the mob, when he suggested the enfranchisement of the Italian allies. Senate and people were alike unwilling to share the profits of empire with any one else. In 121 B.C. Gaius, too, was murdered.

THE CITY INVITES HER SOLDIERS TO RULE

THE fate of the Gracchi proved that reform by constitutional means was impossible. Henceforth the popular leaders were to be soldiers, not politicians. The first of these was Marius (155–86 B.C.), who had risen from the ranks by sheer merit. He proved himself a great general by crushing two barbarian hordes which were threatening Rome from the north (102–101 B.C.). His military innovations were revolutionary. Conscription and the property qualifications for service were replaced by voluntary enlistment. The army was composed of professional soldiers, who took the oath of loyalty to the general and not to the State, and who looked to him for their reward in war and peace. When Marius returned to Rome in 100 B.C. he failed to produce any constructive policy, and went into retirement.

The discontent of the Italian allies boiled over into open war (90–88 B.C.), which Rome ended by granting citizenship to all who wanted it. The effect of the concession was nullified because the new citizens were crowded into a few tribes and could not exercise influence proportionate to their numbers. In any case, most of them lived too far from Rome to be able to come there for the elections, so that disproportionate political power lay in the hands of the dwellers in Rome. The fact was that a city-state had developed into a nation without knowing it. There were two ways in which this state of affairs could have been remedied—by the personal rule of one man or by a system of representative government. The widespread anarchy made the first solution inevitable.

The next military leader was Sulla, a brilliant general and a champion of the Senate, who had himself elected Consul (88 B.C.). After defeating Mithridates, an oriental king who had invaded the Roman province of Asia Minor, he returned to Rome and became dictator. A reign of terror followed, in which party hatred was glutted by confiscations and licensed murder (82–81 B.C.).

Sulla tried to turn back the clock by passing laws which made the Senate ruler of the State (we must remember that senatorial rule had up to now rested only on the custom of the constitution). The powers of the assembly of the people and of the tribunes were made ineffective.

The people found a leader in Pompey, a stolid but conscientious and able organiser who, ten years afterwards (70 B.C.), succeeded in repealing the Sullan legislation. Pompey then put down piracy in the Mediterranean and crushed Mithridates, who had renewed the war in the East (67–62 B.C.).

THE IMPERIAL LINE OF CÆSARS

MEANWHILE a realist had appeared in Rome in the person of Julius Cæsar (102–44 B.C.), who joined the extreme section of the democratic party and was probably behind the attempt of Catiline, a debauched noble, to start a revolution in 63 B.C. This attempt miscarried owing to the activity and eloquence of Cicero, the greatest of Roman orators. Cicero was a true patriot, who advocated a union of classes. Sprung from the Italian middle classes, he had joined the party of the Senate as a friend of constitutional government. Cicero failed to see that the time for this was past.

In 60 B.C., Pompey, alienated by the Senate, joined in a

coalition with Cæsar and Crassus, the richest man in Rome. Cæsar was elected Consul in 59 B.C. and forced through Pompey's settlement of Asia Minor. Crassus received financial advantages in the placing of contracts. For himself, Cæsar secured an appointment for five years as governor of Cisalpine Gaul (the Po valley), and Transalpine Gaul (Southern France). In Gaul, Cæsar discovered his own military genius and forged the army which subsequently won him the Empire. Roman rule was extended to the Atlantic, Britain was raided, and invading tribes from Germany were driven back across the Rhine. These successes made Pompey jealous and uneasy, for he wanted to be the indispensable servant and saviour of the State. The death of Crassus in 53 B.C. left the rivals face to face, and the Senate, playing on Pompey's fears, used him as a catspaw against Cæsar, who was obviously intending to make himself master of Rome.

After some manœuvring for position on either side, civil war broke out in 49 B.C. Cæsar put himself technically in the wrong by crossing the River Rubicon, the boundary of his province, with an armed force. Pompey had no army ready to face him, and fled to Greece with the Senate. There he started collecting a huge army from the Eastern provinces. Meanwhile, Cæsar occupied Rome and agreeably disappointed expectations by refusing to sanction another reign of terror. He first crushed Pompey's supporters in Spain, and then, with his rear secure, he crossed over to Greece and defeated Pompey at Pharsalus (48 B.C.). Pompey fled to Egypt, where he was murdered, and so escaped the ignominy of being pardoned by Cæsar. The free republic was ended.

THE IDES OF MARCH : "AMBITION'S DEBT IS PAID"

THE next three years were spent by Cæsar in campaigns in Asia, Egypt, and Africa, until by 45 B.C. he was master of the Roman world. But, as was shown by his dallying with Cleopatra of Egypt for nearly a year, and by his bombastic three-word despatch after a campaign in the East, " I came, I saw, I conquered " (*Veni, vidi, vici*), success had blunted his judgment. On the 15th, the Ides of March, 44 B.C., he was assassinated by a group of reactionary republicans, headed by Brutus and Cassius. Shakespeare's *Julius Cæsar* gives us a vivid picture of the events leading up to and following the assassination.

Cæsar had formed far-reaching plans for remoulding

and enlarging the empire, but he outraged sentiment by his open contempt for the old constitution. The Senate was increased in numbers and filled with provincials and freed slaves. Rome was not to be superior to the other cities of the empire, and Alexander's cosmopolitanism was to be revived, with the Latins as leaders of the world. The assumption of a life dictatorship awakened the inherited Roman prejudice against kings and caused Cæsar's death.

This event showed how necessary his rule had been. Anarchy and bloodshed followed for another thirteen years, until his grand-nephew and adopted son, Gaius Octavius, known as Augustus (63 B.C.–A.D. 14), restored peace. In 45 B.C., Augustus [1] was only eighteen years old, but he managed to assert his right as Cæsar's heir against Mark Antony, who had been one of Cæsar's followers. The two joined forces and aided by another general, Lepidus, defeated Brutus and Cassius at Philippi in 42 B.C. The Empire was partitioned between the three victors. Antony went to Egypt and fell victim to Cleopatra's lures. Augustus conquered the West, took Africa from Lepidus, and in 31 B.C. beat Antony in a great naval battle at Actium off the west coast of Greece. Rome had fallen under the rule of her wisest son, and the hundred years of agony were over.

THE GOLDEN YEARS RETURN

AUGUSTUS avoided Cæsar's mistakes. He grasped at the substance and let go the shadow of monarchy. His military rule was clothed in republican forms. The Senate conferred on him all the powers of the Republic, and those only for a fixed term of years. These powers were renewed from time to time, not only because he had command of the army, but because with each year the State became more dependent on him. His aims differed from those of Cæsar, who had

[1] The full titles of Gaius Octavius were Emperor Augustus Cæsar. *Emperor* was originally the title borne by Roman commanders of an army, then it was assumed by governors of a province, and finally by the heads of the Roman Empire. *Augustus* was a title bestowed on Octavius by the Roman Senate in 27 B.C. for services rendered the State ; it was afterwards assumed as the first title of his successors. *Cæsar* was the name of the patrician family of the Julia gens (the family of Julius Cæsar) and it was adopted by Octavius as heir presumptive to Julius Cæsar ; it was thus originally a title equivalent to Prince of Wales. It was afterwards adopted as the second title of the Roman emperors.

intended to assimilate Italy to the rest of the Empire, for Augustus came from the old Italian stock and wished to ensure its predominance. The Assemblies were permitted to meet and approve legislation and elect candidates recommended by Augustus. The Senate was purged of provincials and freed slaves, and permitted to retain a share in the government.

This dyarchy (joint rule) had no basis in fact and the Emperors gradually encroached on the functions of the Senate, and removed the fictions which disguised their military and personal rule. Another influence tending to exalt the Princeps (First Citizen) was the cult of Rome and Augustus. After his death he was deified—a cult taken from the Hellenistic kingdoms—and priests of Augustus were appointed in all cities of the Empire. The infection spread even to Rome, for the giver of peace seemed to be of superhuman power.

Augustus preferred to consolidate rather than to extend the Empire. He sought great natural boundaries, such as the Sahara desert, behind the Roman province of Africa, the Euphrates, to mark the division between the Syrian province and the growing empire of the Parthians, and the line of the Rhine and the Danube in the North. This last frontier presented an inconvenient angle at the gap between the two rivers. Augustus tried to straighten it out by advancing to the Elbe, but after the German tribes had wiped out a Roman army in A.D. 9, he fell back again to the Rhine.

HOW AUGUSTUS ORGANISED THE EMPIRE

THIS defeat stopped the Latin civilisation from spreading through Germany, in which event Europe would have been entirely Roman, and Britain might never have been colonised by the English. The army which safeguarded the frontiers consisted of 150,000 men who served for twenty years. The soldiers took their oath to the Emperor and received their pay from him. Auxiliary forces were raised from the warlike provinces and stationed in the districts where they were enlisted. At the end of their service, these auxiliaries were rewarded with citizenship and gifts of land.

The provinces benefited most by the rule of Augustus. Under the republic, the governors had been practically irresponsible autocrats. Augustus made them responsible to himself, limited them to administration only, and appointed

THE BOUNDARIES OF THE ROMAN EMPIRE UNDER JULIUS CÆSAR

Rome

Allies & Protected States

MAURETANIA

SPAIN

Danuus

GAUL

GERMANS

Rhenus

Massilia

MARE

Carthage

NUMIDIA

Rome

INTERNUM

Syracuse

DELMATIA

Aquileia

MACEDONIA

Danubius

GREECE

PONTUS EUXINUS

Byzantium

Crete

PERGAMUM

BITHYNIA

CYRENAICA

LYCIA

PONTUS

Cyprus

CAPPADOCIA

PTOLEMAIC-

Alexandria

ARMENIA

EMPIRE

Jerusalem

Antioch

ALANS

Nilus

Palmyra

Carrhae

PARTHIANS

Tigris

ARABIA

Seleucia Ctesiphon

Euphrates

MARE CASPIUM

MARE

special officials for financial and military affairs. Instead of being allowed to fleece the provincials, the governor was given a fixed salary, and often kept in office for long periods so that he obtained full experience and did not have to leave just as he was beginning to learn the routine. Even from the senatorial provinces, an appeal was allowed to the jurisdiction of the Emperor.

Augustus made a statistical survey of the resources of the Empire, assessed the taxes more fairly, and reduced them in amount. The proceeds were largely spent on the provinces themselves, and were devoted to the construction of roads, bridges, and aqueducts.

In Italy Augustus restored peace and prosperity. In Rome he erected so many public buildings that he boasted that he found the city brick and made it marble. The seeds of a caste system were laid by the grant of different offices to different classes. The Senate, for example, provided the governors for the more important provinces, while the knights, who were appointed by Augustus himself, were given the new offices, such as the Prefecture of the Prætorian Guards, and the governorships of some of the less important provinces. By marriage laws, and religious reforms, Augustus tried to revive the old Roman family life, but he could not undo the effect of two hundred years of unlimited wealth and oriental luxury and vice.

A GLORIOUS POET SINGS A MIGHTY RULER'S FAME

THE glories of the new age were proclaimed by the greatest Latin poet. Virgil (70–19 B.C.) wrote the *Æneid*, the epic of Rome, to show the peace of Augustus as the destined goal of Roman history. The praise of Augustus may appear fulsome to our taste, but Virgil had lived in a world where it seemed as though " earth's foundations fled." We can excuse him for eulogising the man who had " saved the sum of things." Himself a poet of exquisite taste and metrical subtlety, he yet cheerfully acknowledged the supremacy of the Greeks in the sciences and the arts. He rightly saw that the mission of Rome in that age was to make the good life possible, " To impose the way of peace by warring down the proud and sparing the conquered." Another poet, Horace (65–8 B.C.), also enjoyed the patronage of Augustus. He was a cool man of the world who, in his *Satires*, commented shrewdly though kindly on human follies. His

Odes are lyrics whose trite sentiment is concealed by perfect choice and arrangement of words. They cannot compare for spontaneity and charm with those of Catullus (87–54 B.C.).

Virgil was himself inferior in vigour to Lucretius (about 95–54 B.C.), whose poem *On the Nature of the World* sought to free the mind from fears of death, and rebuked men for wasting their lives in empty ambition instead of learning Nature's laws and living the tranquil life of the philosopher. Court patronage, however, stifled the old Republican freedom of speech, especially in oratory.

Cicero (106–43 B.C.) whose debating powers had raised him to the consulship, had no successor. Though lacking the fighting spirit of Demosthenes, his rounded periods and exuberant expression had suited the taste of the times. He had even, when roused, been capable of incisive brevity, and his second *Philippic* against Mark Antony has a stab in every line. His letters reveal him as a delightful friend and a man of taste and feeling. His essays on ethics, though unoriginal in idea, set forth attractively the common code of the liberal-minded Roman gentleman. In history, however, the Augustan age produced a master of prose in Livy (59 B.C.–A.D. 17) who wrote his *History of Rome* " to point a moral and adorn a tale " rather than to find out the exact truth about what had really happened.

THE LEGACY A KING FORGOT TO LEAVE

HAD Augustus made his monarchy hereditary and " by law established " many difficulties that arose later might have been avoided. Whilst his descendants lived, loyalty to his name kept the succession undisputed, but after his family had died out there was often a crop of pretenders who weakened the man-power and the resources of the Empire by bitter civil wars.

On his death in A.D. 14, Augustus was succeeded by his step-son, Tiberius, whose aim was government not for the sake of the governed but for the sake of efficiency. Haughty and morose by nature, he despised the people and, suspecting the Senate of disloyalty, he encouraged informers to trump up charges of treason against wealthy or prominent men. The provinces which were further away fared better and were well governed. After living in retirement for some years at Capri, a beautiful little island in the Bay of Naples, Tiberius died unlamented in A.D. 37. His short-lived and frenzied successor Caligula (A.D. 37–41) was succeeded by Claudius (A.D. 41–54), " the wisest fool " in his Empire. Though clumsy in appearance and speech, Claudius displayed a liberal outlook. Augustus's policy of restricting grants of citizenship was reversed, and Gallic chiefs were admitted to the Senate. Claudius rightly justified this action on the ground that it was a security for the safety of the Empire. During his reign South Britain was made a province. He also began organising an Imperial Civil Service, and appointed special secretaries to attend to home and foreign affairs and to the Treasury.

Nero (A.D. 54–68), after governing well for five years under the advice of Seneca (about 4 B.C.–A.D. 65), a Stoic philosopher, threw over his adviser and gave himself up to art and debauchery. When the Spanish armies revolted and began to march on Rome, Nero committed suicide. During his reign occurred a terrible massacre of the Christians, who were accused of setting Rome on fire. A strange sect, of whom as yet little was known, they were charged with hatred of the human race, and became natural victims of popular frenzy and ignorance. During the years A.D. 14–68, the show of republicanism had begun to wear very thin, for each emperor was now voted his powers for life, instead of for a term of years, as in the time of Augustus.

The Western provinces developed rapidly in commerce and civilisation. The tribes were encouraged to build cities and to adopt the Latin language and civilisation. Already in the first century A.D., Spain sent to Rome such writers as Seneca, the philosopher, and Lucan (39–65 A.D.), the poet of the Civil Wars between Cæsar and Pompey. Native chiefs were being appointed to important governships and, before long, Trajan and Hadrian were to provide the Empire with rulers of Spanish origin. In the East, Rome came as a pupil rather than as a teacher, but she brought peace and prosperity as a fair exchange for Greek learning.

ROME MAKES A UNITED STATES OF EUROPE

ON Nero's death a bloody civil war followed, in which the victor was Vespasian (A.D. 69–79). He was of humble origin, and started a line of kings of whom very few had any hereditary claim to the throne except as the adopted sons of their predecessors. The intended successor hence-forth received the title *Cæsar*. Circumstances, too, made it more necessary at the end of each reign to assume no gap in the succession.

The Senate became a kind of Upper House, which had little influence on action, but appointment to which was a distinction equivalent to the grant of a peerage. There was a Civil Service not dissimilar to our own and a Privy Council, consisting of jurists and high civil servants. This was later called "The Sacred Consistory," a name still retained by a Council in the Roman Catholic Church.

With the spread of one language and one judicial system, local national feeling disappeared. The design of the Roman villa, with its baths and its central heating system which far surpassed any method known until the twentieth century, was adopted everywhere. Roads and bridges made communications easier and fostered commerce. In those days, a man could cross Europe without having to show his passport at ten frontiers. Free trade allowed eastern spices to be exchanged for British tin without restrictive tariffs or quotas. The Roman franchise was granted with greater liberality than ever to whole towns and districts. The old Italian stock had almost disappeared, and Rome was filled with provincials from all parts. In A.D. 211 the Emperor Caracalla took the final step of granting Roman citizenship to every inhabitant of the Empire. In the first century A.D. local patriotism was strong, and citizens competed eagerly for election to the local town councils, and endowed their towns with baths, gymnasiums, theatres, and schools. In the second century, however, the spirit of local independence was weakened by the interference of the central government.

THE HIGH TIDE OF EMPIRE

THE problem of frontier defence became more urgent. The impetus of conquest had long disappeared, and the Emperors were content to keep the Roman Empire secure. Beyond the boundaries, the barbarian tribes were on the move from the Rhine and the Danube right on into Asia. The tide of Roman fortunes had reached its flood, and would soon begin to ebb. Domitian (A.D. 81–96) was faced by a rising of German tribes on the Danube, where there arose the powerful kingdom of Dacia (modern Roumania), whose situation enabled it to threaten the provinces which lay on the road to Italy.

Trajan (A.D. 98–117) revived for a time the old aggressive spirit. He conquered Dacia and made it a province, thus enabling Rome to keep an eye on the movements of the tribes to the west and north. So successful was his policy that there was peace on the Danube frontier for the next fifty years. Hadrian (A.D. 117–138) was a soldier too, but he preferred internal prosperity to unsafe adventures beyond the limits of the Empire. He built a great frontier barrier to close the awkward gap between the Rhine and the Danube, and to keep the legions in closer touch with each other. The Roman wall in Britain from the Tyne to the Solway was built during his reign.

Antoninus Pius (A.D. 138–160) enjoyed a peaceful reign, but his successor, Marcus Aurelius, the Stoic philosopher, whose *Meditations* breathe a spirit of Christian gentleness, had to encounter the first thrust of a united barbarian army. A German tribe, the Marcomanni, united with other tribes, crossed the Danube, and in A.D. 167 were the first non-Roman force for three hundred years to camp on the sacred soil of Italy.

Marcus Aurelius, though handicapped by a plague which ravaged the Empire and by lack of funds, managed to drive back the main body of invaders, but only by resorting to the desperate and dangerous expedient of settling many tribes on land within the boundaries of the Empire, and enrolling their warriors as soldiers in the Roman army. It was the beginning of the end when Rome had to enlist one set of barbarians to defend her against another.

AN AGE OF PEACE AND PLENTY UNEQUALLED

DURING the greater part of this period, the lands of the Roman empire enjoyed on the whole a prosperity and peace unknown before and never experienced since. Literature continued to flourish in the first century A.D. Tacitus (about A.D. 55–117), the historian, wrote a bitter and brilliant account of the early years of the empire. Many of his mordant phrases have become familiar, such as " They make a desert and call it peace." Juvenal's caustic satires have found countless imitators. The letters of the Younger Pliny (about A.D. 61–113) to the Emperor Trajan, asking for advice on how to deal with the new sect of Christians, give a very fine picture of an over-conscientious official and an extremely able and wise emperor. The noble

philosophy of Seneca (about 4 B.C.–A.D. 65) is illustrated in
the sentences, " Love if you wish to be loved," and " What
matters is not how long you live, but how well."

THE COMING OF CHRISTIANITY

IN the last century B.C. peace and justice seemed to have
been banished for ever from the world. People had
sought consolation in oriental worships such as that of Isis
of Egypt and of Mithras, the Persian god of light, a form of
belief which, by arousing religious ecstasy, suggested that
the rewards of the next world would balance the inequalities
of this. During the reign of Tiberius, Christ was preaching
His revolutionary creed which affirmed the equality of all
men in the sight of God. Mankind, He taught, was the
object of Divine Love, and He Himself was its agent.

The new religion, which attacked the narrowness of the
Hebraic and the selfish individuality of the Greek religion,
found a most valuable champion in Paul, a great apostle.
He travelled widely, preaching the faith and attempting
to find a theological basis for the new religion so that it
would withstand the criticisms of the Greek philosophers.
The Romans who were, officially, uninterested in religion,
apart from the formal worship of the Emperor as a token
of loyal submission, at first tolerated the Christians as a
sect of the Jews. Trajan, when consulted by Pliny, forbade
systematic prosecution, but ordered punishment for any
who, when brought before the governor, refused to worship
the Emperor's image. Their refusal to do this, and their
secret meetings, led to occasional persecution of the Christians
by suspicious Emperors. The pagan mob, too, sometimes
massacred the unbelievers who took no part in the popular
religious festivals and shunned the shambles of the gladiatorial
combats.

In spite of repeated martyrdoms, the number of converts
multiplied, and by the end of the second century A.D. it is
probable that Christianity claimed more adherents than
any other single creed.

The third century A.D. saw the Empire on the verge of
collapse. There was a bewildering succession of short-
lived emperors who failed to check repeated barbarian raids.
On the west, from A.D. 213 the German Alemanni and the
Franks swept over Gaul and Spain, whilst their kinsmen,
the Goths, from A.D. 238 overran the provinces south of the

Danube and annexed Dacia. In A.D. 273 Aurelian restored peace temporarily, but it was now impossible for one man to protect East and West at the same time. Under Diocletian (A.D. 284–305), who reorganised every department of the Empire, all the tendencies of the Empire's three hundred years reached maturity. The last traces of Augustus's republican compromise are replaced by an undisguised Oriental monarchy with a crown and royal robes, a throne and a title.

Rome, which had long ago fallen into the background as the needs of war kept the emperors on the Danube or Euphrates, now became a provincial municipality with the Senate as the local town council. Diocletian sought increased efficiency by partitioning the Empire between four rulers, but unfortunately this involved still heavier taxation, for there were now four courts and four sets of officials to maintain. Money was raised by making the wealthy men everywhere responsible for the financial quota of their own district.

Diocletian attempted to prevent evasion of taxes by stereotyping society. A son was compelled to follow his father's trade, and no one might change his home or his occupation without permission. Even the cost of living was regulated by a price-fixing board. By these measures the new despotism crushed all personal freedom and initiative. This was truly " for life's sake to lose what makes life worth living." Constantine (A.D. 323–337) made two epoch-making decisions —the removal of the capital to Byzantium (renamed Constantinople) and the official acceptance of Christianity as the State religion. The foundation of Constantinople, while bringing the capital nearer to the seats of war, hastened the separation of East and West, for Gaul and Spain and Britain were quite out of the orbit of oriental politics. The new city became the capital of the Eastern Roman Empire and outlived the Western Empire by a thousand years.

THE ESTABLISHED CHURCH BECOMES PROSPEROUS

THE change-over to Christianity gave the State more popular support, but raised complicated problems. It restricted imperial authority and materialised religion. Christianity had succeeded because it had offered itself to the sinner and the slave. Henceforth, it became an established church with worldly possessions and a system of government.

Christianity, after its triumph, itself became intolerant, and secured prohibition of the old pagan worship. Its truer spirit was shown when it ended the murderous gladiatorial shows. The Goths, the Franks, and, later on, the Vandal tribes were visited by intrepid missionaries and converted wholesale. If the teaching did not penetrate deeply, it yet enabled the Bishop of Rome to prevail on Alaric, the leader of the Goths, to spare the lives of the inhabitants when he sacked the city in A.D. 410. In the confused years that followed the downfall of the Empire in A.D. 476, the Christian Church upheld, however feebly, the ideal of human brotherhood, and managed to temper a little the savagery of the barbarian conquerors.

In A.D. 364 the division of the Empire so long observed in practice was formally admitted when Valentinian took the West and Valens the East. In spite of a brief spell of peace under Theodosius (A.D. 376–395), the Empire was now in its death throes. Civil and foreign wars and infanticide had depleted the population. In the towns, over-taxation had ruined the prosperity of the middle classes, while in the countryside large areas were laid waste through incessant barbarian raids on every frontier. The peasant had fallen into a state of apathy, where to starve was easier than to sow for others to reap. The Vandals and the Goths, German tribes who had already settled within the Empire, now began to break it up into separate kingdoms.

WHEN BRITAIN WAS INVADED BY GERMAN TRIBES

THE Visigoths (Western Goths) established, with imperial recognition, a kingdom in south-western Gaul. Similarly in Spain, other barbarian tribes had set up new kingdoms which, nominally at least, acknowledged the Emperor of the West as overlord. Britain was lost entirely at the beginning of the fifth century, when the semi-Romanised natives fell victims to raiding Picts from Scotland, and to Angles and Saxons, German tribes from overseas, who seized the land without seeking any recognition from the Emperor. From Spain a section of the Vandals crossed over to North Africa and conquered the country (A.D. 429–440).

Another invasion which threatened Western Europe with heathen barbarism was repulsed in A.D. 451 at Chalons in France, when the Franks and Goths united with the Imperial troops to defeat Attila, leader of the Huns, who came from

Asia. The victory saved Western Europe for the Indo-European races.

Italy, the only land now left to the Western Empire, also became a separate kingdom in A.D. 476 under Odoacer, leader of yet another German tribe. The new king acknowledged the suzerainty of the Eastern Emperor at Constantinople, but he was, in fact, as absolutely independent as the other kings in Gaul, Spain, and Africa.

The Empire's gifts to the world have been permanent. The Romans were the great builders and pioneers of antiquity. They brought the waste lands under the control of man by encouraging agriculture and by building roads and bridges on such strong foundations that many of them have continued in use until the present day. In the sphere of government they had not only given the world peace and security ever since the time of Augustus, but, by bestowing their citizenship on the subject peoples, had made them enthusiastic partners in the Empire. Their language, which Cicero had made into a perfect instrument of dignified and precise speech, had become the mother-tongue of millions to whom Rome was nothing but a name, and was not only the vehicle by which Greek thought was transmitted to the West, but was destined to be the origin of modern French, Spanish, Portuguese, and Roumanian. The scientific and humane code of Roman law which embodied the experience of a thousand years of jurisprudence, remains the basis of the legal systems of many nations to-day. Europe, however, was destined to undergo centuries of travail before she could enter into and enjoy this splendid heritage.

BOOKS ABOUT THE HISTORY OF ANTIQUITY

THE best short introduction to the study of Ancient Times is *The Dawn of History*, by J. L. Myers (Home University Library, Thornton Butterworth Limited), and *Anthropology*, by R. R. Marett (Home University Library, Thornton Butterworth Limited). Both of these books are lucid and illuminating expositions by acknowledged masters of their subjects. A book by Leakey, *Adam's Ancestors* (Methuen), carries the story of mankind further back than it has ever been carried before. J. H. Breasted's *Ancient Times* (Ginn and Co.) should be read also.

A. Toynbee in *A Study of History* has published three

CENTRAL HEATING 2000 YEARS AGO.

Comforts like these were introduced by the Romans all over their Empire. Note the flat bricks and the grill windows.

volumes of what promises to be the greatest and ablest history of civilisation. D. G. Hogarth's *The Ancient East* (Home University Library, Thornton Butterworth Limited), gives a brief but very helpful survey of the history of Babylonia and Egypt. Good introductory volumes to the history of Egypt are published in the Home University Library, Thornton Butterworth Limited, and by the Oxford University Press.

There is a brief history of *The Peoples and Problems of India*, by Holderness (Macmillan), and many histories such as *The Early History of India*, by V. A. Smith and *The Student's History of India*, by the same author (both Oxford University Press). H. A. Giles, *The Civilisation of China* (Home University Library, Thornton Butterworth Limited) surveys Chinese history from 1000 B.C. up to modern times.

The best way to understand the Greeks is to read their writings. Good translations of most of the authors mentioned in the text are to be found in the " Everyman's Library " or " The World's Classics." The most fascinating of all books about the ancient Greeks and Romans is Plutarch's *Parallel Lives of the Greeks and Romans* (Dent), a collection of intimate biographies crammed with anecdotes and incidents. W. Warde Fowler's *City-state of the Greeks and Romans* (Macmillan) is indispensable and can be followed by J. B. Bury's *History of Greece* (Macmillan) which goes down to the death of Alexander. A sympathetic and penetrating study of Greek civilisation is *The Greek Commonwealth*, by A. E. Zimmern (Oxford University Press).

W. Warde Fowler's *Rome* (Home University Library, Thornton Butterworth Limited) is a good introduction to Roman history, and can be followed by H. F. Pelham's *Outlines of Roman History* (Rivington). Longer works are Mommsen's *History of Rome* (Dent) and Gibbon's *The History of the Decline and Fall of the Roman Empire*. The latter is a work of literature as well as a history book. Read it at all costs.

THE GREATNESS OF THE MIDDLE AGES

by R. T. CLARK, B.A.(Oxon.), M.A.(Glasgow)

THE history of the Middle Ages, it has been said, begins with the prehistory of the steppes and continues till the teeming womb of Asia exhausts itself of peoples. It was the impact of Asiatic invasions, either primary, like the inroad of the Huns, or secondary like the westward and southward pressure of the German tribes, which shivered into fragments the noble structure of the Roman Empire. But that Empire had resisted long enough to make the final inroads that destroyed it something more than mere avalanches of savagery. Roman civilisation had penetrated far beyond the formal confines of the *Pax Romana*, and the barbarians who wrecked it came not merely as destroyers but as pupils.

At the end of the fifth century the Roman Empire of the West had vanished for ever, but Roman civilisation remained, and Christianity was the only super-racial religion in Europe. Romanised Britain, where Latin culture was less deeply rooted than on the continent, fought desperately with Jutes, Angles, and Saxons from North Germany; the Frank had flooded Gaul, which was to become France, the land of the Franks; the Visigoths had conquered Spain and Africa; Goths and Lombards ruled Italy. In Rome itself the Pope, the head of the Western Church, drew to himself the prestige, if not the power, of the Cæsars. In the East, with barbarian tribes seeping or raiding into the Balkan countries, and Persians conquering Asia Minor and Syria, an orientalised Romanism, busied more with theological disputation than with government, maintained itself precariously in what is now called the Eastern or Byzantine Empire.

Behind the political barrier of Byzantine, behind the cultural barrier of the Western Church, the tribes ended by coalescing into nations, and into Christian nations, in which the monk and the priest carried on imperfectly, but as well as they could, the tradition of learning inherited from Greece and Rome. The ascendancy of the Pope over the bishops of the West became recognised in the fourth century and was

consolidated during the pontificate of Gregory the Great
(590–604), who converted the inhabitants of Spain and
Lombardy from their Arian heresy (the belief that the Son
and the Holy Ghost were created by God the Father), and
sent missionaries to convert the heathen German tribes
settled in Britain.

When Rome ceased to be the capital of the Roman Empire
in 476 the Pope became the chief figure in the Eternal City,
and the rupture between the Greek and Roman churches in
866, while restricting the region over which he might claim
supremacy, made the realisation of that supremacy a probability. It was the conquest of the barbarian by the Church
that gave the Pope, the head of the Church, his prestige.
Christians looked not merely to the tribal leader but to the
head of their religion, and Rome became the hearth of the
new *imperium*, a power over the souls rather than over the
bodies of men. It was that unifying influence of a universally-
accepted missionary religion that created the first feeble dream
of a European unity and saved classical culture for the day of
a renaissance more splendid than even the days of its greatest
glory.

"DARK AGES" THAT WERE EPOCHS OF ACHIEVEMENT

NO period of becoming, of terrific creative effort at
survival, can fairly be called " the Dark Ages." The
phrase is only a vivid expression of the feeling of later students
who saw in these centuries a period of confused transition,
of a hopeless mix-up of ideals, of what was often apparently
purposeless struggle. They are dark ages only by comparison ; they were, in fact, ages of great achievement and
supreme importance in the spadework of establishing a new
civilisation. The last four centuries of the first Christian
millenium are centuries of active movement and change, of
which many of the details are now lost to us. When they
begin the European nations do not exist ; when they end,
despite all subsequent changes of frontiers and movement of
populations, all the transformations produced by war and
politics, the nations are recognisable as the European nations
of to-day. Let us study briefly that development from west
to east.

In Britain, Roman power to protect the native Romanised
Celts had disappeared long before the traditional date of
the German conquest (449). Wave after wave of invaders

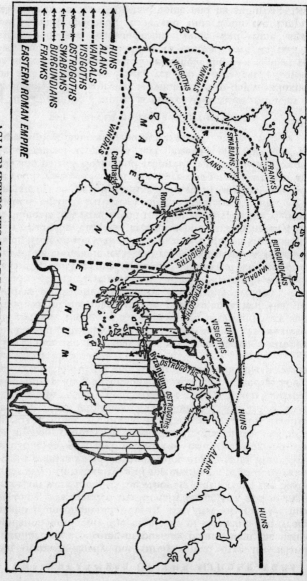

ASIA EMPTIES ITS HORDES INTO WESTERN EUROPE.

from overseas slowly but surely spread over the island, exterminating, absorbing or pushing before them the native population until only the highlands of Scotland and Wales remained unconquered. Kent, the first of the German kingdoms, was founded traditionally about 450, and in rapid succession were founded the other six that formed the Saxon heptarchy. Christianity, still maintaining a precarious existence in Scotland and Ireland, came afresh from Rome with Augustine in 597, and within two centuries England was a Christian country, a devoted daughter of the Church. Christianity meant unity and, although old tribal rivalries died hard, and ambitious chiefs clung to their kingly state, by the ninth century there was one state, a Saxon Christian state, and one king, a Christian monarch, in England, although the organisation of the one was imperfect, and the power of the other sadly limited.

In France the Frankish invaders encountered a stronger political and cultural resistance. They came into an organised and civilised, though greatly weakened land, and they submitted to the influence of the past to an extent that the invaders of Britain escaped or deliberately avoided. Side by side with the last armies of Rome, they fought and beat the Huns; and the kingdom of the Clovises and the Chilperics, with all its Germanic legal and religious traditions, ended by basing itself on the Gallo-Roman culture and on Christianity.

In Spain the Visigoths erected a powerful monarchy, but the Vandals lost Africa, and the Goths Italy, to the vigorous reaction against barbarism of the Eastern Empire. The generals of the great Byzantine Emperor, Justinian (527–546), the codifier of the laws of Rome, reconquered Carthage and Italy and part of Spain, and restored, in part at least, Rome's Mediterranean empire, a feat possible only because the Imperial fleet had command of the seas.

THE MIRACLE OF THE BYZANTINE EMPIRE

THE Byzantine Empire is one of the major miracles of history. The adjective is synonymous to-day with luxurious and corrupt decadence, yet the " decadent " Empire for more than nine hundred years held the pass against the East, and permitted the West to proceed with its task of assimilation and consolidation. Time and time again destruction threatened ; time and time again the Empire was little more than Constantinople and its suburbs ; time

and time again a vigorous ruler pushed the frontiers back
again to the Nile, the Danube, and the Euphrates.

It was while the German invaders, planted amid alien
peoples, were painfully passing from the tribal into the
national state, that the first great attack was launched on the
Eastern Empire. The storm came from the deserts of Arabia.
It was a land of strange contrasts. Arab merchants, with bases
in flourishing ports and on fertile coastlands, held the Indian
Ocean trade ; they had created a state which had become a
Christian state in Ethiopia (Abyssinia) ; they held the east
coast of Africa down to Sofala ; their ships were in every
port from the Persian Gulf to the East Indies and the coasts
of China. The sea lands of Arabia were full of prosperous
little warring kingdoms which had attained a high level of
civilisation. Some were Christian after a fashion, some had
accepted Judaism, some were still heathen ; and behind
them the desert teemed with nomads, fierce, untamable
fighters. Tribesman and town dweller lived side by side
and changed rôles at will.

BATTLES FOUGHT TO GAIN A MOSLEM PARADISE

IT was about 620 that a merchant of Mecca, Mohammed
by name, claiming divine revelation and the succession to
the Hebrew prophets and to the Christ, worked out a new
and simple monotheism, founded on the debased Judaism
and Christianity which he met among his heathen people.
That people would have none of him, and in 622, the year
in which the Mohammedan era of the *Hegira* (" the Flight ")
begins, he departed from Mecca to the more receptive
Medina. The new creed found few followers, but many
persecutors ; yet it survived and, reacting vigorously, helped
to defeat the Meccans in battle and swept through Arabia
like a flame. Backed by the warrior legions of the desert,
who burned to propagate their faith and win a physical
paradise by dying for it, Mohammed sent a proud challenge
to the kings of the earth. He himself died before he could
do more than begin the work of conquest, but under the
Caliphs, " the Successors of the Prophet," the Moslem
storm burst out of its desert fastnesses.

The Byzantine Empire had just been restored to greatness
by the victories over the Persians of the greatest soldier of his
time, the Emperor Heraclius, yet it was in no condition to
withstand this new and more formidable enemy. Jerusalem,

Aleppo, Antioch and Alexandria in turn fell prey to the invaders, who, internal dissensions notwithstanding, swept like a flood over Central and Western Asia and North Africa. Eastward they wiped out the Persian Empire, reached the Caucasus in the north, and, taking Samarcand in their stride, swamped Asia as far as the Indus and the Hindu Kush. Westward they pushed through North Africa, crossed the straits of Gibraltar that still bear the name of their leader Tarik, wiped out the Gothic kingdom of Spain and flung its remnants into the hill fastnesses of the north.

By the end of the seventh century they were at once battering at the gates of Constantinople and beginning to cross the Pyrenees ; the Mediterranean was almost a Moslem lake. Greek fire (a predecessor of gunpowder, which produced flame, smoke, and an explosion), beat them back from the Bosphorus (718), and in the West the wave of invasion, pushed beyond its effective limits, was rolled back by Charles Martel and his Franks at Tours in 732. Tours is one of the outstanding battles in history, not because history would have been very different had Charles lost it, but because it marks the ebb of the invasion. It occurred at the turning-point in the history of the great attack on Christian civilisation. In the West the forces of that civilisation were able to assume the offensive, the offensive which after twelve centuries has not succeeded in expelling the Moslem from Europe.

DISSENSION IN THE CHRISTIAN CAMP

CHARLES MARTEL was " the Mayor of the Palace," the viceroy of the decadent descendants of the great Merovingian house of Frankish kings who had conquered Gaul, and his son Pepin became King of the Franks (751) in name as well as in fact by the grace of Pope Stephen II. It was a step of great importance. The Pope was not yet the holder of any real temporal power, but he was recognised as the conferrer of any title to it. He was the head of the universal Church, a supra-national body which confessed a common religion and used Latin as its universal language. Only in the East were his claims to supremacy not admitted. The relations of the Popes, the rulers of old Rome in the absence of any other claimant, with the patriarchs of the new Rome had long been strained, and both the emperors and the patriarchs of Constantinople had shown increasing reluctance to admit the claim to headship on the part of him whom they styled the bishop of Rome. The emperors refused admission on political, the patriarchs on ecclesiastical, grounds. Quarrel succeeded quarrel, with political issues carefully concealed behind theological niceties. Matters of doctrine and discipline divided Eastern from Western Christianity, and all attempts at reconciliation proving vain, Western Christianity tended more and more to develop on its own European lines and claim universal power ; the Eastern Church was abandoned to become an agency of the Byzantine Empire.

But the universal Church of the West also claimed a temporal power. The Pope of Rome vindicated Rome for his own rule as the patrimony of St. Peter. He might be the Holy Father of Danes, Germans, English ; but he was also an Italian princeling, and to his principality he attached great importance. It therefore became necessary for the Pope to secure possession of his patrimony by acquiring a temporal protector, and it was this need for protection that was the reason for his arrangement with Pepin. The King of the Franks by the grace of the Pope crossed the Alps, subdued the Lombards in the north and drove the Byzantine power from the east of Italy. He had firmly consolidated his power in France, clearing the Moslems finally from the south, and in 771 left to his son Charles the greatest kingdom the West had so far known.

Charles (or Karl) rightly called the Great, or Charlemagne, greatest of German and first of French kings, ascended the throne just when the West was at last able to react on the invaders who so far had threatened it. Fixing the capital of a great empire at Aachen on the Rhine, he pushed south and east with untiring energy. An invasion of Spain proved a task beyond his strength. The Pyrenees were crossed and the Moslems routed, but the disaster of Roncesvalles, where the rearguard of Charlemagne's army was cut off and destroyed, showed that conquest had been pushed beyond its limits. Spain was abandoned and the Christians of the hills took up the fight that was to end by driving the Moslem from the peninsula.

RELIGION AND CULTURE FOLLOW THE SWORD

IN the east the Franks moved slowly but surely into the congeries of pagan tribes of more than one race which inhabited what is geographically known as Germany. They conquered Saxony and Bavaria and pushed on towards the Oder and the Baltic ; in the south-east their empire absorbed Lombardy and established at least nominal domination over Italy. Moving down the Danube it defeated the Hunnic Avars and the Slavs who had been conquered by them, and pushed on as far as the Save. Except for the Moslems in Spain, for the British Islands, and the northern fringes of Germany with their Scandinavian hinterlands, Western Europe was a unity, threatening Asia, carrying the Cross and culture along with the sword, settling and civilising the land as well as devastating it. Aachen, the equal of Bagdad and Byzantium, and recognised by both as the seat of a third and equal power, was a centre of civilisation as well as of government, of a genuinely organised empire such as had not been seen since the Roman Empire perished.

It was in admission of that fact, as well as to serve the Papacy's political ends, that Leo III. crowned Charles in Rome as Emperor of the Romans (A.D. 800). The Holy Roman Empire succeeded to the Rome of the Cæsars, but it was a divided *imperium*. Charles's empire, though it was of mushroom growth and depended for cohesion too much on the strength of its ruler, was none the less a tangible empire with defined frontiers, a political organisation of very definite significance. But it was also a mystical unity, a vision soaring above geographical space, the political counterpart of the universal Church. The one guaranteed the other. The Empire guaranteed the Pope's possession of Rome and supported his universal spiritual claims ; the Pope conferred on the Empire the honour of being the Church's secular arm, the instrument of its spiritual domination. The political influences at work are easy to see, as are the inevitable grounds of conflict in a sphere where the limits of the two authorities were not easy to define. Yet, none the less, the Holy Roman Empire was a triumph of mystical imagination over reality, a triumph that has never ceased to impress the minds of men. To-day, centuries after it has been proved a political chimera, its dream still haunts the mind of the visionary.

Charles the Great died in 814, leaving his empire to his son, Louis, whose three sons, a bickering brood, divided the possessions of their grandfather by the Treaty of Verdun (843). The partition was arbitrary, but it corresponded none the less to new groupings of peoples. Lothair got Lotharingia, the west bank of the Rhine, and Italy ; Louis got Germany, the lands across the Rhine and all that he could add to them ; Charles the Bald got France. These kings quarrelled instead of trying to meet new challenges of paganism. The kingdoms divided, reunited, and divided again. For two brief years (884–887) Charles the Fat restored the Carolingian empire, but the movement towards disintegration on the one hand, and an embryo national reintegration on the other, had gone much too far, and in 887 the empire of the great Charles finally sundered, never to be united again.

THE STRUGGLE FOR MASTERY IN EASTERN EUROPE

IT is time now to turn to the East, where development, as important for European history as that in the West, is much more obscure. New tribes and nations, known but dimly if at all to Rome, appear on the scene. Before the Christian era the north-westward trek from Asia had carried Finno-Ugrian tribes to the Volga and then northward across the north of Russia into Finland and down the shores of the Baltic. German tribes had flowed east and founded short-lived empires in the steppes before returning to assail the West. The Huns had swept over them like a devastating fire, and into the emptiness new invaders emerged slowly from Asia, founding kingdoms. From their original fastnesses in the marshlands of the Pripet, where they had multiplied in security from the nomad horsemen, the Slavs pushed northward, eastward, westward, southward, covering much of Russia and pressing the Finnish tribes northward, colonising Germany to the west of where Berlin now stands, crossing the Carpathians and flooding the Danube plain, reaching the Adriatic and penetrating the Balkans. Long before their expansion was completed, those in Central Europe had been conquered by the Avars who, as a nomad aristocracy ruling a nation of peasant slaves, threatened West and East alike, nearly reached Constantinople, and challenged Charles the Great, only to be defeated and disappear before the end of the eighth century. Earlier there existed a mysterious and somewhat uncertain Slav empire in the Danubian area, but it was not until the domination of the Avars was broken, and on every side the Slavs were coming into contact with Christian civilisations, that the Slavs began to coalesce into states— usually around the old centres of organised political life.

The eighth century saw the creation by the Poles of a state of Poland, by the Czechs of Bohemia, by the Croats of

Croatia, by the Serbs of Serbia. The process was slow. The Slav showed little genius for state building, and his greatest achievements in that respect were due mainly to the inspiration of other races. But Slav heathendom occupied the greater part of Central, South-Eastern, and Eastern Europe, touching the encroaching Western civilisation in the west and bickering with Byzantium and mobile Asia in the east. Slav infiltration into classical Greece was the easier, as the Byzantine empire was again at grips with the Moslem. On the East, Saracens appeared on the Bosphorus; in the West, winning command of the sea, they flooded Sicily, established themselves in South Italy, and compelled the Pope to organise the defence of Rome itself.

For the Slav contact with civilisation was contact with Christianity. Not merely did Charles the Great in his victorious advance eastwards give his enemies, German, old Prussian, and Slav, the choice between conversion or death, but the missionary monk was proceeding methodically to the evangelisation of the pagans beyond the Elbe and the Danube. These Christian priests, some of whom penetrated into the East by the old trading ways—for along the old routes trade still moved as well as armies—preached the Cross and the primacy of Rome in the forests of Poland, on the shores of Pomerania and even on the fiords of Scandinavia. The conquests of the Roman Church roused the Greek Church, but it could not even supply missionaries equal to those of the West in the art of conversion. Cyril and Methodius were men of the East, but when they christianised the nearer Slavs they converted them to Rome, and thus not only added to the adherents of the Western Church the most virile portion of a mighty race, but set up a new dividing line between Western and Eastern Europe.

THE COMING OF THE VIKINGS

Now on still unconsolidated Europe there came a fresh storm. In the eighth century the Scandinavian tribes began to expand. On the shores of the North Sea and of the Baltic they learned to become daring seamen and traders and were not long in becoming equally daring raiders. The Viking period began. In the far north the seamen from the fiords colonised Iceland, from which they were later to colonise Greenland and even reach America. They harried all the North Sea coasts in their long ships. As

kingdoms arose in Scandinavia, they passed from raiding to
conquest. The north of Scotland, the Western Isles and
Ireland became the seats of Viking principalities. In the
ninth century their attacks were shaking even the kingdom
of England to its foundations, and it took the political and
military genius of Alfred the Great, the creator of an early
English navy, to confine them to the north, and make them
acknowledge an English king. Finally, there came the great
organised invasion of the foreign power of Denmark which,
under Canute (1016–35), created an Empire of the North
Sea, an empire which might have lasted, had not the native
English been too strongly entrenched. Under his weak
successors the older stock reasserted itself and, restoring
native kings, began to absorb the invaders.

Across the Channel, the inroads were no less destructive.
The Vikings ravaged and plundered the whole coast from
the Rhine to the Loire. The successors of Charles the
Great did their feeble best, but the defence really rested
with the local nobility. Despite the nobles' best endeavours
the longships were masters on the Rhine, the Seine, and the
Loire, and twice they were beaten back only with the greatest
difficulty from Paris itself, now becoming the capital of the
kings of France. From devastation came once again conquest.
The bands of Rollo were finally bought off with the cession
of Normandy (912). France was spared further Viking invasions, and the Normans took up the task of conquest of other
lands. They were no longer pirates, but state-builders, and
Norman states arose in Sicily and Italy and even in Antioch.
But they did not last. The only permanent Norman conquest
was in England (1066), which ended in the destruction of
the old Saxon rule and the establishment of a Norman
kingdom. Norman rule took nearly a century and a half
to yield to the spirit of the land and by the ensuing fusion
to establish one of the main factors in the creation of the
modern English. In France the effect of the Norse settlement in Normandy was salutary. The weak descendants
of Charles the Great were set aside and the strong man of
the period, Hugh Capet, founded a dynasty which was to
last for centuries and which became a potent influence in
making France what we know it to be to-day.

In Eastern Europe the Scandinavians who controlled the
Baltic appear as fighting traders rather than as freebooters,
though they had no objection to acting as the latter when

opportunity offered. They controlled the carrying trade down the old ways that led to Constantinople. Out of trading posts grew cities ; in Tsargrad, as the *sagas* (old Norse epics) call Constantinople, Viking axemen formed the imperial bodyguard. The Slav tribes of the upper Dnieper, disorganised and exposed to attack from Asiatic invaders, invited the Swedish merchant, Rurik, to be their king. He accepted, and in Kiev laid the foundations of the Russian empire. Kiev soon became a power, and Rurik's successors sought to conquer even Byzantium ; but the effort was too great for the young empire and the outcome was its acceptance of Greek Christianity, the greatest conquest the Greek church ever made.

THE DIM BEGINNINGS OF GENEVA'S PROBLEMS

BUT the Slavs were not the only people on the move in Eastern Europe. The Finno-Ugrian tribes on the Volga had already moved on, and into the places they left went the Slavs, occupying nearly all European Russia except the south-east, which the Asiatics ruled and along the frontiers of which there was perpetual war. These Finno-Ugrians had moved westward in two waves. In the sixth and seventh centuries the Bulgars had gone south-westward, penetrated into the Balkans beside the mouth of the Danube, and in the plain of the Maritza and on the slopes of the Balkan ranges had founded an empire among the less warlike Slav invaders. They adopted the speech and customs of the conquered, to the great embarrassment of later politicians, and, under warrior-kings, created a great Balkan empire which endured until the Byzantium they had threatened rallied under a new dynasty, and under Basil II. (976–1025), crushed them for generations.

The routes and objects of the second wave are less well known. By the end of the ninth century the nomad horse-men of the Magyars were raiding into Germany and even crossing the Rhine. The heavy armed horse and foot of the German nobles were no match for them, until finally the skill of the Emperor Otto I. destroyed their main army in the battle of the Lechfeld (955) and drove them back to found in the Danubian plain a kingdom which was composed of Magyar nobles and a subject population of Slavs and Dacians. Here there was no absorption. The races remained distinct, to contribute to the twentieth century the worst of its nationality problems.

The Magyars were the last menace that the German state had to meet for many a year. While Hugh Capet, as the most powerful noble in France, had founded a dynasty (987) which, in spite of all the turbulence of its vassals, was permanent, the German state to which the title deeds to the Holy Roman Empire had descended had become a prey to the great houses. A strong ruler united the Empire ; a weak one had to struggle with civil war. But, in 911, Henry the Fowler founded a dynasty which lasted a century, and gave to Germany the three Ottos. Under their vigorous rule the Empire expanded eastward and the new Slav states, like Bohemia and Poland, found it politic not merely to accept their overlordship, but also to accept Latin Christianity. The ground plan of modern Europe was being laid down. Under these three emperors the Empire was supreme. The Papacy, which had become the bone of contention between Italian noble houses, was sunk in disorder and corruption which the intervention of the Emperor was powerless to check.

A PICTURE OF EUROPE IN THE ELEVENTH CENTURY

IF we survey the continent of Europe we shall find it in the eleventh century sharply divided into east and west. The religious division is of greater significance than the much more complex political divisions. In the West, Ireland, still independent and governed by a multitude of petty kings with a nominal head king, had subdued its Viking invaders and was about to submit to the invasion of the Normans from England. Scotland was an independent country, painfully seeking a union of three races, the Angles and Britons of the south with the Picts and Scots who had already combined in the north. England was a Norman aristocracy, with a ruling house that attached as much importance to its possessions in France as to its domains at home, with a subject population still unreconciled. In France the king had a small patrimony of his own and the suzerainty over powerful nobles, some of whom had arrogated to themselves much authority, and with whom he was in perpetual feud.

In Spain the Christians of the north had begun to react against the Arab settlement, but they had not yet pushed very far. In the south and centre there was still a powerful Moslem kingdom, the last outpost of the East. Italy was a mass of little principalities, the prey to every adventurer or

ambitious conqueror. The Pope barely ruled Rome; th
Holy Roman Emperor was the nominal lord of Italy, but ha
never made his power completely effective. Norman
Byzantines, and Saracens held now this, now that, part of th
peninsula.

Germany was a land of kingdoms (though their holder
were not always called kings), owing allegiance to the Em
peror, but giving him obedience only when he was able t
enforce it. They had spread Germanism as far as Danzi
and Silesia, and down the Danube to Vienna. To th
north were the Scandinavian kingdoms, Sweden, Norway
and Denmark, now united, now apart, and bitterly quarrel
some. As outposts of the Latin West were the Slav kingdoms
or duchies; Poland, seeking expansion steadily to the north
and east, Bohemia to which was added Moravia, Croatia,
which was soon to yield to Hungary, and, in the very centre
of the Danubian plain, Hungary itself.

Of these four nations the kings were more important than
their peoples. They united or quarrelled; gave each other
kings, made conquests, or were themselves conquered. They
had as yet no national stability. All beyond was the Greek
east. From the White Sea to the Black Sea stretched Russia,
split into a score of kingdoms as the great kings of Kiev
decided to partition their lands among their children, yet
an entity beginning its historic mission of conquest. Between
it and the West there still lay pagan tribes in the north—Finns
in Finland, Esths in Esthonia, Livs and Letts in Courland,
and Lithuanians in the forests around Vilna. Through these
lands Russia sought to reach the sea. The traders' republic
of Novgorod, with its intimate ties with the trading ports of
Germany, fought with the Lithuanians; it was already clear
that the westward movement would be resisted.

In the eleventh century the Swedes were already beginning
to pass into Finland; the Danes had landed on the shores of
Esthonia, and Germans were creeping up the Baltic coasts.
On that dividing line eastern and western Christianity were
to meet in a long and bitter struggle. In the south the
Russian kingdoms were in close touch at once with Asia and
with Byzantium—at this period in a phase of revival under
the " Macedonian dynasty " (867–1057). Russia had been
checked, some Moslems of Asia subdued, and much of the
Balkans recovered. The Bulgarian empire had been crushed,
but to the north-west was the younger power of Serbia which

was to prove a deadlier foe ; and in the Carpathians and the Transylvanian highlands older populations than any of the invaders were beginning to form kingdoms. Beyond teemed the hordes of Asia and the Moslem world, which, divided into a score of kingdoms, stretched from Hindustan over Central Asia, Mesopotamia, Syria, and Egypt to North Africa and Spain. Such is the picture supplied by the political map.

THE EVER-SHIFTING BOUNDARIES ON THE EUROPEAN MAP

POLITICAL Europe has taken shape ; what is more important, Western Civilisation has taken shape and develops culturally and politically in well-defined limits. During the next centuries the map is like a kaleidoscope ; but behind these political changes are stirrings which are later to rise into national movements, which will make Europe present a very different picture by the time the Renaissance is reached.

It is not too much to say that much of the change is very unimportant to the general reader, however fundamentally it may interest the historian. To the former what matters is the Western states, and, however briefly, one must dwell for a moment on their organisation. This differed in the various countries ; but so long as the reader remembers that only a very general picture is attempted, and that the organisation described was not a rigid one but in a constant state of evolution, he will not receive a distorted impression.

In the West in the eleventh century there was only one universal power and that was the Church. It was also the unifying force, for it supplied a universal religion, a universal culture, and a universal speech. From Aberdeen to Budapest, from Bordeaux to Danzig, men believed the same things, studied the same books, and, if they wrote, used the same language. Obedient to the power of the Church, the ecclesiastic claimed a freedom not enjoyed by the layman, and so he came into conflict in theory and often in practice with the king.

The German tribes brought with them a rough theory of kingship. From being the war leader, first among his equals, the chief became, with the acquisition of property, the king. In theory the king owned the kingdom. In practice a war leader shared out the conquered land among his sub-ordinates, whose acceptance of the gift carried with it an obligation, not at first legal, to defend it. Insensibly that

4

original relation merged into that of ruler and vassal; insensibly the tradition of Rome and the patronage of the Church intensified the new conception. The kingdom was a *dominium* (full sovereignty) which the king held from God, and the vassal was a landholder who recognised that *dominium*. But God was the Church, and the consecration of God's anointed was His blessing by an earthly ecclesiastic. Hence the quarrel that raged all through mediæval times : which authority came first—the royal or the ecclesiastical ?

KING AND VASSAL : THE FEUDAL SYSTEM

THE question of the authority of Church or King was never resolved, any more than what is called the feudal system was ever existent in the well-defined forms that a short account must give. The constraints were not absolute. The feudal system was essentially a military organisation. The king needed men to fight. His own revenues were incapable of maintaining a great army. He therefore depended on his vassals, who brought their men when needed, but who perpetually sought to restrict the numbers they brought. When the king was strong, the greatest vassals obeyed ; when he was weak, they became virtually independent princes.

But the theory was never denied ; only the consequences of it were. Thus in the West the feudal system was the prelude to nationalism. The nation was divided into king, ecclesiastics, nobles, and common folk. Inevitably the king came to look for a makeweight against the noble, not in the Church which itself held property, but in the common people. This was why kings were the patrons of traders, who brought them wealth, and later of the towns, in the streets of which were formed the first vocal elements of the third estate or commons, as distinct from nobles and ecclesiastics. But in the eleventh century, although the voice of national feeling began to be heard among the common people, often of a different nationality from their nobles, it was no more than a still small voice, for the common people were without power either of wealth or of arms and were mainly peasants in a state of servitude to the noble owners of the land. It was when the nobles began to be divided into the greater and the less, when the smaller landowner, becoming identified with the soil, became a patriot, that the nations emerged as we know them.

A THOUSAND YEARS OF FARMING

These scenes, copied from an old illuminated manuscript, show that agricultural work has changed little since feudal times. Ploughing, breaking the clods, harrowing, sowing, all go on in much the same way.

Nor did that evolution come until the nations ceased to expand. The king sought to extend his dominions either by conquest or by acquiring vassals, and it was only when the limits of conquest were reached that the internal issue was finally settled. In some countries it was not settled until almost the close of the Middle Ages. It began to dominate the stage in one form or another in the next centuries.

WHEN CULTIVATORS WERE SERFS

THE next two centuries, the twelfth and thirteenth, see the consolidation and development of the feudal system, an extraordinary and disconnected effort of Europe against Asia and the struggle between the temporal monarch and the eternal church. To the reader the story looks like nothing so much as a confused chronicle of war, war which on the surface appears to be the creation of ambitious individuals, but is really the expression of economic, political, and racial forces often obscure, as life seeks to create a synthesis out of a mass of antitheses. The effort of a transition stage is always towards a new unity, an effort hampered by those who see in it a threat to their interests or dignity. We shall see in the succeeding years the failure of the attempt to secure European unity and the success of the attempt, though a success not everywhere repeated, to obtain national unity. The conception of the Crown and the relations to it of the component parts of the nation become clearer, and we arrive at a stage of Constitutional development such as had not been witnessed for nearly a millenium. The abiding fact is the gradual restoration of law to the position which it had enjoyed in the last ancient civilisation.

The term " Feudalism " implies a system of political and social organisation based upon land tenure. Some scholars profess to trace its origins to the Roman *villa* with its dependent cultivators, but its true origin is probably twofold. Feudalism developed "from below " during the troubled times of the Norse invasions of Western Europe, when the practice of " commendation " grew up. By this a man " commended " himself to a lord, offering him homage and service, generally labour-service, in return for protection. From " above " Feudalism was created by royal grant of governmental areas or " fiefs " to great nobles. Both processes were actively at work all over Europe in the ninth century. Development was more rapid on the main-

...land of Europe than in England, so that William the Conqueror, although he did not actually introduce Feudalism into England, brought with him a more developed form of it.

The typical feudal structure of society may be considered as a pyramid with the king as its apex. Below him come his tenants-in-chief, holding land on condition of military service (or knight-service); below them come the sub-tenants, also holding by military tenure and, at the base of the pyramid, the mass of unfree cultivators called *villeins*.

MEN WHO DEVELOPED FEUDALISM IN ENGLAND

Norman knights from the Bayeux Tapestry. Note the long coats of mail and the helmets like those of dirt-track racers. The pictures on the Tapestry deal with the Norman Conquest.

These serfs, living on the manors of their lords, had small holdings of land, generally of about thirty acres each in England, scattered in acre strips in the open fields of the manor; and in return for these they had to work so many days a week for the lord and perform extra labour (" boon-work ") for him at the busier agricultural seasons. They were not slaves, in the sense of being personal chattels, but, on the other hand, their freedom of action, *e.g.* to leave the manor or to marry, lay at the pleasure of the lord, who could not, however, rob them of their land. The lord of the manor or feudal overlord also enjoyed, by royal grant and by virtue of his position, legal powers—the right to hold a court and to try offenders for prescribed offences.

The process of the consolidation and dissolution of the feudal system may best be studied in England, even at the risk of confusing the reader by anticipations, for it is here that we can see the creation of what we mean by a national unity and the creation of constitutional relations between its parts. The Norman Conquest placed a fertile and comparatively undeveloped land in the power of a body of foreign adventurers under a war-leader. The leader became King of England, and he parcelled out English land among his followers, who became his vassals. Some of them were already great nobles with possessions on the continent such as the king himself had ; others were " ennobled " for the first time ; others were ecclesiastics who held land on what may be called secular tenure, owing service and homage to the king for it.

The great landowner sought to be as independent as he dared. He claimed to dispense justice on his own estate ; he parcelled it out among his followers who became his vassals and owed him service ; he sought to limit in every possible way his duty to the King. The power of the King was due very largely to his personal prestige and, though theoretically very great, was actually slight. For power— and in the Middle Ages the King's power meant the armed strength he could put in the field—he depended almost wholly on the nobles. In turn the noble, when asked to supply armed forces, called upon his vassals, and he thus not only maintained a retinue, but a private army with which he could and did wage war on his own account, disturbing " the King's peace " if the King was not strong enough to prevent him. The initial stages of the conquest of Ireland and of Wales were the work of the great Norman nobles.

Duty, expressed ceremonially as homage, practically as the provision of armed forces, was owed as payment for land which was theoretically in the King's gift. Now William the Conqueror was not merely an English king, for he was, as Duke of Normandy, the vassal of the French king. His nobles owed him as its king allegiance for lands in England, and for lands in Normandy as its duke, but they also owed allegiance to the King of France for lands held under the latter's suzerainty. Divided allegiance became a complication that confuses much of mediæval history.

The King naturally sought to organise his kingdom ; he began to create his own civil service and his own law—" the King's servants," and later to increase his own military force. All three naturally came into conflict with the rights claimed by the great landowner on his own land and in his personal actions. A strong king like the first William had no difficulty in bringing recalcitrant vassals to heel. But when there was a weak king or a disputed succession, as in the reign of Stephen, the great nobles were almost the independent allies of whichever claimant to the superior title they found it politic to recognise.

Over against both were the lands held by the Church, and the power the Church claimed over the persons of men in virtue of the power it claimed over their souls. If there were worldly ecclesiastics who were reckoned among the persecutors of the serfs, there were others bold enough to stand up against tyranny and oppression. In England, where masters and serfs were of different nationalities, to use the modern term, it was to the Church and to the Crown that the serf looked for protection against his master, the landowner. All these antitheses were present and it took centuries to work out a synthesis.

THE "LITTLE ENGLANDERS" OF 1066 AND AFTER

IN that process geography was a potent factor. The newcomers became conscious, thanks to the dividing sea, of an entity called England, and those lords who owed homage only for lands in England evolved the ingenious but specious argument that their liege lord could not demand them to serve outside England. In the eleventh century there was already a " Little-Englandism." The wars of the first two Henries were feudal forays which interested only the king and the vassals directly concerned ; " England " was not interested. The vassals who won Tenchebrai (1106) for Henry I. and thereby secured Normandy for him could not be described as an English army ; on the other hand, not so very many years later the little band that Richard Lionheart took to Palestine was conscious, among Frenchmen and Germans, of being English. If an English patriotism such as we find in the fourteenth century had not yet arisen, an island patriotism was developing. Its development meant inevitably the fusion of the races. If on the great estates there were still Norman barons and Saxon serfs, the dividing line was perpetually being crossed as the King's service became English, the Church became English, and the towns became English, with English crafts and English trade. In the opinion of some historians the quarrel of the barons with John (1215) is more than a mere assertion of feudal rights against a feudal lord. The explosion of wrath against the King's appeal to France for

aid is unmistakable. The subsequent quarrel between Henry
III. and his barons under Simon de Montfort (1257) at times
appears almost a struggle between a native aristocracy supported by the people against the foreign mercenaries of the
King. It is significant that the Port of London was the most
violent champion of Montfort and that London citizens went
forth with disastrous results to themselves to the battle of
Lewes. The King beat Montfort eventually, but the victory
none the less remained with the barons and the Commons of
England.

The issues are confused, as always. The nation wants
strong and just government. An oppressive king rouses
against himself the baronage, the Church, and the commons.
A strong king controls the barons, may incur the dislike of the
commons if he interferes with or taxes trading privileges too
highly, and certainly like Henry II. raises against himself the
wrath of the Church. An able tyrant like John can play with
the semblance of a parliament ; the trading classes will support
a baronage, capable of extremes of oppression if it gets the
chance, against competent but exacting royal rule. The
serfs remain still inarticulate.

THE WANING OF THE FEUDAL SYSTEM

BUT in the development of classes, warfare as well as
economics plays a part. To the adventurous or the able,
both the Church and the army offered careers from which
they might graduate to the king's service. War, never so
chivalrous as in the tales about Richard Lionheart, for example,
became professional. To the baron war was still an adventure
or a foray ; to the king and to the nation it became a business
of politics and economics. To carry on a political war on the
old feudal system was impossible. Service was limited by
tradition and was rapidly becoming still more limited as
opportunity occurred to escape it. The practice arose of
hiring the vassals of a noble, of trusting the king's servants to
recruit, of levying not by head but by district for defence.

Here is the nucleus of the king's army, the standing army of
which the English by tradition are so whole-heartedly suspicious.
Thus Edward I., attended by hardly any of his nobles, could
maintain forces in the field all winter and pay and feed them
himself. The test of the new system came with the war with
Scotland. The issue was framed feudally—Was Scotland
a fief of the English crown ? Actually, the determining factor

was Edward's political prescience in seeing the desirability, indeed the necessity, from the point of view of English policy, that there should be only one realm in Britain. The claimants to the vacant throne of Scotland were all connected with the Scottish royal house, but most of them were also English nobles. They accepted Edward's interpretation of the law, and John de Baliol donned the Scottish crown as Edward's vassal (1292). A true feudalist, he rebelled on the first opportunity, and was promptly and mercilessly crushed and deposed. Scotland became an English territory (1296).

THE CLAIM OF SCOTTISH LIBERTY

THE agents of Edward's rule were tyrannical and the Scottish people rose in revolt, not under any of the great nobles, but under a small independent landowner, William Wallace. Wallace himself, with unconscious lack of logic, justified what Edward called rebellion as the defence of the rights of his lawful sovereign, the King of Scotland, rights which that sovereign had never legally claimed. When he had freed Scotland temporarily the gentry and the commons of Scotland and the rank and file of the Scottish church sought to make him king, but he refused, although he took the title of regent. This was an assertion the great landed nobility could not admit, and their " treachery," legal though it was, ruined the cause of Scottish independence, and sent Wallace himself to a felon's death in London.

But here we have novel conceptions. First, that there is something called Scotland which is above the king, and then there follows the conception of its " rights," which its king ought to defend, because they are the title, as it were, to his royal rights, which the people of Scotland, unversed in niceties of feudal law, will defend if he does not. And there also emerges as a doctrine that theory of national liberty as a fundamental divine right which no man may gainsay. Eventually an Anglo-Scottish nobleman, Robert de Bruce, claimed the Scottish throne against his overlord, repudiating feudal ties, because only by such repudiation and by the right of the sword could he hope to win it. He ended the English claims at Bannockburn (1314). The Pope, the only fount of international law, had interfered on more than one occasion on not very legal grounds ; finally, having issued a decision, he threatened a rebellious land with what the modern world would call " sanctions." In reply there came the famous answer of the Scottish parliament, which placed liberty above legal judgment, a note which, echoing through William Tell to Joan of Arc, sounds over a dozen hard-fought fights and was to swell into the triumphant assertion of liberty by Luther.

The reaction on England resulted in the creation of as strong a feeling of nationalism there as in Scotland. When Edward III. arrayed his thin lines at Crécy (1346), he arrayed not a royal army, not a feudal levy, but an English army burning to fight and conquer, not for the sake of any valid or invalid claims of the monarch to the throne of France, but for a similar mysterious entity called England that rose above the king and claimed men's allegiance. Edward was still the feudal king, and feudal kings were to continue till the Wars of the Roses wiped the feudal lords out and paved the way for Tudor absolutism, but feudalism had met and lost to its deadliest foe, local patriotism, the sense of the land, the sense of nationalism.

PAPACY AND THE EMPIRE

THE system was a long time dying. It was helped to die by the quarrel between the Pope and the Emperor, and by the Crusades. It may be said roughly that the feudal system in its full theoretic form never existed anywhere. That it did not, that it was so constantly modified and changed, was due to the fact that feudalism, excellent as a theory, in practice needed universal authority. When the land tenure system of the Germanic tribes was evolving into the feudal system, the endeavour was made to obtain a double overlordship by the strait alliance and interdependence of the Church and the Holy Roman Empire. The Holy Roman Emperor was in theory the elect of God. In practice he was the head of a German feudal system which evolved into a confederation of German states, instead of being the universal emperor who was the overlord of kings. The claim was indeed made by more than one emperor, but it was not recognised, because the quarrel with the Church made any recognition impossible, even if the conception of a transcendent secular unity of Christendom had been granted. The Empire could have become a reality only if there had been a succession of great emperors and great popes fully conscious of the mutual advantage of the dual arrangement, and capable of evolving a practice to suit it.

The tenth century saw a weak papacy and strong emperors. The scandal of evil-living popes and the struggles of Italian noble houses for the chair of St. Peter provoked the intervention of the Empire under the Ottos, who had to intervene forcibly to prevent the Papal government falling into a sheer chaos that might have ruined much more than Rome. By the fault of the Popes themselves the emperor acquired a superior *dominium* which increased, till, in effect, as far as Rome was concerned, the emperor regulated the domestic affairs of the universal Church, and over the Church in his own domain acquired an authority which no Pope worthy of being at the head of a universal Church could brook. Nor could other nations brook the existence of a Papal religious power which was in fact a mere tool of the Empire. Things went so far that the Emperor Henry III. had to depose summarily three ecclesiastics, each of whom claimed to be Pope, and instal his own nominee. That roused the Papacy. It reformed itself by giving the duty of election to the College of Cardinals (1059), and by producing a great Pope in Hildebrand, enthroned as Gregory VII. in 1073.

A GIANT ARISES TO DEFEND THE CHURCH

GREGORY was an ambitious prelate, but he was also fighting for a principle that was higher than mere ambition. The right of investiture, which amounted to a claim on the part of the emperor to choose bishops, was an effective barrier to the reform of the Church, and the same obstructionism was encountered everywhere where kings for their own ends protected refractory ecclesiastics or suppressed rebellious ones. Gregory boldly challenged the Emperor's claim to domination over bishops as their secular overlord. This phase of the Investiture dispute, as it is called, ended in the humiliation of the Emperor Henry IV. at Canossa, where he humbly submitted to Gregory in 1077. But the fight was not over. It ended in wars and alarms, till finally Gregory abandoned it to die in exile. The compromise of 1122 settled the immediate issue, but virtually it was a defeat for the Empire, and so for the whole feudal system. The system was turned against the temporal upholders of it, for the overlordship was now interpreted as giving the Pope what was virtually a feudal overlordship over the secular monarch, a claim that was completely destructive of the system as it had evolved.

The prestige of the system was likewise shaken by the

Crusades, that most extraordinary of all the episodes of the Middle Ages. Their occurrence, though not their form, was dictated by the evolution of Western civilisation. Despite all its feudal wars it was developing the arts of peace at an amazing pace, and in trade particularly it felt the need of expansion. Already its emissaries were finding new fields, and the ports of the North Sea and the Mediterranean were sending their fleets into new seas. In the East the existence of a fanatical anti-Christian power, divided though it was into many kingdoms, was an insuperable barrier. The Seljuk Turks had been pressing westward from Central Asia for centuries, and in the middle of the eleventh century dominated the eastern Caliphate of Baghdad. They had accepted Mohammedanism, but were not patrons of culture such as the old Caliphs had been, and their rule opposed to the West a buttress as formidable as it was irksome. The banning of the pilgrim from the Holy Places, and the claims of trade as well as of religion combined to call upon the West for a united effort to clear a way. It is true that in the minds of the Popes who preached the Crusades and failed to organise them, there was present the noble idea of causing civil wars in Christendom to cease by combining its forces against the infidel, and the ignoble one of giving the Papacy headship over it. But the aim was hopeless of realisation from the first. National evolution had proceeded too far, and the consciousness of a deeper unity than that of mere allegiance to a dominant Church was yet to arise.

THE REAL SIGNIFICANCE OF THE CRUSADES

YET the failure was of itself productive of results. The leader of a Crusade was obviously the emperor, the co-ruler of Christendom. But the emperor had his hands abundantly full in Germany. Nor was any other monarch, despite theoretical willingness to take the Cross, particularly enamoured of leaving his own realm for Palestine. The result was that the Pope had to appeal over the heads of the kings to the barons and the common people. The greater barons had the same reluctance to go, and for the same reasons, as the king, and the leadership of the First Crusade fell to minor barons, honest crusaders or doubtful adventurers, with a following of enthusiasts recruited from all ranks of life. The motley crew that followed Peter the Hermit and the later Children's Crusade were in themselves the symbols of revolt

against the feudal system; to any politico-ecclesiastical
theorist they must have appeared enormities for which there
was no excuse, and he must have trembled when he realised
that the idea of a holy war had caught the imagination of
Christendom.

The course of the crusades is not important to this history,
for the kingdoms of the crusaders are of interest really only to
the historical archæologist and student of war. The First
Crusade beat the Seljuks at Dorylæum, took Antioch—thanks
to their opponents' dissensions—and by winning a crowning
victory at Ascalon entered into Jerusalem (1099). From
Edessa to Sinai the crusaders, as they flowed in, established a
series of little feudal principalities, of which the most important
was the kingdom of Jerusalem.

The reaction of Asia was immediate and the gains soon
imperilled. Bernard of Clairvaux preached the Second
Crusade to war-rent Europe and this time succeeded in getting
both the Emperor and the King of France to take the Cross.
It was a hopeless failure, and the respite enabled the famous
Saladin, who seized the throne of Egypt, to retake Jerusalem. The Third Crusade saw the greatest effort of the
West. It was headed by the foremost figures of this age, the
Emperor Frederick Barbarossa, Richard of England, and
Philip Augustus of France. It failed equally and for the
same reasons. The Emperor was drowned in the waters
that had nearly proved fatal to Alexander the Great; Philip
and Richard quarrelled and their followers discovered that
they were not vassals of a feudal monarch but Englishmen
and Frenchmen each worth six of the other. Although they
took Acre and Richard inflicted on Saladin his greatest
defeat at Arsuf, they were not strong enough to retake Jerusalem. They returned to the West with added reason for
quarrel rather than with the lesson learned of a new unity.

Pope Innocent III. preached a Fourth Crusade which was
the least honourable of all. No king led it; it was financed by
the merchants of Italy, and at the request of Philip of Swabia
it turned aside to assail the Byzantine Empire. The host
stormed Constantinople, set up there a Latin Empire (1204),
and divided classical Greece up into tiny feudal duchies.
The Fifth Crusade was a failure. The leader of the Sixth
Crusade, the Emperor Frederick II., won results by diplomacy
and not by fighting. Egypt surrendered Jerusalem by treaty
and Frederick styled himself, to the great annoyance of rivals

King of Jerusalem. But the treaty remained a dead letter. The Holy Places remained in the hands of the Moslems, but contact between East and West had been re-established.

Some of the later Crusades are of great interest, for they constitute the first overseas effort of France. But they are incidental. St. Louis (Louis IX.) led a skilfully planned though badly executed descent on Egypt, but was disastrously defeated (1249), simply through the complete indiscipline of the feudal baron. St. Louis's second crusade was just an episode; its hero died at Tunis (1270), which is very near France but a considerable distance from Jerusalem. Edward I. of England's crusade of 1271 accomplished little and the Frankish outposts of Christendom were gradually reduced until by the beginning of the fourteenth century only Cyprus and Rhodes remained in Christian hands.

The Crusades were over. The movement had failed of its many objects. Neither merchant not enthusiast, neither pope nor king, had attained what he sought. But besides enriching Italian traders and turning Italian ports into miniature empires, besides giving Europe the produce of the East and opening up new horizons which were never to cease alluring until there was no longer *terra incognita* (unknown territory) on European maps, it enlarged the mind of Europe, intensified nationality, and disturbed the relations of classes. Above all, it created at once a sense of nationalism and difference and of common civilisation and unity.

If we look at the map in 1300 and compare it with that of 1100 the Crusades will be found to have produced no changes except minor ones in the Mediterranean. Not even the Latin Empire lasted ; it was overthrown by Genoa in 1261. In its major lines indeed the map shows less change than the record of wars and conquests would have led one to expect; in the West, minor principalities rise and fall, or change allegiance, and a detailed map would show infinite variation from decade to decade, but the really significant changes are few.

EUROPE AFTER THE CRUSADES

BEGINNING our survey from the Atlantic we find Ireland now to all intents and purposes an English possession, a turbulent and not very profitable one, it is true. The military skill and diplomacy of Edward I. had created a nominal unity in Britain. In France a series of able kings had consolidated the power of the throne. A long struggle with England had ended in victory, but the vassalage of Englishmen for French possessions remained a potential source of trouble, and the English king was still a feudatory of the French. The patrimony of the king had been extended and the King of France was a more powerful person by virtue of his actual political and military strength than Hugh Capet was by virtue of his personality. But it continued possible for the great noble to be to all intents and purposes independent.

The Counts of Toulouse embraced the Albigensian heresy, which among other things denied the incarnation, passion, and resurrection of Christ, and against its upholders Innocent III., sworn foe of infidel and heretic, launched a crusade. It was ruthlessly carried on on the soil of France, in theory the possession of the French king, by a band of crusaders specially raised for the purpose, of whom the father of England's Simon de Montfort was chief ; these crusaders broke the power of the Tolosan counts and defeated their Spanish allies, to the great profit of the French crown. The heart of France was already consolidated and the hour of expansion when France could advance eastward was about to strike. It was only the subsequent war with England which delayed its striking till so long after. Along the Rhine there were still feudal principalities as there were also in the Low Countries, where the trading classes were beginning to revolt against exploitation by the feudal prince.

In Spain there were more serious changes on the map, for here the war against the Moslem intruder was carried on from generation to generation almost as an incident apart from Europe ; a war which is the background of the tales of the Cid and the training ground of Spanish chivalry. By the eleventh century the Moors had been pressed so far southward that Christian kingdoms had been consolidated in Leon, Aragon, Castile, and Navarre. Now united, two or more under one ruler, now in isolation, they advanced slowly but inevitably. Toledo was taken in 1085 ; Saragossa in 1118. A French adventurer wrested part of the south-west from the Moor and founded there a principality of which his successors made the Kingdom of Portugal and which, developing on its own lines, broke the unity of the peninsula. A dynastic change in Moslem Spain gave the enemy strong rulers, and to meet the menace of a great reaction the Kings of Aragon, Castile, and Navarre united their forces and won the epic victory of

Las Navas de Tolosa in 1212. The effect was immediate. Cordova fell to the Castilians in 1236 and Seville twelve years later. The Moors were driven to their last stronghold in Granada, where they were able to maintain themselves against a divided Spain.

A GERMANY DIVIDED AGAINST ITSELF

THE Empire was no nearer unity than before. The Emperor, thanks to his peculiar relationship to the Papacy, could not be a national German monarch, and the doctrine of election made the Imperial seat the prize of contending families. Thus the growth of nationalism in Germany takes peculiar forms. It is not German in the modern sense, although its manifestations are German. The noble houses gradually become transformed into territorial princes, and instead of a German patriotism we find that particularism, Franconian, Bavarian, Swabian, Saxon, which has imposed to this day an obstacle to the realisation of a truly German state. Germany was a land of independent countries nominally bound together in the Empire, actually developing each on its own lines. Worse still, the Empire was not homogeneous. It included Czechs, Poles and other Slavs in the East; Dutchmen, Flemings and others in the West. In the West geography was to settle the issue; in the East politics. The king, often a German, of the non-German territories could aspire to the Empire and therefore had some reason to deprecate attempts to cut adrift from it; on the other hand, there was the persistent tendency, strongest naturally in a non-German monarch, to assert complete independence. The tendency was particularly strong in the Slav peoples, who felt already the menace of the German *drang nach Osten* (" drive to the East "), and were prepared to assert the claims of their own culture.

In these troubled waters the able diplomatists of Rome could fish. We have already dealt with the investiture quarrel, a quarrel in which the essential disunity of the Empire was the Church's best ally. It could, if faced with the threat of an anti-Pope, reply with the threat of an anti-Emperor; it claimed the right to recognise independence by recognising an individual as king and sending him crown and blessing. In 1077 Henry IV., who submitted at Canossa, found himself faced with Rudolf, a great Swabian noble, as rival to the Imperial title. Sixty years later, the House of

Hohenstaufen, which after an interval succeeded to the Empire, was in turn challenged by the Duke of Bavaria. The rivalry between all the German nobles culminates in the long rivalry of the houses of the Welfs and the Weiblingens, the Guelfs and Ghibellines of the older histories.[1]

The great period of the emperors of the House of Hohenstaufen was due to the fact that the first Emperor of the line, Frederick I., surnamed Barbarossa by the Italians, united Welf and Weiblingen in his own person. The effect of the new unity in Germany was ruined, however, by the Emperor's attempt to restore the old empire by conquering Italy. The old kingdom of the Lombards, of which the Ottos had been kings, had gone, and in their place had arisen the communes of Northern Italy under local leaders. They were bitterly hostile to the idea of a restoration of Imperial, or rather German, domination, and formed the Lombard League, which defeated Frederick at Legnano in 1176.

Guelf and Ghibelline acquired new meaning. The Guelf stood for the freedom of Italy ; the Ghibelline sought peace, order, and unity under the Empire, and as things were, the anti-Ghibelline Papacy assumed the curious rôle of the champion of Italian liberty. The Papacy won the first round, and the only success of the Empire was the acquisition by marriage of the old Norman kingdom of Sicily by Henry VI. (1165-97). Frederick II., the grandson of Frederick I., carried his predecessor's dream still further. Lord of Sicily, he dreamed of an Italian monarchy which, had it been achieved, would have made short work of the temporal power of the Pope, now not inconsiderable in Italy. The Papacy excommunicated him and backed the Lombard League against him. It failed to have Frederick deposed, but after his death in 1250 it summoned a French prince who exterminated the house and ended the dream of an Italian kingdom. There was from 1256 to 1273 no emperor at all.

THE EMPIRE THAT WAS ONLY A DREAM

THE effect of the Italian adventure was to increase the disunity in Germany, which now expanded haphazard

---

[1] Originally *Welfs* and *Weiblingens* designated German political parties in the war between Henry the Proud and Conrad of Hohenstaufen. About 1200 the names *Guelf* and *Ghibelline* came into usage to denote respectively the Italian patriotic and Papal Party, and the Party that supported the domination in Italy of the German emperors.

instead of being directed by a great controlling mind. The interregnum was a confession that the whole theory of the Holy Roman Empire had broken down, although the name was to survive for centuries. What had been a statesman's dream had become a political absurdity. When in 1273 Rudolf of Habsburg was elected Emperor the conditions were such as to make an empire of Germany impossible.

Rudolf's election was, however, symptomatic. It was not merely a personal recognition, but a recognition of Germanism's eastern "mission," for Rudolf's duchy of Austria was, in fact, not merely the eastern marches of Germanism but the spearhead of German penetration into the south-east. Situated in the centre of Europe, served by a good river system, with easy access to the east, Germany was a centre of trade, and despite all the political and constitutional confusion, the trading towns gained rapidly in importance and wealth. The Hansa League of the northern seaports was in itself a great power which was the devoted champion of the principle that trade followed the flag of German expansion. Towns like Nuremberg, whose burgomaster was later to be made a margrave, were of far greater importance than similar manufacturing and trading towns further west. In the southeast, German settlers had penetrated the towns of Bohemia and settled in masses on its borders, and had even penetrated into Transylvania ; in the north-east, the proclamation of a crusade against the still pagan inhabitants of the Baltic lands led rapidly to their Germanisation. In the Danubian-Carpathian area, Bohemia, Hungary, and Poland played a complicated game of dynastic diplomacy, the more complicated as beneath it nationalism consolidated and in the end effectively prevented the efforts of ambitious monarchs to make permanent any of their fantastic schemes of unions of crowns.

In the Balkans, where French and Italian adventurers were finding happy hunting-grounds for duchies, Byzantine influence had entirely gone, and the Eastern Empire, despite occasional revivals, had almost ceased to be a power. As the result of the defeat of the Seljuks by the Crusaders, the Eastern emperors had been able to recover not a little of Asia Minor, but the effort was wrecked by the fall of Constantinople before the Fourth Crusade. Although the Latin Empire failed to last, it had completed the ruin of the Eastern Empire. Power in the Balkans passed gradually from the adventurers to the vigorous stock of the Serbs, who a little later were only prevented from putting an end to the Byzantine Empire by the death of their great king, Stephen Dushan, when the van of his army was almost within sight of Constantinople (1355). That feat was left to the Ottoman Turks who succeeded the defeated Seljuks and were already a power in Asia Minor.

STORM OVER CENTRAL ASIA: JENGIZ KHAN

IT was during this period that the last great wave of invasion swept out of Asia. In 1207, in far-away Mongolia, the nomad tribes had produced a leader of genius in Jengiz Khan. At the head of his horsemen he burst like a storm upon Central

EASTERN HORDES AT THE GATES OF THE WEST

The westward drive of Jengiz Khan's Mongols in the thirteenth century. They advanced as far as the Oder and the Danube, while the Ottoman Turks, working up from Asia Minor, overran the Eastern Empire and the Balkans.

Asia. China yielded to him, then Persia, and finally in 1222 his generals reached Russia. The princes of the Russian principalities refused to unite, and a great battle swept the northern kingdoms from history for the time. The invasion was renewed in 1235. This time it was the turn of the southern princes, and Kiev was burned to the ground. The invaders then swept in two swarms into Poland and into the Danubian plain. In 1241 Pesth was taken, and the Danube crossed.

In Poland they were no less successful, and Cracow fell before them. The ravage was continued up to the frontiers of Germanism, and it was only when walled cities met them that the Mongols, thousands of miles from their base, failed. Even then it was reasons of domestic policy, not defeat in the field, that made them withdraw. The eastern marches of Slavdom were a desert and Russia continued for generations in their possession, its remaining native rulers being mere vassals of the Great Khan. The end of the thirteenth century saw Asia brought within striking distance of Warsaw and Vienna.

The effects of the invasion are plainly seen in the next century. Rudolf of Habsburg, more Austrian duke than German emperor and bent on increasing his own hereditary dominions, found himself confronted with weak states. Skilfully taking advantage of their quarrels he allied himself with Hungary to crush the Bohemians on the Marchfeld (1278), and around Vienna created a German state which aspired to eastern domination. It was the tragedy of Germany that events made the Habsburgs become a dynasty and the country cease to be a German state.

A CENTURY OF UNCEASING WAR

THE history of the fourteenth century is one of unceasing war. Wars were still wars waged by kings on kings, but they were also national wars, and they were like the hammer strokes on white-hot metal which create form out of shapelessness. Once again let us trace the history on the map. In far-off Scotland the English dream of one realm of Britain was shattered at Bannockburn, where Bruce asserted the new conception, a popular conception, of nationality. His dream of a Scottish empire of Scotland, Ireland, and Man was only a dream, but he had created a nation. In Flanders, the trading burghers, the middle classes, were able to defeat the chivalry of France which sought to restore the old class domination of the feudal lord, and in Switzerland the mountaineers were able to assert the rights of men to be free against the claims of the Habsburgs. Bannockburn (1314), Courtrai (1302), Morgarten (1315)—these are battles which have not only local

ignificance, but mark a stage in the evolution of Western
Europe.

TWO SPIRITS THAT CLASHED TILL 1914 : ENGLAND AND FRANCE

THE greatest of the wars was the attempt of England to
conquer France. It was to all appearances a war of princes,
and a hundred years earlier would have been little more than
that ; it would have been brought to an end because the
feudal barons would never have responded to the demand
for such an effort. Actually, it was a war of peoples, although
England saw many Frenchmen fighting for her. To the English
it was emphatically a national war ; and on the French side,
despite the divisions which a dying feudalism succeeded in
maintaining, it ended by provoking a lively national resistance.
When it ended, two spirits had been created or awakened
which were to clash for centuries until they were united
in 1914.

England had acknowledged Scottish independence in 1328,
but the dream of union, by the nature of the times a military
dream, did not fade. When her great enemy, Bruce, died two
years later, leaving an infant son, and the heir of the luckless
Baliol made an effort to recover what he considered his
patrimony, he did so as an English vassal and with English
aid. The levy of Scotland was wiped out at Dupplin, and
Edward Baliol actually became king. Here, when England was
again embroiled with Scotland, was a heaven-sent opportunity
for France ; a long Scottish war might well give the French
king the chance to settle to his advantage the question of the
English possessions in France. Philip VI. took the infant
king of Scots under his protection and French aid helped to
dispossess the English nominee to the Scottish crown.
Edward III. indeed won a victory over the Scots at Halidon
Hill (1333) but to him that was a mere preliminary to his final
reckoning with France. His claim to the French throne was
perilously weak, and was fundamentally a pretext, but once
the claim was made war was inevitable and was enthusiastically
approved by the people.

It broke out finally in 1337 and went on until 1453. At
Crécy (1346) a small national English army, containing not
only the great lords but ordinary gentlemen and the archers of
the common people, faced and beat by superior tactics and
superior unity the vassals, levies, and allies of the King of
France, while at the same time at Neville's Cross, the men of

the northern shires in the absence of their king defeated the
invading Scots. Three years later the Black Death swep
over the West with disastrous results to the whole politica
and economic life and made the carrying on of a national war
a national burden. That it was carried on at all stamps it
as a national war. The defeat and capture of Philip's successor
at Poitiers in 1356 seemed decisive. But neither country was
able to continue the war effort, and the French tactics of
avoiding battle succeeded in forcing a peace which was only a
truce. The king of England waived the claim to the French
throne ; the French king admitted him to be lord of Aquitaine,
Ponthieu, and Calais. These were terms neither could permanently admit.

WHEN PEACE AT HOME MEANT WAR ABROAD

BOTH in France and England distress provoked peasant
risings ; there was the *Jacquerie* (from " Jacques Bon-
homme," a nickname for the French peasant) in France and
Wat Tyler's rebellion in England (1381). The latter was
chiefly due to the economic consequences of the Black Death,
which killed between one-third and one-half of the population
in 1348 and 1349 and dislocated the social life of the country.
Added to this, we should note the effects of the vaguely
Socialist views of some of Wycliffe's disciples. But the moment
the national economy recovered and England was ready,
the peace was broken. The French stirred up trouble in
Scotland and supported rivals to the house of Lancaster,
which renewed the claim to the French throne. The moment
was favourable, for France was rent with faction. The royal
house was at odds at once within itself and with its vassals,
particularly its kin, the Dukes of Burgundy, who had succeeded
in carving out a considerable empire for themselves on the
eastern frontiers of France. Henry V. had no difficulty in
repeating the triumph of Crécy at Agincourt (1415), and in
securing a diplomatic success such as had been denied Edward
by obtaining the Burgundians as allies. He proceeded
methodically to reduce Normandy ; he was a precursor of
modern war as well as one of the last of paladin or knight-
errant kings. The murder of John of Burgundy turned the
Burgundians into active allies, and France was forced to see
Paris lost and to accept the humiliating Treaty of Troyes (1420).

Henry married the French king's daughter and was recognised as heir to the French throne, but his premature death

ruined possibilities on which it is curious to look back. War broke out again and English commanders, backed by their people under a by no means popular regency, very nearly succeeded in achieving on the field what Henry had obtained potentially by diplomacy. But disaster produced Joan of Arc, a daughter of the common people, and, though the issue of the war was determined more by the withdrawal of the Burgundians from the English alliance than by the Maid's feats in the field, Orleans (1429) was none the less a worthy if belated successor to Morgarten. Peace was finally made on the basis of the surrender of her claims by England, though she retained Calais ; but the significant thing was the consecration of French nationality. In the West the key states for the future of Western civilisation were now all national states.

In Spain, indeed, nationalism had always been a force, because only on nationalism could the religious struggle against the Moslem be based, but the kings of the Spanish kingdoms not only went on quarrelling among themselves, but were drawn into the vortex of continental politics. They became involved in France and Italy, not always with fortunate results ; they fought each other, and wars like the attempt by Castile to subdue Portugal in 1385, and civil wars like that which led to the invasion of Castile by England's Black Prince and his victory of Najera in 1367, prevented that unity of effort which would have ended Moslem intrusion. The union of Spain under Ferdinand and Isabella in 1479 and the conquest of Granada in 1492 belong really to another epoch, for it was Isabella who made the voyage of Columbus possible, and the discovery of America belongs to modern history. Even then, the union of the peninsula was not complete. The little kingdom of Portugal developed a sturdy nationalism, and under the inspiration of one of the most remarkable men of his time, Henry called the Navigator, (1394–1460), son of King Juan II., began, by sending out explorers to Africa, the age of discovery.

TROUBLED TIMES IN CENTRAL AND EASTERN EUROPE

THE Empire suffered its usual vicissitudes. Germanism throughout the fourteenth century made steady progress geographically and no progress at all politically. The crusaders against the pagans pushed their way north and north-east, and by dint of hard fighting and diplomacy succeeded in exterminating or assimilating the old Prussians and creating German territories in Esthonia and Livonia, with a flourishing trade and an active—often militarily active—Church. The Teutonic Order soon became a first-class Baltic power, cutting Poland off from the sea, and threatening steadily to expand into Slav regions. The pressure from north and west had, however, raised up a new foe by forcing on the quarrelling tribes of the heathen Lithuanian centralisation and unity. Under a series of fighting kings they not only blocked the path of the Teutonic Orders, but, taking advantage of the weakness of Poland and Russia, conquered or rather overran a broad belt of territory reaching to the Black Sea.

Poland, after many divisions, intestine quarrels, and foreign kings, acquired a native dynasty, and when the stock died out in the male line, the Polish nobility, hammered by foreign pressure into being Polish, insisted on the heiress to the crown, Jadwiga, giving up the thought of a Western marriage and espousing Jagiello, the Grand Duke of Lithuania. Jagiello finally accepted Christianity for himself and his people, and under the name of Vladislas V. created a new state, Polono-Lithuania, and added it to Western Christendom. The effect was immediate. At Tannenberg in 1407 the forces of Slavdom inflicted a decisive reverse on expanding Germanism. From that hour the Teutonic Order declined ; Poland had her access to the sea, and it was left to the house of Hohenzollern, a member of whom, the burgomaster of Nuremberg, was made margrave of Brandenburg, the kernel of Prussia, by the Emperor Sigismund, to take up the secular struggle against the Slavs.

The Polono-Lithuanian state was a logical creation, even if its enormous territorial expansion violated all the laws of political geography. It eventually ended the fantastic schemings of the dynasts of East Central Europe. The son of Ottocar, the Bohemian king who fell fighting against the Emperor Rudolf I. at the Marchfeld in 1278, had nearly succeeded in occupying at one and the same time the thrones of Hungary, Bohemia, and Poland, but the Poles preferred a Lithuanian heathen and the Magyar nobles a French Italian ; Charles of Anjou became King of Hungary in 1307. A Habsburg sat on the throne of Bohemia for a brief period, but once again a Westerner was eventually chosen, and a son of the Emperor Henry VII., John of Luxemburg, accepted the crown of St. Wenceslas.

In 1313 the Habsburgs had a furious contest with the

Bavarians for the Empire, which lasted until 1322, when the latter temporarily triumphed. The Pope, John XXII., had sided against Louis of Bavaria, who as emperor elect invaded Italy, had himself crowned at Milan (1314)—thus reviving the claim to the crown of Lombardy—set up an anti-Pope and was crowned Emperor in Rome. The contest was waged with speech and pen by legalists and ecclesiastics seeking to find a formula to express a relationship between Pope, Emperor, and nationalism that would meet the needs of the age, and provoked a memorable declaration that the Imperial authority was derived from God and the electors without any intermediation on the part of the Pope. Clement V. retired to Avignon, and, wiping the dust of Rome from insulted feet, began what is known as the "Babylonish Captivity" (1305–77), during which the Popes at Avignon were under French influence.

THE GREAT SCHISM AND THE GENERAL COUNCILS

LOUIS'S adventure stirred up all the troubled waters of Italy, where cities were now under tyrants and where noble houses with their lands divided into petty states, acquired significance as they became more or less important pawns in dynastic diplomacy. The Guelfs were too strong to allow German rule to be consolidated, but they were not strong enough to prevent princelings and foreigners from ravaging Italy. Pope Gregory XI. ended the "captivity" by returning to Rome, but the advantages of Popes and anti-Popes and of control of a Pope in Rome, had not passed unnoticed by royal intriguers, and on Gregory's death in 1378, there began the "Great Schism," which, by weakening the Papacy and preparing the ground for the Reformation, was to provoke a greater rent in Christendom than any of the schismatics had anticipated. Two Popes ruled, each mutually declaring the other anti-pope, Urban VI. in Rome and Clement VII. in Avignon. Each received strong support, but the support was given purely on political lines. Austria, Bohemia, Hungary, and England supported Urban ; France and Scotland, Clement.

In 1347 Charles IV., the son of John of Luxemburg, added to the throne of Bohemia the dignity of the Empire. The title was a meaningless one, for his rule was hardly recognised, and the parts of the Empire were pursuing their own national policies. On the other hand, he did much for Bohemia, founding the University of Prague, reforming the finances, encouraging industry, and attempting to codify the laws. The result of the weak rule of his son and successor, Wenceslas, was a formidable explosion of Bohemian nationalism on the part of a nation which had to watch Louis of Hungary take Dalmatia from Venice and become the greatest monarch in Central Europe, and Poland set her feet on the road on which she was to become a great power. Wenceslas was deposed from the Empire, which had gone to a Bavarian, Rupert of the Palatinate, but on his death Charles's second son, Sigismund, became emperor, and it was he who in the presence of nationalism and heresy sought at the dawn of the new era to deal firmly with schism.

The house of Luxemburg could produce obstinate men, and Sigismund hammered away at the problem till he got a solution. That it came hopelessly late was not his fault. His father, the Emperor Charles IV., had defined the duties of the electors,[1] and given the electoral college definite status. Individually, the electors might be very minor potentates and venal at that, but collectively they elected, and so in a sense stood above the Emperor. By analogy it was suggested that a General Council of the Church might override the Pope. There were plenty of precedents and, if there might have been hesitation to place an Innocent III. at the mercy of a council, there could be no objection to placing the decision as to the claims of three men to be Pope, each engaged in anathematising the rest, in the hands of a council which would represent the sanctity and the intelligence of the Catholic Church. Sigismund held to the plan with praiseworthy resolution. A council at Pisa deposed both the Avignon and the Roman Popes, and elected Alexander V. to the chair of St. Peter.

But this was only a beginning. Mere arithmetical reduction of Popes reigning simultaneously was not of itself enough to reform a Church that was now being seriously threatened by heresy, and to save a Christendom that was being menaced by the infidel. Sigismund succeeded in having the great Council of Constance summoned. The council deposed Popes, sat off and on for four years (1414–18), passed all sorts of reform schemes, was the scene of a bitter diplomatic conflict between national states, and healed the schism by electing Martin V. But it did something far more epoch-making than end the

[1] *Electors :* the four princes and three Church dignitaries in whom was invested the right to elect the Emperor.

schism ; in 1415 it burned at the stake John Huss, the Bohemian anti-Papal religious reformer.

EXPLOSIVE FORCES THAT UNDERMINED CHURCH AUTHORITY

AMID all the military clamour of the times, learning had gone on, and the human mind, perpetually questioning, questioned, as it had always done, the teachings of authority. All along there had existed an intellectual criticism of dogma, a criticism that was scarcely effective until in the minds of men greater both intellectually and morally than the Head of the Church, it was allied to humanism and social aspiration. The move to " reform " the Church came from men very jealous of its honour, and there was much in Church discipline and government to offend any honourable man. As the Papacy, as a result of the conduct of the Popes and of the corruption evidenced in the schism, declined in prestige, the reform movement made a progress that alarmed not merely worldly ecclesiastics but temporal kings. Intellectual and social criticism fused into a force ; the reformer of social abuses sought the assistance of the scholar to justify reform by appeal to the Scriptures and the fathers of the Church.

The Bible is an explosive book, and it was the Biblical scholar who, as much as any one, was to wreck from his desk the universality of the Church. It was unfortunate from the Pope's point of view that the reform movement coincided more or less in time with the discovery of another explosive force, the printing press. The three combined to make the Reformation not only the religious but the political turning point in European history, as the Renaissance is the cultural as well as the political turning point. As the sources of the Renaissance can be traced back to Dante and Petrarch, so can those of the Reformation to Wycliffe and Huss.

Wycliffe was typically English, a mediæval Wesley, an evangelical as opposed to a churchman. His teaching spread by the Lollards was less important than his translation of the Bible, but it was inspired by a genuine intellectual conviction that certain dogmas had neither the sanction of authority nor of conscience —indulgences and auricular confession are cases in point— that the church had a social mission, and that neither in its personnel nor in its organisation was it capable of performing that mission. In an awakening world where endless wars had set a new value on the individual as well as created a social and a class problem, the teaching found ready listeners, and particularly among the common people.

It inspired the much more bellicose Czech professor. Huss, who contrived to combine theological opinions—opinions with great justice declared heretical at Rome—with democratic nationalism and a fearless attack on the misgovernment and indiscipline of ecclesiastics. His sermons, particularly in their attack on the abuse of indulgences, roused his nation. The Czech nobility, especially the smaller gentry, the middle class and the peasantry, regarded him as a national hero, and when on Sigismund's safe conduct he went to Constance to defend himself against that charge of heresy which no heretic will or can admit is just, and was burned despite that safe conduct, Bohemia rose.

The rising was a strange mixture of fanaticism, nationalist fervour, and democratic aspiration. It produced a leader of genius in Ziska, who taught Europe how to handle guns and proved that the new weapon could put unarmoured peasants in a position to defeat mailed knights. Had not the Hussites quarrelled among themselves they might have changed the face of Europe. As it was, despite being declared the object of a crusade, they brought their king and emperor to his knees, and were for a decade or two the terror of eastern Germany. Finally, after wars and civil wars, they gave Bohemia at long last a national king, Sigismund, a brave flicker of national life before the Habsburg darkness fell upon it, and the Counter Reformation wrecked Bohemian nationalism for three centuries. The abiding merit of Huss is not only to have been the forerunner of Luther, but to have roused his countrymen to such a pitch of national self-consciousness that three centuries of oppression found the flame of resistance as bright as ever.

Sigismund died in 1437. He was a man of both ability and character, but the times were too much for him. At his death the Empire passed to the Habsburgs and they were to hold it until Napoleon ended the farce.

A STOCK MORE DANGEROUS AS ALLY THAN ENEMY

THE failure to organise south-eastern Europe was to have disastrous results. The restored Byzantine Empire succeeded in regaining part of Asia Minor, now that Europe was lost to it. But in 1329 the sultan of the Ottoman Turks who from being subjects of the Seljuks now formed an independent ower, drove it back to the capital and its environs. From nemies they became allies, and were more dangerous in the latter capacity than the former. Called in to aid the Empire against the Serb, they did their work only too well. The advance of the infidel into Christian Europe created a sensation even in the remoter West, and provoked a temporary unity in the East. The Magyars came to the aid of the Serbs to meet defeat. In 1389, Sultan Murad, who was killed in the battle, ended Serbian independence at Kossovo. The Turks were now on the Danube, and Sigismund, a belated crusader, came to the aid of the threatened Hungarians at the head of a motley crew of knights and nobles, some of them from distant France, only to be disastrously defeated at Nicopolis (1396).

The Turk was now master of the Balkans ; it only remained for him to end the Eastern Empire. The advent of Timur the Tartar momentarily wrecked the Turkish Empire, or at least its base in Asia, but the scourge soon passed. In 1422 a great attack on Constantinople failed, but the Greeks were now driven into their last stronghold. An appeal was made to a common Christianity for aid. The Pope, indeed, used emergency as opportunity and secured theological unity and recognition of Papal supremacy, but the Constantinopolitans would have none of it ; they preferred the unbeliever to the Latin. No aid came from Rome or the West. The only aid to be expected was from individuals and from the nation which would next be exposed to invasion. John Hunyadi, a Transylvanian nobleman at the head of a host of eastern crusaders, was the only—though no small—obstacle to Turkish progress. He won a brilliant victory in Serbia in 1443, but he could never persuade quarrelling kings and princes to give him that support which would have enabled him to follow up his victory. He did indeed induce the Polish king Vladislas VI. who was also, by reversion to the old game of the dynasts, King of Hungary, to lead an official Magyar host, but only to his death at Varna. In the general disarray, the Turkish wave surged forward again. In 1448 Hunyadi's last effort decisively failed at the second battle of Kossovo after three days' furious fighting, a result mainly due to the Serbs who fought for the Crescent as Turkish vassals.

There was now no hope for the Eastern Empire save in the thickness of the walls of Constantine's city. A lost outpost of Christendom, it died worthy of its founder after a long and magnificently obstinate defence ; the last of the Cæsars, him-

self a Constantine, met a hero's death on the breached wall
(1453). Except in the hearts of its followers the Greek Church
was now without power ; generations were to pass before it
was once again to be the national religion of a great state. The
result of the fall was the exodus of those scholars who brought
the manuscripts of ancient Greek literature to be printed in
the West in the age that succeeded Petrarch and Boccaccio,
the pioneer figures of the cultural Renaissance. The new age
was culturally and intellectually to be built not merely in
the classical tradition but on the classics themselves.

THE WORLD NO LONGER A VAST MYSTERY

IF we close this rapid survey with a glance at the map in
1500 we find great changes. The Moslems are out of
Spain, but the Tartars are still in Russia and the Turks are
pressing across the Danube. The West and Scandinavia
have national states, with Poland as the outpost of Latin
civilisation. The Czechs are about to fall before the Germans,
the Magyars before the Turks, and Germans and Turks are
to settle the destinies of Danubian Europe in a secular struggle.
Italy is once again to be a battle-ground of ambitions, and
Germany, a congeries of princes, dukes, counts, and bishops,
is about to be rent politically by the Reformation, against
which Rome and the Emperor will once again be allies.
Gutenberg's printing press has produced many another
volume, Vasco da Gama has rounded the Cape of Good Hope.
America is on the map, and Magellan, who will circum-
navigate the globe, is a young man. We are in modern times,
and the world, in spite of the fact that its ships are cockle
shells, is already a tiny place.

THE SPIRIT OF THE MIDDLE AGES

THE mediæval period comes to an end in the middle of the
fifteenth century. If we look back over the thousand
years between the fall of the Roman Empire and the dawn
of the modern world, we may note several broad sub-divisions
of the period. There is the confused epoch following the
break-up of the Western Empire, then a brief interlude of
enlightenment and order in the age of Charlemagne and
Alfred. The clouds again lower during the ravages of the
Norsemen, but the eleventh century sees the beginning of
a religious and intellectual revival which lasts until the
beginning of the fourteenth. These years form the central

eriod of the Middle Ages, and the one during which most
f what is spoken of as being "characteristic" of mediævalism
ourished, before disintegrating and giving way to modernity.
n analysis of the chief characteristics of mediævalism will
onclude our historical survey of the period.

The outstanding feature of mediæval thought is its pre-
ccupation with religious and theological matters ; the in-
ellectual history of the Middle Ages is largely ecclesiastical
istory. Learning was generally confined to churchmen;
nost of the schools were under either monastic or priestly
nfluence, as were the universities, which, beginning with
Salerno, Bologna, Paris, Oxford, and Cambridge, arose in the
welfth and thirteenth centuries. The chief subjects of study
n the mediæval curriculum were the *Trivium* (grammar,
lialectic, and rhetoric) and the *Quadrivium* (geometry, arith-
netic, music, and astronomy). The pedagogic technique
consisted mainly of dissertations and commentaries on
authoritative texts by the lecturer and of "disputations"
amongst the students themselves.

During the intellectual revival, the seeds of which are to
be found in Charlemagne's patronage of scholarship, there
arose that characteristic product of the mediæval intellect—
Scholasticism. This was an intellectual attitude rather than
a philosophical system, and it strove to synthesise the philosophy of Aristotle (called by the Schoolmen " the philosopher," since he was practically the only one they knew)
with Christianity, and to harmonise faith with reason. The
attempt did not succeed, for the later Schoolmen found themselves compelled to withdraw many Christian doctrines from
the realm of rational proof or criticism. Scholasticism produced acute and subtle minds, and gave to the world such
illustrious names as Erigena, St. Anselm, Abelard, Albertus
Magnus, Duns Scotus, St. Thomas Aquinas, and Occam ;
but its emphasis was on order rather than discovery, on the
systematisation rather than the extension of the bounds of
human knowledge. As an experimental scientist, Roger Bacon
(1214-92) was unique in Christendom, which until the
Renaissance lagged far behind the Arabs and Moors in
scientific knowledge.

A CREED THAT CAPTURED THE IMAGINATION

THE pretensions and intellectual ascendency of the Catholic
Church are not surprising when we consider the influence

it exercised over the imaginations and ideals of men, an
particularly over those of the best of them. Asceticism,
encouraged by the Church, was one of the most influenti
ideals of mediæval man. Christian monasticism, originatir
in the Egyptian deserts in the third and fourth centuries, w;
thought to have been brought to Western Europe by S
Athanasius in 340. In the sixth century St. Benedict estal
lished the monastic rule which came to bear his name, and t
spread far and wide.

In the tenth century began what is known as the " Clunia
reformation," originating at the monastery of Cluny, whic
became the chief centre of European religious life in th
tenth and eleventh centuries ; there grew up here not onl
a stricter conception of the monastic life, but also a mor
exalted view of the dignity and authority of the Papacy an
the Church. In 1098 the Cistercian order was established
its ardent originators again demanding a return to primitiv
simplicity, founding monasteries in sequestered localities
to which their enthusiasm for agricultural labour often brough
prosperity.

The last of the great ascetic movements of the Middl
Ages was the coming of the Mendicant Orders of Friar:
in the thirteenth century—the Dominicans, Franciscans
Carmelites, and Austin Friars. St. Francis (1182–1226)
" the little poor man of Assisi," who regarded all created
things as his brethren, and who preached to the birds, is a
figure of the greatest spiritual beauty, and probably the most
exquisite individual product of the religious idealism of his
age. It is to be noted that each successive monastic movement found its justification in the alleged backslidings of the
earlier ones, and the Friars, who constituted the last reform,
did not themselves permanently adhere to the precepts of
simplicity and poverty laid down by their founders who had
sought by instituting a mendicant order to reform the
indulgence that was invading some of the monasteries.

Monasticism produced many saints and heroes differing
widely in character. Hildebrand (Pope Gregory VII.,
1073–85), who brought the Emperor Henry IV. to his
knees at Canossa, was a Cluniac ; and St. Bernard, that
champion of orthodoxy against rationalism and innovation,
the inspirer of the Second Crusade, was Cistercian Abbot
of Clairvaux from 1115 to 1173. Such men made the mediæval
Church what it was in the days of Innocent III. (1198–1216),

or when its great Councils, such as the Lateran Council of 1216 and the Council of Constance in 1414, were synods of the whole of Western Christendom. Its might in moving men to action as well as to the devotional life is seen in the Crusades, which, although we think of them as being chiefly directed towards the recapture of the Holy Land, were also carried on against heretics such as the Albigenses and their leader, Raymond of Toulouse, at whose rich court the troubadours and Courts of Love flourished. Religion could sometimes keep men at peace as well as inspire them to fight for their faith, as we may see in that curious phenomenon, the Truce of God (*Treuga Dei*), appearing in Guienne in the eleventh century and spreading through France to other parts of Europe ; there was to be a truce to all feuds during Christian festivals and from Wednesday evening to Monday morning every week !

THE IDEAL OF CHIVALRY

THE connection between religion and that system of social and military ethics and etiquette denoted by the term " chivalry " was particularly close. Not only was the code of chivalry, with its theoretical reverence for womanhood, much influenced by the cult of the Virgin, but also the actual orders of knighthood (Templars, Order of St. John of Jerusalem, Teutonic Order) were religious—crusading indeed —in origin. What the ideals of knighthood were appear in the pages of Malory's *Morte d'Arthur*, and their more mystical side particularly in the legends of a Parsifal or a Galahad. Chivalry also provided a system of education as well as an aristocratic ideal, for the young squire was supposed to learn playing, singing, versifying, and possibly even reading and writing, as well as etiquette and jousting. In the unsurpassed mediæval portrait gallery of Chaucer's *Prologue* to *The Canterbury Tales* we have a superb description of the " verray parfit gentil knight," who had done doughty deeds against the infidel, yet was in his bearing " as meeke as is a mayde," and of his son, the " yonge squyer," the apprentice in chivalry who carved " biforn his fader at the table."

The romantic side of knighthood must not, however, make us lose sight of the fact that primarily knighthood meant an often tiresome military obligation to a feudal superior, and that its chivalric side was an offshoot. The mediæval mind was, indeed, apt to be niggling in matters of legal obligation

5

or property. The wardships of heiresses and the right to dispose of their hands in marriage were bought and sold as investments, and on the whole the atmosphere seems to have been one of litigiousness and literal legalism. Feudalism, some aspects of which have been already discussed, was a pyramid of contractual arrangements, some implicit and some explicit, and even the king was limited by legal rights and obligations. There was no startlingly novel theory underlying John's sealing of Magna Carta in 1216, for we see what the attitude of the mediæval political thinker was towards monarchy in the Assizes of Jerusalem, the rules of law drawn up in the Latin Kingdom of Jerusalem established by the Crusaders in the eleventh century. The king's power was limited by the law, and he could be deposed if he broke it. Despotism and theories about the Divine Right of Kings have no place in the mediæval world.

HOW THE MEDIÆVAL TRADER OBEYED THE CHURCH

IN one aspect of life in which we might expect to find legal theories more influential than religious concepts we actually find the reverse to be true ; for in the Middle Ages economics was a branch of moral philosophy, and accordingly economic life was dominated by ethical considerations, and even by religious or quasi-religious organisations. The teachings of the Church and its authorised spokesmen condemned the taking of interest—that " breed of barren metal "—as usurious and unchristian. An important postulate was " The Just Price " ; this idea that there was a morally justifiable price for commodities provides an interesting contrast to modern theories of price, based on supply and demand. We have ample evidence that practical commercial morality was no better in the Middle Ages than at any other time, but evidence is equally abundant that there was a code of economic morality, recognised if not universally observed, of a much wider scope than was known in the succeeding period. In practice this code finds its outstanding expression in the Gilds.

The origin of the Gilds is obscure, but they first appear in mediæval history as religious fraternities devoted to works of piety and charity. In the eleventh century we begin to hear of Gilds of merchants in the towns which, at that period, were beginning to free themselves, by means of the purchase of charters, from the control of feudal overlords, and to manage their own affairs. The Gild Merchant laid down regulations for the conduct of business within the town, and dealt diplomatically with the corresponding Gilds of other towns, which were regarded as " foreign " and treated as such in the matter of tariffs and restrictions, except possibly at the time of the fair if one was held, for fairs were of great importance in the Middle Ages. At some of the greatest, such as that of Novgorod, produce borne by caravan or ship with infinite trouble and danger from all parts of the known world changed hands.

Just as commerce was largely controlled by the Merchant Gilds, so was industry (such as it was) by the Craft Gilds, which arose somewhat later than the former. For each trade or " mystery " in each town or city there was a Craft Gild consisting both of employers and employed, between whom there was little economic difference in an age of small-scale manufacture. The Craft Gilds made ordinances regulating prices, hours of work, apprenticeship (which may be viewed as another form of mediæval education), and the quality of workmanship ; and also acted as friendly societies for their members, as well as possessing religious functions, one of the most interesting of which was sometimes the production of Biblical plays. As time passed, the Merchant Gild tended to become identified with municipal government, while the growth of a social distinction between masters and men broke up the unity of the Craft Gilds, which split up into Livery Companies of the employers and Yeoman Gilds of the employed, before ceasing to be of any practical importance in the sixteenth century.

THE CORPORATE SPIRIT OF THE MIDDLE AGES

THE Gilds and the town life of the Middle Ages are interesting as an illustration of the " corporate " spirit that seems to have been prevalent then. Men were not isolated integers as early nineteenth century political thought saw them, nor were they simply members of a State—the conception fashionable to-day ; but rather they were all members of some body, whether gild, fraternity, monastery or manor, which claimed their allegiance (and in the three first cases generally passed it on to the Church) and made its own terms with the secular power of the State. Religion is again the keynote.

The importance of religion in its effects upon Art is nowhere more profusely illustrated than during the mediæval period. Mediæval architecture at its best is practically entirely ecclesiastical, and from one end of Europe to another magnificent cathedrals and abbeys—Byzantine, Romanesque, and Gothic—bear witness to the religious ardour and artistic merits of their creators. Music, too, was mainly ecclesiastical, and mediæval painting was inspired chiefly by religion. Cimabue (1240–1302) was succeeded by Giotto (1266–1336), and the work of Fra Angelico (1387–1435) brings us to the verge of the Renaissance. Literature, particularly vernacular literature, was less under religious influence, although Dante (d. 1321) may be described as the voice of Mediæval Catholicism, and the connection between religious idealism and some aspects of mediæval mythology has already been mentioned. There was, however, nothing particularly religious about those courtly and amorous bards, the Troubadours of France and the Minnesingers of Germany. It is noteworthy that Chaucer, coming at the end of the fourteenth century, not only writes in English (a *national* tongue), but satirises many types of ecclesiastics, servants of the *international* Church.

From the beginning of the fourteenth century we can see the waning of the mediæval heyday. The dream of a Universal Empire is, for a while, obscured. The Papacy is weakened by heresy and schism ; monasticism deserts its pristine simplicity, and, above all in importance, we note the rise of national consciousness, producing national heroes and heroines like Bruce and Joan of Arc, as well as national literature. The Middle Ages had run their course and made their contribution to the story of mankind. A new age was at hand, bringing with it new forces, new ideals, new hopes, and new problems.

SOME BOOKS ABOUT THE MIDDLE AGES

BOOKS on the Middle Ages are legion. The *Mediæval European History* of Dr. Claude Jenkins (Benn) is a useful short summary of fact. A wider view and a summary of great interest will be found in Prof. H. W. C. Davis's *Mediæval Europe* (Home University Library, Thornton Butterworth Limited), and there are other excellent surveys of mediæval life and history in Dr. Charles Seignobos's *History of Mediæval Civilisation* (Benn) and Dr. G. C. Coulton's *The Middle Ages* (Cambridge University Press). All Dr. Coulton's books are excellent and will repay study. Larger textbooks and histories are numerous ; the best and most voluminous of all is the still unfinished *Cambridge Mediæval History*, of which seven volumes have been published —a monumental achievement of scholarship. In it will be found a very full bibliography of the multitudinous special studies which exist in all languages and in which the reader will find all the information he wants. The eleventh edition of the *Encyclopædia Britannica* is most useful for the national histories, for biography, and for the non-European history. The individual nations can best be studied in the works of their own historians ancient and modern, of which full lists will be found in the Cambridge volumes. For maps, the handiest book is the *Smaller Historical Atlas*, published by Philips.

MODERN HISTORY : 1485–1914

by
T. G. Standing, M.A.(Oxon.), Former Exhibitioner
of New College, Oxford

HUMAN history has, so far, been a continuous process; change has never ceased, and it is unwise to say, for instance: " In 1485 English mediæval history ends and modern history begins." Still, between the middle of the fifteenth century and the middle of the sixteenth century (say 1453–1555) an epoch slowly passed away and a new one grew into its place. Spanish, Portuguese, and Italian sailors traced the coasts of Africa and a new continent, America, and traded with India and China. Books were printed in thousands where once they had been painfully copied in twos and threes. The art of warfare was complicated by grimy mechanics who operated tubular instruments from which missiles were shot with much risk to the gunner. North-Western Europe was filled with religious enthusiasts who claimed independence of the Pope and professed novel views of ritual and the way to salvation. A very large number of the monasteries which formerly had been local centres of cultured leisure, education, and charity, were quite destroyed and lay adventurers took their estates. Many laymen learnt more Latin than priests had formerly known : there were men who learnt a great deal of Greek. Law was modified by experts who considered the Roman code of Justinian to be the ideal legal system.

It was impossible for any European who could compare the two periods to doubt that his world in 1550 was a different place from the world of 1450, and on the whole more exciting. Men were beginning to believe in progress. That belief, among other things, differentiates us from our mediæval ancestors.

THE AGE OF PERILOUS DISCOVERY

IT is said that a fleet made its way round Africa about 600 B.C. in the time of the Pharaoh Necho. During the Dark Ages, however, the ancients' knowledge of the world had been forgotten. China and India became lands of fable. Travel was very expensive, and few people travelled except for

RENAISSANCE SAILORS TRACE THE COASTLINE OF THE NEW WORLD

NORTHMEN BEFORE 1000
BARTHOLOMEW DIAZ
COLUMBUS (4 VOYAGES)
JOHN & SEB CABOT(2 VOY?)
VASCO DA GAMA
MAGELLAN
NORTH EAST PASSAGE
COASTS VISITED BY
EUROPEAN NAVIGATORS
UP TO 1522

PACIFIC OCEAN

Manihiki I.

Tuamotu

1520

Strait of Magellan

SPAIN
PORTUGAL
THE POPE'S LINE
OF DEMARCATION 1494.

New Siberia

Panama

West Indies

Vinland

ATLANTIC

1492
1493

Greenland

Labrador

Newfoundland 1497

Azores

Canaries

C. Verdes

1498

1497

LATER ENGLISH & DUTCH
ATTEMPTS TO FIND A N. E. PASSAGE

Scandanavia

OCEAN

1497

C. Verde

1446

1521

Cape of Good Hope
(C. of Storms) DIAZ 1487

INDIAN

OCEAN

Mombasa

1498

Calicut

INDIA

CATHAY
(CHINA)

Java

PORTUGAL
SPAIN
LINE OF
DEMARCATION 1529.

Spice Is.

Philippine Is.

Japan (Zipangu)

Ladrones

PACIFIC

OCEAN

trade, to visit holy places in hope of salvation, or to escape from enemies. In the Middle Ages there was a certain amount of travel by pilgrims and by students seeking knowledge. "Foreigners," even from a few miles away, were generally received as enemies.

Norsemen reached America nine hundred years ago, though nothing came of their voyages. Almost every household was self-contained, but ships carried wine, wool, fine steel, and grindstones across the narrow European seas. A sailing ship was evolved capable of riding out storms and keeping the sea for months—a bluff-bowed, broad-beamed, half-decked, single-masted vessel of fifty or a hundred tons.

Navigation was assisted in the fourteenth century by the introduction from the East of the Chinese compass and later of the astrolabe, which gave the latitude. Small half-decked ships were dangerous craft in which to grope along unknown coasts. Fresh food could not be kept for more than a few days. Salt meat for months on end led to scurvy; it was an even chance that any man condemned to a voyage would die. A host of imaginary and superstitious terrors, fears of devils, whirlpools, sea monsters, pools of flame, and skies of pitchy night, caused exploration when it began to be carried out by crews of sentenced criminals.

IN SEARCH OF WEALTH : THE LANDS OF SPICE AND GOLD

THE most important of all mediæval trades was in spice. Pepper, ginger, nutmegs, mace and cloves, and other eastern products like silk, camphor, opium, frankincense, myrrh, and indigo, were brought out of the unknown by Levantine merchants. Wealthy Europeans would pay very high prices for flavours and preservatives to relieve their winter diet of salt beef. In the fifteenth century difficulties arose as Europe's gold and silver were drained eastward in payment.

A party of Europeans—the Polo family of Venice—spent many years at the court of Kublai Khan of China between 1272 and 1295. Marco Polo's marvellous book of travels was, however, regarded as a collection of lies.

During the years when Henry V. of England was campaigning in France, a Portuguese cousin of his, Prince Henry, attacked the Mohammedan Moors of North Africa in what they called *Bilad Ghana*, "the rich land," from which they drew much of their wealth. After twenty years of feeling their way down the African coast, the ships that Henry sent out from Sagres began to tap the gold, ivory, and slaves of equatorial Africa. *Bilad Ghana* became "Guinea" : the new gold was called " Guinea gold."

Many years after Henry's death, Bartholomew Diaz rounded the tempestuous Cape of Good Hope in 1488. Calicut, the great port of Southern India, was reached in 1498 by Vasco da Gama, who drove his crew of cut-throats to make the voyage out and home in seventeen months : two-thirds of the crew died on the way. Lisbon now took the place of Venice as the spice distributing centre.

The Portuguese, under Almeida (d. 1510) and Albuquerque (d. 1517), organised an eastern dominion with its capital at Goa, fortresses on the coasts of Africa and India, and trading connections all the way from Brazil and the Guinea coast to Japan. For a hundred years they held the gorgeous East in fee, European interlopers being treated as pirates. They wanted trade, not colonies, and they left South Africa alone.

Their voyages drained much adventurous blood, and the little kingdom suffered defeats from the Moors in North Africa, and was conquered by Spain in 1580. Then Spain's English and Dutch enemies, between 1590 and 1620, forced their way East and established themselves in Surat and Java respectively. The Dutch and English fought each other only a shade less fiercely than the Portuguese, or than all three fought the Arabs, and later the French.

THE DARK ATLANTIC

SINCE man first looked westward over the rolling waters he had thought of the Atlantic only as a boundary beyond which lay an abyss or an inferno. Greek scientists of Alexandria had proved that the world was round, but in fifteenth century Europe the world was conceived to be flat, surrounded by Ocean ; Ocean was surrounded by an awful gulf.

The Portuguese found the Azores in Prince Henry's time ; they claim, too, that a Portuguese, Sanchez, sailed farther into the sunset and discovered an island, Antilia ("the land opposite"). Perhaps Sanchez's voyage was known to the Genoese weaver, Cristofero Colombo (Christopher Columbus), who first contemplated crossing the Atlantic. Columbus was a bad sailor, a bad commander, and a bad geographer. The Portuguese rejected his plan and so did Henry VII. of England, but he persuaded the Queen of Spain to give him ships We do not know what he promised to find.

In 1492 he and a much abler seaman, Pinzon, found some small islands, including Hispaniola (Little Spain). Columbus announced that he had discovered the Indies and the shortest route to the cities and empires of Cathay and the ancient East. His " Indies " yielded neither spices nor gold, only naked Caribs who were exterminated by the Christians. Amerigo Vespucci may or may not have sailed with a fleet that reached Brazil in 1500 ; at any rate he wrote an account of it and his publisher called it *Terra Americi*—hence America. Columbus was imprisoned and died.

A THREE YEARS' JOURNEY ROUND THE WORLD

FIFTEEN years after the death of Columbus, Cortez discovered Mexico. While he was conquering the Aztec ruler, Montezuma (1519-22), Magellan, a renegade Portuguese, took a small Spanish fleet through the frightful Straits since named after him, and then across the Pacific, an unknown sea ; they were chewing leather before land was at last sighted. Magellan was killed in the Philippines, but his flagship, the *Vittoria*, reached Cadiz at last with thirteen men out of the 300 who had sailed three years before. They were the first circumnavigators of the globe, though the object of the voyage was a new route to the Spice Islands, not geographical discovery. Some ten years after Cortez, a ruffian named Pizarro discovered the kingdom of Peru, where the Incas with their stores of gold were conquered (1523-33). The enormous courage and endurance of the early Conquistadors were matched by the ruthless greed with which they squeezed gold and silver from the mines at the cost of countless Indian lives.

Portugal and Spain had the New World, East and West, to themselves, because they were strong enough at first to hang intruders. The French and English were left only the bleak north-eastern coasts of North America. Here, annually, fishermen came to catch cod and learn seamanship in a very hard school.

SCHOLARS SAIL UNCHARTED SEAS

WHILE adventurers were facing death on new oceans and on the coasts of fabulous new continents, another kind of adventure and exploration was going on in Europe, where scholars sailed uncharted seas of learning. There were two sides to the New Learning of the fifteenth century, or Re-

A GALLEON OF THE SIXTEENTH CENTURY

naissance of intellectual life : the spread of scholarship and art, and the Reformation movement in religion.

There was, first, the progress which European civilisation always makes in more or less settled times. Towns, superb cathedrals, and universities had grown up. Modern literature began in the fourteenth century with Dante, Petrarch, Boccaccio, Froissart, and Chaucer. Two significant inventions had been made ; gunpowder and printing. Crude cannon were in use, and in 1454, Gutenberg, a German, first cut wooden types for printing. Caxton brought printing to England in 1476. During the fourteenth century there lived Giotto, the first great modern painter, and Donatello, the first great modern sculptor. Italy had a radiant climate, relics of the wonderful Roman world, the capital of a Western Christendom still owing allegiance to the Pope, and contact with Byzantium and the cultured Moslem of the Near East.

It was in Italy, too, that there began the revival of the study of Greek and classical Latin. Mediæval scholars used Latin familiarly, but it was not very good Latin, and the only great work of classical Latin that they had was Virgil's *Æneid*. Greek had survived only at Byzantium, as Constantinople was called, the capital of the eastern half of the old Roman Empire. Towards the end of the fourteenth century, one Chrysoloras came to Italy to teach Greek. Other Greeks followed with manuscript books. In 1453 Byzantium was at last captured by the encroaching Turks, and more of its scholars took refuge in Italy. Thanks to Gutenberg, their Greek books could now be copied in great numbers.

Europe's native literature included a few good English, French, and Italian poems, some good Latin lyrics and hymns, many old knightly romances of some merit, and an arid mass of theology. To such a Europe, eager but intellectually starved, the refugee scholars brought the literature of the Greeks : Homer, in poetry ; in history, Thucydides and Herodotus ; in drama, Æschylus, Sophocles, Euripides ; in oratory, Demosthenes ; in philosophy, Plato and Aristotle. The New Learning overwhelmed the men who received it.

It is perhaps hard for us to understand the really passionate enthusiasm with which scholars strove to master Greek, and correct the readings of the rediscovered classical manuscripts. Grammars and dictionaries were very crude, and much was obscure in the ancient writings even to the Byzantine Greeks. Lifetimes of toil completed the work. Browning has given us a living picture of a Grammarian :

> " So, with the throttling hands of death at strife,
>   Ground he at grammar ;
> Still, thro' the rattle, parts of speech were rife ;
>   While he could stammer
> He settled *Hoti's* business—let it be !—
>   Properly based *Oun*—
> Gave us the doctrine of the enclitic *De*,
>   Dead from the waist down."

HOW THE RENAISSANCE LED TO THE REFORMATION

FOR the next two centuries, the thought and the religious and political life of Europe were deeply marked by the classics, and by a new joy in living, to which was added energy in questioning old things and looking forward to new. First Italy, then France, Germany, and Spain, and, at last, the England of Elizabeth were stirred by them. Barely five per cent. of the population of any of the countries affected can have had any direct contact with the new scholarship, but they were the men whose influence was strongest.

The Revival of Learning perhaps accelerated Europe's

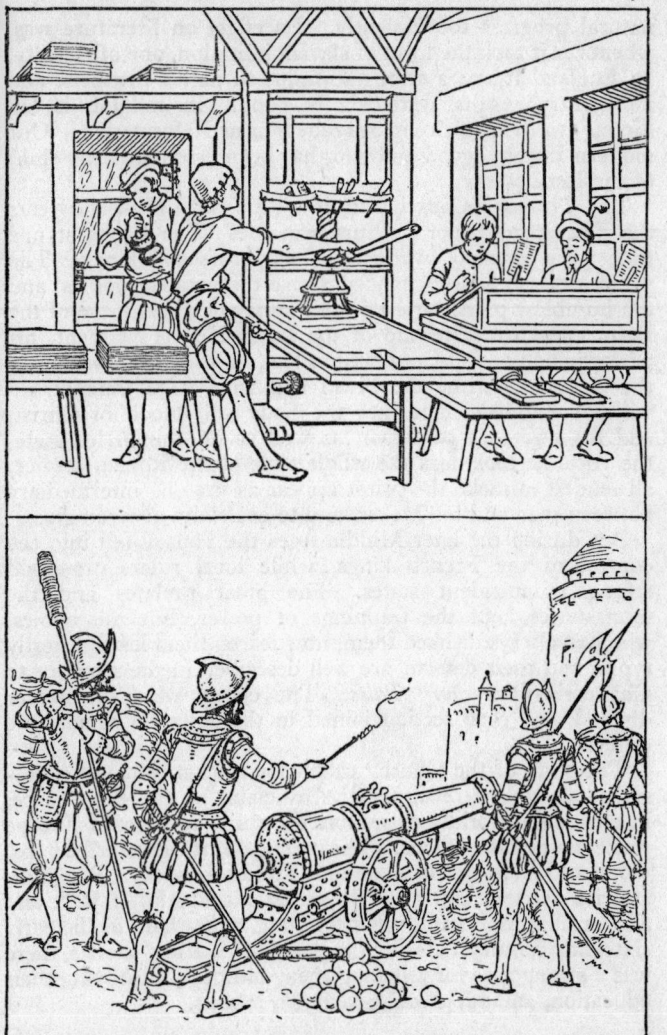

ARTS OF PEACE AND INSTRUMENTS OF WAR

Printing press and field artillery—both inventions characterise the Renaissance, age of intellectual enlightenment and nascent nationalism.

natural progress too violently. Its effect on literature was, whenever it took the form of slavish imitation, one of sterility. In England it was a strong stimulus to native instincts, and its literary results were wholly good. In religion it led directly to the great religious rebellion or Reformation. Our modern Europe, good and bad, has been essentially the child of the Renaissance.

The Christian Church had now been for a thousand years the permanent factor in European life. The Popes at one time were virtually overlords of emperors and kings. The princes of the Church ranked above the greatest nobles, and the humblest parish priest feared no layman. His use of the Latin church service and of the Latin New Testament, his performance of the Communion rite, at which, according to the Roman doctrine the bread and wine were transformed without visible change into the body and blood of Christ, and his duties as confessor, as well as his unmarried state, the vows he took, and the whole style of the Roman service, all tended to make the priest appear as the one intermediary between man and his Maker, and to exalt him accordingly.

But during the later Middle Ages the Papacy fell into the control of the French kings, while local rulers organised strong independent states. The great prelates and the monasteries kept the trappings of power, but the nobles, who had always disliked them, now feared them less. Priestly types, and their defects, are well described in the *Prologue* to Chaucer's *Canterbury Tales*. The clergy were themselves divided, and each section joined in the agitation against the others.

The state of the Church called for reform, but not necessarily for violent revolution. Any claim by the Pope to be, in effect, the worldly as well as the spiritual ruler of Europe was certainly anomalous. The prestige of the greater bishops, too, could no longer be maintained undiminished. The monasteries needed reform, as the ablest bishops knew well, and a reforming movement was beginning in England in the early sixteenth century. As for the parish priests and monks, there was a strong case for reducing their numbers, improving their education, and suppressing laxity in morals.

TOO MANY POPES WEAKEN "THE FAITH"

WE have seen in the previous section how during the fourteenth century the prestige of the Papacy fell almost to zero. A great many concluded that Rome's claims to supremacy were baseless, and that celibacy, transubstantiation, the power to hear confession and give absolution for sin, and, above all, the wealth and worldliness of prelates had no authority in Scripture.

In Italy many cardinals and even several of the Popes adopted the New Learning and devoted their energies to art, literature, and more sensual amusements. Italy went over to a pagan culture which at its best was elegantly unChristian and, at its worst, rather diabolical. The former type is portrayed vividly in Browning's poem, *The Bishop orders his Tomb at Saint Praxed's Church*. The latter type produced the Borgia family, whose interest in poison was perhaps exaggerated by tradition, but whose vice and ambition were certainly not compatible with the Christian religion of which the father, Rodrigo, was, as Pope, the titular head. Italian political morality was expounded by Machiavelli in his handbook *The Prince*.

In theory the Pope was the spiritual and the Emperor the temporal head of Europe. After the destruction of the Imperial power by the Papacy in the thirteenth century the growing young kingdoms became independent and the kings beat down the nobles, assisted by cannon, which battered down baronial castles. Communications improved within each geographical area, so that men of Kent could think of Yorkshiremen as fellow-countrymen. Their speech might still be mutually unintelligible, but national tongues were evolved in all the chief states, usually from a mixture of Latin and the native tribal languages. Most of the little kingdoms possessed some kind of representative assembly—Parliament, Cortes, or States General—in which the nobles and clergy, and a few inarticulate townsmen, obstructed the king's business. Their credit, never very high, sank considerably during the fifteenth century and the time was coming in most countries for their suppression.

The long wars of England against France, and of the Spanish kingdoms and Portugal against the Moors, helped to crystallise national sentiment. Internationalism in Europe was weaker at the beginning of the sixteenth century than ever before or since.

The New Learning unsettled priests and poets, and even the lawyers remodelled their local law in the spirit of the Roman legal system which, under its despotism, had legal conceptions quite alien to those of the oligarchic Middle Ages. *Quod principi placuit, legis habet vigorem*—"What pleases the prince has the force of law." The process was least active in England, which had been inoculated with a small dose of Roman principles four hundred years before. In England the strongest force tending to exalt the king was the intense disgust of all industrious people with the baronial unruliness which had given the country so many years of chaos during the Wars of the Roses (1455–85).

The least united states were those which were the seats of " universal " sovereigns—Italy, where the Pope resided, and Germany, the home of the Emperor. Italy was divided among a dozen kingdoms, duchies, and city republics. Germany, or the Empire, was divided among seven Electors, several dukes and ecclesiastical princes, city-states, and three hundred very small counts and knights. Disunion meant a pitiful contrast with the peace of orderly despotisms like that established by Henry VII. of England. The Emperor had no powers as such, but from 1438 to 1806 the head of the House of Habsburg was regularly elected Emperor ; he was Archduke of Austria by hereditary right, and the energetic, moody, gluttonous man who was Emperor from 1519 to 1556 —Charles V.—was also ruler of Spain, the Netherlands (Belgium and Holland), the Spanish New World, Burgundy, and most of Italy.

LUTHER GROPING IN SEARCH OF THE TRUTH

IN 1517 a Saxon priest, Martin Luther, protested against abuses arising from the sale of indulgences. These were intended as a condensed substitute for penances which the Church required as one condition of absolution for sin, and for the penalties which the Almighty would inflict in Purgatory. Luther was a sincere, violent, and somewhat ignorant German, who seems to have gone on rather blindly, step by step. In 1521 he was condemned at Worms by an Imperial Diet. He was allowed to leave in safety and remained in hiding, translating the New Testament into German (and so beginning the standardisation of the language), pronouncing against the celibacy of the clergy and transubstantiation, and suffering from hallucinations. The King of England, the clever young Henry VIII., wrote a Defence of the Seven Sacraments, and was given by the Pope the title of Defender of the Faith.

Germany was in such disorder that Luther's agitation

precipitated rebellions by the small nobles and peasants, each being suppressed. Luther shunned them; he had genuine reverence for monarchy. Many earnest middle-class men read his German Bible and adopted his "Protestant" views. Many princes adopted them as a cloak for designs on Church property. The Emperor between 1521 and 1546 was constantly absent and at war—with France for Italy and Flanders, with the Turks on the Danube, and with the Moors in Tunis. Journeys were very slow, and it was impossible for Charles to govern Germany with any firmness. Friction with the Pope in Italy also hampered him. Many German abbots " secularised " themselves and their estates, transforming themselves into counts reigning over the monastery's former lands. The Protestant creed was defined at the Augsburg Conference of 1530 by Melanchthon, Luther's able young follower.

ENGLAND DEFIES THE POPE

THE idea of reform found very congenial soil in the Netherlands, but in France it was checked by the king's being dependent on the Pope for assistance against their common enemy, the Emperor. In Spain and Italy it never made any progress at all. No very satisfactory explanation has ever been found for the comparative success of Protestantism in North-West Europe and its total failure in the south. Distance from Rome and lack of sympathy with Latin ideals may have caused it.

Britain soon began to receive the continental doctrines, as merchants and sailors brought them to southern and eastern ports. The national tradition was anti-papal, and Henry VIII. turned against the Pope in 1529, when the latter refused, probably from fear of Charles, to nullify Henry's marriage to Catherine, Charles's aunt. Henry was simply a tyrant, but English public opinion was behind him. He declared himself head of the Church in England, and confiscated the property of scores of monasteries. He was, emphatically, no Protestant, and he burned Protestants who refused to accept the six chief points of Catholic doctrine. But he was persuaded to allow an English translation of the Bible, copies of which were chained in churches.

A small power, such as Britain then was, would hardly have dared to set herself against the policy of the greatest powers of the Continent but for one circumstance : she was an island.   Henry founded the English navy of heavily gunned sailing ships, the first in Europe, and beat off a French invasion with it.   The prestige of royalty was at its height, and Henry had the solid support of the upper classes, especially of those who bought up monastery lands.   His father and his own able minister Wolsey had practically dispensed with Parliament, but his urgent need of national support drove him to summon it regularly (1529-36) and have his acts endorsed by it.   It was thus saved from atrophy and the foundation was laid for future claims.

But the strongest thing associated with the new Protestantism originated in France and matured in the Swiss mountains. Calvin, a clever north-Frenchman, became at twenty-three the ablest exponent of Protestantism, and Geneva, where he settled, the centre of a new propaganda.   Luther had denounced the Catholic doctrine of Salvation by Works, and preached Justification by Faith.   Calvin revived Augustine's doctrine of Predestination.   Every soul was fated at birth either to " election " and eternal life, or to rejection and eternal torment.   There was no means of deciding whether one was of the elect, except by the consciousness of grace, but a devout Calvinist, after brooding over the awful problem of his fate, was almost certain to end in a happy consciousness of his own election.   Geneva adopted a form of government by the upper citizens, enforcing harsh laws against most kinds of harmless frivolity.

This bleak Calvinist creed attracted followers in the German middle class, and during the 1540's it spread into north-western France, the Netherlands, and England, where small congregations met secretly, at the risk of death.   It found its way later to Scotland and proved to be completely to the Scottish taste.   There were also minor novelties of reform, like the Anabaptist sect, which flourished sporadically and was attacked by the bigger Protestant bodies quite as brutally as those bodies ever were attacked by the Roman Church.

ROME RALLIES HER FORCES : THE STRUGGLE FOR SOULS

THE terrible events of 1527, when Charles V.'s mercenaries sacked Rome, ended the cynical paganism of the Italian Renaissance.   The Church began to prepare seriously to meet the Protestants with their own weapons of energy and casuistry.   The Inquisition was revived to destroy heretical books and hear charges of heresy. Ignatius Loyola, a Spanish knight, founded the Society of Jesus, a mobile force of highly trained enthusiasts, for exacting labour-missionary work in Africa or Japan, intrigue against Protestant governments, and for preaching and education in Catholic countries. A great Council of the Church met at Trent, in North Italy, in 1545 : it spent eighteen years in reforming the Church's discipline. This Counter Reformation regained much of the lost ground during the century from 1547 to 1648.

The first effort of the Counter Reformation was Charles V.'s attempt to restore religious order in Germany. In 1547 he was at last at peace with France and Luther was dead. After winning a delusive victory and suffering humiliating betrayals and defeats, he made the Peace of Augsburg in 1555 ; each German prince might enforce his own religion—Roman or Lutheran—in his own dominions : *Cuius Regio, eius religio* (" Whose is the kingdom, his the religion ") was the maxim which summarised the exaltation of monarchy. Charles then abdicated and left the Empire to his brother Ferdinand, already ruler of Bohemia and Hungary. From him the later Habsburg emperors descend. All his other dominions he left to his son Philip II. of Spain. The success of the German princes encouraged the French nobility to begin a similar revolt, and Philip's personality was the prime cause of a rebellion in his Netherlands dominions which soon followed. A forty years' struggle ensued.

The Reformation, which on the spiritual side was an assertion of individual judgment against that of the Church, tended in Lutheran and Anglican areas to the aggrandisement of regal power and the control of the Church by the State—the principle known as *Erastianism*. Where Calvinism prevailed, its tendency was towards republican or oligarchic government, which gave the Church a show of independence on condition of its serving class and national ideals.

TRYING TO DIVIDE POWER BETWEEN THE NATIONS

IMPROVED communications tended during this century to the concentration of national resources for national wars, and the modern conception of Europe as an armed camp really dates from 1494. As war has grown more intense it has, mercifully, grown spasmodic : and it is true also that

aspirations towards a Society of Nations began in the sixteenth century.

Sixteenth-century Europe knew nothing of Russia and
did not recognise the Turk, sprawled over everything from
the Danube to the Jordan, as civilised. The three chief
powers were the great agglomeration of territories which had
fallen by marriage into Habsburg hands, the smaller but
central, fertile, defensible, and cultured kingdom of France,
and the still smaller kingdom of England. There were
princes of some importance in Germany and Italy, of whom
the Pope was the chief as ruler of a considerable Italian
state.

The central theme of modern military history is the opposition of France to the chief German power—the Habsburg
dynasty till 1866, and since then Prussia. England, generally
in alliance with the weaker, has brought down one dominating
power after another—Charles V., Philip II., Louis XIV., the
France of Napoleon, the Germany of Bismarck. In the
absence hitherto of any hope of establishing international
peace by a permanent organisation, this Balance of Power
has mitigated international bullying. But at its worst it has
degenerated into jackalism, any accession of power to a state
being made grounds by its rivals for demanding "compensation," usually at the expense of weaker neighbours.

The bone of contention from 1494 onwards for nearly
forty years was Italy. Charles VIII. of France first overran
the north. France continued to plan a conquest and was
resisted by the rival power of Spain, whose kings had claims
to certain Italian principalities. The wars were conducted
by mercenaries who inclined, as mercenaries generally do, to
reserve their ferocity for neutral civilians. Modern conceptions of the nation in arms and of striking the enemy hard
at his strongest point are out of place in these wars. They
reached their climax in 1525-27, when Francis I. of France
was matched against the Emperor Charles V. The wealth
of the Netherlands enabled Charles to win a victory at
Pavia in 1525 and to sack Rome in 1527. Italy now became
virtually a Spanish province for two hundred years and
provided Spain with the best of her generals and infantry.
The next three centuries of Italian history were torpid, but she
remained the Mecca of scholars and cultured travellers—a
remoter Mecca to Englishmen of that day than London is
to a New Zealander of ours.

FLANDERS SCARRED WITH THE WARS OF SEVEN CENTURIES

THE Emperor's Turkish wars enabled France to continue to encroach on the Netherlands. This process began when France first acquired unity in the Middle Ages, and remained a feature of French policy until 1870. Desultory wars went on for years, small armies besieging small frontier fortresses and marching through what was already the characteristic mud of Flanders. After Philip II.'s accession Spain won a victory at St. Quentin and made peace at Le Cateau in Cambrésis (1559). The part played by St. Quentin and Le Cateau in the war of 1914-18 is a reminder that this area for seven hundred years has never been immune for long from invasion, chiefly because the level plains provide better routes between France and Germany than the mountainous country which separates them in the south-east, and are worth occupying for their own sake.

The part played by Britain in these wars was inconspicuous. The poor but warlike kingdom of Scotland was always ready, as in the Flodden campaign of 1513, to invade the north when her neighbour had a French war. The cardinal principle of English policy for several centuries was to keep friends with the Netherlands, to which she sold her all-important wool, and this meant alliance with Spain when Spain controlled the Netherlands, an alliance which was fortified by the traditional English hatred for Spain's rival, France. Henry VIII. supported Spain before Pavia, partly in hopes of Spain's help in regaining Henry V.'s dominions in France. Though disappointed by Charles, with whom his relations were further damaged by the divorce of Catherine and the breach with Rome, he remained neutral or passively friendly towards Spain. His hands were full enough with the dissolution of the monasteries, his organisation of Wales, Ireland, and the north, and financial difficulties resulting from the rapidly falling value of silver, which drove him to debase the coinage and caused great distress and disorder.

The guardians of Henry's successor, Edward (1547-53), raided Scotland, and Henry's daughter, Mary (1553-58), married the new king of Spain, Philip, as part of her unsuccessful attempt to retrace the steps towards Protestantism taken by Henry and Edward's guardians. Mary's sister and successor, Elizabeth, began her reign with every wish to preserve good relations with Spain, her only support against the Franco-Scottish menace.

"NOT PEACE, BUT A SWORD"

SPAIN, successful in arms, government, and literature, supported by the Austrian branch of the Habsburgs and by Italy and England, was now standing over a France which was beginning a long period of royal minorities and religious wars. Yet the forty years that followed were not successful years for Spain. Philip, who had inherited from Charles V. in 1556, Spain, the Netherlands, the Spanish possessions in the East and West Indies, Mexico and South America, and most of Italy, was a superstitious and sickly dullard, but he had a strong sense of duty and there were very able men around him. Though he tried hard to reconcile religion and politics, the claims of religion drove him to quarrel with the English, to act against his own interests in France, and to provoke in the Netherlands the first and fiercest national revolt of modern times. There were elements of weakness in Spain herself, such as her exclusively military tradition and lack of a solid merchant class.

The Netherlands (our modern Belgium and Holland) were then the richest part of Europe : they consisted of seventeen small states, united only by allegiance to the King of Spain as heir of the Dukes of Burgundy. Calvinism made many converts there, and very great numbers of men and women were burnt or strangled as heretics by the Spanish government. The revolt, which began with riots in Brussels in 1566, was not altogether due to religion. Much was due to excessive taxation, to the misbehaviour of Spanish mercenaries, and the unpopularity of Spanish governors. Many Catholics resented the persecution of their fellow-countrymen by the Spanish Inquisition, and many were led by ambition or restlessness to join the party of discontent. Protestantism was destined to be extinguished in the ten southern provinces, since these provinces were dry, open country, ideal for the operations of Spanish troops, which were handicapped when trying to subdue the seven maritime provinces of the north among their rivers and dykes.

The Dutch revolt was fertile in dramatic incidents, of which the submersion of a wide area to drive the Spaniards off Leyden in 1574 was the most famous. It was distinguished by the career of William of Orange, miscalled the Silent, a national hero who gave his fortune, and finally his life, for the cause which he maintained during twenty years. Spain was served by the infamous butcher Alva, the celebrated Don

John of Austria, victor of Lepanto, and the highly competent Duke of Parma. Flanders proved a grave, both for reputations and their holders. By the end of the century, Spain held the ten provinces which now constitute Belgium, but the seven United Provinces of the north were independent. Their energies were now to be given to successful ventures in East Indian, American, and Baltic trade, and to internal quarrels between monarchists and republicans, Calvinists and Arminians, a religious sect, followers of a Dutch divine, Arminius.

RELIGION AS A MASK FOR HATE AND GREED

SPAIN'S duties as a Catholic state prevented her from supporting the French nobles, who used the Calvinist faith as a pretext for rebellion. During the minority of Charles IX. and the reign of his feeble brother, Henry III., the Bourbons—heirs-presumptive to the throne—posed as the head of the Protestant or Huguenot cause, and the House of Guise led the stronger Catholic party.

A singularly futile series of small wars, assassinations, and broken treaties was given interest by the bloody business of St Bartholomew's night in 1572, when some thousands of Huguenots were suddenly slaughtered at a time of truce. The disorder produced a party of *Politiques* who demanded peace at all costs, and the head of the house of Bourbon, Henry of Navarre, went over to Catholicism soon after succeeding to the throne as Henry IV. (1589). He gave his Huguenot adherents guarantees of toleration under the Edict of Nantes (1598), and France thus achieved a religious settlement much sooner than either Germany or England. The English government encouraged the Huguenots in France and the rebels in the Netherlands ; volunteers served with the Dutch against the Spaniards, and the defeat of the Armada was a considerable factor in the wearing down of the Spanish cause.

At Elizabeth's accession England was small and poor, with no colonies and little trade ; there was religious strife, and much arrant fraud and greed, and these circumstances had by no means all been bettered by the end of the Queen's forty-five years on the throne. Yet there was a spirit abroad of hope, energy, and joy in action which bore fruit in great men and great deeds, produced by a population of perhaps three millions. Much must have been due to the Queen—a vain, false, avaricious woman, but possessed of one quality which wiser and better sovereigns of England have lacked—she was

English completely. Of the positive acts of her government, the bulk must probably be ascribed to her ministers, of whom William Cecil (Lord Burghley) was for forty years the chief. Elizabeth's claim to the throne, as daughter of Henry VIII. and Anne Boleyn, could not be accepted by sound Roman Catholics, to whom the true heiress was Mary Queen of Scots.

The New Learning had percolated to England, so that the men who came to manhood towards the end of the reign had, like Shakespeare, learned a little Latin, if no Greek, and were familiar with translations from French, Italian, and the Classics. The dissolution of the monasteries and chantries had been a blow to education, but some schools survived and others were refounded by Edward VI., Elizabeth, and their subjects. Imagination was stimulated by the discoveries of Columbus and Magellan, by the emancipation of the private layman's judgment which may not unfairly be credited to the Reformation, and by the extreme fluidity then characteristic of language. Finally, a country which is itself secure while wars are going on in all the world around it is probably a stimulating country for a poet to be young in.

SHAKESPEARE : MOUTHPIECE OF A TUMULTUOUS AGE

SHAKESPEARE must, indeed, remain somewhat of a mystery ; no conditions of time and place can adequately account for him. We have to accept him as he was, a fairly successful actor who in the leisure of his employment about the two small London theatres wrote the bulk of his plays and poems. It is unwise to take every line he wrote as hall-marked by genius, but he remains the perfect master of tragedy and of those forms of verse then practised, and the creator of a gallery of human characters beside whom those of any other dramatist of any period seem incomplete. He dwarfs his contemporaries, though they were men of considerable talent. Jonson was his nearest rival ; Marlowe's name has been preserved almost as much for his riotous life and violent death as for his merits. Elizabeth's last years and James I.'s reign, into which Shakespeare and most of his contemporaries survived, was a brief summer for the theatre.

There was a great deal of miscellaneous lyric writing, besides the elaborate verse of which Spenser's *Faërie Queene* was the chief example. Far more talent then went to the writing of sonnets and lyrics than at any time since ; educated people found it natural to sing and to write in verse. Much of the best Elizabethan poetry was meant to be sung, and the madrigal or unaccompanied song for several voices reached its highest development. Musical instruments were few and the spinet or virginals had not yet evolved into the piano, but there was a number of gifted musicians, among whom Byrd, the madrigalist and church composer, was the chief. The prose writing of that time survives in the Authorized Version of the Bible, which, though translated a few years after the Queen's death, fairly ranks as typical of her reign. There were no great English painters as yet : few besides Italians and Flemings practised the art.

ELIZABETH, THE QUEEN WHO KNEW THE BETTER PART OF VALOUR

THE policy of Elizabeth and her ministers may be studied in three main connections—religion, unemployment, and foreign policy. All clergy were required to use the English Prayer Book and to adhere to Thirty-Nine Articles of religion. The clergy were allowed great latitude, and, though fines were imposed, severe penalties were only inflicted for the political offence of refusing to admit the Queen's headship of the Church. It was twelve years before the Pope excommunicated Elizabeth, and ten more before active measures were taken against her. By that time pressure had brought most people to the position held by Burghley and his school—preference for something resembling Catholic doctrine and ritual, without Papal control. Anxiety for their ill-gotten monastery lands doubtless governed many of the gentry. There was, too, a general determination to support the Queen at all costs.

Unemployment, due to the rise of prices and fixity of wages, the change from tillage to sheep-farming, and the dissolution of monasteries, had filled the land with paupers and " sturdy beggars "—armed vagabonds. The restoration of the coinage assisted trade, apprenticeship acts were passed, and, after much experiment, the laws relating to pauperism and vagabondage were codified and defined in the Poor Law Acts, which authorised the Justices of the Peace to collect a small tax on landed property and apply it to the relief of the aged and sick. Able-bodied paupers were put to work ; vagrants were whipped home.

The Justices of the Peace, who virtually carried on, unpaid, the local government of England, gained great authority during the commotions of this century. Thus the English gentry

learned, for good or ill, the habit of self-government (one
might add, of governing other people), which in the next
century they were to apply to the central government.

Elizabeth contrived, while keeping Philip's goodwill, to
lead the French government on, and to remain unmarried,
her hand a potential piece in the game. Relations with Spain
worsened into war, as Roman Catholic emissaries intrigued
in England, while English sea adventurers assisted the
Dutch rebels, and preyed on Spain's trade. Scotland, now
largely Calvinist and controlled by a gang of cut-throat
noblemen, evicted its Queen Mary, the half-French ex-Queen
of France, and arrived at last at a good understanding with
England, which lasted through the reign, while Mary spent
eighteen years as Elizabeth's prisoner.

The remoteness of England and her domestic problems
kept her out of the early scramble for the Indies. Until the
1550's it seemed impossible to interfere with the Spanish and
Portuguese monopolies. About 1530 William Hawkins began
the slave trade, taking prisoners from West Africa to Central
America. In the 1550's schemes to reach the East by a
North-East passage led to contacts with Russia. A North-
West passage was then sought by Frobisher and others, while
a younger Hawkins resumed the slave trade.

The English interlopers were welcomed by the Spaniards
in America, but frowned on by the Spanish government,
which in 1568 destroyed most of a fleet of English slavers at
San Juan de Ulloa. Hawkins remained at home henceforward and helped to reorganise the Royal Navy. His
kinsman, Francis Drake, however, sought revenge and made
very successful raids, the raiders taking the risk of hanging
as pirates or burning as heretics : their Queen and her Council
took no responsibility, and Drake had to slip away secretly
from England on his great voyage of 1577–80, when he
rounded South America, took a million pounds of plunder
off the coast of Peru, and returned across the Pacific by the
stormy Cape. His was the first English ship to reach the
East Indies ; not only the greatest feat of navigation ever
achieved by an Englishman, but the beginning of British
power in the East.

THE ROUTING OF THE SPANISH ARMADA

PHILIP would not make war on Elizabeth as long as Mary
Queen of Scots was alive, with her French affinities and her

claim to the throne. He encouraged rebellion in Ireland and plots in England, and, when the last plot cost Mary her head, the Armada sailed. Most of its hundred-and-thirty ships were transports only very lightly gunned, and packed with soldiers to reinforce Parma's army in the Netherlands. England had nearly two hundred ships, smaller but seaworthy, heavily gunned, and manned only by combatants. They had the windward position and raked the Spaniards from long ranges, driving them up the Channel, and with fire ships out of Calais harbour, to be wrecked by the Atlantic gales as they made their way homewards by the northern route. Spain lost more ships than England lost men.

Spain profited by her defeat and the war lasted till 1604, but England had asserted her insularity. She soon sent fleets eastwards and later founded the East India Company (1600). Her chief attempt at a colony (Raleigh's Virginia) had failed.

The black feature of the reign is that it began the Irish blunder. The Irish chiefs and the obstinately Catholic peasantry provided grounds for massacres and confiscation of tribal lands, followed by rebellion, murder, and further confiscation. Massacres might have been forgotten, but confiscation of lands is invariably a source of future trouble, and the Protestant settlers who were planted in Ireland in this reign and the next half-century failed to maintain the Protestant cause there.

MONARCHIES AND PEOPLES

WE have seen the mediæval inclination towards control of government by oligarchic parliaments displaced by a growth in the prestige of monarchy in the sixteenth century. All over Europe embryonic parliamentary institutions were suppressed. For half a dozen generations (approximately 1600–1750) the theory was elaborately argued that kings were descended from the first rulers whom God gave to mankind, and that resistance to the Lord's anointed was therefore a form of blasphemy.

This view was accompanied by the pre-eminence of France in war and politics and the arts of peace throughout the seventeenth and eighteenth centuries, especially during the manhood (1661–1715) of Louis XIV. His position had been prepared by Sully, Richelieu, and Mazarin—the ministers of his grandfather and parents—and his system, when complete, meant government by royal officials, closely controlled by the ministers of the King, who himself worked hard at administration ; it meant a narrowly national and military outlook, a protectionist policy in trade and industry, the construction of palaces, the maintenance of ceremonial, and the enforcement of orthodoxy in politics, religion, and art. The French system was imitated by every princeling in Europe.

The seventeenth century saw the last religious wars. The uneasy Peace of Augsburg (1555) broke down in 1618, and the war raged throughout Germany until 1648. The Thirty Years' War was relatively the bloodiest of modern times : in it one-third of the German population died. The Roman Catholic cause was supported by the Habsburg emperors, while the weaker Protestant princes received help from Gustavus Adolphus of Sweden and from France, Cardinal Richelieu disregarding the interests of the Church in serving those of the King of France. It ended with France's acquisition of most of Alsace, of which she had already taken part, and was later to take the remainder, and of Lorraine. After this war the independence of the minor German states was complete. The Roman Church could not now hope to crush the German Protestants, and all the heart had gone out of religious faction by the end of this most frightful of all religious contests. England and Holland alone had reason to be glad of it : England, because it kept continental powers from meddling in her Civil war (1642–51) ; Holland, because she gained a lead in Eastern trade.

THE GREATEST STATESMEN OF THE AGE MAKE FRANCE SUPREME

WITH the Empire thus exhausted, and Spain succumbing to a strange torpor, France was drilled by Richelieu, and afterwards by Colbert, into the most efficient State of the day. Her nobles kept their privileges, but were deprived of their powers. France had Turenne, the ablest commander of the century, and Vauban, its greatest military engineer. Roads, canals, and bridges were made, industries encouraged, and some order introduced into the financial system. Louis was capable of using the fruits of these measures in diplomacy and war, but after the deaths of Turenne and Colbert he failed to select good ministers and generals.

The social system of the period was mirrored in the art and

terature of France, and indeed in that of most of the civilised countries of Europe, whose writers and artists closely imitated French models. The regularity of the royal system, its subservience to authority, its hatred for " enthusiasm," its neglect of spiritual experiences, and its ceremonial grandeur found expression in some of Boileau's poetry and in that of his numerous followers. The favourite medium was, in France, the alexandrine (the six-foot line), in England the five-foot heroic couplet.

" Vulgar " subjects and strong epithets were banned; much use was made of conventional adjectives and allusions to the Classics. In the drama, the three unities (of time, place, and action) were rigorously observed in most of the pieces of the French playwrights. The unities, of which only that of action is now considered essential, were taken from the ancient Greek philosopher-critic, Aristotle. Their adoption arose from a misconception of his meaning. For Aristotle did not mean to lay down a rule that the time covered in the action of a play should be the same as the duration of the play's performance ; nor did he mean that there should be no change of scene. He was only describing a certain kind of play which was performed in Greece in his time.

As a consequence of adopting this convention, French classical drama is often unreal, but it was redeemed by two great dramatists, Corneille and Racine, whose plays, if they lack the richness and the myriad variety of Shakespeare's masterpieces, are nevertheless nobly conceived and magnificently executed ; human passions are magnified, but they are not distorted. France also produced in this period one of the greatest comedy writers of any age, Molière.

Milton, and after him Dryden, were the first to introduce the classical spirit into English poetry. Dryden, who forged the English heroic couplet into the instrument it was later to become in the hands of Pope and his eighteenth-century imitators, was completely imbued with the poetic formula of the Romans and their followers in the court of Louis XIV. ; Milton represents the transition stage ; his poetry is more austere than Shakespeare's, but less limited in range, both of metre and subject, than that of Pope and his school.

It was, indeed, an age in which science and knowledge ranked before imagination and enthusiasm. The great intellectual shocks in which the sixteenth century had been prolific now came very rarely. The last new continent was

discovered, and, though progress was made in many sciences
it called for calm persistence rather than for exuberance. /
glory had passed away from the earth, and religious enthusiasm
had apparently reduced itself to absurdity. Men found littl
to deplore, and nothing to aspire to except good manners and
a rational conduct of life. A cheerful atheism made reason ;
substitute for conscience, and even the belief in witchcraf
waned.

But if the literary and religious impetus of the Renaissance
was spent, its scientific effects were now perceptible
Copernicus, the great astronomer of Columbus's day, was
succeeded a hundred years later by Kepler, Galileo, and Tyche
Brahé. They were contemporary with Francis Bacon, who,
though he did very little to advance natural science, wrote
eloquently in favour of careful study of the matter-of-fact
world of sense in preference to speculation on the mystery of
existence, the nature of truth, and other topics of philosophy.
Later, Descartes in France exemplified admirably the natural
scientist and the philosopher; the great Leibnitz in Germany
half a century afterwards continued the same tradition.

Scientific progress is illustrated by a series of English names
of the seventeenth century : Harvey, who discovered the
circulation of the blood ; Halley, the astronomer ; Napier, who
discovered logarithms in algebra ; Boyle of Boyle's Law ;
Petty, the economist ; Lord Worcester, who (possibly) pro-
jected the design of a steam engine ; Wren, the architect and
scientist ; and, above all, the great name of Isaac Newton. In
the company of such men, of prose writers like Defoe, the
father of modern journalism, and of kings like Charles II.,
we are most distinctly approaching modern times. A gulf lies
between us and Shakespeare, and these men are on our side
of it.

THE MIDSUMMER OF MONARCHY

LOUIS XIV.'s armies overran the Spanish Netherlands in 1666
and, when checked by Holland, the French monarch
sought to take a drastic revenge on the Dutch. His invasion of
Holland in 1672, however, called forth another William of
Orange, who, like his ancestor a century before, flooded the
land, and so gained time to collect allies against his cousin Louis.
Louis lost Turenne in the long war that followed, but the peace
treaty (Nymwegen, 1678) was the high-water mark of Louis's
success. He then endeavoured to absorb more German terri-

ry ; he was resisted by the Grand Alliance, or League of ugsburg. Its basis was Dutch gold and the indomitable nacity of William. England, previously for a period sub-rvient to France, began the long series of French wars hich occupied fifty-nine of the years between 1689 and 315.

The League asserted the Balance of Power against Louis. 'he Powers made agreements for the partitioning of the panish Empire between French and Austrian claimants hen its degenerate and childless King Carlos II. should die. Villiam's chief object was to keep the Spanish Netherlands— ne buffer of his own Holland—in any hands but those of France r a French prince. The Spanish ministers had, however, ιo desire for partition, and Carlos left his empire intact ι 1700 to a French prince, or, failing him, an Austrian. ιouis and the Austrians fought for twelve years, England ιupporting Austria chiefly because Louis threatened the Netherlands, maintained the Stuart claim to England, and ιroposed to monopolise Spanish trade for France. There vas fighting all over Europe ; the chief theatre of war was, ιs so often, Flanders. The armies of the Allies were mainly Dutch, but the war was a stage for the ablest of English ιenerals, Marlborough. He won at Blenheim (1704) England's ιirst great Continental victory since Agincourt, and during ιhis war too, Holland allowed her ally, England, to displace ιer permanently as the leading naval power. England made ι separate peace at Utrecht (1713). She gained territory in North America and trading privileges in Spanish South America, but her greatest achievement was to have brought Louis to his knees.

STRUGGLES THAT WERE STEPPING-STONES TO DEMOCRACY

SEVENTEENTH-CENTURY government was the business of the king and his ministers on the one hand, or of the upper class on the other—but not of the whole people. There are grounds, however, for treating the constitutional struggles of the century as steps towards democratic government, or the form of it that was attained in England in the early twentieth century. Such progress as was made was the more striking by contrast with the general extinction of parliaments on the Continent.

The Stuarts reigned in England from 1603 to 1714, and in two hundred and forty years (1567–1806) produced one able

man, Charles II. (or two, if we credit them with William III
Of the rest of the family, none was English in outlook (wi
the exception of Anne) or free from very grave defects
judgment. They were called on to hold their own again
the English gentry and the London merchants, two class
which had attained considerable importance during th
Middle Ages, and had worked hand in hand with the ver
successful Tudors. Expenses of government were the
met from the king's own pocket. He had rents and custom
duties (tunnage and poundage), but the rents were fixe
money was falling in value, and every monarch of the si
teenth and seventeenth centuries found his income inade
quate. Parliament, however, desired to obtain control
policy if it granted extra subsidies (crude property taxes
Very able rulers might have shown results in policy and wa
that would have silenced critics, but the Stuarts seldom gav
value for money.

Religious disputes in many minds bulked larger than th
money question. The upper class, which provided all th
members of both Houses, was in general strongly Protestan
It held lands which had formerly belonged to the monasteries
it liked forms of Church government in which prominen
laymen could share, and its æsthetic inclinations were toward
simplicity in ritual. The Church in England still include
clergy and laity who were strongly Presbyterian in opinion
and there were extremists—Independents, Anabaptists
Brownists—who had openly seceded. The Stuarts, eve
when not suspected of tenderness for Roman Catholicism
were firmly attached to what we should call High Churcl
practices and to autocratic government by bishops, becaus
popular government in the Church was a step towards popula
government on the State.

GRUMBLING TAXPAYERS OF THE SEVENTEENTH CENTURY

JAMES I. (1603–25) united the crowns of England and
Scotland, though not their parliaments or administrations.
He rapidly grew unpopular through his pro-Spanish and
anti-Presbyterian inclinations, and through his attempts to
tax London's trade without the consent of Parliament. His
foreign policy was elaborately absurd, and at his death he
left England floundering in a backwater of the Thirty Years'
War. Charles I. (1625–49) was soon driven by Parliamentary
opposition to retire from the war, as the only condition on

which he could do without Parliamentary grants. For eleven years (1629–40) he raised small illegal taxes, or taxes that were legal but obsolete and vexatious, and encouraged Archbishop Laud to enforce High Church ritual, but did not give his confidence to the very able man who could perhaps have made him a despot, Strafford. The country gentlemen afterwards called this the "Eleven Years' Tyranny," an exaggeration; but they undoubtedly felt a sense of grievance over Laud's religious policy and trifles like the King's Ship Money tax. Laud used various weapons of Church discipline harshly against Puritan clergy and against Puritan laymen who criticised his views of doctrine, ritual, and government, e.g., the celebrated pamphleteers, Prynne, Burton, and Bastwick. This "Eleven Years' Tyranny," however, was a golden age in contrast to the insane bloodshed of the Continent and the turmoil that soon followed in England.

Charles and Laud provoked a Presbyterian rebellion in Scotland and had to ask Parliament's help. Parliament, led by Pym and Hampden, executed Strafford, made Charles agree to several reforms which he would not have carried out, and then split over religion. A bare majority of the Commons wished to introduce Presbyterianism. In 1642 the King, most of the peers, and the strong minority of Commons who loved the English Church more than they disliked arbitrary taxation, raised forces to crush London and the rebellious majority in the House.

In the war that followed, the King's supporters were drawn largely from the north and west of England and from Ireland, Parliament's from London, the south-east, the Midlands, and the seaports. The Parliamentary forces had much greater resources in money, and enforced closer organisation and stricter discipline than the Cavaliers. Moreover, they were assisted by the Scots between 1644 and 1646. They were handicapped by weak leadership, but the Puritan element in their forces displayed a combination of fanaticism and coolness that proved irresistible. Cromwell, the leader of the Puritan element, was mainly responsible for the victories of Marston Moor and Naseby. When it appeared impossible to nail Charles down to pledges, Cromwell took the lead in overriding the moderate Parliamentarians and bringing Charles to the block.

After crushing the Irish and then the Scots, who had originally supported Parliament, Cromwell used the magni-

6

ficent Puritan navy and army in wars against Protestant Holland and Catholic Spain in a manner that Charles and Strafford would have envied. The naval and military expenses of the republic made the government insolvent, and necessitated far heavier taxation than Charles had ever levied. The Puritans tried to suppress drunkenness and various forms of amusement, and these endeavours added to their political unpopularity; the extreme Puritans had never been more than a small section of the upper and middle class, and they held power now only because they controlled fifty thousand excellent troops.

After Cromwell's death, General Monk brought Charles II. back in 1660. Puritanism was defeated; the upper-class Puritans joined the Church of England, while the poorer Puritans kept their separatist or Nonconformist congregations alive, but were subject for some years to penalties and exclusion from public life. The political and financial side of the Parliament's cause was won. There was to be no taxation without consent of Parliament, which was to meet regularly. Its temper was ardently Royalist and Anglican. Catholicism was not tolerated any more than Puritanism.

"GOOD KING CHARLES'S GOLDEN DAYS"

THE king, Charles II. (The Merry Monarch, or, less delicately, Old Rowley), was intelligent and tolerant, but his life of excesses was not compatible with energetic administration. His was, however, a very prosperous reign. Trade with the East grew fast, and many features of modern England go back to Charles's day—the regular army, newspapers, the Royal Mail, horse racing at Newmarket, The Royal Society, Wren's buildings, the Tory party, and the existence of a leisured literary class in London.

Charles and his brother James, with Pepys in the background, maintained the navy of the Puritan republic, and fought Holland twice. Their guiding principle seems to have been a hope of becoming real unparliamentary kings like their cousin Louis, and restoring the Roman Catholic religion to which the one secretly and the other more openly was attached. But an explosion of Anglican anti-Catholic feeling produced the Test Act of 1673, which shut all non-Anglicans out of public offices and emolument. The realist Charles closed down his tentative intrigues, not in time, however, to prevent the anti-Catholic pogrom of 1678-80. He caught public opinion on the rebound, dispensed at last with parliament, and died suddenly in the plenitude of power.

His brother James, who succeeded him (1685–88), assumed the right to tolerate Roman Catholicism, and promote Roman Catholics to office, even in Anglican strongholds. He was for some time childless and the heiress-presumptive was a Protestant, married to William of Orange. A son was born to James and this meant a Catholic succession. The Whigs worked on the Tory anti-Catholic feeling and brought William over to turn James out.

King and Parliament then agreed on the Bill of Rights of 1689 : there was to be no taxation and no standing army without the consent of Parliament, which must therefore meet annually ; the King might not suspend or dispense with laws ; other acts freed Nonconformists from persecution (not from political disqualification), required the King and Queen to support the English church, and allowed judges to hold office without fear of dismissal by the King or by government. This legislation concluded the struggle that had gone on openly since 1603, in veiled forms since 1215 : the monarchy was now limited, and its power divided with the great land-owners who filled the Upper House, and whose relations, dependents, and allies among the merchant princes filled the extremely unrepresentative Lower House.

There was nothing necessarily permanent about the settlement, but fortune sent Marlborough to vindicate the parliamentary governments of England and Holland against the French pattern of all despotisms. Fortune then sent England George I. of Hanover, whose inability to speak English caused him to leave power to a " Prime Minister." Walpole's cautious tenure of this office (1721–42) gave time for the Parliamentary system to consolidate. Had he hurried ahead with desirable reforms he might have strained the system beyond what it would bear. The theory long continued to be that the King was the head of the administration, and it was two hundred years before the Prime Minister's existence was officially recognised. Had an Elizabeth or a Charles II. succeeded to the throne, the monarch might have regained power. However, George II. was almost as unattractive as George I. and the Tory party sulkily tolerated the Hanoverians as a disagreeable alternative to the Catholic Stuart claimants.

George III. tried to regain the old position, but the results of his policy did not bring credit to his system : partly to his blundering administration we owe the loss of the American colonies ; moreover, he made a great mistake in not presiding at Cabinet meetings. So the Parliamentary system was established firmly, against all the strongest tendencies of the age ; to continental observers it was a thing of wonder.

THE AGE OF REASON, BEAUTY, AND TASTE

DURING the eighteenth century, the life died out of the conventional forms in government and literature, and embryonic forms of new life peered into daylight. Yet the satisfaction of men with themselves and with the human race grew steadily. Poetry almost ceased to be a vehicle of music or deep feeling, but the musicians, Bach, Handel, Mozart, and Haydn were in instrumental composition what Shakespeare, Racine, and Milton had been in verse. Germany had almost a monopoly of musical genius, perhaps because the career of one great artist sometimes paves the way for others to follow. England had had such a great musician as Purcell and provided an enthusiastic public for Handel, but her æsthetic energy chiefly took the channel of portrait and landscape painting. In Hogarth, Reynolds, Gainsborough, Romney, and Constable she had the first great English artists, and some of the best European artists of the period. The architects carried on Wren's tradition, and both in the building of small houses and the designing of furniture the century achieved a delightful style, quite distinctive between the clumsy picturesqueness of the seventeenth century and the forms of ugliness which the nineteenth century manufactured. It came as near beauty as proportion, symmetry, and moderation can come. Even in poetry there were signs in Gray, Collins, and Isaac Watts of a return to better taste.

Prose was the instrument which the ablest writers wielded best. It was prose which has not yet lost currency, as that of Clarendon or Isaac Walton has. The prose of Addison, Steele, and Goldsmith was very lucid and simple but there was amongst some writers too great a tendency to employ or invent long Latinised words. Their sentences were elaborate and the sentiments extremely dignified. But as it was used by Gibbon, Johnson, and Burke in England this prose had force and life : Smollett and Fielding used it to write better novels even than Defoe's.

Among the French writers of their time there was one at least who commanded an emotional power such as no

ucceeding political analyst has had. This was Rousseau,
. Genevan adventurer who wrote on several subjects, usually
vell, and his *Contrat Social* (The Social Contract) was the
Bible of the men who made the French Revolution. It
probably influenced events more profoundly even than
Marx's *Das Kapital* (Capital) did a hundred years afterwards.
There has very seldom, however, been a book which would
way men unless it expressed ideas which they already held
ut had not yet put into words. Rousseau's doctrine of
nen's Natural Rights was already known; the other politi-
al writers of his time, too, summed up in lucid and amusing
ashion views already in circulation. Adam Smith, for instance,
n his *Wealth of Nations*, talked a great deal of sound
ense in favour of Free Trade, which can be traced back to
ne merchants who began to carry weight in politics under
Villiam III. When Voltaire poured the vials of his malice
n priests, soldiers, and posturing courtiers, he was preaching
● those willing to be converted. In a hundred volumes of
erse, stories, history, essays, and letters this intelligent,
nergetic, spiteful man fought against priestcraft and tyranny
nd all forms of stupidity, though democracy, as the twentieth
entury sees it, would have been repulsive to him. It is absurd
● think of such writers having any influence on peasants,
nopkeepers, or merchants. But they made a deep impression
n many clever lawyers and priests, and they undermined the
elf-confidence of many people who had an interest in sup-
orting the unreformed state of things.

THE BARGAIN BETWEEN CITIZEN AND RULER

THERE were similar writers in England. At the end of the
seventeenth century John Locke, the mouthpiece of the
Vhigs, in his *Civil Government*, defended the idea of
atural rights and found arguments in favour of subjects as
gainst princes. Absolute government had been advocated
y Filmer, the exponent of the Divine Right of Kings, and
Thomas Hobbes, who in his *Leviathan* ingeniously turned
ne " contract " theory to the support of absolutism. This
ontract theory was an attempt to explain the origin of
overnment on *a priori* (from cause to effect) principles. Men,
was said, had surrendered to government their natural
ght to seek their own interests in their own way. One
chool, typified later by Rousseau, argued that men only did
● in return for definite advantages, their natural state being

one of great freedom and innocence, and, if a governmer
failed to give them these advantages, the contract was at a
end, and men had the right to change their government.

Hobbes, a little less unhistorically, said that the natural stat
of man was brutish and nasty, and that man owed everythin
to government, and, having once made the surrender of h
rights, could not now resume them. Filmer, in his *Patr
archa* really came nearer to the truth, which is that no suc
contract was ever made, and that in primitive times Ma
lived under the most direct of all tyrannies—the tyranny o
his father. The general tendency of eighteenth-centur
thought in England and France was towards Locke
argument.

These social ideas were coupled with the justification o
individualism. The moral individualism of the Protestar
reformers had co-existed with a high degree of state interferenc
in economic life. Throughout the seventeenth and eighteent
centuries there was a strong current of feeling in favour o
non-interference in anything which could possibly be left t
individuals. Adam Smith's *Wealth of Nations* advocate
it very cogently, and there was a school of "Physiocrats" i
France who popularised the principle, as yet untried i
practice, of *laissez-faire*—"leave things alone." The greate
advocate of individualism was Bentham, who at an early ag
published in 1776 his *Fragment on Government*, and wh
later played a great part in the sweeping away of mediæv
lumber in the spheres of law and commerce.

In France the seventeenth century had been a time of toler
tion, and Huguenots had done great things in the nation
service. In his later years Louis XIV. revoked Henry IV.
Edict of Nantes (1685), and by mean forms of pressu
forced a million Huguenots to conform. A hundred thousar
escaped from France and carried their industrial skill ar
their religious persistence to Holland, Prussia, England, ar
America. The French Church, thus unified, did not gai
in health : there was not much active persecution, but the
was no crusading energy. By 1770 the Jesuits were ten
porarily suppressed throughout Catholic countries, so muc
had times changed in two hundred years. Similar apath
came over religion in most of the Latin countries where Jew
Moors, and other heretics had been expelled or made t
conform.

England was more fortunate in that comparatively fe

Catholics or Nonconformists were driven into exile. But during the seventeenth century almost every generation of clergymen had had to adapt their views to those of some new government as an alternative to giving up their livings. Those who retained office were, inevitably, the more pliant. In the eighteenth century parish clergy were sometimes inoffensive, ineffective gentlemen, sometimes sycophantic topers—in either case generally Tories. The bishops, selected by the government, were often time-servers and sceptics, frequently absentees from their dioceses.

It must not be imagined that there was no religious feeling —Dr. Johnson, for instance, was strongly religious. But the commonest belief was a diluted Deism, which recognised the probable existence of a Supreme Being, credited Him with kindly rational sentiments and a preference for the established social order, and tolerated drunkenness and license in private behaviour as well as callous brutality towards prisoners, paupers, lunatics, apprentices, negro slaves, chimney sweeps, sailors, and schoolboys. Life was then rougher for even the wealthiest than it is now, and the sufferings of the poor were proportionately less striking, while many good men who did not interfere to prevent cruelty would certainly not themselves have been cruel. Philanthropists did indeed appear during the century, amongst whom, John Howard (1726–90), the prison reformer, was typical.

THREE YOUNG CLERICS WHOSE ENTHUSIASM SHOCKED THE CHURCH

THE greatest Anglican churchman of the eighteenth century was Bishop Berkeley, a conscientious Irish prelate, whose great work, *Principles of Human Knowledge*, was an unanswerable demonstration of the immateriality of the world of sound and sense. More significant socially were the group of Methodists led by John and Charles Wesley and George Whitefield, three young clergymen who desired to revivify the Church of England and carry religion to the hordes of miners, slum dwellers, and rustics whom the Church was ignoring. The Church either shook its head at such enthusiasm (the eighteenth century still used—and deprecated—" enthusiasm " in its original sense of frenzy) or incited mobs to attack the Methodists. The Methodists ended by establishing independent chapels and instituting clergy of their own.

John Wesley was an indefatigable traveller, who for many

years averaged fifteen miles a day on horseback and daily
preached three or four sermons. His brother Charles wrote
five thousand hymns, many of which are still sung. The
Methodist Church became the largest Protestant denomina-
tion in the world, and its social influence was considerable :
it tended towards conservatism among the middle class, and
against what was to be the atheistical French Revolution,
and it helped the coming change in morals and manners and
the Evangelical movement which restored the vigour of the
Established Church.

THE AUTUMN OF MONARCHY

AFTER Louis XIV.'s death it took another seventy years of
monarchy before the French Revolution arose to destroy
it, and finally restore it in a heightened form as the rule
of Napoleon. In modern government it is possible to see
a contest between two principles, liberty and authority.
Patriotism and efficiency may co-exist with either. Liberty,
veiled in parliamentary and oligarchic forms, is familiar to
us in England and modern France. Authority has been
exemplified by Cromwell, Frederick of Prussia, Napoleon,
the Emperor William II. of Germany, and Mussolini, among
many others. It perhaps seems idle to seek for common
features in such varied systems, but all emphasise the claims
of the State in preference to those of individuals, and the
importance of ends rather than of means. The justification
of authority was, in the sixteenth and seventeenth centuries,
Divine Right—usually hereditary, but to Cromwell given by
revelation. During the eighteenth century, as the force of
the divine appeal diminished, hereditary rulers began to
justify their existence by surpassing even Louis XIV. in
their efforts for efficiency and national power, while avoiding
his excessive ostentation. During the nineteenth century the
emphasis on duty and success grew still greater; the hereditary principle, though not extinguished, was weakened.
Government business grew vast and technical; there have
been permanent officials under all kinds of government, but
bureaucratic power and its abuses have inevitably been
greatest under despotism.

ENLIGHTENED DESPOTS TAKE REFORM IN HAND

THE monarchs of the middle eighteenth century are known
as the enlightened despots. They sometimes owed a

reputation for enlightenment to their ministers, as did Joseph of Portugal to Pombal, and Philip V. of Spain to Alberoni, and as Louis XVI. of France to a lesser degree did to Turgot. But, on the other hand, Frederick II. of Prussia, Joseph II. of Austria, and Peter the Great of Russia were certainly the fountain-heads of their own policies. These despots founded new towns and villages, built roads and bridges, gave sub-sidies to industry, drained marshes, simplified the laws, abolished torture, made imprisonment less horrible, abolished tolls and other barriers to internal trade, destroyed the influence of nobles and priests, and established elementary schools in the villages ; then they employed the strength of their re-formed countries to gain territory and prestige. Before the century was out, the work they had left unfinished was accelerated by the French revolutionary reformers.

Even despots are open to suggestion. They all owed something to the writers commonly known as the French philosophers, whom we shall describe more fully later. Politically, though these writers prepared the way for the Revolution, most of them proposed to carry out reforms through the agency of enlightened despotism.

The eighteenth century is full of wars, fought in slow time by small well-drilled armies ; but national feeling, at any rate among educated people, was not acute. Foreigners ruled in England, Russia, and Spain ; Irish Catholic exiles and Scottish Jacobites made careers in several continental countries, and civilians could reside unmolested in war time in " enemy " countries. All people of rank talked French, and French books, dress, and manners held them together in a kind of freemasonry.

The chief importance of the wars of this period lay in the struggle between England and France for the control of India and North America, a conflict that will be described more fully later. In Europe the wars showed a common tendency for a group of strong powers to partition a weaker one, often on the pretext of disrupted succession to the throne. Sometimes the thing was an elaborate plot, sometimes one power took the lead and the others intervened in the name of the Balance of Power. After the war which determined the succession in England (1689–97), we have seen the war over the partition of Spain, and there was a smaller war over Sweden.

After 1739 an Anglo-Spanish trade war merged into the

War of the Austrian Succession (1741–48), the least successful contestants in which (Austria and France) fell on a too successful rival, Prussia, in the epic Seven Years' War (1756–63). Great Britain, having in her turn done too well, three continental powers assailed her during her American War (1775–83). Meanwhile the partition of Poland began. The War of the Austrian Succession (1741–48) began with a scramble to divide the dominions of which a woman had just succeeded to the throne. The tendency grew stronger as the century wore on : its most famous example was in the almost bloodless partitions of Poland. In modern times we have seen Africa and the Pacific partitioned with more justification.

THE HARDEST WORKER AMONG MODERN KINGS

PRUSSIA, a small State in the barren north of Germany, was the creation of the Great Elector of Brandenburg (1642–88), and of his eccentric grandson and namesake King Frederick William I. (1713–40), who made no war, but hoarded money, created an enormous standing army and competent civil service, and warped the whole nature of his son Frederick, who became the ablest soldier, the most ruthless schemer, and the hardest worker among modern kings. Frederick seized Silesia in the War of the Austrian Succession, and with some help from England held it during the Seven Years' War (1756–63). He exacted appalling sacrifices from the Prussian people, but he gave them peace and efficiency afterwards, and settled many of them on territory appropriated from Poland. The characteristics of Prussian administration and policy had already been evolved.

THE TSARS WHO BROUGHT CIVILISATION TO RUSSIA

THE State of Muscovy, or Russia, had been populated by Norse and Slavonic settlers who were later brutalised by Tartar oppression. Ivan the Great laid the foundations of a modern state in the fifteenth century. During the life of that frightful fiend, Ivan the Terrible, a contemporary of Elizabeth, trade with England began. Peter, Tsar from 1696 to 1725, was a boor in manners and a coward in war, but he extended the territory of Russia, suppressed the nobles, established Azov on the Black Sea and Petersburg (Leningrad) on the Baltic, westernised the language and dress of his subjects, and collected technical experts from civilised countries. He left an organisation and a political testament on which

Russian policy was modelled for several reigns to come. Russia was still in the rudimentary stage of civilisation ; popular education, for instance, played no part in the policy of her rulers.

Russia, which originally no more counted as part of Europe than China does to-day, took part in the alliance against Frederick the Great, helped to partition Poland, and began her hundred-year attempt to partition Turkey. At the end of the century she had reached the North Pacific coasts where other civilised powers already had interests, and soon afterwards she took part in several campaigns of the Napoleonic wars.

THE BOON DENIED TO HAPLESS POLAND

POLAND, in the Middle Ages a State stretching from the Baltic to the Black Sea, still retained a considerable territory situated between Russia, Prussia, and Austria. Her military traditions were long and splendid : she had helped to hold back the Turks, and had delivered Vienna itself from them. But in a Europe where the modern reorganisation of industry was beginning, she remained a poor agricultural state, dominated by poor and unruly nobles. There were few towns : trade was carried on by Jews who remained un-Polish. She had an elective monarchy ; every candidate for election tended to promise away some of the crown's diminished resources in return for the votes of the nobles who elected the king, and the elected king had no family interest in leaving the kingdom stronger at his death. The Diet of nobles retained control of legislation and a unanimous vote was required for the enactment of laws.

In 1772 the three big neighbours of Poland agreed to annex large areas of her territory, and in 1793 and 1795 the partition was completed. Prussia administered her new territories more successfully than England administered Ireland, where conditions were parallel, and Austrian rule was not unpopular, but Russian unpopularity was increased by the hostility of the Greek and Roman Churches to which Russia and Poland respectively belonged. The annexation can hardly have been either a material or a moral wrong to the Jews and peasants. It was bitterly resented, however, by the ruling class. To do them justice, they had tried towards the end to reform their government, and under Kosciuszko they resisted the final partition with some energy.

THE RACE FOR EMPIRE

THE growth of European control over the other four
continents can from some points of view be taken as
the most important political process of the modern era. For
five centuries the initiative remained with Europeans, whose
energy contrasted with the passivity of Indians, negroes, and
Chinese. Tartars, Moors, and Turks, who in their day had
pressed so hard on Europe, shrank into obscurity. Two
European inventions were indispensable in this process—
gunpowder and the improved warship. The process was
marked by the utmost jealousy between competing European
nations, and they generally treated their overseas dominions
strictly as private appurtenances. Great Britain in the late
nineteenth and early twentieth centuries gave political liberty
to the Europeans in her overseas settlements, and freedom of
trade to all-comers in her non-self-governing possessions. The
usual practice of all other European powers, however, has
been to give little political liberty to their settlers, and to
employ their overseas dependencies for the advantage in the
first place of the parent country. France, for instance, has
always, except for a short period in the mid-nineteenth
century, been rigidly " protectionist " in her policy. The
laxer policy of Great Britain, though defensible on many
grounds, would hardly have been adopted by a nation
struggling through such difficulties as those encountered by
continental states. In the sixteenth century the exclusionist
policy was coloured by religion. During the seventeenth and
eighteenth centuries, when co-religionists began to fall out,
it was justified on economic grounds.

The greatest of the " mercantile " school of statesmen was
Colbert, who lived in France from 1619 to 1683 ; the object
of these men was to collect great stores of bullion by exporting
much and importing little. Each principal country and its
overseas dependencies were to supplement each other and be
in combination self-supporting. The principal country would
not grow crops to compete with those of the dependency,
which, in return, was not to compete with the principal
country in manufacture or in the carrying trade, or to sell
to others any products that the principal country wanted
(especially those useful in war), or to buy from others any
product that the principal country had to sell. The system

was invariably modified by extensive smuggling. It was always unpopular with colonists, and trade actually improved when principal and dependencies were separated, as England was from her American colonies in 1783. The system in England was embodied in certain " Navigation Laws," first enacted by Cromwell. In these circumstances, wars were fought to secure trade and colonies, and trade led to more wars. The flag followed trade and trade followed the flag. Similar conceptions were largely responsible for the war of 1914–18.

A "NEW FRANCE" ACROSS THE ATLANTIC

FOR two centuries colonial rivalries were mainly coastal in their scope, and naval strength was inevitably an important factor. The coasts of America (North and South), India, Africa, China, and Japan were known, but little was known of the interiors, or of Australasia. Some European countries were overpopulated in proportion to their productive capacity at that time, among them England ; but the intention of early imperialists was to get trade and wealth, not to settle surplus population overseas, except as an aid to the more important aim.

Portugal held some African and Indian ports and Brazil, while Spain (her overlord, 1580–1640) had the rest of South and Central America. Neither power was strong enough to extend its territorial possessions in contention with the nations that now began to compete—France, England, and Holland, and to a very limited extent Sweden, Denmark, and Prussia.

The land which was—rather obscurely—named Canada was discovered by Cabot, and further explored by Verrazano and Cartier in the early sixteenth century, though no permanent settlement was made till 1604. The French founded Quebec and Montreal, fought the Iroquois redskins and tried to convert them to Christianity ; they had numerous wars with the English during the seventeenth century. There were small stations in the woodlands surrounding the lonely Great Lakes. A missionary reached the upper Mississippi (1678), and the great explorer La Salle journeyed down two thousand miles of it to the Gulf of Mexico, where New Orleans was founded. The French were fortunate in their governors, of whom Frontenac was the greatest, and they proposed to use the river routes of the vast Mississippi basin

to link the St. Lawrence settlement with New Orleans, so
holding the British settlers of the east coast back from expansion westward.   It was necessary only that they should
hold the gap at the watershed between Lake Erie and the
headwaters of the Ohio.   " New France " was controlled by
royal officials and missionaries, and it had a very small
population—some eighty thousand hunters, trappers, and
peasants, subject to feudal conditions of land tenure.

A "LAND OF SICKNESS AND SORROW"

ENGLAND had sent generations of cod-fishers to the Newfoundland Banks and had sought the North-East and
North-West passages to the Spice lands : when Raleigh
founded Virginia in 1584, one of his avowed objects was to
find a route through the continent to the Pacific.   Virginia
failed, but was revived in 1607 while Raleigh languished in the
Tower of London.   The hardships of the early settlers were
dreadful, but they finally became prosperous on the cultivation of tobacco.   To the south there were Spaniards in
Florida.   Further north the Dutch and Swedes made settlements, and in 1620 Plymouth in Massachusetts Bay was
founded by Puritans who left England to escape petty persecution.   Many settlers followed, who, from economic
motives more than anything else, migrated to this

> " land of sand and sickness and sorrow
> Short allowance of victual and plenty of nothing but
> Gospel."

Colonies grew up—Massachusetts, Connecticut, and New
Hampshire—known collectively as New England.   Unlike
the Anglican planters of Virginia, who were very soon importing slaves from Africa, these settlers cultivated small
farms of the English type and had no slaves.   From early
days they were keenly interested in education, printing, and
litigation, and in the first two respects, at least, they differed
from the Virginians.   Their Puritanism was not coupled with
toleration for rival sects, and they continued to stone moral
offenders and burn alleged witches until the end of the seventeenth century.   One colony, Rhode Island, was founded as
a haven for religious refugees of every creed, and another,
Maryland, to tolerate even Roman Catholics, a condition
which did not last.   There was money in colonies, and
Charles II. and James II. encouraged the seizure of Dutch

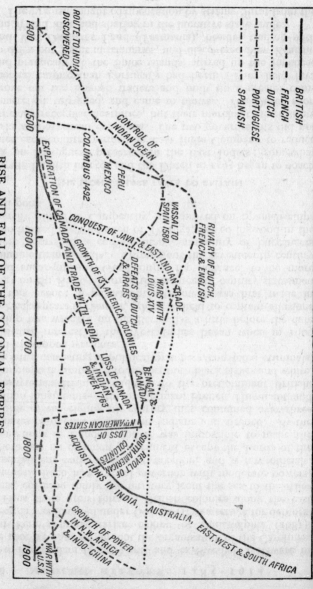

RISE AND FALL OF THE COLONIAL EMPIRES.

New Amsterdam (New York) and ex-Swedish Delaware in the 1660's ; they set on foot the organisation of the Carolinas, and Penn's humanitarian colony of Philadelphia (1681). Georgia was founded under George II. as a refuge for debtors.

Thus there grew thirteen British colonies along the east coast, covering thinly the territory from the sea to the Alleghanies. Each had a royal governor with moderate powers, a parliament with control of taxation, and a few officials. There was no common government except the Lords of the Plantations in London, and it was impossible to make the colonies co-operate against the Indians and French. By the middle of the eighteenth century they contained over three million inhabitants—Dutch, German, French, Huguenot, and Presbyterian Irish, in addition to the predominant British. The planters continued to import both black slaves and white, the latter consisting of political prisoners, convicted criminals, and kidnapped wretches.

British interest in the West Indies began when in 1609 a ship was wrecked on the Bermudas a little before the date of Shakespeare's *Tempest*, which is held to contain allusions to this event ; a permanent settlement was first made in 1623 on St. Kitts. During the eighteenth century statesmen held sugar-growing Guadeloupe, for instance, to be more valuable than Canada. Throughout the seventeenth century there flourished a cosmopolitan community of buccaneers who hunted the wild oxen of Tortuga, hewed logwood in the marshy jungle of Campeachy, and preyed on Spanish ships and ports.

THE LION'S SHARE FALLS TO BRITAIN

THE English in 1591 and the Dutch in 1595 began to poach on Portuguese preserves in the East Indies ; somewhat later each country formed an East India Company to reduce risks and overhead expenses. The two governments did not officially recognise hostilities, but their merchant adventurers quarrelled, intrigued, and came to blows. The Dutch soon drove out the English traders and built up a greater commercial empire than Portugal's had been. They held Java and practically all the Spice islands, stirred up the Japanese to drive out Jesuit missionaries, and discovered New Zealand and Van Diemen's Land (Tasmania), besides trading with the West Indies and sharing in the lucrative slave trade.

The English sought compensation by seizing Surat from the

Portuguese (1614) and trading with the petty rajahs of the Malabar coast. It was a hundred and fifty years, however, before England was even to give promise of ever dominating the whole of India. During the seventeenth century she acquired half a dozen small stations round the Indian coasts, where a few merchants lived uncomfortably in fortified " factories " and traded in calico cloth, spices, silks, muslins, jewels, and saltpetre. The principal French station was Pondicherry, near Madras. There was, originally, no design of conquest.

India was still ruled in name by the Mogul Emperors, the most recent of the conquerors who had come down on India from the North. After the death of Awrangzeb in 1707 the Empire was broken up. Viceroys and governors made themselves independent princes, and mercenary and plundering hordes ravaged large areas. This was the state of India when in 1720 Dupleix was sent by the French Government to Pondicherry as an official, and began to measure the situation.

The century between 1713 and 1815 decided whether England or France should control India, Australia, North America, and South Africa ; the contest was most acute between 1742 and 1763. France had a population three times as large as England's (perhaps twenty-four million as against eight million) a unity of command and a great military tradition. Yet England won. Sea power was the chief factor. The French navy lost the most important battles and campaigns for the simple reason that the English fleet, confident of victory, took the initiative and the windward position in battle.

The comparative healthiness of British taxation and finance was a considerable asset in war. The French government tried to play a great part both in Europe and overseas, while England concentrated her efforts on the colonies. England was overpopulated for its resources and for that reason the Englishman was ready to leave his native land. The size of the population of the American colonies made it easy to raise armies on the spot. Though parliamentary government, both in England and the American colonies, meant irresolution and procrastination, it did in a measure allow men to rise, and in Pitt, Wolfe, and Clive, England found three men of destiny. The French enlightened despotism lacked between 1715 and 1763 the one essential working part—a driving force at its head. Its king, Louis XV., a morbid pleasure-seeker, was

under the thumb of mistresses whose influence on his administration and foreign policy was wholly bad.

THE CLERK WHO LED AN ARMY TO VICTORY

DURING the Austrian war of 1741–48, England and France
fought each other rather pointlessly in Germany, in
Canada, and in India. An intractable young clerk at Madras,
named Clive, obtained military employment at this time.
French interests in India were guided by Dupleix, who made
alliances with Indian princes, lent French contingents to turn
the scale in Indian wars, and gained territory and privileges
for his government. The English followed the same policy, but
with little success until, in 1751, Clive volunteered to seize
a key position, Arcot. He held it for seven weeks against
odds of twenty to one, and then won a series of victories
which caused Dupleix's recall and gained a great reputation
for the English.

Meanwhile in the far West the French were occupying the
wild country between Lake Erie and the Ohio, and a British
force which tried to check them was cut to pieces. Chicago,
Detroit, and Pittsburgh were represented by no more than
blockhouses in the woodlands.

When Frederick of Prussia challenged the enemies who
were planning his destruction in 1756 he was able to call on
England for support under a recent treaty of alliance, and
because their colonial rivalry made it inevitable that England
should fight France. The English government of the day was
feeble, and the war began with British defeats in Germany,
the Mediterranean, India, and Canada. The great William
Pitt then became Secretary of State in 1757 ; his policy was
ruinously expensive but it was vigorous, and he took expert
advice from Admiral Anson and Field-Marshal Ligonier.
With his haughty features, his organ-like voice and disdain of
pettiness, the Great Commoner inspired the House of Commons
and the country and browbeat his Cabinet colleagues. He
was incomparably the greatest of war ministers. Clive had
already conquered Bengal at Plassey (1757), and the French in
India were finally beaten by Coote at Wandewash (1760).
Canada was invaded in 1758 by the three possible routes—
up the St. Lawrence, by Lake Champlain and by Lake Ontario.
Wolfe's marvellous victory at Quebec in 1759 was completed
by the arrival of a British fleet next year and the fall of Montreal.
Sea power, without which neither Bengal nor Canada could

ave been taken and held, was affirmed by the naval victories
of Hawke and Boscawen.

Meanwhile Pitt had been " conquering America in Germany " by subsidising Frederick lavishly and absorbing the
strength of France. George III., on succeeding in 1760 to
the throne of an England which was reeling towards bankruptcy, was glad to lose Pitt's services in 1761 and to make
peace behind Frederick's back in 1763. France—by the
Peace of Paris—was to retain her stations in India unfortified
and to surrender Canada, her other North American territories in the Mississippi basin (east of the river to England,
west of it to Spain), several West Indian islands and some
West African ports useful for the slave trade. She might
still have regained everything, but the wars of the next half-century confirmed the results of the Seven Years' War.

AMERICA BEGINS TO SLIP AWAY FROM BRITAIN

THE Treaty of Paris ironically enough led directly to the
loss of the American colonies. Probably it only forestalled
an inevitable separation. Most of the American colonists
were descended either from British emigrants who had left
their homeland with bitter feelings, or from continental exiles
whose ties with England were negligible. The actively
rebellious elements were supplied mainly by New Englanders
of British ancestry or by recent Presbyterian immigrants from
Ulster. There was a strong pro-English party in the colonies,
but it was small numerically, and some at least of the upper
class, who would have been most attached to the British
connection, were alienated, as Washington was, by the
arrogance of British officers during the Seven Years' War.
Wolfe regarded the colonial troops with contempt, and men
like Washington did not forget the insults they had
received.

American opinion was beginning to be governed by the
frontier outlook, with its westward inclination and impatience
of European control and European entanglements and
standards. Even before the Seven Years' War the Navigation
Acts, which allowed goods to be carried in English ships only
and not in colonial or French vessels, had been tolerated only
because their more irritating provisions were nullified by
smuggling. The most respectable merchants of Boston were
implicated in the traffic and found the high tariffs a distinct
advantage to them in selling smuggled duty-free goods.

Perhaps the worst difficulty was that the mutual jealousy of the thirteen colonies made it impossible to establish a united government. When grievances were to be expressed there was no one entitled to speak in the name of all thirteen colonies, and receive more respectful attention from the British Government than the representative of Massachusetts could obtain.

THE LAST DAYS OF A BRITISH AMERICA

THE colonies had been kept loyal to England mainly by fear of the Catholic and military power of France. The final defeat of the French (in which the Americans claimed perhaps more than their proper share) removed this menace. The new government in England proposed to maintain a force in America for defence against the Indians : for this purpose, and to recover some part of the enormous expense that had been incurred (the colonists said unnecessarily) in the war, they hunted round for revenue and tightened up the anti-smuggling machinery. In Canada the French peasants who remained were very wisely given complete toleration for their religion. Very wisely, too, an elected Parliament was not yet established in Canada, and immigration thither and into the ex-French territory west of the Alleghanies was restricted. This far-sighted policy aroused furious disgust amongst New Englanders who had expected to flood Canada and the West, and set up a Canadian parliament.

England had as king a stupid and overbearing young man, George III., who was busy between 1760 and 1770 in breaking up the Whig party which had governed England, not unsuccessfully, since 1714. A succession of feeble Whig governments held office during this period when attention was distracted by domestic scandals and disputes. In 1770 George got a congenial Tory ministry under North, who did as the King wished for the next twelve years. They were years which spoiled for good any hope there might have been of restoring the active monarchy of Charles II. or William III.

One of the feeble Whig governments—Grenville's—imposed a Stamp Duty on the colonies. It required newspapers and other documents to carry stamps. The total amount of the tax was only a shilling or two a year per head of the colonial population. The Americans, however, like Hampden —the old Parliamentarians were much in their minds—sus·

ected the thin edge of a wedge, as indeed it probably would ave been. Their slogan was " No taxation without repre- entation." Realists in vain pointed out that not more than ne per cent. of the British population was directly represented n Parliament. A few members in either House would have atisfied them, the colonists said, but it is hardly likely that hey would have been content for long.

The Stamp Act was repealed by a new government, which exatiously declared that it retained the right to tax, while nsisting that it never intended to use it. Another new government imposed small extra duties on certain imported goods, which the colonists refused to use ; all the duties were removed except that on tea, which was disguised by allowing he East India Company to convey it directly to America from China at a reduced cost. A violent protest was organised in Boston by certain vested interests, and there ensued the " Boston Tea Party," in which a number of men disguised as Indians boarded the Company's ships and threw the tea overboard. Severe penalties were imposed on the riotous city—it was no longer to be a port of entry. The Quebec Act, which in the same year (1774) guaranteed the language and religious rights of French Canadians, caused nearly as much resentment. The anti-English party in New England prepared for war. Fighting began in 1775. There was a conference of the colonies other than Georgia that year, and in 1776 a Declaration of Independence was issued that dis- owned the rule of George III.

The grounds of rebellion were perhaps inadequate, and had greater men been ruling England the quarrel might well have been healed. But it is obvious that there were many colonists who were only waiting for an opportunity to strike for independence. It is unlikely that the colonies could have remained subordinate to Great Britain as they grew, or that any form of friendly partnership could have been, at that stage, evolved.

ENGLAND ATTACKED ON EVERY SIDE

THE colonies were, as before and afterwards, disunited ; they hated to hand local forces over to joint control, and they nearly broke the heart of Washington, the very able Virginian who was already known as the best soldier in America. There were, too, many neutrals and some active loyalists, especially in the South, and the well-to-do colonists

were not willing to serve in the ranks. Washington's whole
force was at one time down to one man per thousand of the
colonial population.

But the colonists were too numerous to be held down
except by a very large force, and England's population was
barely three times theirs—England, too, was six weeks away;
the country was favourable to the colonial style of warfare
(consisting largely of " sniping "), and there was no enthusiasm
in England for the conflict; the Whigs were actively against
it, from mixed motives; lastly, the British Government and
forces were, on the whole, in the least competent hands that
ever guided them.

What turned the scale was that England's enemies fell on
her as soon as it was seen—at Saratoga in 1777—that the
colonists could hold their own. Cornwallis carried on a
campaign successfully in the southern and more loyal colonies.
But France, Spain, and Holland came into the war against
her, the Baltic powers formed an Armed Neutrality, and
England lost control of the sea. Suffren, the great French
admiral, kept Warren Hastings cut off in India, though
Hastings and Coote were fully a match for the French there.
Gibraltar was besieged for three years, and French control
of the West Indian waters compelled Cornwallis's surrender
at Yorktown in 1781. Rodney's great naval victory off The
Saints (Dominique) in 1782 enabled England to make peace
in 1783 with the loss of very little except the American
colonies and the territory west of the Alleghanies. It was the
lowest point in international credit to which Britain had
fallen since Charles I.'s reign, but at any rate the French
Canadians had remained loyal and had repulsed American
invasions.

The war bankrupted France and Holland, and six years
later the French Government had to call its creditors together
in the famous States General of 1789. It had sent troops to
America, including volunteers from the French nobility,
who were impressed by the prosperity and equality of the
American farmers, as contrasted with the state of the peasants
in France. It seemed to them like the Golden Age of which
Rousseau wrote, before kings and priests had corrupted
man's natural happiness. The American Revolution was the
link between the rebellion against Charles I. and the French
Revolution; it was very widely copied in Europe and America
during the next fifty years.

COLONIES LIKE FRUIT THAT RIPENS FOR THE FALL

THE loss of the colonies led directly to the foundation of a new colony in Australia, and, by concentrating English interest on the East, it led England to seize the Cape from the bankrupt Dutch East India Company. It also affected Colonial policy profoundly. One school argued that the colonists had rebelled because they had been given parliaments and too much liberty. Another said it would be wiser to treat colonies generously. But events seemed to prove the view that colonies were like fruit and would drop off when they were ripe. During the next fifty years England was driven, by military reasons chiefly, to occupy several more territories, but the theory during this period, and the practice during the fifty subsequent years (1830–80), was that great expense and trouble should not be incurred for colonies; they should be encouraged to shoulder their own responsibilities as soon as possible.

The victorious colonists had promised not to molest those of their fellow citizens who had been "loyal," but the loyalists were subjected to persecution and outrage, and about eighty thousand were compensated by the British Government with land in Upper Canada, in the peninsula between Lakes Erie and Huron. They were at once (1791) given parliamentary government, as was the older province of Lower Canada inhabited by the French settlers. The number of new settlers corresponded with that of the original French, and, as immigrants came in from Scotland, Canada became substantially British.

In the eighteenth century serious crimes (if the criminal was caught) were punished by death, minor crimes by transportation for life or a term of years to an American or West Indian plantation. The American plantations being closed, the government decided to send convicts to the remote new land that had recently been placed on the map by the great Captain Cook. An expedition first landed at Botany Bay in New South Wales in 1788. Many convicts were venial offenders, but imprisonment, the convict-ship voyage, and the conditions in Australia were brutalising. Settlements were made for convict stations round the south-east coast and in Van Diemen's Land; free settlers arrived in 1793, merino sheep were introduced before the end of the century, and inland exploration into the almost empty continent began.

New Zealand, discovered two centuries before, still remained,

unexplored and unsettled, inhabited by warlike Maori tribes
but missionaries and rather disreputable traders were now
coming to its shores, and in 1825 settlement began. Both in
Australia and New Zealand, England anticipated France
merely by a narrow margin, but had France arrived first
England's sea power would have led to her dispossession soon
afterwards.

THE THIRTEEN STATES CARVE OUT THEIR DESTINIES

THE thirteen American colonies were now to establish
a new nation, not wholly unfettered by the past, but with
very wide scope to do as it pleased. They soon were coming
to blows among themselves over boundary disputes, but the
abler leaders succeeded in mastering State feeling and establishing a united government in 1787. But the States surrendered
only certain powers to the federal government—army, navy,
customs, foreign policy. They retained their sovereign powers
intact in education, justice, and divorce laws ; and all future
topics of interest that might arise were to fall in the sphere of
the States, not of the Federal government. The tendency,
however, has been to increase the powers of the Federal
government, especially as communications have improved.

The President was to be chosen for a term of four
years by representatives elected directly by the people.
It was expected that they would be chosen for their general
wisdom and then select their President, somewhat as the
College of Cardinals chooses a Pope, but in practice they are
elected to vote for a certain candidate only. The President was
to have considerable powers, modelled on the theory of the
King of England's powers then current ; in war time he was
to be almost a despot. Washington was inevitably elected
President and served for two four-year terms : he could
have remained President indefinitely, but he retired and
set a precedent which none of his successors has broken.
Washington was great in his positive talents and in the
moderation which saved him from overreaching ambition
and faction. He displayed indeed a degree of honesty and
calm wisdom very rare even in less troubled times.

GOVERNMENT-MAKERS WHO MISTOOK THEIR PATTERN

IN accordance with what French writers wrongly held to
be the English practice, the power of making laws possessed by the Senate and House of Representatives was
separated from the administration of them. This was

entrusted to the President and his ministers, who could not be members of either House. In the Senate each State—large or small—was to have the same number of members—two. The Senate had great powers, especially in treaty making, and it has preserved far more importance than the English House of Lords. The weak part of the Constitution was the House of Representatives, a short-lived ineffectual body. The severest commentary on the defects of the Constitution was to be the bloodiest civil war of modern times.

The Supreme Court of Federal judges was given the power to disallow legislation if it conflicted with the fundamental principles embodied in the Constitution. Unfortunately, this has caused the obstruction of reforms if they appear to be in advance of the conceptions of the eighteenth century—for instance, certain legislation for the protection of labour, which, pedantically, is an infringement of the human being's right to " life, liberty, and the pursuit of happiness," guaranteed by the Constitution. It was sound practice to separate the judiciary from the other branches of government.

The Constitution was not by any means the worst of the hundreds that have been framed since 1653, but it had the defect of rigidity. Amendments could only be made by the agreement of a two-thirds majority of both Houses of Congress and three-quarters of the States.

A golden opportunity was lost when, at the opportune moment, the slaves of the southern states were not set free, or when, at least, the importation of new slaves was not forbidden under effective penalties. Many men desired it, and it could have been done at this time with no great inconvenience. A few years afterwards it was too late.

REVOLUTION IN PEACE AND WAR

THE Industrial Revolution goes back to the first use of fire and the wheel. But common usage has applied the words to the mechanical and social changes which began in the eighteenth century, and of which the use of steam was the central factor. The Revolution is, in fact, still in progress ; it reached a " plateau " in the middle nineteenth century, however, and its first phase was completed during the reigns of George III. and his sons (1760–1837).

During the same period the old agricultural system disappeared. The English village community had for ten centuries cultivated as a rule three great fields in common : one field lay fallow each year, and the villagers had each a varying number of strips scattered about the cultivated fields. There was no chance of improving methods under these conditions. The lord of the manor might possess an enclosed estate, but the rest were tied together in a traditional system of co-operative farming ; and there was a general unimproved " waste " of pasture and woodland. Most villages had squatters who had settled on the waste land, but had no rights. The yield of land was low, the quality of cattle poor, the standard of living miserable, but the villagers had independence and a livelihood.

In the early eighteenth century agriculture was a paying industry, and great landowners devoted their energies to agricultural development. In the course of the century they improved the breed of sheep and cattle and vastly increased the productivity even of poor land. Agriculture was further stimulated, extensively rather than intensively, by the shortage of foreign wheat during the wars of 1793-1815.

It is only natural that the persons who were best fitted to exploit land should covet the large tracts which were being misused, as it seemed, by every village community. The acquisitiveness of the bigger landowners had been satiated during the earlier centuries by monastery lands, Irish tribal lands, and the transferences of estates caused by the Civil War.

In the eighteenth century the appropriation of village lands grew common, and reached its climax about 1800. A few years later practically all village lands had been enclosed. The enclosure process, covered by private Acts of Parliament or by the general Enclosure Act, meant that the village lands were pooled and divided. Even if done with accuracy, it left the smaller villager with a patch which was useless to him because he could not afford to fence or drain it. He generally sold it, spent the small proceeds, and became a hired labourer, or, if young and energetic, migrated to a town. Probably the apportionment was not always accurate, and if it was not it erred in favour of the big landowner. He frequently annexed much of the waste land, and the squatters, who had no legal status, were turned out.

These changes increased productivity considerably, but they handed over the land of England to a smaller number of

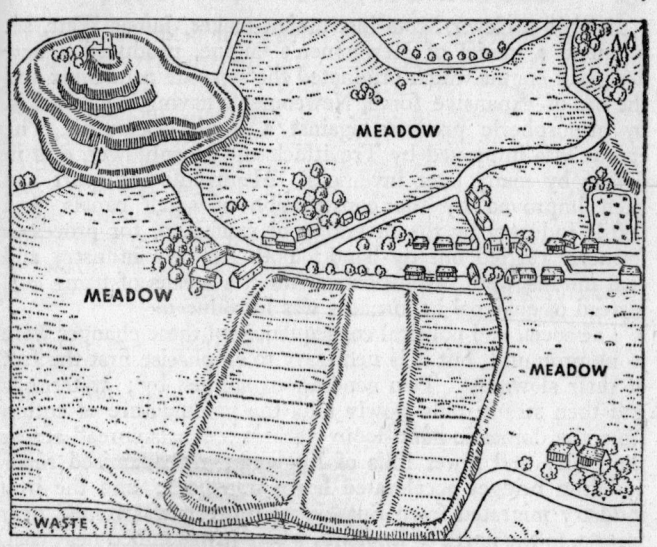

SHARE AND SHARE ALIKE: AN ENGLISH VILLAGE COMMUNITY

Two of the three fields in the foreground (foreshortened for diagrammatic purposes) were cultivated, the third remaining fallow. Wheat was sown in one field, and various cereals in the other. The castle was inhabited by the Lord of the Manor.

owners, proportionately, than is found in any other European country, and they separated the agricultural labourer from ownership of the soil he tilled, thus removing the chief incentive to industry and permanence. The drift towards the towns and overseas has been an inevitable consequence.

THE AGE OF IRON AND STEAM

MATERIAL progress between Roman times and the eighteenth century had consisted merely in the accumulation of materials and the improvement of designs. Printing and explosives, indeed, had marked new departures. At the beginning of the eighteenth century Newcomen and others made a slow, feeble steam engine which was employed with moderate success to pump water out of mines.

In 1768 a clever Scots instrument-maker, James Watt, set to mend a model of Newcomen's engine, produced a new design of engine which originated the separate condenser and the use of expansive force, Newcomen's having been worked by atmospheric pressure against a partial vacuum. The engine was improved by Trevithick and Hornblower, and in details by many later inventors. Meanwhile transport had been improved by the construction of small canals, and textile industry by the invention of machinery for processes formerly carried out by hand ; both the iron industry and coal mining were revolutionised when a means of using coal instead of charcoal in furnaces was introduced.

The social and political consequences of these changes were to be profound, but it is necessary to emphasise first the fact of their slowness. Two generations slipped by ; watermills and then steam mills slowly took the manufacture of cotton from the domestic hand-loom workers ; canals spread across the plains and lower hills of England ; macadamised roads and iron bridges accelerated horse transport ; and the iron industry migrated from Sussex, where iron was mined near forests, to the north of England, where it was mined near coal. The changes influenced each other—materials, transport, power, and manufacturing process, each as it was improved, helped in the improvement of the others. But not until 1825 did the first steam engine ply for hire. Electricity was still little more than an interesting toy.

Canals had been known in Europe for centuries before an English mine-owner decided in 1759 to build one for his coal transport; their development was fatally cramped by short vision. The first railways aroused great opposition because of their anticipated effect on the nerves of dairy cattle. The objections to change were sometimes economic, as when hand-loom weavers broke labour-saving machinery, but in general they arose from the plain man's distrust of anything that stirred the emotions which had formerly been aroused by fears of witchcraft. There were, moreover, special difficulties in organising the first steps towards industrialism. Trials and errors had to be made, and the early machines did not work when first set up, but had each to be coaxed into activity, a process which took weeks. There was a remarkable absence of precision in design and manufacture, materials wore quickly and unevenly—there was a good deal of wood in the early textile machinery, parts were not

andardised or replaceable—and there were few skilled fitters
and engineers. Some of these circumstances reappeared in
Russia during the first Five Year Plan.

SECURITY THAT MADE BRITAIN THE WORKSHOP OF THE WORLD

NEVERTHELESS, no other nation approached England in the
speed of her industrial development. The torpid
southern nations and the war-exhausted German countries
could not compete. It is, however, more surprising that
France, Holland, and the United States of America did not
keep pace. But Holland was in a phase of apathy, and her lack
of coal, iron, and water power put her out of the new developments. The United States was still a small agricultural
republic, and the energies of its citizens went chiefly into
the opening up of new territory for agriculture. France had
produced inventors at the same time as England, was ahead
of her in textiles and transport, and could certainly have
copied the steam engine very quickly. But there came the
French Revolution and the wars of Napoleon. In the
extremely disturbed political conditions of 1789–99, no one
would hazard savings in new enterprises, which even in
normal times were risky. Under Napoleon, France was
unprofitably absorbed in European wars. England, meanwhile, enjoyed security and political stability, and she had
always been inclined towards commerce rather than war,
thanks to her island position and comparative freedom from
invasion, and also to the early disappearance of internal tolls.
She was able from 1793 to 1815 to trade with overseas
markets and sources of materials, while the commerce of
France was interrupted by the English blockade. England's
continental trade was indeed affected by the extension of
French control over much of the Continent, but this mattered
less.

As a result, " the nation of shopkeepers " gained a considerable start. To him that hath is given, and England
continued to hold her lead until about 1880. She was again
assisted, especially between 1848 and 1871, by the internal
disturbances and foreign wars in which her potential
European and American rivals were engaged. In her turn,
she was destined to lose during the War of 1914–18 a part
of her industrial primacy to nations which were less deeply
involved.

INVENTIONS TRANSFORMING THE FACE OF BRITAIN

THE England of the early eighteenth century with i
population of five or six millions was an agricultura
country, self-supporting in all essentials. Its overseas trad
was largely in eastern luxuries (including tea, which then wa
a luxury) and in carrying slaves from West Africa to America
London had perhaps 500,000 inhabitants, but other towns
in proportion, contained fewer people than now, and th
biggest ones were county towns of the south and east. The
century between 1760 and 1860 saw a very considerabl
increase in population in most European countries, bu
especially in England ; families remained large, generally
from six to twelve, while great improvements were now made
in sanitation, water supply, inoculation against smallpox
and other branches of medicine. People now lived longer
and fewer small children died. There was, too, a marked
displacement of the balance of population. The north of
England had nascent textile, metal, and mining industries,
but it had hitherto been sparsely populated. The inventions
concentrated industry in those areas where coal and iron
were found together, and where mountain streams were
numerous ; the iron industry left Sussex, mainly for the
Midlands and the North-east coast ; the textiles of East
Anglia and the West of England were eclipsed by those
of South-east Lancashire and West Yorkshire. The metal
industry of South Yorkshire and Birmingham grew rapidly,
as did the coal mining of South Wales and the industries of
the Scottish lowlands and Clyde valley. Population was
attracted more perhaps from neighbouring rural areas than
from the south, and in the growing northern towns it increased fast. During the nineteenth century the population
of England and Wales rose from nine millions to nearly forty
millions, besides providing many millions of emigrants to the
United States, Canada, Australia, and New Zealand.

THE GROWTH OF THE TOWNS EXPOSES WRETCHED LIVING CONDITIONS

THE new industrial conditions, in which machinery and mass
production were the main factors, increased the profits
of those with capital to take advantage of them. Domestic
labour was now displaced by factories employing hundreds
of people. The typical factory owner was a self-made man,

cial conscience was uncommon, and there was a strong
radition against legislative interference. He was there-
re free to make hours long, wages low, profits enormous
: failure spectacular ; to disclaim responsibility for death
r accidents sustained by his employees from unfenced
machinery or mine explosions; to use insanitary and ill-
entilated sheds for factories; to run up towns of insanitary
ovels ; to employ children in cotton mills almost as soon
s they could walk, and to have half-naked women hauling
rucks underground in coal mines.

However, these things were not new. They had always
xisted in domestic industry, while towns had always been
nhealthy places. The ugly new northern towns simply
xposed such conditions on a large scale and in a concentrated
rea. The health of the population actually improved, and
eal wages probably rose, despite periods of distress, due
mostly to the Napoleonic Wars, with their high prices,
hortage of supplies, and post-war unemployment.

The parliamentary system, giving representation chiefly
o the landed interest and to the south of England, had been
due for reform in Cromwell's time. Agitation for reform
revived in the 1780's and then was deferred for half a century
by the reaction against the principles of the French Revolution. Meanwhile the Industrial Revolution gave importance to new unrepresented areas and to a new class of wealthy
factory owners, distinct from the landowners and the London
shippers, and extremely impatient of landowning pretensions. The political consequences of this will be dealt
with later. Meanwhile the Industrial Revolution provided
funds which enabled England to fight France for twenty years
and to subsidise any continental state willing to assist.

Had Napoleon's energies been devoted to industry and not
to war, or had he even organised war on modern lines, he
might have driven industrial change ahead faster in France
than it progressed in England. But he did not. France
began after his fall to adopt English methods, Germany and
Belgium followed France more slowly, but the other nations
hardly industrialised at all. The United States went ahead
with inventions in their own agricultural domain and took
up railway construction with vigour. The continental nations
were compelled at first to import English engineers and
mechanics, even English capital and managers ; their people
were often reluctant to enter factories in the English way

and unable to accomplish such feats of labour as those pe
formed by the English "navvies" during the railwa
construction period.

RUMBLINGS OF REVOLUTION IN FRANCE

THE French Revolution did not break out because th
French peasant was worse off than any other peasant: fc
one thing it was not a peasant movement, and for anoth
the French peasant was better off than the peasants of an
other continental state. It came, rather, because in Franc
surviving abuses and injustices were more irritating than i
countries where few people had the intelligence to perceiv
the anomaly, or had ever been accustomed to anything bu
oppression. An additional reason was that the Frenc
despotism was suffering from the ultimate sickness of al
despotisms—the absence of a capable despot. Whateve
happened in France interested all Europe and produce
commotion; the disturbances, however, ended with fewe
changes in Europe than had seemed likely at first. A fev
intelligent men had predicted the Revolution, but most peopl
had been quite blind to its coming: the evidence of chang
would nowadays be thought sufficient, but Europe was no
used to revolutions on such a scale. There must, however
have been a very strong disposition towards revolution in
many minds, and there is some indication of conspiracy in the
deeds of violence that occurred.

The way had been prepared by the clever writers of the
eighteenth century. For instance, a group under Diderot who
published an Encyclopædia in which common objects and
institutions were used as pegs on which to hang critica
disquisitions. A series of unsatisfactory officials had acted as
chief minister, chiefly influenced by the unpopular Austrian
Queen, Marie Antoinette. In 1774 Louis XVI. had made
Turgot minister. Turgot was a very able administrator who
had written an excellent introduction to economics, but his
proposals for reform caused so much opposition among
vested interests, especially among the nobles, that he was
dismissed. Calone was the worst of his successors. Necker,
another of them, however, published the true state of the
government's debts. The American war and the Queen's
extravagance had brought the government to bankruptcy.
Louis at last consulted a Council of Notables and then
summoned the States General or Parliament in 1789 — the

irst time since 1614. There had been bad harvests, and
nosts of unemployed and vagabonds collected in Paris.

THE MEN WHO MADE THE FRENCH REVOLUTION

THE Revolution was made by the educated middle
class or bourgeoisie—certain lawyers, doctors, priests,
some small landowners, and a few merchants. The French
middle class paid taxes, but was barred from high civil,
military, and diplomatic employment and was subject to
social slights. It was small in numbers—five per cent. of the
population perhaps. It had read Rousseau, Voltaire, and
Diderot, and was full both of grievance and idealism.

The bulk of the population (ninety per cent.) were peasants,
conspicuous for hard work and attachment to their property.
In many parts of France they owned land, and they were
much better off than German or Spanish peasants. But
their very " prosperity " made them more impatient of the very
heavy burdens they had to bear. The royal government
taxed them and demanded road labour and military service.
The lords of manors, even if they had sold their lands, retained
manorial rights ; there were, too, tithes to the Church. In
all, three-quarters of a peasant's income went in miscellaneous
dues. But the peasant, though not unintelligent, was not
likely to have made a national movement.

There was a quarter of a million nobles (one per cent. of
the nation), some very great lords, others mere honorary
noblesse. Many were hangers-on at the palace of Versailles,
and their bailiffs squeezed the peasants : others did the
squeezing directly. Where the nobles retained the paternal
feudal way of life, as in Brittany, they and the clergy were
popular. The nobles had privileges but no powers : government at Versailles and in every province was carried on by
ministers and officials usually selected from the nobility,
but unpopular with the other nobles, who indeed were
nearly as full of grievances as the middle class. Some were
followers of Rousseau.

The higher clergy were usually of noble birth, clever
worldlings, appointed while young to abbacies or bishoprics.
Their posts carried great emoluments. The humbler priests
were usually very poor, of peasant origin, and conscious of
the need for reform. Neither clergy nor nobles, though best
able to pay, paid direct taxes. The taxes were " farmed "

7

to contractors, a vicious system. No wonder that the national revenue was inadequate.

The States General contained three Houses—Clergy, Nobles, and the Third Estate or Commons, who were embarking entirely unprepared on great changes. Mirabeau, an unscrupulous but astute noble of great energy and ambition, took the lead in the Third Estate, and forced the other Estates to join it in a National Assembly. The King meant to dissolve it by military force, but the Paris mob forced him to come to Paris, where he remained under guard. Meanwhile the Assembly abolished feudalism and the privileges of nobles and clergy. The peasants were already burning castles and title deeds. The Assembly with much windy rhetoric abolished the old provincial boundaries and provincial tolls, and set committees to work to prepare other reforms. But, like the English parliament in 1641, they now ran into difficulties over the Church. They took all its property in France, issued paper money called *assignats* on the security of the lands, promised to pay all clergy reasonable salaries, and set up a new Church, with Catholic doctrine and ritual and government by elected bishops. The Pope and all loyal Catholics refused consent, churches were closed, and a large section of the country was alienated.

Probably no one could have saved the King and Queen, who were sulkily plotting revenge. Mirabeau, who might have done it, died in 1791. Soon afterwards the royal family made off to join the royal princes and nobles who had already fled to Germany, hoping to get the military assistance of the Queen's brother, the Austrian Emperor. They were caught, and henceforward were not trusted. Elections for a new Assembly took place that year. It had been agreed, unwisely, that no members of the States General should sit in the new Assembly, which was filled with unpractical young men. A party known as the Girondins took the lead, extreme reformers but not so violent as the Jacobins, a political group who were gaining influence.

The King was forced in 1792 to declare war on his Austrian and Prussian friends, who invaded France, hoping to gain territory but determined not to be involved too deeply, since the second partition of Poland was pending. The nation was roused by the famous hymn, " The Marseillaise," sung by a regiment of revolutionaries from Marseilles; its bloodthirsty words echo the panic produced by the menace of invasion.

The invaders drew back after an abortive battle at Valmy, many suspected royalists were murdered in prison, and a new parliament, the Convention, was elected, with the Jacobins in the ascendant (September 1792).

ROBESPIERRE : EVIL GENIUS OF THE TERROR

ROBESPIERRE, the Jacobin leader and a successful barrister, was now for nearly two years the master of France. He was a vain, foolish man but an honest and forceful one, possessed by a blood lust, like an appalling number of his contemporaries. The Jacobins raised large armies by compulsion ; the armies were ragged but enthusiastic, and marched far on short rations, while their numbers told in battle. They gained victories, especially when Carnot took charge of the war, but until the middle of 1794 France was in great danger, fighting to repel invasions from the Austrian (formerly the Spanish) Netherlands, and from Germany, and to repress royalist rebellions in France. The revolutionaries executed Louis and his Queen and declared a general war on European kings, including George III. of England, to whom their occupation of the Austrian Netherlands (Belgium) was provocation enough. This desperate state of things led to the amazing Reign of Terror. Two or three thousand persons were guillotined in Paris and many more were murdered in the provinces. Some were aristocrats, others were suspected of royalist leanings, others were revolutionaries who profiteered in corn. Some were merely Jacobins whom Robespierre disliked or feared, like Danton. In the middle of 1794 Robespierre's actions became openly unbalanced, and his party executed him and his close friends.

The surviving Jacobins rather unwillingly desisted from executions ; Prussia and Spain made peace, and a new constitution was set up, the Directory, controlled by the old Jacobin gang (1795–99). They discovered a useful collaborator in an ambitious young artillery officer, Napoleon Bonaparte, who crushed a Paris rising of royalists and other anti-Jacobins. The revolutionists' work had not been merely a butchery. They had planned reforms in education and justice, abolished the old irrational weights and measures, and introduced the decimal system. They began the simplification and codification of the law of France. Their revolutionary calendar with new month-names, a new era, and a week of ten days, was a typical break with the past but did not last long. Reform, however, was pushed into the background under the Directory. The Jacobins were always unscrupulous, and the less corruptible ones were now dead. Those ruling France were kept in power by the army, to which they promised employment and loot.

Their European campaigns in 1795-98 against the Allied forces (Austrian chiefly) were not successful. Bonaparte, however, sent to command in Italy, won a series of victories and soon the Revolution was merged in his own amazing career. For five years, from 1789-94, the Revolution had moved towards extremism ; from 1794-99 it was moving back towards monarchy, and in 1799 the destiny of France was in the hands of this enlightened despot, the perfect product of the eighteenth century.

WHAT THE WORLD THOUGHT OF THE REVOLUTION

WHAT then survived ? The land of France had been transferred almost completely to the peasants ; every one was equal before the simplified law and in eligibility for public employment under the more efficient government. It was conceded that henceforward there must be some kind of elected parliament and some pretence of respect for the public welfare. These were considerable gains and they placed France socially ahead of England.

The Revolution was, of course, popular in the United States and it stimulated the Spanish colonies in South America to rebel. In England, enthusiasm for the old revolution of the 1640's was only slowly awakening from a long night of disrepute. Whigs and young poets sympathised at first, but anti-French feeling had always been strong, especially among the Whigs, and the Whig nobles were shocked by attacks on noble property, while the Puritan middle class were shocked by atheism. The Tories were revolted by the whole thing, and the bulk of the nation was Tory. Sympathy for the Revolution in France and desire for reform in England practically died out as the old military ambitions of France began to reappear more strongly than ever.

But elsewhere in Europe the Revolution was welcomed wherever there was a middle or upper class who were glad to get rid of an unenlightened native or foreign despotism. In Spain and Russia, however, the strong national feeling of a priest-ridden population was incapable of persuasion, and neither French armies nor French ideas were popular.

The Revolution alarmed and infuriated the opponents of change : in England reforms which were pending in the 1780's were delayed to the 1830's, and the wars which arose from the Revolution left the usual legacy. But in the long run the Revolutionary period stimulated change, invention, and reform : it broke the conventions of centuries and started the modern policy of planned, logical change.

THE CONTROVERSY ROUND THE CHARACTER OF NAPOLEON

NAPOLEON has continued for more than a century to recede in reputation from the extremes both of greatness and vileness. We can see first the romantic, unkempt young man, the enthusiastic student of Rousseau and Euclid ; later, romance giving way to megalomania and unkemptness to pomp ; then the awakened somnabulist of St. Helena. This Corsican adventurer of Italian extraction had enormous powers of work and digestion (which broke down under abuse), supreme confidence, decision, and tenacity, an excellent memory, considerable military and organising ability, and hints of rarer qualities, which were extinguished by success. He was unscrupulous and untruthful, callous and vain, vulgar and hypocritical, and his judgment was sometimes grievously at fault. He was, emphatically, one of the most successful men working in the eighteenth century conventions rather than the precursor of anything novel, and even his generalship, which, judged by results, was supreme, derived from eighteenth-century antecedents, and did not improve when it departed from them. Napoleon's later manner was not his best, and it was unfortunately his later manner which the nineteenth century copied.

THE SPLENDOURS AND MISERIES OF NAPOLEON BONAPARTE

HIS public career began in 1795 : he was twenty-six and had twenty-six years ahead of him. His successful Italian campaign of 1796–97 and his great military reputation enabled him after his abortive descent on Egypt in 1798–99 to abolish the Directory and assume the powers of King (nominally " First Consul ") and a few years later Emperor. For eight years everything went very well with him. He forced a general peace on France's enemies in 1802 : France kept the Austrian Netherlands and the left bank of the Rhine and was suzerain of vassal states in Holland and Switzerland,

and completed several reforms foreshadowed by the Jacobins, including the codification of the law (the *Code Napoléon*). When he goaded England into war again in 1803 he was perhaps forestalling the inevitable, but English money, English mobility of transport, the English blockade, and finally an English general were to ruin him. He beat England's continental allies decisively in 1805–07, and though his scheme of invading England had failed, he was in 1807 at the pinnacle of success, with Germany and Poland added to the French empire (which now included Italy) and Russia in alliance.

But the next eight years saw him stumbling towards the pit. In order to destroy one source of England's wealth by cutting off her continental trade, he invaded Portugal and Spain (1807–13) and Russia (1812); he would bring the whole Continent under control. The geographical difficulties and the national resistance of these countries (not only their governments and mercenary armies, but their civilians) gave the opportunity for Germany and Austria to fall on him in 1813. After his exile in 1814 he returned, reigned again for the Hundred Days, and met his match in Wellington at Waterloo (1815).

THE DESTROYERS OF MONARCHY ELECT A KING

THE French, after the great plans and preparations in 1789–94 for a new egalitarian republic, returned in 1799 to an imitation of Louis XIV.'s monarchy, with a hierarchy of nobles, even—the one thing that the early reformers hated most. The French were not yet ready for parliamentary government, which requires a nation educated to moderation on the part both of majorities and minorities. However, the French never entirely gave up the Parliamentary idea. Even Napoleon kept going a system of what pretended to be popular assemblies, and in future France was generally at least on a level with England as regards the degree to which public opinion controlled policy. In the late 1790's, having gained certain very big and positive things from the Revolution, the French did not trouble very much about liberty : they now for a time returned to the old autocratic government that they had known.

Napoleon's system contained a nominated Council of State, where his ablest civil servants worked out details of

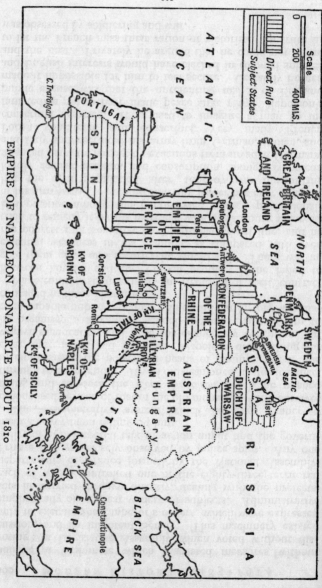

EMPIRE OF NAPOLEON BONAPARTE ABOUT 1810

Scale
0
200 MLS.
400

Direct Rule
Subject States

ATLANTIC OCEAN

C. Trafalgar

PORTUGAL

SPAIN

KM OF SARDINIA

Corsica

Lucca

Rome

KM OF NAPLES

Corfu

KM OF SICILY

GREAT BRITAIN AND IRELAND

London

NORTH SEA

Boulogne

Paris

Antwerp

EMPIRE OF FRANCE

SWITZERL'D

Milan

KM OF ITALY

Venice

CONFEDERATION OF THE RHINE

ILLYRIAN PROV.S

AUSTRIAN EMPIRE

Hungary

DENMARK

SWEDEN

BALTIC SEA

SWEDISH POMERANIA

PRUSSIA

Tilsit

DUCHY OF WARSAW

RUSSIA

OTTOMAN EMPIRE

Constantinople

BLACK SEA

policy; a Tribunate which discussed measures without voting; a Legislative Assembly which voted without discussion, and an impotent Senate. This machinery existed only to execute the Emperor's orders, which were expressed emphatically on a great variety of subjects. Administrative acts he carried through directly, dealing with the prefects, each of whom controlled one of the eighty-three territorial departments of France formed by the National Assembly. Private life was closely observed by police spies. Any one guilty of anti-Imperial talk or action might find the government's heavy hand falling on him.

The administrative system which he gave France—a rationalised version of that of the old monarchy—still survives there, and so does the *Code Napoléon* which he pushed through to completion. It was old-fashioned, as, for instance, in emphasising the powers of heads of families, but it was clear, systematic, and uniform. Napoleon did nothing for women's education and little for elementary education, but he organised a secondary school and university system to train capable public servants. The study of history was discouraged in these institutions.

Napoleon's system existed in virtue of a tacit contract between himself and the French people. If he failed to give them glory and security he would fall. There was an essential weakness in his position, as compared with even the poorest representative of a legitimate royal line, and he tried to remedy it by his marriage with a Habsburg princess. His prestige among the long-service veteran professionals of his army was the greatest that any leader has ever enjoyed, but the civil population after 1805-07 was murmuring loudly against taxation and conscription, though Napoleon financed his wars largely by exactions from invaded Germany and Italy and recruited his army from German, Italian, and Polish volunteers and conscripts. Very many French conscripts deserted. It is hard to imagine a man so infatuated as not to have made peace after 1807. Napoleon's public excuse was that the unrelenting malice of England made it impossible for him to feel secure. Certainly French and English interests would have clashed in colonial spheres and the East. Privately he argued that he could not afford to let the French miss their ration of victories. In truth he was obsessed by soldiering and war.

A WAR THAT THE WHOLE OF ENGLAND APPROVED

GREAT BRITAIN gave the French their first national resist-ance, for, from the beginning of the war, people of all classes were prepared to make sacrifices for victory. This spirit to some extent spread to the rank and file in the army and navy, and probably made some difference between their conduct in action and that of continental troops, whose heart was sometimes not in their work. This does not mean that every able-bodied man of military age was ex-pected to be " engaged in work of national importance " as in 1914–18. The regular army was not more than a few hundred thousands strong, though a large number of regi-ments for home defence underwent perfunctory training. Farmers and landowners were able during the enforced shortage of Russian and German wheat to sell corn at high prices and to bring large tracts of poor land under the plough. Their standard of living went up very much and they found it hard to revert to pre-war conditions after 1815. Their prosperity did not extend to their labourers.

England was governed under George III. by the younger William Pitt (1793–1800); after Pitt's resignation, by Adding-ton, Pitt again, Grenville, Portland, Perceval, and Liverpool in succession. These are not great names, except for Pitt's : and Pitt's chief title to fame had been his peace ministry (1783–93) when he had curtailed expense, kept national accounts, and supported—very gingerly—some pressing reforms. Unlike his famous father, he was not a good war minister, but he shared with his father the gift of unshaken confidence. The details of England's military activities are of small interest before 1807, and Pitt's repressive measures at home are perhaps better forgotten. In 1800 his agents bribed the Irish Parliament to vote for amalgamation with the English Parliament at Westminster, as the Scottish Parliament had been amalgamated in 1707. Restlessness in Ireland had led to rebellion and an abortive French invasion in 1798. The King, rather treacherously, refused to let Union be followed (as Pitt meant it to be) by the liberation of Irish Catholics from all the penalties and burdens to which they were still liable. They were emancipated in 1829, but it was too late. George with his Tory prejudices and interest in farming was far more popular with the aristocracy than the earlier Hanoverians had been, and his righteous and sober

private life endeared him to the middle class, but he did ;
much to break up the British Empire as a much worse ma
might have done. Few merits can be attributed to his soi
who was Prince Regent from 1810 to 1820 and King Georg
IV. from 1820 to 1830. Some indication of his personalit
can be gathered from his fantastic and vulgar palace a
Brighton, the Dome.

HORRORS THAT MARRED THE NAVY'S GLORY

SEA power damaged French trade, drove Napoleon into hi
Spanish and Russian blunders, and enabled England t
maintain the Peninsular expedition and to attempt other les
successful ones. The navy enjoyed great popular esteem, an
Nelson, who rose with dazzling speed to command its chie
fleet, was the greatest popular hero of modern England
Sailors in the Royal Navy of those days were frequentl
" pressed " on shore or taken from merchant ships, seldon
got leave, were paid much less than merchant rates, and wer
fed on hard weevily biscuit and salt pork. Wounds wer
dressed roughly with boiling pitch : shattered limbs wer
sawn off without anæsthetics. There was plenty of rum
but also inhuman floggings. The gruesome conditions provoked mutinies in 1797, after which year things were improved
a little.

Between 1803 and 1805 the French fleet, in conjunction
with the navies of Spain and Holland, seemed formidable.
After Trafalgar (1805) France never fought another general
action at sea. The British blockade, however, caused discontent in the United States, which were also annoyed by
the British practice of stopping American merchant ships and
taking out any English seamen on board to make up their
own crews. There was a savage little war for two years
(1812–14), during which some ship duels were fought, and
some land fights and destruction of cities took place. The
war did harm to Anglo-American feelings, and continued to
be a bitter memory in America for a century to come, long
after it had been forgotten in England.

Wellington described his troops as very base material, but
added that discipline had made fine men of them. They
broke out of hand badly on occasion, and frightful scenes
took place after desperate actions like the storming of Badajoz
in the Peninsular War. The armies were small : it was impossible to feed very large armies, except in fertile and well-

disposed country. Napoleon invaded Russia in 1812 with four or five hundred thousand men, but he lost ninety per cent. of them through exposure and hunger. Armies generally mustered one or two hundred thousand men. At Leipzig in 1813 there were four hundred thousand ; in the Waterloo fighting about a quarter of a million. Movements were slow, scouting and communications depended entirely on the horse in the days when that side of staff work which depends on large and accurate maps, carbon copies of typewritten orders, and telephone and wireless conversations did not exist. England, as usual, began her wars with indifferent commanders, but also, as usual, gradually picked out a number of able men. Moore was the first of these to make his mark, and after Moore's untimely death (1809), Wellington achieved a fame second only in his day to Nelson's.

WAS NAPOLEON UNLUCKY AT WATERLOO ?

WELLINGTON invites comparison with Napoleon as a soldier, and the evidence is tantalising. Wellington had an unbroken series of successes against other commanders, while Napoleon had a much longer and more brilliant record, ending in 1813–14 with a few defeats against overwhelming numbers, so brilliantly resisted as to be moral victories. When they met at Waterloo Wellington won, with inferior numbers and a force of good Germans, bad Netherlanders, and some English, mostly half-trained. Napoleon admittedly was in a hurry and did the attacking, and but for the great Prussian numbers might have fought again. Perhaps he was not quite his old self. Wellington was not merely a cautious formalist who fought by the book : in India and Spain he was perhaps too daring. He was not a great innovator, nor was Napoleon. It is doubtful whether the Wellington of 1796 could have shown the qualities which Bonaparte, his exact contemporary, displayed that year in his Italian campaign, but when he reached maturity it was another matter. Napoleon emerges with a record of more successes, but it is by no means certain that he would have beaten Wellington had they met on equal terms at any date between 1805 and 1814.

Credit for wearing down Napoleon must largely go to Austria. The government of that ramshackle Empire resumed the conflict against him repeatedly, at the cost of much hardship to its subjects. After invading France with the Prussians in 1792, the Emperor carried on the war on France's frontiers until in 1797 Bonaparte's conquest of North Italy and invasion of Austria forced him to make the peace of Campo Formio. A second coalition was broken up by Moreau's great victory at Hohenlinden (1800), and Napoleon's more questionable one at Marengo in the same year, after which Austria again made peace (Lunéville). In 1805 Pitt, unwisely perhaps, gave Napoleon a target and an opportunity by persuading Austria and Russia to form a third coalition. It did not last long: while Nelson's fleet was struggling home after Trafalgar, Napoleon was destroying one Austrian army at Ulm and then the chief Austro-Russian force at Austerlitz. Austria again made peace (Pressburg). When the French were entangled in Spain she once more attacked Napoleon, and in 1809 he was actually defeated at Aspern, but retrieved his fortunes at Wagram. Peace was made at Schönbrunn, and was cemented by Napoleon's marriage to an Austrian princess, Marie Louise. Metternich, who became Chancellor at this time, was quite Napoleon's equal in diplomacy, and in 1813, when it proved impossible to make Napoleon accept reasonable terms of peace, Austria helped to drive him back into France and to abdication.

The prestige which Austria now claimed was not, on some grounds, unmerited. She had made it a condition of helping Prussia and Russia in 1813 that Germany should be restored substantially to its condition before 1789. The destruction of Napoleon was a co-operative effort, in which England and Austria played the chief parts, with help from Russia, Spain, and Prussia.

RESTORATION OR RECONSTRUCTION ?

As the deluge receded, the surviving representatives of Old Europe assembled to construct a New Europe which should resemble the old as much as possible. Most of them proposed to go back to 1789. The Congress which met at Vienna was mainly concerned with the establishment of new political frontiers, with the usual regard for dynastic interests and the balance of power, not for the wishes of the inhabitants. Austria, England, Russia, and Prussia very nearly went to war with each other, and their dissensions were skilfully exacerbated by the French representatives.

The Allies professed to have been fighting Napoleon, the Corsican usurper, in order to restore the legitimate dynasty in France, and wisely did not make the event unpopular in that country by associating it with reprisals. The very able French representative, Talleyrand, insinuated himself among the " Big Four " on a footing of equality, and played on their divisions.

While young, Talleyrand had been pushed in pre-Revolution days into a bishopric, and had joined the Revolutionary party in 1789; he had been exiled before the worst of the Terror, and had later taken service with the Directory and Napoleon : he had broken with the latter after 1807, and he assisted in bringing back the Bourbons. Like many other ex-Jacobins and servants of the Emperor the supple renegade now served under the restored government.

England was represented by Wellington and the Foreign Secretary, Castlereagh, a well-meaning person whose vision stopped short at temporary measures for preserving the peace of Europe. Russia had its Tsar Alexander, who had been influenced in youth by French philanthropy and philosophy, and who had already carried out a number of reforms in his half-barbarous empire. He was destined to be soured by the ingratitude of human beings, but in 1814–15 he was still full of high principles, backed, however, with a very clear determination to take all that Russia could claim and a readiness to use the large and untired Russian army to get it. Hardenberg, the representative of Prussia, the state which had suffered most from France, had a very good record as an administrator in Prussia, whose government had carried out many useful reforms in its struggle with Napoleon. Prussia, however, did not carry much weight. Austria was in a strong position and consistently opposed her.

The Austrian Emperor's representative was Metternich, Chancellor since 1809, a man destined to play the leading part in European politics for four decades. To two generations of reformers he was the incarnation of tyranny. Conservatives see in him a cautious upholder of working realities against fantastic demands for change. Even his enemies would admit that he desired international peace. Yet his admirers must agree that he propped up an effete despotism by a system of spies and harsh penalties.

AN EARLY ATTEMPT TO KEEP THE PEACE

THE Vienna settlement aimed at preserving peace and restoring " legitimate " rulers. France was not to have been penalised at all, save in returning to her 1792 boundaries, but after Napoleon's Hundred Days she had also to pay a small indemnity and restore art treasures stolen from Prussia. As France had fought most of the campaigns since 1793 on foreign soil and made foreign populations support her armies, she escaped very lightly and her national debts did not become very heavy.

The Allies reunited the Netherlands under a Dutch king, so that France should be held in check in the north by a strong state, while Prussia took over the Rhine frontier to hold against the eternal aggressor. The Netherlandic kingdom, however, was composed of incompatible partners. The Dutch were largely Protestant and Dutch-speaking and had a heavy national debt, while the Flemings and Walloons of the ex-Austrian Netherlands were Catholic, Flemish- or French-speaking, free from debt, and very pro-French in feeling.

Prussia was given half Saxony and her old possessions, or most of them, in Poland. Russia took most of the rest, including Finland. Sweden, for supporting the Allies, received Norway from Denmark, which had supported Napoleon. Austria gained, besides part of Poland, Lombardy and Venice ; and Austrian princes were given small Italian dukedoms. The Pope and the King of Naples again misgoverned their old dominions, and the unity and efficient government which Italy had enjoyed under Napoleon, gave way to disunion and maladministration. Germany, which had also been unified by Napoleon as the Confederation of the Rhine, became a Bund or League, a little better organised, perhaps, than the old Holy Roman Empire had been. There were to be thirty-nine German states as against the former three hundred and sixty-five, and Austria was to preside over a system of government, whose powers in Germany corresponded to those of the League of Nations, as established in 1919, in Europe. Prussia was to play second fiddle, though it was already time for her to take Austria's place as the chief German power.

The Tsar persuaded most of the powers (except the Prince Regent of Great Britain and the Pope) to join a Holy Alliance, whose members should act towards each other and their subjects on Christian principles—that is, in the spirit of enlightened despotism recovering from over-indulgence in war. He was especially anxious that they should repress revolution, which seemed to be the great cause of war. They assented in mild scorn or in stupid good faith. More important was Metternich's plan of a permanent Concert of Europe, or a Congress System. Congresses were to be held every year or two years to discuss current affairs. Possible disputes could be talked over and talked out. It was a system which would give scope to his special gifts for intrigue and persuasion. This interesting anticipation of the League of Nations was launched; Europe settled down to its new order, at least recognising the principle of international co-operation, which had been so long disregarded.

THE FLAG AND THE VOTE

Two forces had been developing during the three centuries preceding the French Revolution. One was Liberalism, which went much further than oligarchic parliamentarianism. It was a demand by the whole educated middle class to share in government. It was not what the twentieth century would call democracy; its demands were merely for some sort of elected parliament, freedom of discussion in speech and in the newspapers which were springing up, and trial by jury. Given these, most " liberals " would have been—for the time being—content. There were few countries where these things were obtained without a long struggle, bloodshed, and suffering. Even in England, freedom of speech and of the Press was an acquisition of the late eighteenth century and was usually suspended in wartime.

The other force was military and political nationalism as distinguished from cultural nationalism. There had been plenty of international brawling between states, but now something more intense had emerged—the acceptance of the idea of nationality, its embodiment in flags and names, and the cheerful willingness of national groups to fight, suffer, and oppress other groups.

England developed this feeling as early as Elizabeth's days, though it was still only an English nationalism; Scots and Irish did not share it. France and the Dutch did the same. Similar feeling in Spain and Russia was shown during Napoleon's invasions. Germany and Italy had never hitherto known unity or nationality, but the French first broke down many internal state barriers and then goaded the inhabitants by taxation and conscription to prefer even bad native kings rather than the oppressive French.

During the nineteenth century this national idea appeared in many parts of the world. The new nations, like the old monarchies, scrambled for territory and trade, on the assumption that national groups have personality apart from the assembly of individuals of which they are composed, and that it is natural and right for them to obstruct each other's good if there is the smallest danger of themselves being in any way damaged or disparaged by it. Nationalism made the World War of 1914-18 and its conceptions were embodied in the Versailles Peace of 1919, when internationalism was already coming to the fore. We now condemn the peacemakers of 1815, who ignored nationality and thought only of dynasties and the balance of power. Future Europeans will probably say that the peacemakers of 1919 were also guilty of an offence against mankind when they allowed groups of politicians and soldiers to set up new national states, which frequently tyrannised over alien minorities.

SOMETHING FOR WHICH A PEOPLE WILL DIE

IT is difficult to explain the "national" principle except in terms of crowd-hypnotism or, more kindly, as something for which people will die. Switzerland, with four languages, proves that common language is not essential. Nor are blood and common descent, geographical unity, common religion, common racial type, common institutions, military or literary traditions, or commercial interests. However, no national sentiment could well arise where some of them were not present.

Roughly speaking, national unity has usually preceded liberal institutions. In the early nineteenth century there was no question in Western countries like France and England of having to struggle for national unity, but the Western nations were the scene of violent efforts to liberalise the national institutions and sometimes to go further and win some kind of Socialist or Communist organisation. Ideas of this kind were less active farther East.

CLASHES BETWEEN THE RULERS AND THE RULED

BOTH Liberalism and Nationalism were resisted by the vested interests of kings and aristocracies. Metternich and his like said, in effect, " If we yield an inch they will ask for a yard. We would rather perish in a glorious crash after trying to hold everything than give everything away in a series of compromises." Most oligarchies probably did not reason even thus far. In each of the numerous instances when a nation was divided or ruled by foreigners, the interests of one or more monarchs directly and of all monarchs indirectly were affected. Nationalism was particularly repulsive to Austria, whose Emperor ruled over Germans, Magyars, Czechs, Italians, Poles, Slovenes, Slovaks, Serbs, Ruthenians, Rumanians, and others, most of whom, if national principles were followed, would join other groups or would at any rate resist Germanising tendencies in language and administration. Had the Habsburg empire been an enlightened despotism, as under Joseph II., the resistance to nationalism might have been one that we could wish to have succeeded, but from 1815 to 1918 it was in the hands of rulers and ministers who compare very unfavourably with English government at its worst under George III. in the 1770's.

Ugly though many of the works of nationalism have been, for instance the erection of tariff walls all over the old free trade area of the Habsburg empire, we must chiefly blame the statesmen who preferred to let foreign or un-national rule be generally associated with misgovernment. National leaders themselves were guilty of much narrowness and folly. We shall see how, in the middle of the century, a group of statesmen enabled nationalism to win its desires in several countries at the cost of some of the Liberal aspirations which in the beginning had been generally associated with it.

Among the states of Europe peace was maintained almost unbroken from 1815 to 1854, twenty years of war and revolution having exhausted the participants. Metternich's scheme of periodical conferences broke down after a few years' experiment when it encountered a really serious problem in which national passions were heated, but it was revived whenever a European problem grew acute, and it frequently helped to keep the peace. Metternich's chief conferences were held at Aix-la-Chapelle, Troppau, Laibach, and Verona, at intervals usually of a couple of years. In 1818 France was admitted to the Congress group. Her accession was counterbalanced by the withdrawal in 1822 of England, whose foreign policy was controlled under George IV. by the Prime Minister, Liverpool, and the Foreign Secretary, Castlereagh. They took a dislike to Metternich's scheme for repressing incipient revolution in European states by the forces of more stable neighbours—as was later done, for

instance, in 1823, when France sent an army into Spain to
subdue a revolt against the worthless King of Spain, Ferdinand. The dislike of English Tories for this policy was due
not so much to sympathy with Liberalism as to their traditional insularity.

DISCORD IN THE CONCERT OF EUROPE

AFTER Castlereagh's death in 1822, the Continental powers
proposed to assist Spain to recover her American colonies,
which had been in revolt since 1810; Canning, Castlereagh's
successor, opposed this plan and obtained the co-operation
of the United States president, whose statement of policy
was the famous Monroe doctrine (1823). It was announced
that the United States would not permit European powers to
acquire new interests in the American continent, though
existing interests would be respected. This was coupled in
American minds with a resolve to keep aloof from European
affairs, which they now did for nearly a century. Their
attitude was an extreme form of the English one, and genuine
objection to the autocratic misrule of Austria and Russia had
a good deal to do with it. British policy was largely due to
the much freer trade that the new republics would give, in
place of the exclusionist policy of the old Spanish government.

The remainder of the Congress group split over a national
question. Since the fifteenth century the Ottoman Turks
had ruled over most of North Africa and South-Eastern
Europe up to Belgrade and the borders of Hungary. They
collected taxes from the subject Greeks, Serbs, Roumans,
and Bulgars—but allowed them to practice their religion
(Greek Orthodox), and treated them with a blend of indif-
ference and savagery. In 1821 a rebellion among Greek
seamen and pirates attracted sympathy from Russians, who
belonged to the same Church, and from English statesmen
who transferred to the modern Greeks the enthusiasm they
felt for the great Greeks of the fifth century B.C. Metternich,
however, disapproved of rebellion even against an infidel
Sultan, and he was profoundly jealous of any extension of
Russian influence, such as might follow if Greece were made
independent. The break-up of the Turkish Empire had
begun fifty years before, and Austria and Russia remained
rivals for its possessions till 1914. Austria never favoured
the displacement of the Turks by small states of native
Christians, since as members of the Greek Church their

affinity would always be with Russia. Both powers were looking much too far ahead—the cause of many wars—but Turkey's expulsion from Europe was a desirable thing. It was virtually accomplished in 1918.

Metternich appealed to the Powers to ignore the affair as something outside the pale of civilisation, while the Tsar indignantly withdrew from the Congress group and sent troops and ships to support the Greeks. A British admiral took the responsibility of destroying at Navarino (1827) an Egyptian fleet which was sailing to crush the Greeks. The other Powers soon afterwards recognised the independence of Greece, which began both the disintegration of the Turkish Empire on its western side and the assertion by small nationalities of claims which had been neglected for many centuries.

This was the end for the time being of attempts to regulate European international relations. It was perhaps unfortunate that Metternich's scheme did not survive till it could be used by a less reactionary set of diplomats. Metternich, however, remained the uncrowned Emperor and the keeper of the conscience of the German princes, until in 1848 the ground gave beneath his feet.

THE EARLY STRUGGLES OF BOURGEOIS LIBERALISM

WHEN the Peace of 1815 was made, the German enthusiasts (middle class students, professors, journalists, and lawyers) were given a form of German union, the impotent *Bund*, and concessions to Liberal ideas were made in the states of Germany outside Austria. Within a few years, however, the princelings were suppressing their Diets or Parliaments and the Carlsbad decrees of 1819 announced the opposition of Austria and Prussia to political discussion, especially in those hotbeds of Liberalism, the German universities. It was not surprising to find Prussia on the side of military reaction, but her subservience to Austria between 1813 and 1858 was entirely due to the weak character of her two kings who ruled in these years. Prussia did indeed form a Commercial Union (the *Zollverein* of 1818), which all her small neighbours gradually entered, until most of Germany was enjoying internal free trade ; the dislike of Prussian manners was neutralised by commercial ties. The governments of the smaller states, however, continued to support Austria.

Meanwhile in France two brothers of Louis XVI. reigned in succession. Louis XVIII. did something to modify the zeal of the ultra-royalist and Catholic party which gained control and which desired to take revenge on adherents of Napoleon. The second brother reigned as Charles X. (1824-30) and endeavoured to undo the Revolution by giving national money to buy back the estates of nobles and clergy which had been confiscated, by depriving the Press of the right of free discussion, and by assuming the right to make laws. The students and workpeople of Paris rebelled, the troops sympathised, Charles went into exile, and various leaders, including some figures of the Revolution of 1789, took charge. They offered the crown to Louis Philippe, a distant member of the Bourbon house, who had learned more than its other members from the Revolution. He became King of the French and promised to rule as a Citizen King.

THE TREATY THAT BROUGHT BELGIUM INTO BEING

THE news of the Paris Revolution caused the pro-French clerical party to rebel against the Dutch King of the Netherlands, who was very rapidly driven out. The party desired union with France or independence under one of Louis Philippe's sons. England, Prussia, and Austria, however, after some years' skirmishing and diplomatic argument, compelled them to accept and the King of Holland to recognise Prince Leopold of Saxe-Coburg as King. It proved an admirable choice. The new state was called Belgium, after its ancient inhabitants the Belgae ; its Government promised not to make war, and the five great Powers, including France, undertook not to make war on it. This treaty was the " Scrap of Paper " of 1914. This affair and the Greek rebellion were settled by the Powers with greater dignity and disinterestedness—and therefore more success—than was usual in the eighteenth century.

The year 1830 was one of minor revolutions elsewhere. In Germany there were attempts to force kings to " grant constitutions" (which was taken to mean some kind of parliament) and to exact a promise from them to act more or less in accordance with its wishes. These movements were suppressed by military force. So was the anti-Russian movement in Russian Poland, where misgovernment aggravated a desire to regain national independence. Henceforward, the Polish language, flag, and other national institutions and emblems were proscribed, and resentment accumulated.

Attempts of a similar kind were being made in Italy. That "geographical expression" included (1) Austrian Lombardo-Venetia and various Austrian dependencies, of which Tuscany was the chief: (2) Sardinia, *i.e.* Piedmont, Savoy, Genoa, and Sardinia, a kingdom ruled by a native Italian prince : (3) the Papal States, stretching across central Italy and ruled, very badly indeed, by the Pope : (4) the Kindom of Naples, that is the South of Italy and Sicily, where the worst misgovernment of all took place under a line of Bourbon degenerates. Italy had forgotten the great traditions of Imperial Rome : the country was divided geographically in an inconvenient manner by the central mountains : there were several very different, and mutually unfriendly, types of Italian in the North, Centre, and South : the Austrian garrison, police, and spies, as well as the Pope, stood in the way of unification, which was the dream of a few eager young men of the student class. They used the old secret society of the *Carbonari* (literally " Charcoal Burners "), and in 1830 there were outbursts in several cities, as there had been in Naples in 1820. They were suppressed, as the 1820 revolt had been, by Austrian forces.

After 1830 Metternich still ruled unshaken, the supreme foe of Liberalism and Nationalism in Germany, Italy, and the miscellaneous dominions of Austria. However, Liberalism had held its own in France, Nationalism had triumphed in Belgium and Greece, and reformers were winning what seemed to be a definite triumph in England. The English Reform Bill will be described later. In Germany, Italy, Poland, and the Austrian dominions, ardent nationalists continued to work in secret, at the risk of imprisonment. In most countries there was agitation for Liberal reforms, and in England there was the " Chartist " movement which demanded a fully representative parliament. In France reformers were preaching Socialism.

PIONEERS OF SOCIALISM

THERE were early Socialists in various countries, for instance, the Levellers in Cromwellian England and the followers of Babœuf during the French Revolution. Both had been extremely unpopular with the official Republicans, whose reverence for the rights of middle-class men of property had, in fact, made rebels of them.

During the first quarter of the nineteenth century, while

Owen[1] in England was developing ideas and schemes which were known, rather loosely, as Socialism, two French writers, Fourier and Saint-Simon, originated what became the chief revolutionary movement of the next hundred years. They assumed or disregarded the merely *political* side of democracy (one man, one vote, or more correctly, one head of a middle-class family, one vote) and looked forward to *social and economic equality*. With the optimism of innovators they proposed Utopian schemes which have not yet been realised, certainly not in the diluted form of State Socialism which has been set up in Russia. They intended to reorganise society in groups of producers, with roughly equal remuneration. The enormous productivity of modern industry, and its unequal division of profits, infliction of unemployment, and neglect of slum conditions were already clear to be seen. Socialists or Communists (the term can hardly be distinguished at this stage) desired to give mankind the benefits of productivity with none of the evils that arose under the industrial system (as yet almost unregulated and entirely competitive).

The three chief writers of the early Socialist movement in its second phase (Lassalle, Marx, and Engels) were all born before 1826. They grew to manhood with the worst aspects of the early Industrial Revolution around them in France and Germany, and they advanced beyond the romantic, Utopian, William Morris views of Fourier and Saint-Simon. The effect of their propaganda (and that of less famous men) in the 1830's and 1840's was to rouse the working-class to demand political rights as a preliminary to a Socialistic reorganisation of society. The appeal of such schemes was strengthened by the widespread starvation which inevitably followed the great wars. It was felt everywhere, and in Great Britain there was much unemployment, low wages, and very acute suffering in the twenties and thirties.

1848: THE YEAR OF REVOLUTIONS

THE year 1848 passed fairly quietly in England, thanks to industrial recovery and an anticipated reduction in the price

[1] In 1799 Robert Owen established his co-operative, communistic cotton-mills in New Lanark, Scotland. In 1844-5 the first of the modern co-operative stores was opened in Rochdale, Lancashire. It belonged to the type of co-operation that has flourished best in Britain—the Consumers' Society. Any one may become a member by taking one or more £1 shares, payable out of the dividend. All goods are sold at the current retail prices, the profit, with expenses deducted, is divided among consumers according to purchases.

of bread. In almost every other European state there were revolutionary movements. Afterwards there was a tendency for new rulers to compromise with reform and work with the more adaptable of their old opponents.

A rising in Austrian Poland in 1846 had been put down by the Viennese government with the help of the Galician serf population : the serfs, once roused, were difficult to appease. But the great revolutions started as usual in Paris. Louis Philippe ruled to the satisfaction of the bourgeoisie, but there was much corruption. The King's foreign policy, directed to promoting the interests of his sons rather than those of his country, was unsuccessful, and his minister, Guizot, refused to enact overdue constitutional reforms. Industrial troubles added to the discontent. A riot in Paris unexpectedly became a revolution, and the king fled. Two parties had overthrown him, the radicals and the new Socialists led by Louis Blanc, but they soon divided, and the radicals got the better of their rivals with much bloodshed. A Republic was set up under bourgeois auspices and an ambitious person named Louis Napoleon Bonaparte, whom nobody took very seriously, a nephew of the first Napoleon, was made Prince-President.

The King of Prussia had already increased the powers of the old Provincial Diets, and in 1848 he gave them greater powers still. Liberals were jubilant. In almost every capital of the small German states the rulers were driven to make similar concessions, and a movement for unifying Germany began. Even in Vienna, Metternich, entirely to his amazement, found the city in revolt, and the Habsburgs were quite ready to throw him over. He had concentrated on himself the hatred of idealists for thirty years, but he was perhaps the victim of conditions. The Viennese revolutionaries sent members to a National German parliament at Frankfurt.

It seemed that the Habsburg empire would disintegrate. The Magyar landowning class in Hungary, led by men like Szechenyi, Kossuth, and Deák, demanded self-government, though by this it meant government by itself and not by its more numerous Ruthenian and Rumanian serfs. The same was done in Bohemia (the Western part of modern Czecho-Slovakia), where the Czechs were fully enfranchised and a national government was set up at Prague. Revolution started in Italy, and the King of Sardinia joined in a national attack on Austria, very much as the King of Prussia consented, in

defiance of Austria, to be the head of the reformed and unified
German state.

THE HABSBURGS LEARN TO "DIVIDE AND RULE"

THE Habsburgs, however, were served by able men, who
took advantage of the antipathy that existed among the
insurgent nationalities. It was quite easy to use ignorant
troops from any portion of the Empire to repress any other
part. Jellacic, Ban of Croatia, employed its barbarous population in defence of the Empire. The Viennese stood by
while the Imperial forces subdued Prague, then they themselves were dealt with, and the Italian forces were defeated.
Finally, with the assistance of the Tsar, the new Emperor,
Francis Joseph, who had succeeded to the throne at the age
of eighteen, saw his servants trample down the Magyars and
punish them with merciless outrages. The Austrian army
had saved the Habsburg empire. Very little seems to have
been learned from this narrow escape.

The King of Prussia, after agreeing to become Emperor of
the new Germany, withdrew, overcome by fear of Austria
and shame at having deserted his fellow-kings. The Prussian
constitution was again limited, the National Parliament at
Frankfurt talked for a time longer, and was then dissolved by
force. All over Germany revolutionaries were executed or
exiled.

Charles Albert of Sardinia led an Italian league to expel
Austria from North Italy, and even the King of Naples and
the Pope joined it. But it broke down against the Austrian
fortresses and the strength of the non-Italian Austrian forces.
The Italians were defeated in battle and Charles Albert had
to abdicate as a condition of peace. His son, Victor Emmanuel,
succeeded him. The other princes had already withdrawn.
Idealists like Mazzini and Garibaldi and Manin, who had
already plotted and fought for Italy, raised revolts in Rome,
Venice, and elsewhere, and fought to the last moment of
hope, escaping narrowly with their lives. The revolutionary
Prince-President of France sent troops to restore the Pope's
authority in Rome. Italy, singlehanded, was incapable of
beating even an Austria handicapped by rebellions in all its
dominions, even if Italy herself had been united and enthusiastic, which she was not—the national movement was in
general frowned on by the Church and of no interest to the
peasantry.

The Revolutions of 1848 thus seemed to have gained little
.cept the dislodgment of Metternich. The reformers had
:en betrayed by the King of Prussia in Germany, and the
absburg tyranny in Italy and Central Europe seemed un-
akable. In France the Citizen King had been displaced
y a bourgeois republic under the ominous headship of a
onaparte. Actually an impression had been made. Certain
sing men in the old governments were prepared to forward
me of the reformers' desires, at a price, and the surviving
formers were learning to adapt ends to means. So, within
venty-five years, a great deal of what was fought for un-
uccessfully in 1848–49 was to be put into effect.

FREEDOM SLOWLY BROADENS DOWN

DURING the nineteenth century, that age to which the
twentieth century is apt to look back rather wistfully,
ontinental nations were torn asunder by revolutions and
rampled on by foreign armies, but Great Britain enjoyed the
nost peaceful period in her long history. She had small
:olonial wars, but her army—very fortunately for her military
restige—only once met a European enemy in the localised
Crimean War of 1854–56. Internal politics were lively, but
here was common ground between the parties. In the thirties
nd forties there were riots which were mild by contrast with
:he tamest of the frequent demonstrations that Paris, for
nstance, saw.

Great Britain was certainly more prosperous and content
than continental countries. She had no thwarted national
aspirations, her constitution was the pattern for advanced
continental Liberals, and, according to current standards, her
population lived well. Political progress was slow, but overdue reforms were sooner or later carried out. The International Exhibition of 1851 might show that the Continent
was rapidly catching up in certain branches of industry, but
substantially England remained not only the workshop but
also the bank of the world. The rigid caste system of pre-
revolutionary France which survived into the nineteenth
century in Prussia, Austria, and Russia, with its military
proclivities and feudal relations to peasants, had died out in
England ; England's castes were fluid. Its oligarchy courted
popular esteem, hat in hand, at parliamentary elections,
earned applause in manly sports and, when necessary, sur-

rendered something by due form of law. The security con
ferred by the narrow seas and the unquestioned supremac
of the Royal Navy prevented any military gang from tradir
on national apprehension, as they could do abroad. An
despite periods of distress, especially 1815-46, real wage
and the standard of living were rising throughout the centur

THE UGLY SIDE OF PROGRESS

BUT nineteenth-century England, especially during i
characteristic period between 1830 and 1880, had i
ugly sides. There was great self-congratulation over th
perfection of her constitution, industries, social life, an
moral principles. It was punctuated by criticism from almos
everyone whose opinion we now value. Dickens's contemporar
novels were full of angry satire and sentimental denunciation
Matthew Arnold in his prose works harped more fastidiousl
on the same string. Carlyle and Ruskin advocated fantasti
alternatives to the grubby ideals of their generation. It was
pleasant land for those of ample means and strong nerves
For the great mass of people who were poor, and the smalle
number who disliked ugly buildings, hypocrisy and pompou
absurdity, it was less pleasant. Still, in most respects i
compared favourably with the Continent.

Without attempting to describe the events of 1815-191
chronologically, we shall sketch their general tendency in
Great Britain under five headings—economic development
political changes; social development; the new British
Empire; and finally (the black exception to the genera
prosperity) the story of Ireland.

Railways, originated by the great Trevithick and made
practicable by George Stephenson in 1821-30, slowly spread
over England. Vested interests opposed them and were
bought out at a price; speculators saw to it that the usual
semi-fraudulent features of a " boom " were not absent;
and the stiff English objection to planning development ahead
and to interfering with everybody's right to do as he pleased
with his property had not yet been curbed. So railways
remained in the hands of a large number of private companies,
and at first there was much waste in competition, and adequate
reserves were not accumulated.

In almost all matters there was complete (and fallacious)
faith that the operations of supply and demand would cause
enterprising producers to meet the needs of discriminating

FORERUNNERS OF MODERN TRANSPORT

Shillibeen's omnibus and Trevithick's steam engine. Trevithick drove his locomotive in Euston square and wagered that no one could catch him on foot.

consumers for goods and services, with cash as the univers
lubricant. In this spirit private companies were allowe
to project schemes for canals, often impracticable and e>
pensive, with insufficient and unstandardised width an
depth, so that frequent changes of boat made costs excessiv
The railways were allowed to buy up the canals and discour
aged traffic on competing routes.

However, communications in general became very good
The stage coaches died out and for many years (about 1850
1900) there was very little road traffic, except local hors
traffic, with cycle traffic from the 'seventies onwards. Th
Royal Mail began to convey letters for a penny in 1840—
the charge had been formerly a shilling or so—and the tele
graph made faint beginnings about the same time. Moto
travel began in the eighties. All this time railway service:
improved in speed, comfort, and frequency.

THE ENGLISH TRADER SELLS TO THE WORLD

STEAM had been applied to water transport as early as 1802,
in the form of the paddle-wheel steamer, later supplanted
by the screw. Accurate measurements, better steel (later the
Bessemer process) and standardised parts all contributed to
improve manufacturing processes in the textile and hardware
and heavy engineering industries. The mines, potteries, mills,
and foundries of the industrial North, Midlands, Scottish
Midlands and South Wales continued to grow in numbers
and size. Their products were sold to all parts of the earth ;
English engineers and mechanics were employed in mining,
making railways, and erecting factories in Europe, South
America and newer countries ; English capital was invested
all over the world, while English vessels did a very large amount
of the world's carrying trade. By the end of the century
foreign countries were competing successfully in many
industries—Germany in glass, hardware, and chemicals,
France in the finer cloths, Belgium in light engineering—
but, all in all, England retained the lead.

Her banking system, developed stage by stage since Charles
II.'s days, reached maturity after the Napoleonic War, when
the cheque, the gold reserve, control by the Bank of England,
and most of its other characteristics were established very much
as they remained until 1914. The system was superior,
probably, to that of most continental countries and the
United States.

Industrial development was paid for by smoky skies, polluted rivers, a grimy countryside, and towns full of stunted people. The shocking conditions under which men and women and children originally worked were gradually improved, but industrial life at the best has its sordid and monotonous side. Facts disproved the theory of those who argued that the race would die out after three generations of town life unless vitalised by rural blood, but it is obvious that in the slums, where children live in overcrowded, verminous houses, the human race cannot breed healthily.

During the first half of the century England gave up her system of trade regulation and protection. After 1815 new Corn Laws were imposed to keep up the price of corn to something nearer its old wartime level. There was a long struggle, principally during the thirties and forties; the Corn Laws were opposed by the masters and men of the industrial areas— by some of the former in the hope that cheaper bread would mean lower wages, by some out of dislike for the landowning class. The leader of the landowning Conservatives, Peel, finally abolished (1846) what remained of the Corn Laws, without producing any very marked effects one way or the other for some time. Free trade in almost all commodities was adopted at that time—steps towards it had begun in the 1820's—and even continental nations and the United States temporarily relaxed their protective systems. Free trade certainly suited an England at the height of her industrial supremacy.

NEW DESIRES GUIDE THE TREND OF POLITICS

THE years after Waterloo saw a governing class in England overcome by the same sort of fears as continental aristocracies. Liverpool, Prime Minister from 1812 to 1827, Eldon, Lord Chancellor from 1801 to 1827, Castlereagh, the Foreign Secretary, and their colleagues, were not bad or foolish men, but they opposed more than one necessary reform and enforced several repressive measures such as the Six Acts against popular demonstrations. The reactionary side of their policy was typified by the Peterloo massacre in Manchester (1819), when an orderly demonstration was ridden down and many men and women killed. After 1822 less reactionary Tories (notably Canning, Peel, and Huskisson) tended to control the Cabinet, while the Whigs' stock recovered from the depression of fifty years out of office and " Radicals " urged reform.

Peel mitigated the savage penalties of the old criminal laws and
reorganised the police. Wellington as Prime Minister was
forced in 1829 to free all Roman Catholics from the restrictions
of not being allowed to vote in elections, sit in parliament,
be magistrates or officers, or hold office under the Crown.
Protestant dissenters had also been freed (1828). The
measure was of most interest to the Irish.

The old party allegiances of Whig and Tory were now
breaking up and a new alignment of parties, corresponding
to the realities of a new era, was soon to come about. The
Whigs had stood for the limitation of the king's power and for
a policy favouring the interests of commerce rather than those
of agriculture. The Tories had been the party with high notions
of the king's place in the constitution, fervid in their loyalty
to High Church principles, and opposed to war waged against
France in the supposed interests of trade and overseas dominions. Many of these issues were now moribund, and new ones,
born of the French Revolution, were taking their place.

The new parties were to be the Liberals and Conservatives,
which may be broadly said to have represented respectively
desire for change and the opposition to it. The ancestry of
the Liberal party was mainly Whig, but not entirely so, since
many Whigs had been influenced by Burke's anti-Jacobin
diatribes at the time of the French Revolution, and became an
ingredient of Conservatism. The Liberals who were descended
originally from the left wing of the Whig Party, stood for
Parliamentary reform and freer trade. They therefore received
a great infusion of new blood, chiefly of distinctly radical hue,
when the great Reform Bill was passed, enfranchising the
industrial North and Midlands.

MAKING A PLATFORM FOR THE PEOPLE

IN the year 1830, when the Whigs introduced the Reform
Bill, the right to vote was possessed by about one citizen
in a hundred, but the qualifications varied from area to area ;
bribery of individuals and corporations took place, and seats
were bought and sold ; voting was public, so that the effect
of bribery and pressure could be noted, and certain areas
were respectively under- and over-represented. The worst
scandals had been, at one end of the scale, Old Sarum, with
two members, one absentee voter, and no inhabitants, and,
at the other, Manchester, with no members and a hundred
thousand inhabitants. However, some of the worst " rotten

oroughs " had been disfranchised already, and the House of
Commons was not altogether unrepresentative, nor altogether
eglectful of its duty, for it voted its own reform.

The Bill was forced through both Houses after two years
of agitation by the firmness of Lord Grey and Lord Durham,
the probability of revolution, and the promise of the new King,
William IV., to override the House of Lords. It gave the
vote principally to heads of families occupying houses rented
at £10 a year, a fairly large sum then—in other words, the
richer five per cent. of the population. Some redistribution
of seats took place, though the constituencies still varied
greatly in size.

The working class soon realised that the mills of the
reforming Whigs were going to grind exceeding slow, and
they began agitation, backed by threats of rebellion, for the
People's Charter—six further reforms which would have
given much the same conditions as were established after
1910, with the additional concessions of annual parliaments.
These demands met with strong resistance among the middle
and upper classes, and the Chartist movement was ruthlessly
repressed by the Government of the day.

After 1848 agitation died out. Public voting, intimidation,
and bribery in cash or kind remained customary until about
the time of the Second Reform Act of 1867. This Act,
passed by the Conservatives, enfranchised large numbers of
town working men. A Liberal Act of 1884 gave the vote to
country labourers, and an Act of 1918, the result of bitter
agitation between 1906 and 1914, gave it to women over
thirty. The Parliament Act of 1911 took away the power
which the House of Lords had enjoyed and, on the whole,
abused, of killing or mutilating Bills sent up by the Commons.
It retained after 1911 the power of suspending other Bills
for two years, but was denied this right of delay in the case
of Money Bills.

During the century the business of Parliament grew much
greater and more technical, hours of work lengthened in-
ordinately, party machinery, previously slight, became
elaborate and exacting, and the status of the private member
declined. The authority and prestige of the Prime Minister
grew greater. Probably the period of Parliament's greatest
prestige was between 1832 and 1867, when the cautious
Victorian householder elected a House of Commons still, as
it had been for centuries, mainly aristocratic or plutocratic

and usually Whig. After 1867, the " swing of the pendulum
was visible, the two parties getting majorities in turn fc
roughly equal periods. The Conservative ministries, fc
example, of 1895-1905 were followed by a series of Liber
governments which would possibly have ended in 1915. Thi
is generally ascribed to the whims of voters, who saw n
difference between the parties, and grew dissatisfied wit
each. Each party in turn after 1867 felt that it must justif
its existence by new departures in policy, and always estrange
certain vested interests or lost credit over some entanglement

SOCIAL REFORM PROCEEDS APACE

IN the 'thirties, the Whig Government emancipated all slave
throughout the British dominions; abolished the Poor Law
system which since 1795 had been liable to gross abuses, and
put in its place a cheap but harsh system of Union work-
houses; established elected Borough Councils, and gave a
small grant to education. Peel in the forties permanently
established the graduated income tax, which did not weigh
on the poor, as did the old indirect taxes raised largely on
imported foodstuffs. Reform stagnated for many years under
Palmerston's influence, but Gladstone's ministry of 1868-74
passed the Ballot Act for secret voting, restricted the sale of
liquor slightly, made elementary education for the first time
compulsory, and made appointments to the Civil Service by
competitive examination instead of, as formerly, by nomina-
tion and favour. Disraeli (1874-80) specialised on housing
reform. Elected County Councils began in 1888—rural areas
had been administered by nominated magistrates—and at
different times Acts were passed which made elementary
education free, raised the age limit, and set up secondary
schools, while the ancient universities, public schools, and
grammar schools were reformed by Act of Parliament. In
the early twentieth century the Liberals granted very small
old age pensions to very old working people, organised working
class insurance against unemployment and sickness, and
established Labour Exchanges. Some of the best reforms
were due to the efforts of private members, as when Samuel
Plimsoll brought in his measure to prevent the drowning of
sailors by their employers overloading ships.

Throughout the century there was a series of Acts to
regulate scandalous conditions in industry. The regulation
of cotton factories dated from 1819, that of mines from 1842.

. very large number of Acts of widely separated dates have
revented the employment of children under twelve, forbidden
ven men to work more than nine hours a day, as against a
ossible eighteen a century ago, prevented women from
working in mines, and compelled employers to ventilate
actories, fence machinery, assume liability for accidents, and
rovide sanitation. Industrial diseases and sweated labour
urvived into the twentieth century, but the diabolical aspect
f the early factories was mitigated. Model employers since
he days of Owen have often shown how good conditions are
not, as was once thought, incompatible with efficiency and
profits. Much was also due to pressure by trade unions
which, after their underground existence in the early nine-
eenth century, gained full recognition in the early 'seventies
nd have since risen to a position of very great power. But
many of the hundreds of small legislative reforms which have
become law since 1829 were due to philanthropists and
enthusiasts, usually sneered at in their day as cranks, who
ought for ideals against much obstruction and at considerable
ost to themselves.

There are few changes as striking as the rise of women in
legal and economic status—partly a matter of social custom,
partly of law. It began in the last quarter of the nineteenth
century, with women's entry to the medical profession, and
women's colleges at Oxford and Cambridge.

BRITAIN'S INTERESTS OVERSEAS

STEAM made ocean journeys very cheap, manufacturing
wages provided small sums of capital, increased population
provided a surplus for emigration, and after 1870 refrigeration
made farming in remote colonies more profitable. There are
now in the United States, the British Dominions, and South
America more people of British descent than in the British
Isles. The overseas dependencies belong to the British Empire
largely as a consequence of British naval strength, and this
strength during the past century was due to trade and the
Industrial Revolution. It could not have been maintained
by a poor country, however good its human material. The
interest and value of these dependencies began to grow, and
though they were encouraged to take responsible government
as soon as possible in order to free the Mother Country of
expense, it began to be expected that they would remain

8

attached to her voluntarily. After 1880 the Imperial idea wa
cultivated and unwritten obligations were acknowledged b
the Dominions during the wars of 1899–1902 and 1914–1
Economically, however, the Mother Country and th
Dominions diverged.

The two original provinces of Canada were united in 184
after much friction between old and new British settlers, an
between the old-fashioned French Canadians and the British
officials. Friction continued, but virtual self-government wa
conceded to Canada by the governor, Lord Elgin, acting i
the spirit of the famous Report which Lord Durham had
signed in 1839. In 1867 the Dominion of Canada wa
established, and soon included all the scattered Canadia
colonies except backward Newfoundland. When railway
were introduced, it became possible to administer Canada
Before the transcontinental lines were built there was n
communication between East and West coasts except by se
round Cape Horn. The Dominion of Canada was a Federa
Union, the provinces retaining great powers, like the American
States, while the functions of the central Parliament wer
modelled on the British Constitution.

MODERNISM FINDING A HOME IN ASIA

IN 1861 an eminent scholar, Sir Henry Maine, remarked that
Europe was the only *progressive* continent, but he would have
had to revise his view fifty years later. America, in particular
the United States, was rapidly eclipsing Europe in the
material arts which Europeans imagined to be the same thing
as progress, and Asia was adopting European dress, firearms
machinery, newspapers, motor cars, and cinematographs.
There was no apparent reason why Asiatics should not
develop their material resources and make scientific and
commercial discoveries, as Europeans had done. Their religion, law, and philosophy were also undergoing change.

With the advent of the steamship in the mid-nineteenth
century contacts between Europeans and the East became
frequent. The educated classes of India and China at first
behaved, when confronted by the overwhelming force of the
West, as they had done under similar circumstances in Roman
times :

> The East bow'd low before the blast
> In patient, deep disdain ;
> She let the legions thunder past,
> And plunged in thought again.

However, force and trade contacts broke down barriers.
The Europeanisation of the East is still very superficial, but
unless Europe herself collapses it will increase.

Between 1798 and 1856 the greater part of India was annexed
by the East India Company in a series of half-forgotten wars.
Its annexation of Oudh was one of the causes of the Indian
Mutiny of 1857–59, when discontented princes stirred up a
revolt among some of the Bengal sepoys or Indian troops.
The Mutiny was confined to one district and one class, and
the English were assisted by many civilian Indians and
Sikh troops, but it was the fierce resolution, the amazing energy
and courage of British generals and troops that held India.
Among them John Lawrence and John Nicholson were pre-
eminent. The East India Company's trade monopoly had
gone in 1834 and the Mutiny caused the Company to be
relieved of its governmental functions. Disraeli arranged
in 1876 that Queen Victoria should become Empress of
India.

There have always been frontier wars in the North-West
—roughly one a year—but the military side of government in
India has gradually been hidden by the political and economic.
During the nineteenth century plague and famine still
occurred regularly ; it was the chief triumph of British rule
to make both less common, the one by means of sanitation,
the other by irrigation.

The Government of India remained until 1909 an enlightened
despotism. The despot was the Viceroy and his Council
(partly representative after 1892) under the Secretary of State
and his Council in London. Under the Viceroy were the
usual hierarchy of provincial governors and legal and financial
officials. Officials of the lower grades were all Indians, but
Indians seldom reached the higher grades, though eligible,
partly because they rarely did well enough in the competitive
examinations on which, after 1870, appointments were made.
Local self-government by town councils began in the eighties.

A NEW LIFE FOR THE ENGLISHMAN IN INDIA

BEFORE steam and the overland route, Englishmen sent to
India usually remained there till their retirement, and were
semi-Orientalised. In later times they kept in close touch
with England, and imported English ways. Wealthy Indians
took to copying them or were educated in England. In 1834,
Bentinck, the Governor-General, had made Indians eligible

for Government employment, and Macaulay, then a member
of Council, secured that Indians should be educated in the
language and literature of England, not of Hindustan or
Persia. The study of Burke and Milton was perhaps destined
to affect India politically, but this education has remained
alien to Indian life : only one Indian—Tagore—has ever
written anything of merit in English. A department of
public instruction was first established by Dalhousie about
1850. The class of educated Indians was never large
—even to-day barely 20,000,000 Indians out of 353,000,000
can read or write, and fewer than 2,000,000 know any English.
However, the educated class soon became too numerous for
the employment that a poor agricultural community could
offer. Low wages, unemployment, and a tendency to live by
journalism were therefore common.

Since the 1880's India has been disturbed by the same
National and Liberal aspirations that we saw at work in Europe
fifty years before. But while the ruling despotism was far
more humane and generous than, for instance, the Austrian
Government, India itself is a jungle of races, compared with
which the Habsburg empire was homogeneous. Racially it
contains all types, from black Dravidians to fair hill-men,
and its languages number nearly a hundred and fifty. Two-
thirds of the population are Hindus, so divided by castes
as to have little cohesion, while the Moslems, though less
than one-third as numerous, are more than able to hold their
own, thanks to their physique and courage. They supply a
very large proportion of the native troops, while the Hindus
supply most of the clerks. The small sect of Parsees also have
disproportionate importance, thanks to their great wealth
and ability. Indian princes whose views may be national
but are seldom Liberal, rule one-fifth of the population.
These facts have made it easy to " divide and rule," but they
make it difficult to hand over control as has been done in
colonies of Europeans.

English sympathisers inspired educated Indians to hold
the first Indian National Congress in 1885. During the next
twenty years unrest of the European "anarchist" type
increased. In 1909, when Morley was Secretary of State
and Minto Viceroy, the first big reforms were made. They
were followed in 1919, as the reward for great Indian services
during the World War, by Montague-Chelmsford reforms,
which introduced self-government into the Provinces and

creased the representation of Indians in the Viceroy's
Council and Legislative Council.

There had been unrest during the War, and measures against
sedition (the Rowlatt Act) provoked resistance organised by
Gandhi, in the course of which a serious riot took place at
Amritsar (1919) with much loss of life.

A BACKWARD PEOPLE SUPREME IN CULTURE AND ART

THE enormous State of China had become an empire
before the time of Christ, and with many vicissitudes it
remained united. Its last ruling dynasty, the Manchus, arose
in the seventeenth century. The Portuguese and other nations
traded with its southern ports from 1511 onwards and the
English East India Company built up a considerable trade,
taking tea from China and importing Indian products,
including opium. Two wars were fought over this opium
trade, which did not contribute to the credit of England. She
gained a port, Hong Kong, in 1842 and other ports were
opened to foreign trade. The barbarous and grotesque side
of Chinese life as compared with Western culture must not
hide its achievements : it had a tradition of civilisation much
longer and less broken than that of Europe, and had done
great things in art. Its religion (Confucianism) was one of
the best of the non-Christian religions, and its bureaucratic
government by the most highly educated persons had all the
virtues of bureaucracy, if it also had the defects.

During the nineteenth century Russia encroached on the
Amur and Usuri, and Great Britain, France, and Germany under
various pretexts obtained naval and commercial bases. Even
Japan was able to bully her big neighbour, organise immigration
from Japan into Manchuria, and provoke a war in 1894 which
gave her Formosa and other territory and made Korea independent. As a climax, Russia deprived Japan of part of her
gains.

European powers encouraged their business men to obtain
concessions and make loans, and much exploitation, along
with some beneficial development, occurred. Meanwhile the
exasperation of the Chinese ruling class had not been diminished by the excellent work done by missionaries of the various
Christian churches. The old Empress took the government
from her nephew in 1898, suppressed a Chinese reform party,
and encouraged a society of " Patriotic Fists " (hence called
the Boxers) to murder foreigners, particularly missionaries

and converts. An international force was sent to relieve t'
besieged survivors in Peking. After some heavy fighting t'
Chinese Government gave way and made reparation.

For some years the Government tried to modernise t'
education, administration, transport, and army of the
cumbrous empire. The reform party in 1911–12 brush
the infant Emperor Pu Yi's Regency Government aside an
set up a Republic, with a President, Vice-President, Executi
Ministry, and House of Representatives. The difficulties
welding a state of such size soon became obvious, and twen
years of anarchy followed. This empire with its vast numb
of inhabitants with their strength, intelligence, and capaci
for discipline, must inevitably affect world history during tl
twentieth century.

AUSTRALASIA: FROM BUSHRANGER TO TEST MATCH DAYS

THE coasts of Australia were explored and mapped (
considerable risk to small sailing vessels), the interi
was explored, and the great central desert was crossed. Settle
made good, in spite of drought and the hardships of a ne
country. The several Australian colonies established in tl
1820's and 1830's were given self-government comparativel
soon. The last State to receive it was Western Australia
1890. The discovery of gold in 1851 in what became tl
State of Victoria, and later in Western Australia, brought man
immigrants, including a large Irish element. In its earl
lawlessness Australia resembled the Western States of Americ
and the bushranger, or armed mailcoach and bank robbe
survived into the Test Match era.

The Australian Aborigines, small tribes of Stone Age peopl
who at one time numbered nearly a million, have been reduce
to fewer than a hundred thousand. This is the same fat
as has befallen the far more warlike and predatory Indians
North America. In both cases the process of extirpation wa
assisted by their susceptibility to diseases to which European
have developed resistance, and by the European's liquor.

After the dwindling away of the Aborigines large tracts c
Northern Australia were very thinly populated, and towards th
end of last century this almost vacant territory became c
considerable interest to the rising power of Japan, whos
territory was by European standards already overpopulated
The urgent necessity of a common policy towards Japa
overcame the reluctance of the Australian colonies to federat

fter their individual attainment of self-government.   Local
eeling was very strong.   The colonies, placed round the coast
f the great island, were not in close touch with each other.
ach could trade direct with the world and control its own
ustoms duties, and railways had been built with different
auges in order to reduce contacts.   However, in 1901 the
Commonwealth of Australia was formed.   Like Canada,
t left considerable powers to the separate States, and the
ountry was overgoverned.   Although New Zealand did not
oin the Commonwealth a unanimous anti-Japanese policy
vas effectively maintained in Australasia.   The most striking
eature of Australian development is the concentration of
opulation in a few big cities.

New Zealand has a cooler, damper climate than Australia,
and its lack of minerals has given it a different economic
development and social life.   It is also different in having a
strong native race, the Maoris, of Polynesian origin.   There
were long Maori wars, originating in disputes over land,
since natives, as is not surprising, often find difficulty in
maintaining existence without it.   New Zealand was given
self-government in 1852 and was very fortunate in at least one
of her early Governors, Sir George Grey.   The Maori wars
ended in 1870, and, after a period of great financial difficulty,
New Zealand became prosperous.   Its population has grown
to more than one million, and it is distinguished for its advanced
social legislation.

DUTCH AND ENGLISH CLASH IN AFRICA

THE Dutch calling station at the Cape of Good Hope was
first occupied in 1795 in the interests of the British East
India Company.   The small population was mainly Dutch
in nationality and Dutch-German-Huguenot by ancestry.
In 1836–38 its more restless element trekked across the Orange
River to Natal and across the Vaal River, partly because they
were squeezed out by British settlers, partly because they resented the abolition of serfdom among Hottentots and the
emancipation of slaves.   Natal was annexed as a British Colony.
Small quantities of gold were discovered in the Matabele
country and in the Transvaal in 1867–73; diamonds were
found in Griqualand in 1869 and the biggest gold reefs of the
world in the Transvaal in 1886.   The economic life of the barren
and droughty interior was revolutionised.   Meanwhile, there
had been wars about land with the stubborn Bantu tribes, and

an attempt in the 'seventies to federate South Africa led to small British war with the Transvaal and the celebrated skirmish of Majuba (1881).

For the next twenty years the history of South Africa could be written as that of a duel between Kruger, the Boer President of the Transvaal, and Cecil Rhodes, the young Englishman who made £6,000,000 out of diamonds and gold and became Prime Minister of the Cape Colony. The Transvaal was hemmed in as England annexed Bechuanaland and coastal territory, while Rhodes annexed Mashona-Matabeleland (1890–93); the two territories were re-named Rhodesia. Rhodes had very far-reaching plans for the extension of British dominions during the general scramble for Africa. Impatience caused him to promote a plot in 1895 to conquer the Transvaal in the interests of the "Uitlanders" or foreign immigrants (mostly British) who had gone into the Transvaal to work in the gold mines, and to whom the Boer inhabitants displayed reluctance to give representation in their parliament. Rhodes' lieutenant, Jameson, against orders, invaded the Transvaal prematurely and failed. The incident was not unpopular in England, but it gave continental nations an excuse for loosing their accumulated dislike of their exasperatingly rich neighbour. From this incident, in fact, Anglo-German enmity dates. The Uitlander question led to war in 1899, an unexpectedly long and inglorious struggle. The Boers surrendered on very favourable terms in 1902, were given self-government in the Transvaal and Orange Free State in 1907, and in 1910 the Union of South Africa united them with the Cape Colony and Natal.

THE MISTAKE ENGLAND MADE ABOUT IRELAND

THE English policy of three centuries had left Ireland at the beginning of the nineteenth century with a strongly Presbyterian settlement in Ulster, a class of Anglican landlords in the South, and nearly eight million Catholic peasants, dispossessed of their lands, existing in appalling poverty. The history of Ireland henceforward was a local specimen of the nationalist and agrarian problems which were common on the Continent. Catholic emancipation in 1829 came too late: it had been extorted by threats of rebellion. The famine of 1845 led to a reduction of nearly fifty per cent in the population, partly by death, partly by emigration. These Irish emigrants, needless to say, took with them to America and Australia

a keen dislike of England and intensified whatever unpopularity of England may have existed, while in London the repute
of Parliament was lowered by the campaign in favour of
Irish Home Rule carried on after 1880. Home Rule, as then
advocated by the Irish and their Liberal allies, was a much milder
thing than the independence which Ireland has enjoyed since
1922. It was unpopular with (probably) a majority of English
people because of the strong anti-Catholic feeling that still
existed, and because it appeared to be impossible to disentangle
the Protestants, either in Ulster or in the South, from the
Catholic population. The Home Rule scheme was therefore
delayed, though measures for promoting the welfare of the
Catholic peasantry and enabling them to buy land were put
into force.

STRUGGLES FOR NATIONAL UNITY

AFTER the failure of 1848 in Italy, the realist, Cavour, in
1852 became Prime Minister of Sardinia under the new
king, Victor Emmanuel. He carried out Liberal reforms in that
small state, and, in the Crimean War of 1854–56, assisted England and the Emperor of the French, Napoleon III., as Louis
Napoleon Bonaparte had become. Napoleon had a quite
erroneous theory that the tradition of the great Napoleon
demanded the protection of small nationalities, and was
anxious to gain reputation by setting up some kind of national
state in Italy, provided that it was not strong enough to rival
France. An agreement was made in 1858; France and
Sardinia were to fight Austria, add Lombardo Venetia to the
Kingdom of Sardinia, and form an Italian federation under
the presidency of the Pope. France was to receive Savoy and
Nice. Next year Cavour goaded Austria into declaring war
on Sardinia, to whose help France at once came.

There was a brief campaign in North Italy, but a distaste
for carnage was a pleasing trait in Napoleon III., and the effect
of the bloody scenes of Solferino was strengthened by Prussian
activity on the Rhine. Tuscany and the small duchies of
north-central Italy also invited Victor Emmanuel to annex
them. This, too, was disconcerting to Napoleon. He abruptly
made an armistice with Austria, the terms of peace including
the cession to Sardinia of Lombardy, but not of Venice. He
obtained Savoy and Nice, and withdrew. Garibaldi then
raised a rebellion in the Kingdom of Naples.

AN UNPRACTICAL LEADER WHO OVERTHREW KINGDOMS

BESIDE the practical, judicious, far-sighted Cavour, Garibaldi was a strange, romantic figure, devoid of judgment, but able to lead men and to overthrow kingdoms. He had previously, as a republican, been in conflict with the Sardinian monarchy. Sailing secretly from Genoa with his thousand red shirts, he raised a revolt in Sicily. The Bourbon government's mercenary troops were outmatched by Garibaldi's irregular forces. England discouraged Austrian intervention. Garibaldi overran Sicily and Naples, proclaimed himself Dictator, and prepared to invade the Pope's dominions. Victor Emmanuel and Cavour persuaded Napoleon that it was essential that they should occupy the Papal States, which they did, and Garibaldi in the south was prevailed on to accept Victor Emmanuel as king. He then withdrew to live in the small island of Caprera. The Pope retained Rome and its immediate vicinity, Austria held Venice, but the rest of Italy—twenty-three million souls—was now unified, and amid genuine enthusiasm from every part of his very heterogeneous dominions, Victor Emmanuel opened an Italian parliament at Turin.

Very soon afterwards Cavour died at the age of fifty-one. The union of Italy was his work more than any one else's, and he is also entitled to credit for his Liberal policy in Piedmont and the Liberal features of the Italian constitution.

His king, Victor Emmanuel, had the princely qualities of discernment and modesty. He was destined to complete Cavour's work and save it from the reaction which might easily have followed. The republican, Mazzini, the other great name of this *Risorgimento*, or resurrection of Italy, would not acknowledge the work of Cavour and Victor Emmanuel. He had for thirty years been engaged in republican plots against the Sardinian government (in its unregenerate phase before 1848) and against the Austrians, and he condemned Garibaldi's compromise. No one did so much to keep Italian nationalism alive during the 'thirties and 'forties, or to gain it the goodwill of educated people in England. He regarded Cavour and Victor Emmanuel as cunning materialists who stole the fruits of other men's devotion, and made a tool of the unsubtle Garibaldi. Though he might with advantage have remembered the fable of the dog who lost the bone for the shadow, he expressed the noblest side of national feeling, and emphasised the duties as well as the rights of man.

Greatly though these eminent men disliked each other, they agreed in subordinating other hatreds to detestation of Napoleon III. Specimens of invective can be found in the verse of Swinburne. Yet mixed as Napoleon's motives were, he alone made it possible to fight the Austrian army. He obtained no gratitude ; French nationalism was alarmed by the strong rival state in the Mediterranean area, while French clerics did not welcome the humiliations inflicted on the Pope. Rome had now to be garrisoned by French troops.

THE POPE RETIRES FROM POLITICS

VICTOR EMMANUEL was harassed by repeated attempts on Garibaldi's part to seize Rome, and by the knowledge that Austria would soon strike back. He found an ally in Bismarck, the Prussian Chancellor, and in 1866, therefore, while Prussia was defeating Austria in Bohemia, Italy attacked her by land and sea, and, though Italy was defeated, Bismarck saw that she got Venetia. The withdrawal of the French garrison from Rome during the Franco-Prussian War of 1870 gave Italy her traditional capital. The step was ratified by a suspiciously unanimous plebiscite, and the Pope became henceforward a voluntary prisoner in the Vatican. For a time the temporal power of the Papacy was ended, to be restored in miniature form in 1929, but the doctrine of Papal Infallibility had been confirmed by a recent Church Council, and the spiritual power of the Pope has increased considerably since.

Austria still ruled some Italians in the Trentino, but Italy was virtually united. Her actions as a nation between 1870 and 1915 did singularly little to justify the spiritual claims of Nationality advanced by Mazzini.

FRANCE UNDER NAPOLEON III.

NAPOLEON III. was now to be the chopping-block on which a stronger man than he or even Cavour hacked out a united Germany. Detested by his Liberal contemporaries as an unscrupulous plotter, which he certainly was, though an unsuccessful one, Napoleon was at the same time a man of much culture and kindliness, who was the victim of the military tradition which Napoleon I. had associated with the family name. Having been elected President of the French Republic, he broke all his pledges and forcibly made himself first President for ten years (1851) and then Emperor (1852). Each *coup d'état* was ratified by plebiscite, but there was always a party which detested him, and it grew. He tried to give the French what he believed they most wanted—military glory abroad and good government at home. His attack on Russia in the Crimea was successful, and his war in Italy produced victories. Meanwhile, he rebuilt Paris, encouraged commerce and industry and enacted social reforms, while keeping up a parliamentary system which was partially representative but did not include responsible government, its powers corresponding roughly to those of the House of Commons under James I.

During the 'sixties France remained to all appearance the leading state of Europe, but the despot, the vital spark of the whole organism, was losing his hold on events. He suffered from stone in the kidney, and pain incapacitated him from work and decision. In these circumstances the influence of the Empress Eugénie increased, an influence as disastrous in its effects as that of Marie Antoinette or of Charles I.'s queen, Henrietta Maria.

BISMARCK : A MASTER OF FINESSE

IN the year when Napoleon made his compact with Cavour, the feeble King of Prussia gave way to a regent, his brother William I., famous for having shot down rebels in Berlin in 1848. The Regent (king after 1861) began by setting Roon, the War Minister, and Moltke, the Chief of Staff, to enlarge the army. The Prussian Diet, which was largely Liberal in composition, disliked the increase of taxation necessitated. William in 1862 appointed Otto von Bismarck to be Chancellor and empowered him to collect taxes without the authority of parliament. As Moltke carried through his army reforms, Bismarck looked round for material with which to pacify the indignant Liberals. These Liberals were further disgusted by the support which Bismarck gave the Russian Tsar during the Polish rebellion of 1863 : the Tsar suppressed it with ferocity and remained under an obligation to Prussia.

Bismarck's mastiff countenance and habit of wearing uniform represented one side of his character, but his success was due to a *finesse* generally associated with Renaissance Italy rather than with modern Germany. His achievement was to take one of the aims of the German Liberals, the union of

Germany, which the Prussian monarchy had hitherto thwarted, and, by helping them to attain it, to defeat their Liberal aims, and impose the military and autocratic character of Prussia on all Germany. Any dislike we may feel for the Prussian system should not blind us to the energy of its servants—nobles, soldiers, and civil servants, and perhaps above all, its efficient schoolmasters, with their inculcation of military patriotism.

In 1864 a dispute over the sovereignty of Schleswig and Holstein caused a war between the German *Bund* and a rashly confident Denmark. The Prussian and Austrian forces overran the smaller country. The war gratified most people in Prussia, and Bismarck now found support against the Liberals. Out of the occupation of the duchies Bismarck fomented a quarrel with Austria in 1866. Europe expected the war to be long and indecisive. It ended decisively, in seven weeks, in favour of Prussia. Napoleon III. had intended to intervene when the combatants were exhausted : he did not get the chance. Bismarck made a very lenient peace ; the cession of Venetia to Italy and the withdrawal of Austria from the German *Bund* left Francis Joseph with very little desire for revenge.

In place of the *Bund* a new North German Confederation was formed, an enlargement of Prussia, which absorbed all the smaller supporters of Austria, while a number of States in the south-west (principally Bavaria) remained independent.

ONE EMPIRE ENDS AND ANOTHER BEGINS

THE accession to power of Prussia caused such alarm in France that Napoleon made proposals to Bismarck for " compensation " in Bavaria or Belgium, according to the balance-of-power principle. The French ambassador committed these suggestions to writing, and in 1870 Bismarck published them, to the fury of Bavaria and of Belgium and her friends, particularly England. The discontent which is endemic in modern states was now in France turning against the Emperor.

In 1869 the Liberal Empire began, with a completely responsible ministry under Olivier ; but it was too late to free the Emperor of responsibility. His Liberal subjects had been annoyed in 1863, when he failed to protect the Poles, though his avowed sympathy with them added to the enmity of the Tsar. His " Mexican Adventure " of 1864-67 had brought him disgrace : he had persuaded the Archduke Maximilian, a rather unruly brother of the Austrian Emperor, to become Emperor of Mexico as a tool of French financiers. When the United States ended its Civil War and demanded his immediate withdrawal in accordance with President Monroe's principles, Napoleon ordered the return of the French army and left Maximilian to be overcome by his native Mexican opponents and executed.

Napoleon had ventured to play a part for which he had neither the ability nor the nerve. Like the first Bonaparte he had an enormous faith in his destiny, but the first Napoleon had done everything that human energy could to assist destiny. Against the Emperor of the French was Bismarck, backed by the force that even in weaker hands would have decided the issue, the Prussian army of Moltke.

An excuse for war came unexpectedly in 1870. Spain had got rid of its disreputable Queen, Isabella, and was looking for a royalty to take her place. The *Cortes* (Spanish Parliament), possibly instigated by Prussian agents, offered the crown to a Hohenzollern, a Catholic, more nearly related to Napoleon than to the King of Prussia, but a Prussian officer. The French government demanded his withdrawal, which was agreed to by Prussia, and then in deference to newspaper excitement demanded an undertaking that Prussia would never allow the prince to renew his candidature. The King of Prussia at Ems politely informed the ambassador that he really could not promise anything of the sort; then Bismarck insulted France by publishing the news in a courteous but somewhat abrupt form. The German and French newspapers did the rest. The French ministry, misled by the Minister of War, declared war. It was the first war to be made by newspapers, but not the last. France was technically and morally the aggressor, but her opponent was overjoyed to be attacked.

Within seven weeks the Prussian and German armies had overwhelmed the French, who were brave and well armed, but badly mobilised, badly led, and somewhat outnumbered. Napoleon surrendered at Sedan. A larger force surrendered later at Metz. Paris set up a provisional government and stood a six months' siege ; meanwhile Thiers unsuccessfully tried to get allies, and Gambetta raised large armies, which had small success against the Germans. Paris surrendered in January 1871, and peace was made in the following

May, France paying a comparatively small indemnity (£200,000,000) and ceding Alsace and Lorraine—two provinces which had once been part of the Holy Roman Empire and were still largely German. Sentiment in them was in general opposed to the transfer, and the French vowed to recover them. At Versailles itself the German princes invited the King of Prussia to become German Emperor, and on his reluctant acquiescence he was crowned there in the splendid palace of Louis XIV. The ceremony was almost entirely military.

The Constitution of the new German Empire allowed Prussia to control the military forces, but not the civil administration of the kingdoms and small states which were included in it. The Parliamentary system resembled that of James I.'s day in England, or that of the United States or a British Crown Colony : the Chancellor and ministers were officials, responsible to the Emperor and not to the *Reichstag* or Chamber of Commons. The Federal Senate represented the separate state governments. Under modern conditions power falls (in the absence of parliamentary control) into the hands of bureaucrats, civil and military, and this was what happened in Germany.

A COMMUNIST INTERREGNUM

A DIRECT outcome of these events was the incident of the Paris Commune. A republic was set up, but a strong party under Thiers wished to restore the Orleans monarchy. Another party wished to restore the Bourbons. The republic defiantly ordained the establishment of government by local communes, and in the Commune of Paris [1] the elected leaders proposed further reforms. The royalist and orthodox republican parties employed the army to suppress them. Paris was reconquered at an appalling cost in bloodshed, both in action and in executions. She lost in all eighty thousand lives. McMahon, an avowed royalist, became

---

[1] In the Marxist interpretation of history, the institution of the Paris Commune takes a most important place, for not only is it held to be the first revolt of the industrial working class against the capitalist system, but it also offered valuable lessons to the communists in their pursuance of the Class Struggle. It is held by the Marxist to have failed chiefly because of the indecision at vital moments of its leaders, the intellectuals, among them the famous socialist thinker, Louis Blanc.

president in 1873, but a royalist restoration was obviously unwelcome, and the republic continued. The constitution of the Third Republic, which has lasted to the present day, was largely a copy of the English constitution of the same period. The President is invested with advisory and exhortatory powers. The Senate, corresponding to the House of Lords, has a longer and more continuous life than the Chamber of Deputies, corresponding to the House of Commons, to which ministers are responsible.

Despite the short lives of French governments, there has been strong continuity in French policy. The French constitution has proved that there is nothing in the French national character incompatible with parliamentary government, but that fitness for parliamentary government is a matter of time and training. The chief political weaknesses of modern France have been corruption among officials and politicians and the hostility to the republic of the clerical and military party, while the system of numerous small parliamentary groups makes for bargains and illicit arrangements.

HOW ENGLAND KEPT TURKEY'S EMPIRE ALIVE

WE have seen something of the long struggle of the Tsardom and Turkey for Balkan territory. Turkey, whose westward progress had ceased after her defeat at Lepanto in 1571 and her failure at Vienna in 1683, could count during the nineteenth century on the support of the Conservative politicians in England. Less open than the Liberals to the sentimental and humanitarian appeal of oppressed nationalities, they cherished profound fears of Russian designs on India, the Levant, and (after 1876) the Suez Canal, and therefore were willing to condone Turkey's lapses if she would obstruct the expansion of Russia. But for England's support, the Turkish Empire would have disappeared from Europe about 1860.

Nicholas I., Tsar from 1825 to 1855, alarmed the English with his proposals for the partitioning of the property of " the sick man of Europe," as he called Turkey, and in 1852-3 the Emperor of the French picked a quarrel with Russia. There was old and bitter enmity between the Tsars and the Bonapartes. The origin of the new dispute was the rival claims of the Greek and Roman Churches, backed respectively by the Tsar and France, to guard the sacred places in Jerusalem, but it was aggravated by the claim, tantamount to that of overlordship, of the Tsar to be the protector of all Christians in the Sultan's empire. But both parties were ready to fight on any grounds, and so was England, while Sardinia presently entered for reasons of her own. It would to-day be regarded as a perfect instance of a mistaken war, but English people were almost unanimous in demanding it, and the few men who opposed it, notably John Bright, ran the risk of violent treatment.

It deserves to be remembered as the worst-managed British expedition of the last three centuries. France and England sent small armies to the Crimea—they also shelled some Baltic towns—the War Office providing neither shelter nor clothing nor food above summer field-day scale. The sufferings of the troops, principally from sickness, but also in a number of bungled battles, gave an opportunity to Florence Nightingale and other ladies to organise a nursing service, and incidentally to open a new employment to educated women.

The terms of peace, made at Paris in 1856, were all broken within a few years, including the promises made by the Sultan to ameliorate his government, but the English object of checking Russia was gained for a time. Two outlying Turkish provinces, Moldavia and Wallachia, inhabited by Christians, were declared neutral states. They united a few years later as Rumania. The disgraces and administrative scandals of the war helped to kill the Tsar.

The new Tsar, Alexander II. (1855–81), extended his territories to the south-east and in 1861 abolished serfdom in Russia. Alexander realised the need for reform and was prepared to override obstructive nobles and officials, but lacked the vigour that such a task demanded. In 1863 he repressed a Polish revolt with ferocity, and renewed cordial relations with Prussia. Then in 1872 Bismarck went on from his triumph over France to form the famous *Drei-Kaiserbund*, or League of Three Emperors, between the Tsar, the new German Emperor, and his former enemy, the Emperor Francis Joseph of Austria. It placed the recently created German Empire in a position of extraordinary strength, confident in its great army, allied for defence to the two other great military powers and on very friendly terms with the naval power, England; while France had no friend in Europe. Bismarck nearly entered into another war with France in 1875, but was restrained by the Tsar.

1878—A LANDMARK IN THE EASTERN QUESTION

THE chief national masses under the Turk were of very varying racial origins, religion, traditions, and even language ; they were full of intense hatreds for each other as well as for their common enemy, the Turk. The Sultan's savagery towards his Bulgarian subjects in 1876 gave an excuse for Russia to employ diplomatic methods against him, and on their failure, to invade Turkey. The Turks fought well, as usual, but were beaten and agreed by the Treaty of San Stefano (1878) to give up the greater part of their European dominions. Disraeli, the Prime Minister of Queen Victoria, was prepared to go to war to save Turkey, while his Liberal opponents were in favour of expelling the Turks " bag and baggage" from the provinces which are now Bulgaria. Austria watched in considerable discomfort and jealousy, and Bismarck, as Chancellor of a power with no direct interest in the Eastern question, invited the other parties to a conference at Berlin. He took Disraeli more seriously than Disraeli's contemporaries usually did, and together they compelled Russia to agree to terms very advantageous to Austria. Despite the League of the Three Emperors the time very soon came when Germany had to choose between Russia and Austria, and she chose Austria, because that power was believed to be more docile and dependable than Russia and because it was difficult to be friendly with Russia and England together.

The Treaty of Berlin (1878) bridged the way from the little Crimean War to the epoch of big wars between 1911 and 1922—wars all linked with the Eastern question. By the Treaty Austria was given the administration of Bosnia and Herzegovina ; the territories were to remain under Turkish sovereignty, but Austria, after conquering them from their own rather unruly inhabitants, was to give them the blessings of Christian rule and to see that no massacres occurred. Russia restored Eastern Rumelia, which was given autonomy, as was Bulgaria, the latter under a German prince tributary to the Sultan ; Eastern Rumelia and Bulgaria were very soon united. Rumania, which had supported Russia, gained the recognition of her independence, but had to cede Bessarabia to Russia and in return was given most of the Dobrudja, to which she had no claim on ethnological grounds. Great Britain obtained Cyprus, and Disraeli was able to return and

to revive a sixty-year-old phrase about " peace with honour "
to describe the balance-of-power bargain that he had struck.

PROGRESS IMPEDED BY IGNORANCE AND SAVAGERY

TURKEY and Russia had always lagged behind the civilised
countries of Europe, and their rate of progress had for
many years been slower. The Turks, a race of Central
Asiatic origin, lived as peasants in Asia Minor or soldiered
and " administered " subject Christians in the Balkans, amid
relics of the Roman and Byzantine Empires. The Turk had
some of the virtues of the Mohammedan man of arms, and
these qualities sometimes endeared him to foreigners. But
his ignorance, laziness, and savagery were not to be explained
except by downright stupidity. The Moslem religion and
the Turkish dress, language, and alphabet tended to sever
him from civilising European influences, and to maintain the
feeling that he was an alien intruder.

Even in Russia there was an Asiatic strain under the
Western varnish of the Government and Court. There was,
too, more than a hint of Asiatic savagery in the methods of
rule. Until 1905 there was no pretence of parliamentary
government. The Tsar, in theory, ruled as Napoleon or
Louis XIV. had done ; in practice, he was in the hands of
his officials and generals ; and the central and provincial
governments were considerably more military than even those
of Germany and Austria. The secret police and spies, the
exile of political offenders, and the frequent use of bayonets
and the lash were regarded as legitimate and necessary
weapons against revolutionary movements. These movements, however, were to a large extent a natural reaction
against obsolete methods of government, whose corruption
was demonstrated clearly by the failure of Imperial Russia
during her wars—the Crimean War, the Japanese War of
1904–05, and the World War of 1914–18.

During the nineteenth and early twentieth centuries Russia
was the object of intense detestation by Liberals in western
countries. In England this feeling dovetailed with Conservative apprehensions about India and the Mediterranean
—the Russians were menacing the North-West Frontier and
the Bosphorus—and produced an anti-Russian opinion which
remained solid until overcome by fear of Germany. In
Germany there were also Liberals who disliked tyranny in the
abstract, and by all Germans, Liberal or militarist, Russia's

enormous area and population were assumed to be capable of producing immense forces in war.

MURMURS OF SOCIAL DISCONTENT : FABIANS AND ANARCHISTS

DISTURBANCES under the Tsardom before the 'seventies had mainly been national affairs—in Poland or Finland, for example—but there had long been a Liberal section among the small educated class, lawyers, journalists, certain civil servants and a few nobles ; Russia now became the home of the most extreme reforming movement of recent times. Socialism had been crystallised by Karl Marx during his exile in England (1849-83). His book *Das Kapital* (1867) expounded the influence of material conditions on the social development of Man, the production of all value by labour, and the tendency for employers or capitalists to absorb everything above a bare subsistence allowance for the workmen. Marx also popularised the term " proletariat " as a description of the working class.

His book was more vigorous than any apologies that capitalism could then make. Marx and his various colleagues and rivals gained considerable followings on the continent and there were writers who, secretly in Russia, and more openly in exile, advocated similar views, with much dispute as to Marx's meaning. Stepniak, Bakunin, and, later, Kropotkin were among revolutionary leaders, and Tolstoy, the great novelist, without being actively revolutionary, was sympathetic. Freedom of speech and of the press did not fully exist in Russia : the censorship was active spasmodically, and open advocacy of reform might be grounds for exile.

The revolutionary movement of the last quarter of the nineteenth century included academic socialists at one extreme, like the highly respectable English Fabians, who proposed to reform capitalist society gradually and by persuasion ; at the other were the persons known as Nihilists in Russia and Anarchists in Italy and other countries. In theory they desired the destruction of all forms of government—the negation of Socialism, in whatever sense that word is taken, but in practice their views had something in common with what we call Communism. They rapidly made an impression by a series of assassinations in the 'eighties and 'nineties. Tsar Alexander was assassinated in 1881, after which the Russian government repressed Nihilism with much rigour. The French and American Presidents, the Empress of Austria, and the Kings of Italy and Portugal met the same fates in the 'nineties. Many other political murders were attempted and " terrorism " was well known in Europe before the end of the century. Lenin, an able young bourgeois, was already active, though not as a terrorist.

AMERICA : THE FEUD BETWEEN NORTH AND SOUTH BEGINS

THE United States of America had by the middle of the century a population, still recruited mainly from North-Western Europe, larger than that of Great Britain. It included four million negro slaves in the Southern States of the eastern (Atlantic) coast. Settlement had spread westward, over the Alleghanies and across the plains, until the Mississippi was passed. The discovery of gold in California in 1848 caused a rush by land and by sea to the goldfields, and several States were established on the Pacific coast. The gap between the Mississippi and the Rockies was slowly settled on between 1867 and 1910.

The American settlers rapidly developed local allegiances. This was most marked in the Northern and Southern States of the east, the boundary between which was the southern border of Pennsylvania, the Mason-Dixon line : south of it were the States where slaves were owned, north were those which had no slaves and, usually, on whose territory a slave could not remain a slave. This question of slavery was not by any means the main cause of enmity between the groups, but it rapidly focused it.

The Northern States with their industry, small mixed farms, good education, energy and acquisitiveness, detested what they regarded as the drawling insolence of the Southerner, whether he were one of the plantation owners who had inherited, or more probably assumed, the Cavalier tradition, or one of the more numerous types of poor white. The South despised and disliked the North for its hustle and crudity, and it needed only a dispute over economic interests to lend these social animosities deep meaning.

Two such disputes arose. The first was the desire of the South, which lived by exporting cotton, to admit European and particularly English manufactured goods at low rates, while the industrial Northern States desired heavy tariffs. The second was slavery. Public opinion in the Northern States consistently condemned slavery on moral grounds, while the South regarded slavery as an institution of vital economic importance and of divine origin. Disagreement on these questions was absorbed in the general question whether State or Federal law was to prevail, and whether States not in agreement with the majority could secede from the Union which they had made.

Now that the very name of slavery has an unpleasant sound, it is often attempted to represent the American Civil War as a contest about anything else and to stress the fact that there were many anti-slavers in the South, who fought solely for State rights. The North certainly detested slave owners more than it loved slaves, but to construe the anti-slavery movement as merely spiteful is quite unfair to the great body of intelligent and humane opinion in the North. The Southerners who disliked slavery generally regarded it as perfectly good if managed on Christian principles ; and the great mass of Southerners, both those who owned slaves and the much larger class who did not, simply regarded the negro as dirt, with none of the rights or feelings of a man.

It is argued sometimes that slave owners did not maltreat slaves, because it did not pay them to do so. This argument does not hold good if the slave owner can get a large supply of new slaves ; he will then find it pays to use up slaves quickly. Even if he cannot, the relationship usually brings out a sadistic strain similar to that which in Latin races is sometimes roused by power over animals. At the best, this economic consideration would not touch the worst injustices of slavery, the prostitution of slave women and the separation of slave families. Apart from moral considerations, slave labour cannot be efficient ; and it is always enervating to the ruling class. The South was destined to be ruined by the cost of the Civil War, but the liberation of the slaves was, economically, a blessing.

TARIFF AND SLAVERY ADD FUEL TO THE FLAME

THE European nations had abolished the actual trade in slaves at dates between 1801 and 1815, but American ships continued the trade, with the horrors of the passage and of the native wars which it stimulated. In 1820 the famous Missouri compromise was made. Missouri was admitted as a slave state, but all the states existing or still to be formed north of the latitude 36° 30′ were to be free. This gave twelve slave and twelve free states. The future, however, rested with the free party, as the area open to them for expansion was much greater than that open to the slave states.

A fierce quarrel occurred in 1828–32 when the Federal government, controlled by the North, enacted a heavy tariff on imported goods, which South Carolina defied, in the end with success. A war with Mexico was fought in 1846–48, largely in Southern interests, and territory was gained for slavery. California, however, came in as a free state. A further compromise was made in 1850 providing for the return of runaway slaves, and in 1854 the Missouri compromise was set aside, Kansas and Nebraska, north of the line, being allowed to decide their condition by vote. There was a local civil war of murders and ambushes between the two parties, who included the usual large proportion of plain gunmen, passionately devoted to causes which they did not well understand. Whether or not John Brown was one of them, or something better, is uncertain—most probably the latter. After taking a bloody part in the Kansas disorder, he tried to raise a slave rebellion in Virginia, failed, and was hanged in 1859.

Meanwhile there was a growing demand in the North for action to end slavery. The Southerners might easily have ignored it, since it could not have obtained the necessary majority of States, House of Representatives, and Senate, required by the Constitution to carry such an amendment, but the last straw came when Abraham Lincoln, an Illinois politician who had been a leading advocate of abolition, was elected President in 1860. Lincoln's rise to prominence was in the teeth of great handicaps and formidable rivals, and the whole question of his motives is rather obscure. It seems fairly clear that at first he intended to prevent the extension of slavery, but not to abolish it where it existed. The South, however, took alarm and early in 1861 South Carolina seceded from the Union, and was joined by the other slave-owning states. Practically all the non-slave states supported Lincoln, though the support of the new West was not active.

THE TERRIBLE COST OF THE FOUR YEARS' WAR

LINCOLN fought, not on the moral question of slavery, but on what he may have thought was the surer legal ground, that a state or states had no right to secede from the Union. It was a time when the discovery and unification of new nationalities was, as we have seen, the chief interest of statesmen, though Lincoln's view may seem to outsiders to be baseless in law. As the eleven states persisted in their secession, they were, as rebels, disfranchised, and the liberation of all slaves in the United States was enacted by the Federal government in 1865 by the necessary majorities.

The war lasted four years (1861–65) and was in many respects a foretaste of the World War—in the size of its armies, their lack of training, the frequent badness of the generalship, and the heaviness of casualties. And it bore some resemblance to the World War, and to the old Civil War in England, in the position of the combatants. The South, full of natural soldiers and well led, had all the opening successes, but it was outnumbered by two to one, blockaded, outlasted in money, and finally worn down as the North discovered capable leaders. The war cost a million lives ; there were two thousand battles and skirmishes, the cost in money and loss of trade was gigantic. The South emerged ruined. The negro slaves on the plantations remained quiet even when their masters were all away.

When his cause seemed quite hopeless and his followers completely unwilling to go on—mutinying against conscription—Lincoln never yielded in his calm will to win, and he completed this attitude by the generous policy he was prepared to adopt when the war was won. Foreign aristocracies sympathised with the South, but the English working people saw only the issue of slavery, and gave the North their moral support, just as they had supported Garibaldi. The Northern blockade cut off supplies of cotton and there was severe unemployment in Lancashire.

The Confederate States, as the seceding states called themselves, were well served by Lee—as great a soldier as Wellington or Marlborough and as great a gentleman as Haig—and by " Stonewall " Jackson, whose nickname, suggestive of the unenterprising cricketer, is a very misleading epithet for a daring and skilful soldier. The North was remarkably slow, even allowing for its Anglo-Saxon origin, in finding Grant and Sherman, who played their winning cards well.

The principal battles were fought over a comparatively small area between the rival capitals, Washington and Richmond. Lee's last drive at the North was held up in the terrible battle of Gettysburg in 1863, but more important was the capture at the same time of Vicksburg, far away on the Mississippi, by the Federal forces, who had invaded the South from New Orleans. They now had the South between two claws. Next year Sherman marched across Georgia, destroying everything deliberately. The Southern resistance was collapsing during 1864. Lee surrendered in 1865. He could have carried on guerilla war for years, but was too wise. Unfortunately, Lincoln was assassinated by a fanatic, and his moderating influence was conspicuously absent during the next years. However, his great fame may perhaps be partly due to his escaping the ordeal of the reconstruction period.

ECHOES IN ENGLAND OF THE AMERICAN FEUD

SEA power had been almost decisive in this war. The Northern blockade had ruined the South, whose funds largely depended on the cotton trade. The war produced the " ironclad " battleship in a crude form. It also saw the usual friction between the United States and England about the freedom of the seas. The United States Navy, for instance, held up the *Trent*, a British vessel, to seize two Confederate emissaries, while England allowed Confederate raiders (notably the *Alabama*) to be equipped in British ports. The former incident very nearly led to war, but good sense on both sides prevailed. The *Alabama* case was submitted by Gladstone to arbitration, and the grotesque American claims were discharged for a few millions. There still were large numbers of English people who would have preferred to spend a few hundred millions on a war.

Lincoln's more or less accidental successor, President Johnson, fought hard to mitigate the terms imposed on the South, but his Congress, maddened by the four years of civil war, impeached him for his pains. The emancipation of all slaves was a reasonable condition of peace, but Congress also enfranchised the liberated slaves, and Northern adventurers (the original " carpet-baggers ") were elected by their votes to offices which gave them control of Southern State funds. The Southerners, notably in South Carolina, formed a terroristic society, the Ku Klux Klan, which, with the usual blend of buffoonery and murder, succeeded in preventing negroes from voting.

The financial effects of the war were made good inside twenty years, and even the South has progressed rapidly in recent times. The racial stock of the United States, however, was perhaps irreparably damaged by the killing, and it is not altogether certain that the negroes gained anything by being enfranchised in that particular manner.

ROMANCE REVIVED IN LIFE AND LETTERS

THERE was in the nineteenth century a great increase in the production of books—closely associated with the cheap manufacturing processes introduced by the Industrial Revolution and with the wider spread of education. There was much great poetry still to be written when the century began, but the epoch especially developed two hitherto little-known forms of literature—the Novel and the History. The century continued what is known as the Romantic Revival in verse and prose. It had begun in the eighteenth century, principally in Germany and England, and was fiercely resisted in France until the 1830's. Briefly it meant a taste for novel verse-metres, simple, not to say crude, language, and very often an interest in past times or distant places—the Middle Ages, the gorgeous East, the untrodden plains of America, or rustic life nearer home. It aroused remorseless combats between " classicists " and " romanti- cists."

There are many great names among the romantics : Goethe in Germany stands above them all. The fashion was reflected in religion with a strong revival of the Catholic and missionary spirits ; in art with Constable, Corot, the Barbizon school, and the pre-Raphaelites ; and in architecture with the re- surrection of Gothic which can be seen in half the public buildings of England, most prominently in the Houses of Parliament, planned to order by Sir Charles Barry, whose own tastes were for the Italian Renaissance, and marvellously bedizened with Gothic detail by his collaborator, Pugin. The mid-century saw industrialised tastes prevailing in archi- tecture, art, furniture, and those forms of literature which are most influenced by supply and demand. These were displaced towards the end of the century by a conventional prettiness in tangible things. Literature reacts quickly to changes in taste, and in the last decades of the century the cult of what the twentieth century languidly calls " red- bloodedness " became popular in Robert Louis Stevenson and Kipling.

Music also experienced changes. Beethoven, Schubert, Schumann, and Brahms used the old forms to express

Romantic feeling, while Liszt and Berlioz expressed their Byronic emotions in descriptive or " programme " music. In the 'forties and 'fifties the uncouth genius of Wagner created the same storm in the world of music as Victor Hugo, the leading Romantic, had created in literature. His final triumph, however, has not reduced the prestige of his great predecessors. Towards the end of the century the subdued mystical harmonies of Debussy led the way to new departures.

A THEORY THAT CAN BE HARNESSED TO MANY IDEALS

IN philosophy there was a strong reaction against the individualism which had asserted itself in the opposition to divine right and enlightened despotism. Hegel, after Kant, the greatest of German philosophers, a contemporary of Napoleon, was the great advocate of the claims of the State, and his views agreed with the tendency to erect or hold together national states and with the growing tendency towards stricter government, which was facilitated by improvements in communications. His theory of conflict was the philosophic basis of the Marxist doctrine of the Class War. It was acceptable to the military and aristocratic governing classes in Germany and Austria. In fact, it can be harnessed to many different ideals, and it has to be judged largely by its works. Its works have generally tended towards a belief in size and force.

Unfortunately, it was associated with the most exciting intellectual discovery of the century, the theory generally known as Darwinism. One now discredited development of Darwin's research (for which the great scientist was not responsible) was a belief that as human history was a tale of the survival of the fittest, therefore brute force and animal cunning, as leading to survival, were the qualities most worthy of admiration. It is obvious that social qualities, such as self-sacrifice and co-operation, have contributed equally to survival, but this was frequently overlooked.

The mixture of Hegelianism with degenerate Darwinism was typified in Germany. The unimaginative military energy of Prussia now succeeded in perverting the intellectual life of Germany. Intellectual freedom and romantic, generous, and unpractical Liberalism did not wholly die out in Germany, but a very large number of the type of German which might have stood by them now became supporters of Prussian militarism and preposterous Prussian theories about ruling races and the will to power, which in our own day occupy a prominent place in the theories of the Nazis.

Liberal and sceptical writers, of course, persisted in various countries, and all the men and women who stood for the new Socialist ideas were at any rate hostile to military dominance. But there was a widespread impatience with the old respect for individual rights, and a tendency to favour the use of force, though rival classes and nations proposed to use it for different ends.

HOW THE SEEDS OF FASCISM WERE SOWN

THE aims of the Liberalism of the early nineteenth century were not sufficient for the regeneration of society, and there was already a demand for something new. In the early twentieth century almost everything that had been demanded a hundred years before had been attained ; life had been improved, but the chronic discontent of mankind remained and vented itself, as it usually does, on institutions. The times were preparing for the age-old theory of enlightened despotism to clothe itself in the least convincing of all the disguises it has ever worn and appear as Fascism.

Parliamentarianism failed in most countries because it demanded more civilisation than they possessed, or because the reactionary forces (as in Germany in 1914) plunged the state into a catastrophe from which everything emerged discredited. Even in the countries where the " representative " theory has survived, it is difficult for any one really to represent any one else—especially the thousands who make up his constituency. He may conceivably be the ablest man among them—though that is not probably so—but even if it were so, the assembly of the elected is merely an aristocracy of talent with certain obligations to the governed. Even if the assembly were representative in the sense of being typical, it could hardly be desirable to reproduce the limitations of ordinary people in their governors. Continental elections, in any case, were often corrupt. In France and England and the United States, the elections are correct enough in that the voting is by secret ballot and the votes are accurately counted. But the elections take place at long intervals, and too often reflect some moment of excitement, and the influence of demagogy or newspaper hysteria.

The gravest defects arose, however, in the actual working

of Parliament, and are exemplified by the development of parliamentary government. Its business became so vast and technical that what was done was often botched ; much could not be done at all. The independent member of parliament became rare, and the private member of one of the official parties had no influence. Power lay with the teams—often unseen—of civil servants who controlled departmental business, and with the groups who controlled parties. The defects of the British system were fewer than those of any other known system of government, but man's usual ignorance of his past and reckless expectations of his future always encourage discontent with his present.

PARLIAMENT MENACED BY IRISH UPHEAVAL

THE worst discredit to the British system was the case of Ireland. Ireland was represented in the House of Commons by a hundred members, eighty of whom belonged usually to the Home Rule party, being representatives of the Southern Irish Catholics. They were usually gentlemen who would normally have been Conservatives but who, for the sake of Home Rule, were prepared to ally themselves with Liberals and to employ revolutionary tactics. During the second half of the nineteenth century the claims of Ireland were asserted by organisations such as the Fenian Society, which organised rebellions—always abortive—and assassinations. Campaigns of outrage and intimidation were carried on in Ireland against the Protestant landlords, and at Westminster the Irish members under Charles Stewart Parnell's leadership, set out to make business as nearly impossible as they could, by systematic waste of time within the legal limits, and when that failed, by hooliganism.

They at last induced the Liberals to support their Home Rule proposals. Those proposals were resisted by some of the Liberal party, who would not hand over the Irish Protestants to a Catholic majority. The scheme failed in the 'eighties and broke the Liberals, but was revived actively between 1906 and 1914. It was now resisted in arms by the Ulster Protestants, with the active support of their numerous English sympathisers. At the same time, some of the advocates of Women's Suffrage were employing methods resembling the Irish tactics of the 1880's. There can be little doubt that these resorts to violence encouraged England's continental rivals to think that the Parliamentary system was collapsing.

EXPLORATIONS IN THE FIELDS OF KNOWLEDGE

MODERN science had begun with the observers and specu-lators of the seventeenth century. In the eighteenth century their work had been carried on by men like Buffon the French naturalist. As travel became safer and easier and the printing of books cheaper, scientific work made progress since it largely depends on the observation of numerous natural facts, their classification and the dissemination of the results. The early observers had to undergo much expense and hardship in their travels, and when they first attempted classification and generalisation they were working in the dark. They persevered with their work up and down their own countries, in far places of the earth and in laboratories, adding to human knowledge of botany, geology, entomology, and zoology, while stay-at-home scientists pressed on with chemistry, physics, astronomy, and mathematics. There have, of course, always been people of scientific bent, but in modern times they have been given opportunities which they never had before. During the last quarter of the century science made its way at last into schools in the form of elementary chemistry and physics and Nature study.

Towards the middle of the century the great conflict, as it is called, between science and religion began. Its issue turned on the Book of Genesis. Was the world created "catastrophically," that is, at one effort, by the Almighty a few thousand years before Christ, or did it evolve, as the geologists said, from molten matter in the course of millions of years? The problem caused acute distress to people who regarded the Bible as a literally inspired record, and their difficulties were increased as the Bible underwent the higher criticism of archæologists, historians, and philologists—mainly German—who, by applying the methods of secular study to the sacred writings, discredited many of the accepted ideas about their authorship and inspiration. The new scientific knowledge was (rather unnecessarily) thought to impugn the value of the Bible as a guide to morals.

Matters grew worse in the 'sixties after Darwin published his *Origin of the Species*, the result of many years of travel and observation. This great work put it beyond doubt that all animal species have evolved from earlier undifferentiated types, and that Man himself has evolved in the same way. Evolution was thought by Darwinians to have been carried out through the survival of the fittest, natural selection acting on small variations in living creatures. Before Darwin, and again since, there has been a tendency to believe rather in organic modification through the influence of inward impulses. The supporters of the official religious view displayed little intelligence or magnanimity, and despite the howls of ridicule and denunciation, the advocates of Darwinism made rapid progress. Wise Churchmen sacrificed Genesis and a good deal besides, or tried to reconcile it with the scientific point of view. This policy has in general prevailed, and the value of the New Testament has if anything been increased by the tendency to jettison parts of the Old Testament.

But on the whole there was a marked waning of religious ardour towards the end of the century. This does not mean that vice was rampant. On the contrary, morals and behaviour continued to improve under the pressure of education, improved methods of detecting crime, and the greater respect for public opinion which comes with a rise in social status. It may also be doubted whether the alleged cynicism and disillusion of the 'nineties was really great. It happened that there was a wave of unusually morbid affectation at the time, but its counterpart could have been found in many earlier periods. The amount of disinterested earnest endeavour was probably greater than ever before. It will be realised that a different outlook on life must result from the knowledge that Man, far from being the perfect and finished work of the Creator, is a being who has developed from something much cruder and has probably a long process of development still before him. Similarly, a new humility came from the work of the astronomers and physicists who have made plain our earth's apparently insignificant position in the Universe.

THE LITTLE RENAISSANCE OF ENGLISH EDUCATION

THE change in outlook was strongly marked in education. The old education in Latin and Greek—very unintelligently taught—which had been originally devised for a few clever boys in the fifteenth century had become the staple education for all boys able to afford a good education (one in fifty, perhaps). Elementary mathematics in schools made a very feeble beginning about the beginning of the century; modern history and modern languages, taught very badly, crept in during the third quarter, and science and geography were finally recognised. At the end of the century, however, clever boys were more often than not still kept on a diet of classics during their whole school and university career, and it appeared to give satisfactory results. It often left them ill-informed of the world, both in its scientific and economic aspects, but it served to select a type of intellect efficient in administration and politics. In other words, a person who could fight his way through a classical education could do anything that depended on the competent use of the arts of reading, writing, and speaking.

The Victorian Age was, on the whole, a time when England began to take an interest in intellectual things, though scholarship and intelligence were never respected as much as they were in France and Germany. Something of the little renaissance which occurred in English education was due to the Prince Consort, an excellent type of the intelligent German, who, but for his early death in 1863, would have made a much deeper impression on English life, and perhaps on the British Constitution, than the Queen after whom the period is named ever did.

1914 : THE GREAT CATASTROPHE

by T. G. STANDING, M.A.(Oxon.), Former Exhibitioner of New College, Oxford

THE great European and American Wars of 1854–71 were
followed only by small wars which served to show the
advance of military technique. Weapons were improved.
Gatling's crude machine-gun was superseded by the Maxim
gun, and bigger cannons were cast, while the single shot rifle
of the 'seventies gave way to a magazine rifle. Meanwhile,
conscription, first used by the French during the 1790's,
was now enforced in time of peace on nearly all young men
on the continent. Even with all possible economies the cost
was from £50 to £100 a year per man. At a day's notice
France, Russia, or Germany could have an army of four
million men preparing to move. The complicated process
of mobilisation was prepared in all details. Formerly it took
months to collect a small force and transport it to the scene of
war. Now, within a fortnight, millions of men could be
assembled, equipped, and hurried to the frontier. A few
hours' start in the first days might win or lose a campaign.
This conduced to a state of nerves and to precipitancy when
it at last appeared as if the moment had come.

There had always been humanitarian and pacifist critics
of war, and a number of significant comments on the new
warfare were made. Humanity caused international agreements to be made giving privileges to ambulance services,
and at the suggestion of the Tsar conferences were held at
The Hague (1899 and 1907) which agreed to certain mitiga-
tions of warfare—humane treatment of wounded and prisoners,
and abstention from the use of poisonous gas. War, as fought
in South Africa in 1899–1901, was not as cruel as it was at
Waterloo or in the Crimea, but it horrified a generation less
accustomed to blood, death, and pain—for among the scientific advances of the century had been the discovery of anæsthetics and a remarkable improvement in preventive medicine
and surgery.

There were certain writers who wondered what the effects
of the new discoveries would be. Bloch, a civilian, prophesied
in the 1890's that the defence, aided by the machine gun, the

9

trench, and barbed wire, had gained such advantage over the attack that war would end in stalemate. The professional went on dreaming of cavalry charges and decrying machine guns, and even the Germans, whose officers were more intellectually enlightened than those of most other nations, had not really grasped the defensive possibilities of modern weapons. People paid only lip-service to the writings of Norman Angell, who told a war-minded Europe in 1910 that under modern conditions the victor would lose as much as the vanquished and could not receive indemnities except at the expense of his own trade.

CAUSES OF WAR THAT LIE DEEP IN MEN'S MINDS

THE causes of war lie deep in the mind and traditions of man, much too deep to be driven out merely by proof that war is horrible or silly. Even this view was not generally accepted. The ceremonial and pageantry of all the great nations was military; soldiering gave a social as well as romantic stamp to a man, and there were vested interests which lived by fomenting wars. The generals and admirals lived by and for the possibility of war. Every year after 1871 took the nations further away from knowledge of what a great war really meant, made them readier for bloodletting and added to the international friction as international contact grew.

The main causes of the War of 1914–18—granted always the nationalist assumption of rivalry—were first and foremost the old feud of France and Germany : secondly, the Eastern question and the Balkan rivalry of Austria and Russia thirdly, the new commercial, colonial, and naval rivalry of Germany and England. But it must be clearly understood that, given the nationalist assumptions, and the war traditions, the causes of conflict were mainly accidental. Had those causes not existed others would have been found, though the alignment of the nations might easily have been different and the date of the war earlier or later.

As Europe settled down after the Treaty of Berlin, Bismarck continued to ride his two restive mounts, Austria and Russia. Austria made a second alliance with Germany in 1879 ; and her old enemy, Italy, angered by the French annexation of Tunis, made it a Triple Alliance (1881). Russia still could not quarrel with Germany since England was her inveterate enemy, while in France, an old foe, the best elements detested

e tyrannies of Russian government. But the situation was
npossible, and, in a Balkan War of 1885–86 (the atmosphere
f which can be studied in Bernard Shaw's *Arms and the Man*),
ustrian and Russian officers were commanding the opposing
rmies. The League of the Three Emperors was renewed
n 1881, and when it expired in 1887 Bismarck made his
amous reinsurance treaty with Russia, by which he secretly
hrew Austria over. But by 1891 France and Russia were
wallowing their antipathy and lending and borrowing money
espectively. Bismarck had ceased to control German policy
n 1890 : for many years he had clung fast to the principle
f keeping friends with Russia, but he had allowed personal
lights to spoil his relations with the Russian Ministers, and
he third-rate men who succeeded him, particularly Holstein,
eem almost of set purpose to have driven Russia and France
etween 1891 and 1897 into their Dual Alliance, while the
ameson Raid in 1895 gave the occasion for Anglo-German
hostility to flash forth.

GERMANY'S FEAR OF THE RUSSIAN BOGY

GERMANY thus found herself between two enemies, and
the exaggerated views generally held of Russia's military
strength gave military careerists a popular pretext for the
burden of military training. A generation of Germans grew
up with a bogy ever before it—the half-civilised hosts of
Russia on the other side of a long and vulnerable frontier.

By the end of the century the German Government had
dug its own grave, but Germany was still the strongest state
in the world. The new Empire was a huge area of free
internal trade, and the richest districts of its European
neighbours lay near it. It was very well supplied with coal,
iron, zinc, potash, and other raw materials, both above and
below ground ; in fact, as the World War proved, it contained
much ampler national resources in proportion to population
than Great Britain did. With industrialisation the population
grew rapidly, in spite of emigration. It rose from forty
millions in 1871 to sixty-eight millions in 1914. The Germans
were full of confidence, the French indemnity was largely
employed to finance industry, and above all the excellent
schools of Prussia were developed. German education was,
as always, largely classical, but the Government anticipated
other countries in encouraging scientific study (particularly
chemistry) at modern and scientific schools and at the numerous

universities, and in organising scientific industrial research. The Bessemer steel process, which greatly facilitated engineering progress, the use of local phosphatic ores, and the utilisation of by-products were various forms that it took.

The result was a great development of German industry which was based in some branches, *e.g.* dyes, on superior skill, and in others, like hardware, on cheap labour and hard work. German shipping took its share of the carrying trade. There had always been many emigrants from Germany to America: over ten per cent. of the population of the United States was of German extraction, and German influence also became very strong in South America. The sleepy, backward, picturesque German cities of the early nineteenth century were modernised: and Germany, from being a romantic vagabond among the nations, became a sophisticated *nouveau riche*. The final predominance of Prussia over the South produced an uncouth arrogance, and as individuals the new Germans were not popular.

German thought was influenced by historians like Niebuhr, Mommsen, Sybel, Treitschke, and Droysen, and by philosophers like Nietzsche, who employed their learning—often in defence of force and absolutism, whether the Cæsarism of Ancient Rome or the military monarchy of modern Prussia. These views had been current for years before Bismarck's decade of war (1862–71), and had contributed very largely to the triumph of his policy, as confidence and will-to-power in a nation do contribute, if controlled by calculating minds in the highest places. Bismarck himself said that his wars had been won by the schoolmaster.

HOW BISMARCK PACIFIED BOTH RICH AND POOR

THE old King of Prussia, now Kaiser Wilhelm I., reigned till 1887, Moltke continuing to control his armies and Bismarck his state business. Bismarck's unbroken tenure of power (1862–90) was not disturbed by such incidents as the monarchist intrigues of contemporary France or the Irish troubles in contemporary England, or the Nihilist plots of contemporary Russia. But, despite his great prestige, he was soon involved in a sharp quarrel with the Catholics over the control of education, in which they worsted him. He had hitherto tried to use the " National " Liberals as an additional support for his Conservative followers, but he now turned to conciliate the growing Socialist or Social Democratic Party

The franchise was so regulated that the upper classes had proportionately more votes than the middle and lower. The powers of the Reichstag, which had universal suffrage, were small, but Bismarck thought it worth while to introduce social measures, such as old age pensions and health insurance. It was to buy the support of the new Colonial Party that in the early 'eighties he began an acquisitive colonial policy.

The old Kaiser died in 1887. His son, the intelligent and moderate Frederick III., reigned for a year, and was succeeded by the Kaiser Wilhelm II., who reigned from 1888–1918. His withered arm and accidents of upbringing brought out much that was unsound in Wilhelm's Hohenzollern and Hanoverian ancestry. He very soon got rid of Bismarck.

Before tracing the events of 1895–1914 we must complete the preliminaries by describing the scramble for Africa. Until the middle nineteenth century Africa had remained unexplored, protected by its diseases, wild beasts, insects and reptiles, coastal swamps and distances. The existence of the Great Lakes, the snowcapped mountains of the Equator, and the grasslands of the interior was not suspected. Modern firearms, modern medicine, the modern desire for adventure, the modern supply of money to finance such projects, and the modern missionary and humanitarian spirit, between 1850 and 1875, combined to cause the chief features of the continent and its potential wealth to be explored. The achievement would have been impossible in the sixteenth century; it was done at the cost of great hardships in the nineteenth; it could have been done in a few weeks with aeroplanes and cameras now in the twentieth. Livingstone, who was among explorers what Nelson was among sailors or Shakespeare among poets, was the greatest of a hundred men of all nationalities, mainly soldiers or missionaries, whose work aroused interest among statesmen, speculators, and among ordinary people alike.

Between 1876 and 1911 Africa was partitioned by the Powers, whose rivalry had been much accentuated by the events of 1871. France wished to balance her losses by gains in North Africa, while Germany and Italy, coming late into the race for colonies, wanted sources of supply, markets, and reservoirs of recruits in war. Russia continued to expand in Asia, the United States in the Pacific, while Austria-Hungary was busy with Bosnia.

THE AFRICAN CONQUEST THAT ENGLAND REFUSED

ENGLAND between 1815 and 1870 had refused to incur trouble or expense in Africa. Even in 1876 when Stanley offered her the Congo, Disraeli's Conservative Government entangled in South Africa, refused it. Stanley then went to the King of the Belgians, Leopold II., a ruthless speculator who, using an International Congo Association as stalking horse, contrived to annex the Congo Basin, shut out foreign trade, and perpetrate abominable outrages on the native inhabitants. French, Belgian, and Portuguese agents competed for the Congo in the late 'seventies, England supporting Portugal, and Germany her rivals. Belgium, as we saw won, but France gained part of the north bank of the lower Congo. France meanwhile was extending from Algiers across the Sahara towards the Guinea coast.

English interest in the scramble began. In 1875 the bankruptcy of the Khedive of Egypt (a vassal of the Turkish Sultan) caused the governments of France and England, to whose subjects he owed money, to take over the financial administration. In 1881–82 the Egyptian population rose against French, British, and Turkish control, and Great Britain's forces bombarded Alexandria and won a skirmish at Tel-el-Kebir, France remaining diplomatically aloof Britain then assumed control of Egypt and evacuated the Sudan, the great area of desert south of the second cataract of the Nile. The operation was disgraced by the death of Gordon in 1885, but in 1896–99 Kitchener reconquered the Sudan The administration of Egypt remained nominally Egyptian, but it was in effect an enlightened despotism of the best type under the British Consul-General, Lord Cromer. Egyptian wealth and population increased considerably, but feeling remained anti-British and pro-French.

Meanwhile Bismarck entered the Colonial race when in 1884, having got from the British Government a statement that it did not claim the territory of the Herreros and Damaras in South-West Africa, he annexed this area. The intrusion of a great though friendly military power was one stimulus to Cecil Rhodes' successful proposals for the occupation of Bechuanaland and—in disregard of Portuguese claims— the great area now called Rhodesia. Germany took Kamerun and Togoland in West Africa and a very large area in East Africa (now Tanganyika) as the price of her support for

Great Britain's Egyptian policy. Great Britain meanwhile was pushed into annexing Uganda, British East Africa (now Kenya Colony), and Nigeria. Interest was further encouraged after 1886 by the discovery of the Rand gold mines and the hope of finding other goldfields in tropical Africa. A Conference in 1890 delimited boundaries and agreed that occupation should not be recognised unless " effective." Soon afterwards Italy made a futile attack on Abyssinia and was defeated with much disgrace at Adowa (1896) but kept a footing on the uninviting coast adjacent to the Red Sea, where France and Great Britain also held territory.

The partition of Africa did not at any rate cause a European war ; it may or may not have been to the benefit of the ninety million native inhabitants. All civilised powers joined in putting down the slave trade still carried on by Arabs, though it survived until the nineteen-thirties. The partition was, however, with the Eastern question, to be the main point on which international dislikes were centred during 1895–1914.

ENGLAND DISCOVERS SOME DRAWBACKS OF ALOOFNESS

ENGLAND retained her commercial importance, but trade had bad spells, and, although the growing importance of her miscellaneous overseas dominions was shown at the Queen's Jubilees in 1887 and 1897, there were drawbacks to her aloofness from European alliances. She was, apparently, irreconcilably hostile to France and Russia and traditionally friendly to Austria and Germany, while the Kaiser Wilhelm's mother was Queen Victoria's eldest daughter. Unfortunately, this connection seems, if anything, to have bred dislike in the mind of the Kaiser. When his uncle, Edward VII., became King of England, and even during the lifetime of his grandmother, he behaved with deliberate hostility to England, not with any idea, probably, that such conduct might form a contributory cause of war, but in order to assert himself against his relations.

A crisis arose over the Jameson Raid of Dec.–Jan. 1895–96. Opinion all over the Continent was favourable to the Transvaal Boers, partly out of pure jealousy of Great Britain. Germany professed to be particularly interested because of her own footing in South Africa, and when Jameson's raid began demanded that the *status quo* in South Africa should not be disturbed, in other words, that the Transvaal should remain independent. The failure of the raid caused her ultimatum to be recalled unread, but the Kaiser cabled congratulations to President Kruger on his victory, and aroused considerable resentment in England. In 1898 Germany began the naval development which was to be an important contributing factor to enmity later. Her navy hitherto had been very small, but, having now colonies and many merchant ships, she not unreasonably proposed to enlarge it. This navy never was equal to much more than half the strength of the British Navy, even in 1914, but the policy caused alarm, as did the formidable personality of Admiral Tirpitz, its organiser.

However, as Milner and Chamberlain conducted the long negotiations which led to the South African War of 1899, France remained England's enemy. France established herself (in 1883–96) in Madagascar, close to the British sphere. In 1898 war was almost caused over the Fashoda incident. Kitchener, reconquering the Sudan, found a French force which had marched across from West Africa with the intention of claiming a wide belt from the Atlantic to the Red Sea, and which had probably been sent in order to forestall the British advance. France gave way after being on the verge of declaring war : the deterring factor was the certainty that Germany would fall on her at once.

A WAITING GAME THAT WAS PLAYED TOO LONG

WHEN the British forces in South Africa were wearing down their elusive enemies, the whole Continent was impotently united in hatred of England. The British Navy made intervention impossible. The war ended with British credit at a low level, her military difficulties not perhaps being appreciated abroad. The Conservative Government, in which Chamberlain was the strongest man, felt that it was imperative to find dependable allies. The affinities between the crowns and the ruling classes of England and Germany were still close. Between 1898 and 1901 Chamberlain made repeated requests for alliance. He gave warning that if they failed, his Government would approach the Franco-Russian group. Germany's rulers played too clever a game. They feared to be used for England's ends against Russia and they fondly expected to bring England in on very humble terms if they kept her waiting. It seemed unthinkable that England could ever sink her differences with Russia or France. They did indeed extract a series of concessions from her, but in 1902

he turned to Japan as the only available (if rather reluctant)
lly.

Anglo-German commercial and naval jealousy was supplemented by the vivid personal dislike of King Edward for his
xasperating nephew, which he expressed pungently. The
German enthusiasts who talked wildly about their new fleet
vere perhaps surpassed by Sir John Fisher in England, who
proposed to seize it before it grew more dangerous. Such
alk bore less relation to serious policy in England than in
Germany, but Germans did not make allowances for this.

As Germany—or rather the Kaiser, Bülow, the Imperial
Chancellor, and Holstein—had not responded, Chamberlain
and his colleagues now attempted the formidable task of
coming to an understanding with France. There was no
commercial or naval rivalry to impede such a possibility, and
England agreed that France might absorb Morocco, if she
vould give England a free hand in Egypt. King Edward's
share in promoting the *Entente* was secondary, it may be
added.

THE POWERS OF EUROPE CLASH IN THE EAST

MEANWHILE the Eastern question was taking on a new
colour. Bismarck had ostentatiously kept clear of it,
but after 1892 Germany began to foster the interests of her
business men in Turkey and the Near East, and to raise
objections to any activities by British subjects. The Kaiser
visited Damascus in 1898 and proclaimed himself the protector
of all Moslems—an announcement of much interest to the
rulers of India. As communications improved, Germany's
numerous ambitions began to include a *Drang nach Osten* or
Eastward Ho project for a Berlin–Baghdad railway, passing
through a string of more or less vassal states—Austria, Serbia,
Turkey—to the Persian Gulf and the neighbourhood of India.
It caused alarm in Great Britain and involved Germany in
an anti-Russian policy in the Balkans. Thus German policy in
Eastern Europe came into line with that of Austria, which was
based on opposition to Slav nationalism patronised by Russia.

The Russo-Japanese War of 1904 very nearly led to war
between Russia and England, owing to the sinking of some
British fishing vessels which the Russian fleet thought were
Japanese torpedo boats, but Russia made amends and her
defeat aided the movement which England was making, under
the Conservative Government and after 1905 under the

Liberals to come to an *entente* with Russia similar to the Frenc *entente*. The Kaiser challenged France's designs on Morocc and forced the French Government to sacrifice its Foreig Minister as the price of securing a footing there with the hel of British diplomacy. The Kaiser, who had a certain persona ascendency over the Tsar, got him to sign a treaty of allianc with Germany, which was intended to include France later

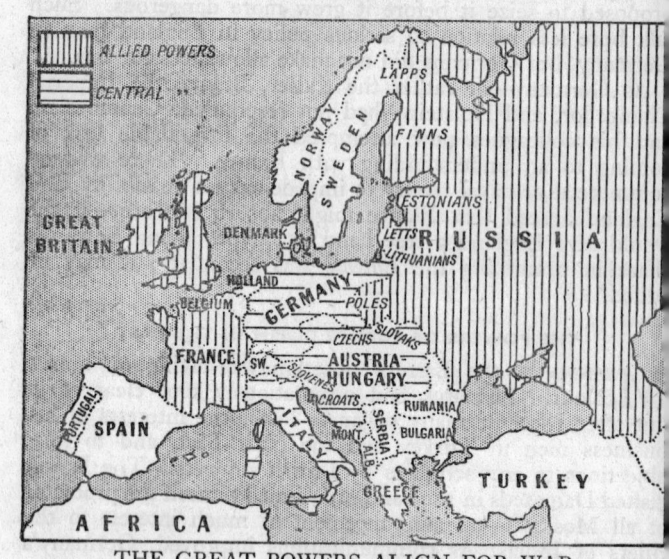

THE GREAT POWERS ALIGN FOR WAR
*Political rapprochements before the world catastrophe, 1914.
Observe Italy's original alignment with the Central Powers ;
and the nationalities in Eastern and Central Europe absorbed
by Germany, Austria-Hungary and Russia.*

but which neither the anti-French German Ministers, nor the anti-German French Ministers would ever have accepted. This new Tsar was Nicholas I., who had since his accession in 1894 followed the traditions of his house in opposing reform and in shedding blood unnecessarily. He was apparently a weak, well-meaning, ill-informed man.

In 1907 the final attachment of England to the Franco-Russian *entente* took place, the event which Germany had thought impossible, and which many English Liberals disiked. Its implications, however, were uncertain. The British Government knew quite well that it could not fail to support France and Russia without damaging British credit irreparably. France relied on Great Britain and the two General Staffs began to work together. But the great majority of people in England, including most Members of Parliament, knew only the official theory that the *entente* was emphatically not a binding alliance. In Germany there remained doubt whether England need be taken seriously, a doubt which was fortified in 1914 by the unchecked preparations for civil war in Ireland and the defiance of the Government by militant suffragettes. Thus France and Germany were both encouraged. Some line of conduct to deter both would have been difficult to find.

Austria in 1908 annexed Bosnia and Herzegovina, which she had been administering since 1879. Her Minister, Aehrenthal, deceived and humiliated the friendly Russian Minister, and Germany with much Imperial bluster warned Austria's rivals not to interfere. The annexation infuriated Serbia. For many years feeling had been growing in favour of the unification of the Slav races. Austria already kept many Slavs under foreign domination (that of Germans or Magyars) and now annexed in Bosnia several millions more, all of whom the Serbs thought should be Serbian.

JAPAN MAKES UP FOR LOST TIME

THE Japanese are a race of very mixed origins and physical types. Their civilisation was much younger than China's, and largely derived from it. The strong west winds of the Pacific are said to have discouraged contact during the sailing ship era ; at any rate, Japan remained feudal and military much longer than China, and produced less art and literature. Portuguese traders and missionaries entered Japan in the sixteenth century, but were murdered or driven out in the seventeenth, largely at the instigation of the Dutch, who obtained a few trading rights in the island of Deshima. Japan was closed to foreigners for two hundred years. Firearms and cannon were known, but the sword and armour remained conspicuous in the private wars conducted by the nobles and their *Samurai*, or knightly retainers. The Emperor (Mikado) enjoyed semi-divine status, though the government was carried on by the Shogun, a sort of hereditary Prime Minister.

In the middle nineteenth century the United States and

European powers forced the Shogun, under pressure of bombardment, to admit foreign traders again. The first commercial treaty was made in 1853. But the Chinese story was not to be repeated. Fifteen years later the nobles began to reform the government. Between 1868 and 1889 they abolished the Shogunate, set up a constitution of the European limited monarchy type, and modernised education, army and navy, communications and industry. It was not at all difficult to find foreign instructors, for instance, German officers, to train the army, but it was remarkable how quickly the European industries were mastered, including the war industry. Japan fought China successfully for Formosa in 1894, and for the Liao-Tung Peninsula, having, however, to give up the Peninsula under pressure from France, Russia, and Germany.

In 1902 Great Britain persuaded Japan to make, though reluctantly, a defensive alliance, safeguarding either power against attack by more than one other. Soon after (1904), Japan attacked Russia, who had continued to interfere in Manchuria. Europeans knew the courage and endurance of the Japanese, but were startled at their efficiency. Russia was handicapped by the distance of the seat of war. There was very heavy fighting, which on land was not decisive ; but the destruction of the Russian fleet after its voyage from the Baltic drove Russia to make the Treaty of Portsmouth. The terms were not very favourable to Japan, as Manchuria was to remain under China, Japan taking the Liao-Tung Peninsula. Korea was annexed by Japan in 1910. The real significance of the war was that for the first time in four hundred years European arms had decisively failed against an Asiatic power now using European methods ; and throughout India and the East, Europe's prestige suffered a reverse which has had a lasting effect.

The Pacific Ocean, which stretches across half the circumference of the globe, had attracted few European explorers and traders until Captain Cook in the eighteenth century mapped it. In the early nineteenth century missionaries, traders, and slave-dealers began to visit the islands. Improved transport and wider naval interests caused a demand for trade and bases. During the century the Pacific Islands were divided among the United States, Great Britain, France, and Germany. Holland retained her possessions in the East Indies. Spain kept the Philippines until 1898, when a war with the United States about Cuba caused their transference, followed by a movement on the part of the inhabitants for national self-government. With the apportioning of the Pacific the European powers finished the process of partition which they had started in the time of Vasco da Gama. The Pacific was now the link between the awakening East and the American outposts of the West.

RUMBLINGS OF THE GREAT VOLCANO

BY 1909 there was a general feeling that the costly race in armaments could not go on much longer. France soon increased the period of conscript service from two years to three ; Russia was re-organising her forces—insufficiently—after her defeat by the Japanese ; the British Government had capped the German naval scheme by building a new type of big ship and planning to maintain their two-to-one superiority. The small British army was also being re-organised. Meanwhile certain of the military and bureaucratic cliques on the Continent were feeling a slow tide of Socialism lapping round their boots, and were toying with the idea of war to give themselves a new lease of prestige. Germany was in a weaker position than she had been since 1866, and even the Triple Alliance was dissolving, as Italy, with her long coast and lack of coal, could never take sides against Great Britain. A myth was spread in Germany that her enemies planned to encircle her, England's alleged motive being commercial jealousy. The very weakness of Germany's position was made the excuse for a gambler's attempt to fight before things got worse. It would have been more intelligent to wait for things to come right again, especially as German industry and commerce gained ground by means of " peaceful penetration " with every year of peace.

The Kaiser, with his bad choice of Ministers and his ill-calculated irruptions into politics, was a cause of trouble, but his energy, high spirits, and apparent intelligence impressed many people—and not only his own subjects. He was a much less sinister figure than the aged Francis Joseph. Since 1848 the Austrian Emperor had done very little to make his numerous subject races more content with Austrian rule : and, although he was by 1910 too old to take much part in business, he cannot be pardoned for his very bad selection of Ministers, in particular that of Berchtold, the Foreign Minister.

The agreement reached about Morocco in 1905 had been skilfully misconstrued by the French, and in 1911 Germany made a fresh protest and sent an absurd little gunboat to back it up. There was a new crisis and this time France was openly supported by England. France finally compensated Germany with territory adjoining Kamerun.

In England, a German invasion was prophesied in much detail by writers of fiction and others. The publication of pre-war records which has occurred since 1918 has not shown that it ever occurred to the Germans to invade England by sea, but the German scare was worked up by advocates of conscription, and the importation of cheap German hardware became very unpopular. In 1914, ironically enough, better feeling began to prevail. But the fundamental cause of trouble, the old Franco-German feud, remained.

CURTAIN-RAISERS TO THE WORLD TRAGEDY

WAR began in 1911 when Italy attacked Turkey and occupied Tripoli in North Africa. It was an unscrupulous action and the Italians outdid the Turks in atrocity. Next year four Balkan States—Montenegro, Serbia, Greece, and Bulgaria—fell on Turkey and began to drive her at last out of Europe. Great Britain and the other Powers intervened and in the interests of public peace required Serbia to give up Albania, a distinct ethnological unit, which received independence. Serbia was compensated at the expense of Bulgaria. The Balkan powers fell to blows again and Rumania helped the others to despoil Bulgaria, Serbia now gaining territory which obstructed the Berlin-to-Baghdad scheme, while Turkey recovered Adrianople.

During 1914 Great Britain was absorbed in Irish affairs, and even the Continental powers were thinking of other things when on June 28th the heir to the Austrian throne, the Archduke Franz Ferdinand, was assassinated at Serajevo, the capital of Bosnia. He was in favour of reconciliation with the Slavs, and was unpopular with the German-Magyar clique which controlled Austria-Hungary and kept down the Czechs, Rumanians, Serbs, Croats, Italians, Slovaks, Slovenes, Poles, and Ruthenians. The plot to kill him was framed by a secret society which was opposed to the Austro-Hungarian Government. Austria had an excuse for war now and determined to crush Serbia finally, either brushing her friends out of the way, as in 1908–09 or, if need arose, fighting them.

Accordingly, the Government sent an ultimatum which made almost impossible demands on Serbia. Serbia was a semi-civilised state, with a bad record for assassination : she aimed at the union of all the Croats and Serbs—two-thirds of them being in the Austrian Empire—her press had been vilifying Austria for years and her Government was suspected of knowing about the plot. The ultimatum was meant only as a step to war. Russia's Balkan interests, her reputation and sympathy with her Slav ideals, demanded that she should support Serbia. Germany, France, and Great Britain were immediately involved in the order they have been named.

THE STORM BREAKS

DURING the last ten days of July a tangle of messages and suggestions were crossing each other, to and from Petersburg, London, Paris, Vienna, and Berlin. The steps by which each day brought war nearer are, in a sense, of no great significance : it is quite possible that the same result would have been reached had negotiations followed a different course. Given forty years of international arming, and a constant assumption that war must come sooner or later, continental statesmen certainly wished to look as if the war was being forced on them, but neither side was ready to submit to humiliation as the price of peace. The British Government, of which Sir Edward Grey was Foreign Secretary, did everything that persuasion could do to hold them back. One reason why his efforts failed was that they had no substantial military backing. No one thought that the British Army would make much difference or that even the Navy would affect a short War. Even had the statesmen given way, the generals were at hand to scare the Emperors and Cabinets with dire pictures of what delay meant. Had they foreseen a four years' war, some of them might have drawn back. But no one expected a war of more than four months. It is remarkable how modern wars are always " forced on " people in the summer, the best campaigning weather.

The responsibility for events in July and August 1914 lies on about thirty men, of whom some, had they been prepared to sacrifice their careers if necessary, could have averted war. Active responsibility probably rests more with Berchtold than any one—the man of straw who was the Austrian

Foreign Minister. Behind him was the much stronger Conrad von Hoetzendorf, the Commander-in-Chief, whose great influence was for war. The same part was played in Germany by Moltke, nephew of the victor of 1870, the feeble heir of his uncle's great reputation. The three Emperors were half-hearted or inclined for peace, but they were weighing *pros* and *cons* in the balance, not rejecting the idea of war with decision.

England did not declare war until three days after Germany had declared war on Russia. There were many people in England, including some Cabinet Ministers, who did not consider that continental feuds need concern Great Britain, and did not appreciate the nice point of international prestige involved in British obligations to France. There was talk of merely protecting the French coasts with the fleet. The Liberal Government, in which Asquith, Grey, and Haldane were dominant, would probably have supported France even with a divided nation, but the Germans played into their hands by striking at France through Belgium. They were willing to refrain in return for a guarantee of British neutrality, but England demanded an unconditional guarantee, which was not given. The Belgian Treaty of 1839 bound the signatory powers not to attack Belgium, but not necessarily to attack any one who violated her neutrality. However, the sentimental appeal of a small nation, the light which the incident threw on German methods, and the old English policy of not allowing a strong power to hold the Belgian coast, turned wavering opinion solidly against Germany, and war was declared with a united nation, even the Irish parties making a truce.

TACTICS DOMINATED BY TRENCH AND BARBED WIRE

THE War far exceeded all previous wars in its opening rapidity of movement, but the day was past when a victory over an army would lay a country in the dust. The success of defensive arms enabled any loser to play for a stalemate. The battles of all wars up to the war of 1870 had been won by gunfire or the bayonet and turned into routs by cavalry charging broken infantry. But a few machine guns could now destroy almost any cavalry charge. The full realisation of what trenches and barbed wire could do, negatively, dominated the tactics of the armies till 1918, when " open " warfare and rapid movement again became possible.

The armies were thirty or forty times the size of the armies of a hundred years ago, modern transport and communications having made it possible to feed, control, and move such numbers. Probably the numbers had really grown too large for effective handling. But their size also enabled them to stretch their wings from one natural defence to another, for instance, from the sea to the Alps. It was thus only possible to outflank an army partially by making a very deep angle in its line, which was sometimes done, or by " amphibious " operations combining land and sea movement, and this was hardly ever attempted.

WHAT GERMANY MEANT TO DO IN THE WAR

GERMANY, greatly outnumbered, proposed to hold the Russians in the East and crush France ; had any one but Moltke been in command she might have done it. The Franco-German frontier being so fortified as to be almost impassable, it had been decided long before, when Schlieffen was in command, to march through Belgium—preferably bluffing the French into doing so first. There was nothing very subtle in this, but Schlieffen proposed to employ seven-eighths of the German force on his right wing to make the enveloping move through Belgium. The left wing was to make no advance against the French fortresses ; in fact, it was rather to fall back and draw the French forward, while the right wing curled down on their flank and rear. The French assisted this plan by an eager offensive against the German left, which repulsed them with appalling losses, and by neglecting the Belgian frontier. Moltke, however, lacked the moral courage to stake everything on the Schlieffen plan.

During the years since the *Entente* was made, the British General Staff, largely controlled by Sir Henry Wilson, had agreed that the six or seven divisions of the British Expeditionary Force should operate on the left flank of the French. It was hardly large enough to make much difference as between armies of ten or fifteen times its strength, and the situation was altered when Belgium became an ally of France and England and proposed to resist. Had the British force landed in Belgium and helped the Belgians on the German flank, it could hardly have failed to produce greater effect than it did, and at no greater cost. Actually it was the rumour of Allied forces in that quarter, as much as the reality of the British Expeditionary Force in front, that caused the German march on Paris to collapse.

On the Eastern front the Russians and Austrians both had plans for vigorous offensives which were unsuited to the nature of their forces—the Russians because of their very weak organisation and slow collection of strength, the Austrians because a large proportion of their troops were anything but loyal or enthusiastic, and were held together only by the German and Magyar officers and non-commissioned officers.

TWO MILLION GERMANS POUR INTO BELGIUM

FOR a fortnight the trains packed with troops and material rumbled westward at the rate of a hundred a day over all the Rhine bridges until two million German troops were pouring through Belgium. They were delayed there, but were soon wheeling through North France and driving Lanrezac's Fifth French Army and Sir John French's British Expeditionary Force back by weight of numbers and artillery in the long and confused retreat to the Marne, almost within sight of Paris. The check they received was, perhaps, due less to the vigorous action of Gallieni, the Governor of Paris, and to the penetration of a gap in the German front by Sir John French's force than to the Germans having outmarched their food supplies, as also to their being thoroughly alarmed by rumours about activity on their flank in Belgium, and to the excessive caution of their commanders, or rather of their chiefs of staff. They could probably have held their ground, but they fell back to the Aisne and took up a strong position from which they could not be dislodged. Very soon both sides began to stretch out to the Channel coast and the trench line became deep and continuous.

The hardest work that the British were called on to do was the defence of the Ypres salient against the first attempt to take it. It was to cost 250,000 British lives in the next three years. It may not have been worth holding. By winter both sides were settling into the permanent trench lines which were a novel feature of this war. The great German offensive had failed ; Moltke had been displaced by the autocratic Falkenhayn, and the siege warfare phase, which was to last for three years, had begun.

Meanwhile the Russian offensive in East Prussia began very well ; extravagant beliefs were entertained of what the Russian hordes would do. But their success in August over smaller German forces caused the local German commanders to be recalled in favour of the two central figures of the War.

Ludendorff, a trusted staff officer, who had shown energy in Belgium, was sent off across Germany to take over the command, picking up on the way a retired veteran of Bismarck's wars, Hindenburg, to be his nominal commander. The partnership had political as well as military consequences, for they proceeded to win the biggest single victory of the War, the battle of Tannenberg and the Masurian Lakes. The Germans took over 90,000 prisoners and ended the Cossack menace. To Germany, the victory was Hindenburg's, though other commanders and the mistakes of the Russians really produced it, and his generalship soon became an article of faith. He seems, in fact, to have been a valiant, unimaginative Prussian, with an iron constitution, great resolution, and wisdom enough to leave things to Ludendorff.

NUMBERS PITTED AGAINST EFFICIENCY

BETWEEN 1914 and 1918 the beleaguered fortress of Germany and Austria, soon joined by Turkey and later by Bulgaria, was attacked at fresh points as Italy (1915) and Rumania (1916) came into the War, but until the besiegers were reinforced by the gigantic resources of the United States of America (1917) the odds were on the defenders. They had the interior lines of communication, which as regards movements from the Russian to the French front were quicker than the Allies' sea and land communications ; they had nearly complete unity of command, and the initial French mistakes had given them most of the northern French industrial areas. Their forces were inferior in numbers, the Allies' advantage being usually about six to four, but the advantage in organisation, training, and equipment was with the Central Powers for the first three years. At the end, they were markedly inferior in numbers and equipment, and four years of active service brought the training of all the chief armies to much the same standard.

During 1915 Falkenhayn sat on the defensive in France and Belgium, except for a badly prepared experiment with a gas attack at Ypres. The German authorities had already established amongst their enemies a reputation for brutality, and the use of poison gas, forbidden by the Hague Convention, added to it, as did the air raids on unfortified cities, and the torpedoing of merchant ships. Much of the propaganda issued by the Allied Governments and press to work up the war spirit in peaceable people was crude in the extreme ;

but there seems to have been some justification for the charges which were made. Big French offensives and small British attacks came to nothing and the Germans were able to use their strength in the East, where they drove the Russians almost out of Poland. Italy joined the Allies and attacked Austria, with the object of gaining the Trentino and other territory to which she had a much weaker claim. She was unable to pierce the Austrian mountain defences, but at least occupied some of Austria's strength. Despite all their other anxieties the Germans collected an army in the autumn which crushed Serbia, Bulgaria assisting them. The Serbs fought with wonderful courage during a retreat which involved frightful losses in battle and from exposure.

This year, when hopes were still running high, saw the Dardanelles expedition. The plan (a flank attack in the East on the Central Powers through Turkey) was in essence sound, though much was done to spoil it by premature naval operations and the despatch of an attacking force barely equal in numbers to the defenders. Sir Ian Hamilton fought the campaign with what for this war was brilliance, but he was badly served by some of his assistants. The climate and geographical conditions were perhaps the worst that any troops had to fight under, and the Turks were well led by Liman von Sanders and Mustapha Kemal. Still, the expedition was within an ace of success, and there is no reasonable doubt that its success would have shortened the war.

IRELAND ADDS TO ENGLAND'S TROUBLES

EARLY in 1916, the " Easter Rebellion " in Dublin occurred. The official " Nationalist " party had supported the British Government, but a wing of extremists, aggrieved by the suspension of the Home Rule Bill, had plotted an outbreak. The rebels held parts of the city for a time, but were suppressed, and executions followed. Leaders, amongst whom Griffiths and De Valera were the chief, survived, and the extreme party, now known as Sinn Fein, grew in strength. For the last two years of the War it continued to gain ground on the old Nationalist party, and in the general election held at the end of the War it captured nearly all the old Nationalist seats. Its new Members of Parliament, some of whom were prisoners or outlaws, did not go to Westminster, but went on organising their rival system of government and undermining the British system in Southern Ireland.

In 1916 there were great battles on the Austro-Italian front, while the last Russian offensive, under Brussilov, was defeated after some success. Russia had reached the end of her strength. She raised, in all, some ten million men, of whom at least a quarter lost their lives. They were very short of artillery, even of rifles and ammunition, the rank and file were illiterate, so that good non-commissioned officers were scarce, and the leadership was inadequate. Russia's allies could have supplied the necessary munitions, acute though their own needs were, but it was impossible to convey large quantities of material, the normal Baltic route being, of course, closed. There occurred the usual corruption and inefficiency in the use of what materials there were. The Russian Revolution arose directly from the military and economic collapse of the old Tsardom, which had inflicted untold suffering on its armies and people during the two years of war, and completely demoralised both.

During this year a British offensive in Mesopotamia failed tragically, a very bad start was made with a new campaign at Salonika, and Rumania having joined the Allies, the Germans again found means to free one hand, hard pressed though they were, and crush her. The conquest was effected by Falkenhayn, whose place as Chief of the General Staff (in other words, Commander-in-Chief) was taken by the idolised Hindenburg, whom Ludendorff accompanied to Headquarters.

But the biggest battles of the year were two indecisive offensives in France. Falkenhayn began the year with an attack on Verdun, which consumed a quarter of a million French and German lives in seven months. His aims are difficult to decide : they may have been far-reaching, but he did not achieve more than the temporary exhaustion of France, which was shown in 1917. The French defence was a supreme effort of heroism, but it left her worn out. Partly to relieve the pressure on the French, but largely in real expectation of breaking through to Berlin, the first big British offensive was launched, on the Somme, when the fine divisions of Kitchener's army, at last fully trained, were used. It lasted for five months, and the enormous casualties were not merely out of proportion to the gains, but were heavier than those of the hard-pressed Germans. The miseries of the troops were increased by rain, which meant that later phases of the battle were fought in thick mud.

The Somme was the final demonstration that something new in tactics was needed. It was still the British practice to send forward attacking infantry in regular lines, closely spaced, excellent targets for machine-guns. Protection was supposed to be given by battering the German trenches with heavy shell fire for several days previously. But this barrage gave full warning of the attack and seldom broke up the defence. Even the creeping barrage, which advanced in front of the attackers, had to cease in time to avoid killing its own infantry and therefore to give the defending machine-gunners time to emerge from their dug-outs. The German losses were increased by their sometimes making counter-attacks on the same principle, but they were able to hold their own with little withdrawal.

IRONCLADS OF THE FIELD : THE TANKS

ONE solution of the infantry problem was now produced—the tank. It was the result of nearly two years application by General Swinton, who, for various reasons, was exceptionally well placed for getting his ideas attended to, but who met with consistent and highly blameworthy opposition from nearly all his superiors except one or two civilian Cabinet Ministers. He at last translated his plan into practice, and the minds controlling the British forces in France then insisted on a premature use of the tank—similar to the German mistake about gas—which threw away most of the value of surprise. However, the tank was to be one of the chief British assets henceforward, and even in its primitive state it almost restored mobility to warfare. The German Command affected contempt for the new machine, but would have copied it had they been able to spare workmen and materials. They hoped in any case to win the War quickly by other means.

The year 1916 was, on the whole, one of deep disappointments for the Allies. At the end of the year the British Prime Minister, Asquith, was displaced, and Lloyd George became Prime Minister. Famous before the War as a pacifist and reformer, he had shown great energy in various capacities since the War began, especially in stimulating efforts to make good the deficiency of shells with which Great Britain, more than the other combatants, was handicapped. The change from Asquith to Lloyd George was probably necessary, if only because the press had undermined confidence in the former, but its effects in domestic politics were to divide and weaken the Liberal party after the War.

A planned German retreat to the very strong "Hindenburg Line," which was carried out skilfully, marked the beginning of 1917. This year was the most dismal of all, heavy rains adding to the heartbreaking ordeal which the troops in the Western theatre endured. The morale of the French broke

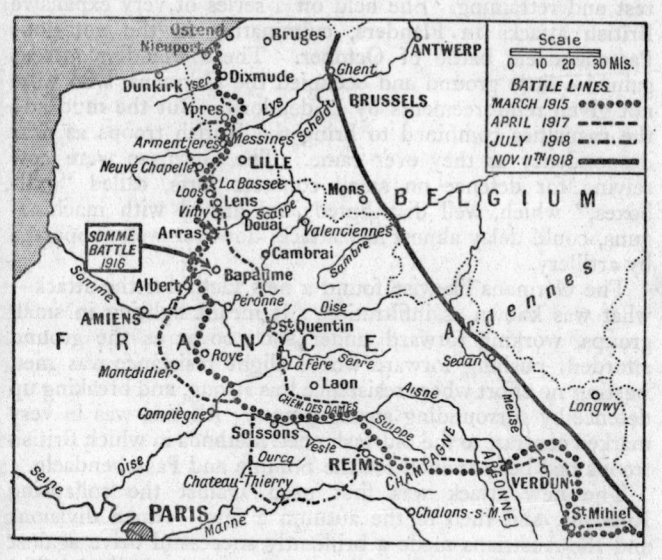

WAVERING LINE OF THE WORLD'S FATE : 1914–18

The four fronts shown in this map indicate (1) the position after the German occupation of Belgium, (2) the German retirement to the "Hindenburg" line, (3) the last desperate German advance, (4) the position at the Armistice.

down after an unsuccessful offensive, and mutinies had to be repressed by executions and appeals. The morale of the British remained excellent, but the more sensitive type of civilian-soldier was feeling a war-sickness which was best expressed at the time by the verse of Siegfried Sassoon. The spring of this year saw the climax of the submarine campaign, which, until defeated by the convoy system, was threatening to starve Britain.

RUSSIA GOES OUT—AMERICA COMES IN

THE final collapse of the Russian Army took place, the Tsardom was overthrown, and the Allies made no attempt to back up the new Liberal Government in Russia. Germany was able to enforce hard terms of peace on Russia, and, more important, to release large bodies of troops for rest and retraining. She held off a series of very expensive British attacks in Flanders, culminating in the notorious Passchendaele battle of October. These Flanders attacks gained a little ground and occupied the Germans, who were not given reinforcements by Ludendorff. But the mud and the casualties combined to bring the British troops as near despondency as they ever came. The Germans were now relying for defence on small concrete forts, called " pill-boxes," which, well distributed, and armed with machine-guns, could delay almost any attack, however well supported by artillery.

The Germans likewise found a new tactic for the attack—what was known as infiltration. It meant fighting in small groups, working forward under such cover as the ground afforded, pushing forward where slight resistance was met, wasting no effort where resistance was strong, and breaking up defence by surrounding strong points. All this was in very marked contrast to the old-fashioned methods in which British troops had been trained for the Somme and Passchendaele.

The new attack was first used against the collapsing Russians, and then in the autumn a few German divisions and the Austrians made a brilliantly successful drive against the Italians. This defeat (Caporetto) cost the Italians half a million casualties. Much of the German success was due to propaganda which had, added to war-weariness, brought the Italians to the verge of mutiny. The victory failed to achieve decisive results, however. Meanwhile in France there had been a sudden British advance at Cambrai, in which tanks played a brilliant part, followed by a successful German counter-attack—an earnest of the war of movement which was to recommence.

Perhaps the chief allied success of the year was the entrance of the United States into the War, goaded by German attacks on shipping, and by the idealism of President Wilson, into giving up the lucrative neutrality in which she had been maintained by the amount of pro-German and Irish anti-

British feeling among her people, and by friction with Great Britain over the blockade of Germany. The United States Navy was immediately of service. The United States army was small, and though America's human and material resources were enormous, little immediate benefit was obtained, the American Government refusing to allow their troops to be used piecemeal under Allied commanders in reinforcing the worn-out Allied troops. They insisted, instead, on creating their own army, complete in all branches, a process which took at least five times as long as the training of infantry to reinforce experienced troops. However, the potential presence of 2,000,000 American troops in 1919 compelled Ludendorff to race with time in 1918. In Mesopotamia the offensive was resumed against the Turks who were being worn down by the insurgent Arabs, aided by T. E. Lawrence, and by Allenby's advance from Egypt into Palestine.

FRESH TACTICS BY LAND AND AIR

THE Germans meanwhile were re-organising and training their infantry in infiltration, and selecting " storm troops," or picked men for attack, a policy which paid in the short run, but weakened their units later. It was perhaps no worse than the British wastage of junior officers. All the armies by this time were largely reduced to recruits who would normally have been too old or too young or medically unfit, and in France and Germany there were very few of any kind still to come. Very few units contained more than ten per cent. of their original members. Aeroplanes had attained a deadly proficiency, and the great phase of air fighting associated with the names of Ball, Bishop, McCudden, Richthofen, Boelke, Immelman, and Fonck was at its height. Regular raids on the areas behind the lines and on towns in France, England, and Germany went on, and London suffered especially heavily, but it is doubtful whether all the air fighting had any decisive effect.

1918 : THE END APPROACHING

ALTHOUGH 1918 was not expected to end the War, the German command were growing desperate. Food was short, even for the troops, and quite inadequate for the wretched civil population of Germany. In spite of all that German scientists had done to organise her resources and provide substitutes, essential commodities like rubber and brass were also scarce. With 1918 and the strength of the United States at last applied, the end was inevitable. Accordingly, Ludendorff resumed the offensive which had been broken off at Verdun in 1916. He was obliged to spare some troops to conquer the Ukraine with its food supplies, and to leave others on the less important fronts, but he had nearly two hundred divisions in France. His rifle strength was very little above that of the Allies, who were now able to use a few American troops, but by skilful preparation the German Staff repeatedly achieved complete surprise in their attacks, disguising the necessary movements for weeks, while they concentrated overwhelming forces at given points.

A very long controversy has raged over Ludendorff's offensives in March, April, May, and July. His choice of ground was not always the best, but the most serious weakness lay in a tendency to panic which the desperate situation produced in a tired man. He had laid down the same principle that Foch did later, of striking a series of blows at successive points before any attempt was made at a decision, stopping each as soon as the initial phase of rapid progress stopped. The attacks, however, succeeded too well and offered opportunities which the forces originally used were not strong enough to take : more troops were then used, but too late. Either policy would have been better than this half-measure. The hundred and sixteen days of the German offensives, from the start of the first (21st March) to the start of the last unsuccessful drive across the Marne on 15th July cost enormous casualties, and though the Germans gained very much ground, the Allied armies remained solid.

Desperation drove the French, British, and Americans to appoint a supreme War Council and then a supreme officer to co-ordinate their efforts. Foch received this post and converted it into that of Commander-in-Chief, though the detail of all orders was left to Haig, Pétain or Pershing (U.S.A.), In contrast to the German General Staff's way of working all orders out in detail, Foch, as Ludendorff had done in 1917, continued to leave weakened armies to retreat, making the best resistance they could, while he built up a reserve. He was able to hit the fourth German offensive in July so hard that it collapsed. This second battle of the Marne was the turning-point. The Allies were now ready to strike back, using the German " infiltration " tactics.

The remaining hundred and sixteen days of the War

(18th June to 11th November) were filled with the Allied advance to victory, beginning with the very successful tank and infantry onslaught of 8th August. This defeat coupled with the imminent collapse of resistance to Allied offensives through Turkey, Bulgaria, and Austria-Hungary, caused a physical and nervous breakdown in Ludendorff, who for a moment despaired and urged his Government to make peace. He soon regained confidence and proposed to fight on, retiring in good order into German territory, but he had disillusioned the civilians, and war weariness now overflowed.

No nation in modern times has had to bear the slow torture that the Germans stood for so long, and such anti-military feeling as had always existed was now reinforced by general despair. Throughout the autumn one hammer blow followed another, delivered irresistibly by Haig and Pétain. Moreover, the Americans were now taking part. At an appalling price in casualties the Allies rolled the German line back. But the Germans fought extremely well to the end and were not fully beaten in a military sense. Ludendorff was dismissed in October, the German Government meanwhile making overtures for peace, on the basis of President Wilson's Fourteen Points, laid down the previous June. These included an end of secret diplomacy, freedom of the seas, removal of economic barriers, reduction of armaments, full restoration of Belgium and of French territory, including Alsace-Lorraine, cession of Italian territory by Austria, and an Association of Nations.

SURRENDER AND THE CRUSHING BURDEN OF DEFEAT

AUSTRIA collapsed before the Allies accepted the German overtures, and revolution broke out in Germany. The Kaiser fled, new generals and ministers took over the Government, and the fleet and troops at home mutinied. Only Hindenburg remained. German delegates received by Foch accepted harsh terms which were still rather better than they had expected. Pershing had wished to go on into Germany, but Haig and Pétain desired peace at once, Haig not wishing to drive the Germans into the arms of Bolshevik Russia. Foch accordingly gave the armistice, retaining the right to increase penalties later. The Germans were able with some show of justice to say that they had never been properly beaten. Complete victory would have meant another

year of war, after which a generous peace would have been
even less likely.

The Armistice terms required Germany to withdraw her
troops beyond the Rhine, hand over the bridgeheads for
occupation, surrender all submarines, and two-thirds of her
other war vessels, surrender five thousand guns, thirty thousand
machine-guns, two thousand aeroplanes and a large amount of
transport material. The blockade was maintained as an additional safeguard, which the Germans had not expected.
Fighting and looting were going on in Germany, much as they
had done in Russia in 1917.

As Germany failed to win the War on land in 1914, it was
decided at sea. Beyond any possible doubt the chief force in
wearing her down, both materially and morally, was the
merciless blockade. The German Navy had not much more
than half the strength of the British, and from the outbreak
of war it was closely watched in its base at Kiel. A few
German cruisers which were on foreign stations were soon
hunted down, after doing a little damage to merchant shipping.
The chief unit, Count von Spee's fleet, sank two British ships,
outranged, off Coronel (1914), and a month later, itself outranged, was wiped out near the Falkland Islands.

A CONTROVERSIAL NAVAL ENCOUNTER

BUT the German commanders were prepared to take risks
in order to fight on terms which gave them a chance
of victory. Several small raids and bombardments of
undefended coastal towns took place; there were small
destroyer actions, a bigger cruiser action on the Dogger Bank,
and in May 1916 the only big naval battle of the War was
fought off Jutland. The Germans tried, with considerable
courage, to draw part of the British fleet on to their own main
force and destroy it. They were extremely lucky not to be
annihilated in doing so. Actually, they inflicted more
casualties than they suffered, but they were very glad, and
surprised, to get home, and, after one more abortive attempt,
they never tried the scheme again. It is often argued that
if Jellicoe, the British Admiral, had taken risks he could
have sunk the whole German fleet, and given England the
opportunity to occupy the German coast. On the other
hand, if he had failed and himself been seriously weakened,
the consequences to England might have been fatal.

As it was, he was able to apply the blockade. All transport from Germany to the outside world was barred or impeded, and before long neutral countries were also blockaded, their imports being restricted to their normal consumption— or what was available, since transport even for Allied needs ran very short. The Germans early resolved on the use of submarines to sink merchant ships, and early in 1915 they were sinking ships at sight, the torpedoing of the *Lusitania* causing such indignation in the United States that the submarine campaign was given up for a time. Its premature start had enabled the Allies to concert measures against it.

Later, it was resumed, the German Naval Staff assuring Ludendorff that it would starve England out. Submarines had now been greatly improved in the distance they could travel, but so had machinery for dealing with them, which included the use of mine-fields, aeroplanes, patrol craft, disguised armed merchantmen (" Q boats "), net barriers, smoke screens, hydrophones, and depth charges. The last destroyed 35 of the 156 submarines which were sunk, but by far the most effective answer to submarines was the convoy system, which had to be forced on the Admiralty against their determined opposition. The losses from submarines were most serious just before and just after the United States entered the War early in 1917 ; they were the chief cause of her entry. Afterwards, though submarines continued to operate in the Atlantic, the seas round England were cleared of them. The morale of their crews fell, as may be imagined. Callous though the policy was, some of the submarine commanders behaved humanely. The submarine base at Zeebrugge was blocked by a brilliant raid in April 1918.

Shortage of food and materials was felt to some extent in England among civilians, but it was nothing to the suffering of the blockaded enemy countries. They were helped at first by good harvests, but by the end a generation of children had been permanently stunted. These conditions were the main factor in bringing Germany down. Even the troops were going hungry and in very poor clothing. In Austria and Russia and East Europe the combination of famine with war conditions led to plague and typhus. The blockade was continued to June 1919. One consequence of sea power was that all the German colonies fell to the Allies, though a small German force held out until the Armistice in East Africa.

RED DAWN : LENIN GIVES A MEANING TO BOLSHEVISM

THERE was born in 1870, of a Civil Service family in a
town on the Volga, one Vladimir Ilitch Ulianov, who,
after a very successful school career, became a revolutionary.
His elder brother was hanged for joining in a plot against the
Tsar's life.   For some years afterwards this Vladimir Ilitch
Ulianov pursued his studies and took part in revolutionary
propaganda, doubtless under close police supervision, and
at twenty-five was exiled to Siberia for three years.   He
afterwards lived abroad with his wife in England, Switzerland, and France : they had a small income from revolutionary funds, and he quietly read and wrote.   We know him
now as Lenin.

In 1903 the Russian Social Democrat party, at their Conference in London, split over the question of Marx's doctrine
and over policy.   Lenin and the *Bolsheviks*, or majority
party (the first obscure use of the now familiar name) began
to work for revolution through the Social Democrat party.
Lenin was in Russia in 1905, when the disgrace of the Russo-
Japanese War caused agrarian disturbances, strikes, and
riots, which were bloodily suppressed.   This was the year
when the Tsar promised to grant a constitution and made
arrangements to call the impotent *Duma* (Parliament).   Lenin
was soon abroad again, working from Paris and Cracow and
writing and speaking energetically on behalf of his own policy
against not only reactionaries, but Liberals, terrorists, and all
who were not prepared to support his programme of organised
work for the transformation of Society in accordance with
Marx's view and alliance with the peasants, not the bourgeoisie.
Revolutionary material in plenty was lying about in Russia,
and the Social Democrat party, especially its Bolshevik wing,
was growing rapidly.   Terrorism was abandoned as futile,
and serious " underground " propaganda went on.

Lenin was deported to Switzerland by the Austrians when
the War began, and spent three years attacking all Liberals
and Socialists who made peace with their governments and
supported the War.   He called on them, without the slightest
success, to rebel.   But in Russia the War broke down the
Tsardom.   It hardly needed the suspicions of court intrigue
with Germany and the scandals of the Rasputin phase to
cause the general collapse of March 1917, when Tsar Nicholas
abdicated.

Lenin at once returned, the Germans assisting his journey, and, though he was unknown in Petrograd, was soon swaying public opinion. He was silenced for a time by the supporters of the new moderate Government under Prince Lvov, but as the Government fell to the next stage of weakness, under Kerensky, his propaganda went on. The country was swarming with demobilised soldiers, entirely out of hand, who were engaged in robbery and disorder. During 1917 one minister after another failed and the whole "moderate" policy—reform but continuance of the War—became impossible. The soldiers would not fight any more and the proletariat, conscious of its strength, meant to have a new society and not merely a new government; at least a fairly large and energetic body, Lenin's Bolshevik Social Democrats, did.

The last Russian offensive, under Brussilov, came to nothing, and in the autumn Lenin and his ally Trotsky were the recognised leaders of the Soviets, or local councils of soldiers and workers. The fall of the Moderate Kerensky Government and the transference of power to the Soviets of soldiers, peasants, and workers occurred at the beginning of November 1917. Kerensky fled; Lenin was proclaimed President of the Council of Peoples' Commissars, and Trotsky was appointed Minister of Foreign Affairs. They met the Germans at Brest-Litovsk and, in March 1918, signed peace on hard terms. They then turned to meet the Japanese and the counter-revolutionary forces which were mustering. There had been the usual use of force in their advent to power; they were considerably assisted by certain Lettish regiments, which were the only troops in or near Petrograd when the Bolshevik revolution of November 1917 took place.

The Revolution meant that the peasants at once seized the land of the nobles, and that an anti-bourgeois movement started. There were a number of murders, carried out in a casual, sordid way, like that of the Tsar and his family. Relations with the Allies were soon hostile, and the situation of the Soviet Republic bore a resemblance to that of the French Republic in 1793-94. The food shortage of the Tsardom's last days had grown much worse, and an appalling famine existed in the cities.

Lenin's enemies have never been able to charge him with any offence more serious than writing dull books. He was, in fact, a man of exemplary frugality, industry, and self-

command, a very good linguist and economist, who wore
himself out in advocating his ideals. He was no terrorist
but ruthlessness was inevitable in him, and he was a most able
practical revolutionary. He was unversed in administration
however, and so were his colleagues, who with him now set
out to make their Marxist (or Communist) state and spread
their views over the world.

SOME GREAT BOOKS ON MODERN HISTORY

THE first work to be consulted, one which is necessarily
large, but which can always be obtained in a reference
library, is the *Cambridge Modern History*, in thirteen volumes.
It is the standard work on its subject, and is an indispensable
book of reference. Two great historians who have tackled
their subject from an Olympian height, surveying the whole
course of history, are Oswald Spengler, whose *Decline of the
West* (George Allen and Unwin) has probably had a greater
sale than any other history of recent times, and A. J. Toynbee,
who brings vast scholarship and balance of judgment to bear
in his *The Study of History* (Oxford University Press). Lord
Acton, perhaps the greatest of modern historians, has written
a masterpiece in *Lectures in Modern History, 1453-1797*
(Macmillan). These books are solid, though brilliantly, and,
in Spengler's case, dramatically written. Good books on
specific periods are A. F. Pollard, *Henry VIII.* (Longmans),
for the Reformation ; G. N. Clark, *The Seventeenth Century*
(Clarendon Press) ; G. M. Trevelyan, *The England of Queen
Anne* (Longmans Green) ; Hilaire Belloc, *The French Revolu-
tion* (Home University Library, Thornton Butterworth
Limited) ; B. Croce, *History of Europe in the Nineteenth
Century* (Allen and Unwin).

The best short modern histories of England are Hilaire
Belloc's *Shorter History of England* (Harrap), Professor G. M.
Trevelyan's *History of England* (Longmans), and A. F. Pollard,
The History of England (Home University Library, Thornton
Butterworth Limited). For further bibliography, a visit to
the reference room of any public library will give access to the
Encyclopædia Britannica, which includes bibliographies on all
subjects.

THE CENTURY OF HOPE DEFERRED

by W. E. SALT, M.A., B.Com., Head of the Extra-Mural Department of Bristol University

THE nineteenth century, which, as an historical period, may be regarded as continuing until 1914, has been described as the Century of Hope. If this is an appropriate title, it suggests as a suitable description of the twentieth century, as far as it has already gone, the Century of Hope Deferred.

The Armistice of 11th November 1918 was greeted by the ordinary citizen of the allied countries with unmixed relief. It brought to an end the uncertainties and sacrifices of the preceding four years and left him free to rebuild his shaken world nearer to his heart's desire. Had not his political leaders promised reforms both of government and social organisation ? And had they not promised that streams of wealth would soon pour from the vanquished nations in the form of tribute, and be available for easing immediate difficulties and for a more thorough-going reconstruction of industry ? The outlook was distinctly bright. The nightmare was over and pleasant dreams followed.

This optimistic faith in the future was not shared, however, by the defeated peoples. They had suffered more from the effects of the War and were in a condition of exhaustion difficult to imagine. Nor did their situation receive immediate relief on the cessation of hostilities. The continuance of the blockade, the persistence of riot and revolution, and the curtailment of their territories, not only worsened their condition, but induced an attitude of despair which was an active hindrance to improvement. The Peace Treaty itself did nothing to alleviate the gloom, for its penalties exceeded the worst fears of the vanquished.

Although the threats to European civilisation were more serious in 1919 and 1920 than was generally recognised at the time, an amazingly rapid recovery was made in the succeeding years. In the economic field, advance was particularly swift. The devastated areas were rebuilt, the broken-down systems of finance and trade were repaired and again set in motion, and the organisation of industry and agriculture was improved considerably. This economic reconstruction was accompanied by many hopeful developments in the political field. The foundation of the League of Nations and the adoption of new and more co-operative methods of settling differences between nations offered substantial promise of a period of unbroken peace for the world.

In the realms of thought and art, an outburst of vigour took place which contrasted with the comparative sterility of the War years. In literature, music, painting, architecture, new movements appeared, breaking away from the forms and limitations of pre-war days and striking the eye and ear with unfamiliarity, sometimes arousing hostility. Scientific speculation and discovery proceeded at a rate even more rapid than that of the nineteenth century. Wireless communication, the improvement of the motor car, and the growth of aviation represent only a few of the more common practical results of these advances.

It seemed not improbable, therefore, in 1925 that the world was entering upon an era of material progress and prosperity which would eclipse that of any previous age. All the necessary ingredients appeared to be present ; the prospect of peace, industrial and financial stability, and intellectual vigour. For some years, wealth and prosperity grew, giving to the common man more steady employment and higher standards of living than he had known for several years, in some cases than he had ever known before. Nations, recently at one another's throats, were drawn closely together by the bonds of trade and financial interdependence. Conferences on disarmament, on economic affairs, and on health, proclaimed the new solidarity of mankind. Outwardly, the appearances were extremely hopeful, and, since most people are prone to accept things at their face value, they were content and optimistic. In Europe, a boom in trade and share speculation developed. In America, confidence in the discovery of the secret of unending prosperity was a first article of faith.

THE BLACK CONSEQUENCE OF FOLLY AND GREED

BUT underneath, much was rotten. The economic reorganisation which had taken place immediately after the War was little more than a hurried and flimsy patching-up of a broken-down machine. The perilous con-

THE DANGER SPOTS IN EUROPE.

1. *Memel, ceded by Germany to Lithuania in* 1919, *and reabsorbed by Germany in* 1939. 2. *Danzig and the Polish Corridor.* 3. *Sudetenland, ceded to Germany in* 1938, *that cession leading to the occupation of Bohemia-Moravia in* 1939. 4. *Italian Tyrol.* 5. *Italy would like seaports here.* 6, 7. *Hungarian Minorities in Rumania and Yugoslavia.* 9. *Bulgarian claims in the Dobrudja and former Bulgarian access to Mediterranean.*

dition of Europe had demanded haste. There was no time to give to radical alterations. Yet, when recovery from post-war distress occurred, the general public, business men, and political leaders alike were deceived, and mistook the appearance for the reality. They regarded the temporary repairs as the equivalent of a complete reconstruction. As a result, they failed to take the opportunity to carry through more deep-seated reforms, and, when the first severe strain was placed on the economic system, it again broke down. The whole painful process of reconstruction had to be begun once more.

In the political field, too, the trend of events was similar. The post-war settlement proved to be no settlement at all. The vanquished powers accepted the conditions imposed upon them with reluctance and with the clear determination to secure revision at the first possible moment. Several of the allied powers were discontented with their share of the spoils of victory. Far from healing old wounds, the Peace Treaties opened new ones. The machinery devised for remedying grievances and for securing an amicable settlement of international issues did not work well, mainly because of a lack of desire that it should succeed. While protesting an unswerving love of peace, most nations continued to pile up armaments. While swearing unswerving loyalty to the ideal of international co-operation, they pursued policies of the utmost selfishness. The result was that when the world most needed disarmament as a means of reducing the crippling burden of military expenditure, and when it needed international co-operation in order to check the spread of world depression, both were absent.

The world depression was in part the product of the folly and selfishness of mankind in the post-war years. But even this black consequence failed to teach its lesson. On the contrary, it served to confirm nations in the paths which they had chosen. " Each for himself " became the watchword of every country. Everywhere short cuts were sought which would lead the nation more quickly to the desired goal of independence and enable it to isolate itself from the shocks of the world slump. New movements arose which preached a return to more primitive ideals and habits. And all the time gloom deepened and privation grew steadily worse. The following pages will give some clue to the currents of thought and events.

A WORLD UNSKILLED IN THE ART OF LIVING

ONE fact stands out prominently from this dark tragedy. The misfortunes of the modern world are entirely man-made. The bounty of Nature has not been less than in former times. Indeed, if anything, under the stimulus of scientific discovery, Nature has yielded her fruits with embarrassing lavishness. Nor is there anything uncontrollable in the relations of nations. The inescapable conclusion is that our troubles are due to the failure of man to understand and control himself. The increase in our knowledge of the material universe in modern times has been marvellous. Has there been a corresponding growth in our knowledge of economic relations and, still more, in our readiness to apply this knowledge? Is there any discernible desire to submit the relations between countries to the rule of law in the same way that the behaviour of individuals is controlled?

Throughout the post-war period, there has been a prevalent sense of uneasiness. Whether this is the direct product of the War cannot easily be decided. But there is not the slightest doubt that since the War a general atmosphere of disillusionment and uncertainty has prevailed. Old beliefs and loyalties have been destroyed or abandoned and have not been replaced by new ones. There is a widespread feeling that the modern generation is groping blindly in a world which is too big and complicated for it to grasp and control.

All this augurs ill for the future. The economic and social systems do not run themselves. They require the directive force of man. If he is excessively diffident of his own powers, or if he is apt to be diverted to the pursuit of narrow, particularist aims, the forces at his disposal are bound to be misused or wasted. The advances which the world most needs to-day are not in medicine or chemistry or engineering, but in the ordinary arts of living. One of the most hopeful lines of progress is to interest the common man and woman in the nature and problems of the world in which they live, so that they may be able to exercise their influence in a wise and restrained manner. For this, some knowledge of the historical development of the modern world is necessary, since it gives the background of our current problems; also, some introduction to the contending social forces.

PEAKS AND DEPRESSIONS OF ECONOMIC UPHEAVAL

by E. J. PROPERT, M.A.

THE signing of the Armistice in 1918 closed the door on four years of ruinous fighting, and it then became necessary for the countries of Europe to turn their thoughts from destruction to restoration. The nations, heartily sick of war, looked for a speedy return to the conditions which they had enjoyed before 1914, with all the additional benefits which statesmen had described as the reward of returning heroes. On the surface, this seemed a not impossible aspiration, especially for the victorious countries ; for, despite the tremendous outlay on armaments, the War period had been one of great activity and apparent prosperity. For a year or two the illusion lingered, in Great Britain at any rate, that the transition to peace conditions could be quite easily effected. But the realisation was soon to be forced home that only by great effort and determination, and only at the cost of much individual sacrifice, could the economic machine again be put into normal working order.

The War had, in the first place, greatly impoverished the belligerent nations. For four years they had concentrated on the production of armaments for purely destructive purposes, and only the current needs of life had been catered for. Like imprudent housewives, they had ceased to bother about the future. Practically no building had been done to provide for increasing populations. Machinery was not replaced unless immediately needed, and every available factory was commandeered for the production of munitions. In addition to this failure to keep up the normal rate of economic progress, much actual destruction had taken place.

TRYING TO BUILD WITH BROKEN TOOLS

EVERY nation suffered alike the loss of a high proportion of its most vigorous manhood—the total death roll among the fighting troops being between eight and ten millions—which resulted in a lowering of standards of efficiency. France, as the battlefield of Europe, suffered particularly heavily, and " No Man's Land " was a scene of desolation and ruin, requiring years of work before the land could again be brought under cultivation or the shattered towns and villages be rebuilt.

In Germany still worse conditions were to be found. The long blockade had reduced the country almost to starvation point, and industry was practically at a standstill. Indeed, throughout Eastern Europe the state of the people was appalling. The continued shortage of food supplies and the lack of proper attention had so lowered the vitality of the people that disease spread, causing terrible distress, while thousands died of sheer starvation. Perhaps Russia endured the worst conditions of all, for her difficulties were intensified by civil war, and the privations of her people were indescribably severe.

It was against a background of this kind that Europe had to attempt to rebuild her prosperity, and it is not surprising that the means at her disposal proved quite inadequate for the task. The resumption of trade was impossible with broken-down transport facilities and a general atmosphere of instability. At first, too, governments tried to finance peace as they had financed war—by borrowing and by printing new money. This led to a rise in prices, wages, and profits, giving at first a fictitious appearance of prosperity. But very soon came disillusionment. In the defeated countries money almost ceased to have any value, so that production and trade were reduced to a minimum and millions were completely impoverished. In the victorious countries prices collapsed in 1920 and a period of trade depression, unemployment, and falling wages began ; the task of reconstruction was made still more difficult.

While Europe was intent upon the process of self-destruction, important changes had been taking place in other countries, making the post-war world very different from that of 1914 and before. Perhaps the most significant change was that which transformed the United States from a dependent and borrowing country into the greatest financial and industrial power in the world.

Undoubtedly, this transformation would have occurred in any case ; but it was greatly accelerated by the War. Refraining from entering into hostilities until 1917, America contented herself with supplying the Allies with munitions and other goods, and with finding openings in overseas markets previously supplied by the Allies. As a result, the U.S.A. emerged from the War with a greatly increased export trade and with an enormous volume of debts owed to her by Europe.

OBSTACLES THAT BARRED THE PATH TO PROGRESS

ALTHOUGH this enhanced prosperity enabled America to take a prominent part in relieving the distress of the stricken European nations, economically it involved a serious hindrance to the recovery of Europe. For the permanent loss of markets in the United States and elsewhere meant that even if the effort were made to rebuild European industry it was no longer possible to rely on selling its products abroad in sufficient quantities to guarantee full employment for men and machines.

Changes which affected Europe economically were also occurring elsewhere. Japan, for example, with her low wages and standards of living, had adjusted herself rapidly to Western methods of mass production, and was already threatening to become a serious competitor, especially in the textile industries. Even the colonies of the British Empire, which had long provided a safe outlet for the products of British industry, had travelled a long way on the path to economic independence, and were not prepared to welcome as before the exports of the Mother Country. Not only therefore, had Europe the task of rebuilding on shattered foundations and with poor materials, but in addition she had to adapt herself to a different world, in which other countries were setting the pace.

Europe's difficult path of restoration, thus outlined, contained a number of other obstacles resulting from the War. In the first place, industry had to be re-organised. During the War, ordinary peace-time needs were neglected, and a disproportionately large amount of labour and capital was directed to the production of ammunition and other war necessities. When these were no longer required, there was inevitably a period of dislocation before workers and capital could be transferred to other occupations.

The demobilised soldiers also presented a very serious problem. Many of them had never been trained in any peace-time occupation and were, therefore, useless in any skilled branch of industry. Others were anxious to return to their previous jobs, only to find themselves unwanted. The docking industry, for instance, had been maintained

t full strength during the War, and when the influx of former
lockers occurred after demobilisation, a difficult problem of
rganisation arose on account of the over-supply of labour.
But although problems of this kind were fairly general,
causing many disputes and hampering reconstruction, they
were only temporary.

There were other and more serious obstacles, however.
Of these probably the most serious was the loss of trade to
other countries. As already mentioned, Europe had lost
markets which she could never hope to recover. It is not
possible to measure exactly how much Europe's share in
world production and trade was affected by the War, but
a few comparisons show that it dwindled considerably.
Taking the world as a whole, population increased between
1913 and 1923 by about 5 per cent., while total production
rose by a slightly larger amount. Although there was a
small increase in the population of Europe during this period,
the volume of European production actually diminished.
In the production of raw materials (including foodstuffs),
Europe sustained a fall of 16 per cent.—the drop being far
more severe in Eastern Europe than in the West—while the
corresponding figures for North America show an increase
of 29 per cent.

This change in the economic importance of Europe was
not, of course, necessarily permanent, and, indeed, a great
recovery was made in the following years. But she has not
recovered, and probably never will recover, her former
industrial supremacy. Furthermore, the necessity of fighting
against rivals of growing efficiency and power, who had been
able to start with all the advantages of European invention,
made the path of recovery a continuous, and sometimes a
losing, struggle.

THE NATIONAL "EGO" STRIKES AT TRADE

A LARGE part of the trade of the European countries had
always been confined to the Continent itself. Great
Britain, for example, had in 1913 found 33·5 per cent. of her
foreign markets in Europe. The recovery of this trade was
made very difficult by the nature of the Treaty settlements.
In the first place, post-war Europe was divided up very
differently from the pre-war Continent. Some countries,
like Germany, had been pared away, while others had
been given additional territory, and some more or less new

countries, like Czecho-Slovaki aand Jugo-Slavia, had made their appearance.

This re-arrangement, expressing as it did a ferment of political and racial feeling, frequently resentful, had far-reaching effects upon trade relations within Europe. It initiated everywhere a policy of national consolidation and the building up of home industries, and an intensely nationalistic outlook which at first found its expression in protective tariffs and trade barriers, and afterwards led the way to a highly dangerous national egoism.

The political situation reacted in other ways upon European industry. The course of German production and trade, for example, was to a considerable extent determined by the reparations exacted by the Allies. In the long run, the only way in which Germany could pay the sums demanded of her was by exporting more goods than she imported, thus securing a credit balance abroad. German reconstruction after the War was, therefore, forced into the channels of her export industries, and a tremendous outflow of manufactured goods at very low prices resulted. These manufactures came into competition with the products of other industrial countries, and particularly with those of Great Britain.

The political disharmony and scarcely concealed hatred which survived between France and Germany was a further obstacle. In 1922 Germany found it impossible to continue her cash reparation payments. Although France agreed to a moratorium, she seized the opportunity of a technical default in deliveries in kind to invade the Ruhr. This step met with passive resistance from the Germans.

THE MARCH TOWARDS PROSPERITY

DESPITE many obstacles, however, Europe, as a whole, made a rapid recovery from the depression of 1920–21, and by 1925 it appeared that the leeway lost during the War had been completely made up, and the conditions of prosperity firmly established. Subsequent events, unfortunately, showed that the revival in trade was built on very insecure foundations. Nevertheless, the rapidity with which Europe recovered from the perilous conditions of 1919 and 1920 showed that the economic system possessed great powers of resistance and recuperation. The rebound from threatened collapse to comparative prosperity was truly remarkable.

There are many indications of the level of economic conditions at any time. Probably the most valuable are the volume of production and trade, the standard of living, and the amount of unemployment. In all these respects, Europe in 1925 showed a marked improvement over previous years. The volume of production had reached a level slightly higher than that of 1913, while trade had improved to an almost equal extent. Standards of living also compared favourably with those of earlier years, although, for various reasons, unemployment remained high. It is important to realise, on the other hand, that had the War not taken place, very much more material progress would have been made. The truth of this statement is made apparent by a comparison of Europe with the rest of the world. In 1925, the volume of production in the world, excluding Europe and North America, was about 24 per cent. higher than in 1913, while trade showed an increase of 26 per cent. The corresponding figures for North America were even higher.

But, while it is true that the War on the whole retarded economic development, in certain directions it actually hastened advance. The demand for large quantities of standardised goods, especially munitions and equipment, and the comparative shortage of workers, stimulated the invention and adoption of machinery in some industries, and accelerated the arrival of what we have learned to call the " Machine Age." In those industries which were readily adapted to machine production, therefore, potential production was greater as a result of the War.

TWO BIG STRIDES TOWARDS THE GOAL

THE improvement in European conditions was accompanied and made possible by the temporary settlement of some of the most pressing immediate problems. Apart from the practical work of relieving poverty and physical distress, in which America played a very active and generous part, and the rebuilding and repair of land and equipment, the two most outstanding achievements were the resumption of the gold standard and the debt and reparations agreements. The restoration of a stable international means of exchange made it possible for trade and financial transactions between countries to be carried on once more with some degree of confidence. Great Britain did not enjoy an unmixed gain from this development, however. As the gold standard was more extensively adopted, world prices fell. Great Britain, with her high and rather rigid levels of wages and other costs of production, was unable to reduce her export prices accordingly, and suffered a severe loss of trade. The vexing problem of reparations was temporarily settled by the acceptance in 1924 of the Dawes Plan. This scaled down the payments to be made by Germany to a level more within her ability to pay. It was combined with an international loan from the allied countries to assist in the restoration of a sounder financial position in Germany. Together, they helped materially in improving Germany's industrial situation and in removing a serious drag on the economic recovery of the whole of Central Europe.

Thus by 1925 Europe seemed to be well on the road to recovery. Given political stability and reasonable freedom of intercourse between the nations, there seemed no reason why material progress should not be substantial and unchecked.

PROSPERITY RIDES ON A WAVE OF RECKLESSNESS

THE year 1925 seemed to be a favourable turning-point, and whereas the years before had been chiefly marked by the struggle to regain pre-war standards, the time which followed was one of rapid advance in many directions, leading up to the spectacular boom of 1928. This advance, while it helped to eradicate some of the more dismal impressions left by the War, and enabled new traditions to be built up, was nevertheless a very critical period in the world economic situation. It evoked, in the first place, a spirit of optimism which at times might more truthfully have been called recklessness, and secondly, it set up a severe strain, not clearly perceived at the time, on the economic system. For the growth which took place in some directions made more serious the maladjustments which remained elsewhere, until ultimately the strain became too great for the weaker links, and the chain snapped. A slower and more even advance might have been in the end more satisfactory.

An examination of conditions between 1925 and 1928 shows that there was, on the surface, ample reason for optimism. Compared with the rationing and high prices of the War, and the frequent scarcity and starvation of the years that followed, the world seemed indeed to have become a land of plenty. On all sides, production was increasing in relation to demand.

The situation is best understood by looking in turn at the markets for foodstuffs, raw materials, and manufactured goods. In the case of the more important foodstuffs, for example, the demand per head of a population does not grow or decline very much, unless a very great social change is taking place, such as the substitution of wheat for rice in the diet of the Chinese. A rise in the standard of living, in fact, generally tends to turn demand away from the more elementary foods, such as wheat or rye, towards more luxurious foods, such as meat and fruit, but even then the demand for these is fairly limited.

THE MOCKING MAKE-BELIEVE OF PROSPERITY

BUT during this period the production of foodstuffs and particularly of grain was very much increased, owing to a number of circumstances. Large-scale farming was developed, and the increased use of agricultural machinery, new seed varieties and fertilisers, as well as the cultivation of new land in Canada and elsewhere, all helped towards increasing supplies, while demand lagged behind. As a result, there was a constant tendency for large stocks and surpluses to accumulate, and, as prices were not for a time allowed to fall, there was an appearance of great wealth and prosperity.

The market for raw materials was in a similar condition. Production was increasing at about the same rate as in pre-war years, but here, too, demand held back. The demand for raw materials arises from the demand for the manufactured goods in whose production they are used—for example, the demand for rubber mainly depends on the number of motor-car tyres that can be sold. An increased demand for raw materials, therefore, presupposes an increase in the sale of manufactures.

But as it happened, the tendency at this time was for consumers to buy goods of better quality rather than in larger quantity, so that in the market for raw materials also there was a tendency in certain cases for supply to outstrip demand. In the manufacturing industries, too, potential production was well ahead of what could be sold, on account of the rapid introduction of more and more efficient machinery. It might have been expected that these increases in productivity would lead to still greater advances in national and individual prosperity, and it seemed likely that this would be the outcome.

One important aspect of this period of post-war prosperity was that standards of living in almost all countries were appreciably higher than before the War. Wages in particular, when expressed in terms of the quantity of goods they would buy, had risen, although it is not possible to measure the exact extent of the rise in different countries. This general increase in the incomes of individuals made a distinct change in the character of spending. Before the War, the majority of wage-earners had only a very small margin of money left over after buying the conventional necessaries of life—food, clothing, lighting, and so on—and this usually had to be saved for a "rainy day." But, since the War, the safe-guards which have been erected against poverty, such as insurance and unemployment relief, have made it more easy for people to spend their larger margin over necessities on comparative luxuries. This has enabled industries producing such commodities as wireless sets, automobiles, artificial silk, and films to expand at an amazing rate, giving employ-ment to a large number of workers as well as contributing to a much more comfortable standard of living than most people had hitherto enjoyed.

At this time, too, international relations were from the economic point of view much more satisfactory. Much of the suspicion and nationalistic feeling of earlier years seemed to have disappeared, and confidence was largely restored. International lending was resumed on an even larger scale than before the War, although the financial situation was not really as sound. There was a constant demand for loans from those countries which needed foreign assistance in rebuilding their industries. But the frequent defaults of the previous years made creditors more wary, and unwilling to tie up their capital abroad, indefinitely. A very large proportion of international lending, therefore, took the form of short term credits, which fluctuated considerably in volume, and were liable to be withdrawn at very short notice. Inter-national trade also received a tremendous impetus. During the period under review, world trade increased by 19 per cent., compared with an increase of only 11 per cent. in world production, while European trade alone grew by as much as 22 per cent. This advance was largely due to a growth in the trade in manufactured goods.

THE FIRST DANGER SIGNALS APPEAR

IT has been pointed out by economists that probably at no time would it be true to say that stable conditions existed in the world. But although trade depressions occurred before the War, and although changes were continually taking place, yet some kind of normality was to be found which has since been lacking. In the period before 1928, a number of danger signals pointed to the existence of hidden threats to the continuance of prosperity.

The most unsatisfactory aspect of this period seems, on looking back, to have been the inability of the World to cope with its own increasing powers of production. This was more serious in the agricultural and raw material producing industries than in manufacturing, partly because supply is less easily controlled in the former, and partly because the growth of new demands had provided fresh outlets for the latter ; for example, the motor-car and artificial-silk industries were expanding rapidly.

When supplies increase relatively to demand, the normal effect is a fall in price, which at the same time tends to discourage production and to stimulate demand. Unfortunately, this was not allowed to happen. For instance, while, for a number of reasons already outlined, the world production of wheat was increasing, there was a distinct attempt by monopolist interests, especially in Canada, to prevent the price from falling as much as it would have done under free competition. As a result, supplies were not scaled down, and the world stocks of wheat became dangerously large, despite poor harvests in 1926 and 1927. When, therefore, in 1928 an exceptionally good harvest was reaped, the situation at once became critical, and a sharp fall in prices could not be avoided, involving wheat growers in serious losses. Similar conditions were to be found in many of the other " primary " industries.

A further weakness in the economic structure was caused by the restoration of the gold standard. Although the re-establishment of a stable international monetary standard was essential to world trade recovery, this was only achieved in most countries—France being a notable exception—by a considerable rise in the value of the monetary unit, or, to express it differently, by a fall in the price level, which had risen as a result of the War. This, however, meant that all debts contracted during the period of high prices now had a much greater value in terms of goods.

Now the most important debtors under the existing system are governments and industrial concerns. Most govern-

ments had borrowed heavily during the War. Consequently
after the War, taxation was unusually high in many countries
because of the debt charges. The higher rates of taxation
did not seem particularly onerous as long as incomes were
high also. But, with the fall in prices, most incomes suffered
a reduction, and the burden of taxation became correspond
ingly greater. In some industries, for example, the Lanca
shire cotton trade, a large proportion of the capital by which
they were financed had been borrowed at fixed rates of interest
As prices and profits fell, the burden of these charges also
increased. Thus, through the relative increase in fixed
charges, a greater burden was imposed on the taxpayer and on
industry.

SYMPTOMS OF THE WORLD'S DISEASE

THESE maladjustments which lay below the surface had
also their visible signs. Of these, the most important
was the persistence of unemployment. Unemployment was
not a new problem. For at least a century before the Great
War, successive trade depressions had periodically thrown
many people out of work. But, because of the absence of
adequate statistics, the actual number of unemployed men
and women was never known with any degree of accuracy
The post-war situation, however, was very different. The
War had caused the removal of millions of workers from
their normal occupations. And, unfortunately, even in
1928, the most prosperous year since before 1914, the re
adjustment of industry in the world was not sufficiently
complete to absorb again all those who had been displaced.

The seriousness of the unemployment problem at this time
varied widely between different countries. In Canada, for
example, where " home " industries were being fostered by
means of protection, the percentage of Trade Union member
registered as unemployed fell from 3·3 in 1926 to as low as
2·2 in 1928. In Germany also there was a considerable re
duction, owing to her rapid recovery just then. Neverthe
less, in 1928 she still had 6·6 per cent. totally and 6·9 per cent
partially unemployed workers. Great Britain suffered most
on account of the great loss of export trade which she had
sustained, and here the proportion of unemployed was in 1928
as high as 11·4 per cent.

The unsteady nature of industrial recovery was also re
flected in the growth of monopolistic tendencies in many

industries. This, as indicated in the case of wheat particularly, was prompted by the fear that prices would, if left to
find their own level, inevitably fall. An attempt was therefore made by groups of producers, sometimes national and
sometimes international, to maintain prices at a profitable
height, and frequently the effect of this was to keep in existence firms which could not have survived under free competition, thus aggravating rather than curing the tendency
to over-production in these industries, and storing up more
trouble for the future.

THE VAIN HOPE OF "MAKING GERMANY PAY"

BUT serious attempts were made during these years to
solve some of the more outstanding and urgent problems.
War Debts and reparations were still a difficulty, for it was
becoming more and more obvious that Germany could not
continue to make the large payments demanded of her
without injuring the manufacturing industries of other
countries which were not intended to help to pay for the War,
or continuing in the farcical practice of first borrowing the
money from the United States. Clearly the idea of " making
the Germans pay " had to be abandoned, or at least very much
modified, and the time was now ripe for a new settlement.

For, with the passage of years, much of the wartime hatred
had faded away, while the revival of industry opened out a new
prospect of prosperity to the world. In this spirit, a revised
agreement, known as the Young Plan, was accepted in 1929.
It was unfortunate that despite good intentions this was in
some ways a less satisfactory settlement than that of 1924, its
chief weakness being that, although the payments were still
further reduced, no provision was made for adjusting the
amount of the payments in accordance with movements of
prices. Since prices did fall almost immediately afterwards,
the payments became very much heavier in terms of goods,
and a correspondingly greater burden to Germany.

An effort was also made to restore the trading relationships
between nations to something like the pre-war footing. To
this end, a good deal of re-organisation had to take place in
the world's monetary systems and in tariff policies. During
the War the monetary systems of the belligerent countries
had been cut adrift from the gold standard and from one
another, and it was now taken for granted that they could only
be held together satisfactorily by a gold link as nearly as

possible of the pre-war pattern. Between the years 1925 and 1927, therefore, nearly every country got back to the gold standard either, as in England, by drastically cutting down prices, which had risen on account of the War inflation, or, as in France, by establishing a lower gold value for the currency unit.

But this was to prove insufficient. As a result of the War, a remarkable re-distribution of the world's gold had come

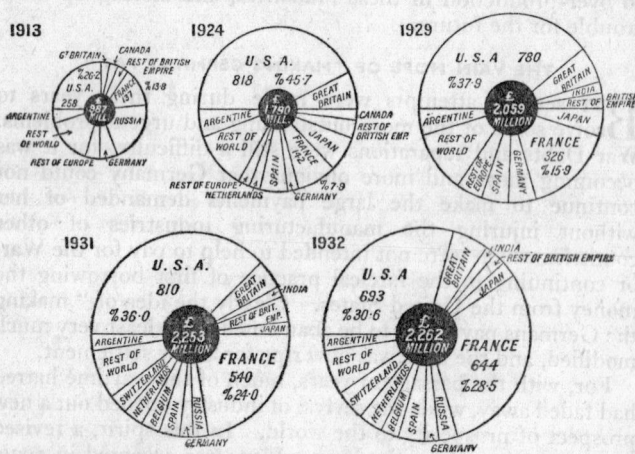

GOLD RESERVES OF THE CENTRAL BANKS

Notice how the gold accumulated in two countries, the United States and France, until, at the depth of the world depression, these two countries between them had collected 60 per cent. of the world supply. Notice also how the stock increased.

about, and this was only aggravated when the use of gold as a basis for currency was resumed. In earlier years, London had been the financial and Great Britain the industrial centre of the world, and England had followed a policy of steady investment abroad to balance her large surplus of exports, which the recipients would otherwise ultimately have had to pay for in gold. Large international movements of gold were, therefore, unusual, and a division of the world's stocks between nations was preserved approximately in proportion to their internal needs.

After the War, New York and Paris rivalled London as financial centres, but they were not prepared to adopt the same policy. America's increased export trade, and the large debt payments made to her, caused a flow of gold in that direction, as she was not prepared to continue indefinitely making foreign loans; while France made a deliberate policy of building up her stock of gold, to consolidate her position in the event of a future war. In 1928, despite improvement in the distribution, the stock of monetary gold in America was $4,141,000,000, in France 1259, in Great Britain only 754, and in Germany 666 million dollars.

AN HONEST ATTEMPT TO SAVE THE WORLD

DESPITE this maldistribution, however, the international gold standard was once again an accomplished fact, and it was to be hoped that with the further return of confidence, and better organised and freer trade, a more balanced position would work itself out. With such idea in view, a World Economic Conference was held in 1927, its aim being to discuss and make proposals for reducing the barriers to trade which already threatened to cut short the revival of industry. It recommended and thought practicable a general reduction in tariffs.

This conference represented an honest attempt to improve the condition of the world, to consolidate the advance made since the War, and to open the path to further progress in the future. Its efforts were lost in the economic catastrophes which followed. It is to be hoped, however, that its task may be resumed in less troubled times.

DEPRESSION : THE BLACK WAVE ROLLS ROUND THE WORLD

THE substantial but unbalanced recovery which the world had made by 1929 gave place during the next year to the most severe trade depression ever experienced. It is not possible to say exactly what was the cause of this collapse, although certain features stand out prominently, distinguishing this depression from any that had occurred before. A slump was not by any means a new experience in the world. For over a century industrial countries had been subject to a succession of booms (periods of good trade and rising prices), and slumps (periods of bad trade and falling prices) which, although they had occurred with almost clockwork regularity, had never been adequately explained. A depression had been due to appear somewhere about 1915, but the intervention of the War had so altered the course of industry that it had not materialised. The 1929 depression showed the world that although the War had caused and fostered many radical changes in economic affairs, it had not suppressed the trade cycle.

A period of trade depression is one of unemployment and hardship. But under existing conditions it does serve at least one useful purpose. When business is good, and high prices are being obtained for all kinds of goods, producers are tempted by the promise of increased profits into extending their businesses and producing on a growing scale. The cumulative result is that after a time more is being produced than can under existing economic organisation be sold profitably. For the present system of distribution is such that increases of production can only be gradually absorbed. This excess of goods over the power to consume means that productive effort is being used wastefully.

The sooner, therefore, that prices fall, damping down the activities of producers by reducing their expectation of profit, the sooner can the over-production be remedied. A slump provides the required incentive for bringing back the volume of production within the limits which can be utilised by society. It is admittedly a wasteful and clumsy method for achieving this end, since it brings in its train a progression of bankruptcies, capital losses, and unemployment. But, in the absence of a more successful control of the economic machine, it seems to be an inevitable one. Some economists have even compared the trade cycle with the ruthless but apparently essential working of natural laws.

1929 : THE SLUMP BEGINS

IN 1929 the tendency to over-production was becoming more and more marked in the world. This tendency, as already explained, was more prominent in the case of raw materials and foodstuffs, the supply of which is not subject to immediate control, and the demand for which is not easily stimulated above its normal level, than in manufactured goods. The first recognition of the situation by producers led to an attempt, by the establishment of monopolistic agreements to prevent prices from falling. But this naturally only had the effect of worsening the over-production, and making still more severe the inevitable fall in prices when it did arrive. In the autumn of 1929 the prices of raw materials fell sharply. The extent of the fall varied in different places and between different commodities, but its severity can be judged from a few typical examples. The prices in the world's markets of wheat and cotton, for instance, had dropped by nearly

	GT BRITAIN	U.S.A	GERMANY	FRANCE	ITALY	U.S.S.R.
WHEAT MILLIONS OF QUINTALS (AVERAGE) 1928-30	13	234	37	76	63	233
COAL MILLIONS OF METRIC TONS 1929	262	552	163	54		38
SHIPS STEAM & MOTOR THOUSANDS OF GROSS TONS LAUNCHED 1929	1520	112	249	79	71	34
MOTOR CARS (IN THOUSANDS) NUMBERS PRODUCED 1929	239	5,358	135	250	91	
COTTON MILL CONSUMPTION THOUSANDS OF METRIC TONS 1929-30	574	1,386	295	286	221	442

PEAK YEAR, 1929 : WORLD PRODUCTION

This chart shows, by means of pictures drawn in proportion to the figures, the production of important commodities by some of the leading countries in the year 1929, which was the peak year of post-war prosperity.

30 per cent. by June 1930, while those of wool and of rubber had declined by over 40 per cent.

This movement in wholesale prices was only the beginning of the slump, however, and its effects soon spread to industry as a whole, having in the end an almost paralysing influence. Despite the post-war tendency in many countries to concentrate on home markets, foreign trade was still very important, especially to the manufacturing countries. One of the most usual channels of trade was the exchange of the industrial products of countries like Great Britain for the raw materials and foodstuffs of the primarily agricultural countries like Australia and the Argentine. But when the world prices of these primary commodities fell, the income of their producers was correspondingly diminished, and they were not able to go on buying industrial goods to the same extent as formerly. The impoverishment of these countries, therefore, led to a decline in the demand for manufactured goods and consequently to a fall in their prices.

THE SHADOW CREEPS FROM LAND TO LAND

ONE of the most striking features of the depression was that all countries alike were affected by it. It might have been expected that whereas Germany, for instance, crippled by war, defeat, and the exacting demands of her recent enemies for reparation, would quickly succumb, the United States, which had become more and more prosperous since the War, would easily withstand its onslaught. Yet actually it was in America that the slump first set in, only spreading subsequently to Europe.

The post-war period had been so good in America that the belief was generally accepted that the secret of permanent prosperity had at last been found. The condition of industry was so flourishing that the dividends obtainable on investments were exceptionally high, averaging something like 12 or 13 per cent. at the beginning of 1929. Unfortunately, this only concentrated attention on the most unstable of all markets—the Stock Exchange. Investment became so profitable that speculation was attracted, and the prices of shares began to soar. An orgy of speculation followed. It was said that even the secretaries in New York offices borrowed on the strength of their slender earnings, in order to buy shares. Many new companies were formed, some of them having titles reminiscent of the South Sea Bubble. Then the point was reached where the banks began to realise the unsoundness of the situation, and to restrict their credits. There ensued a panic and a spectacular crash in which thousands of people were ruined. The effects soon spread to Europe, where a subsidiary Stock Exchange boom had been going on. It was this occurrence, in October of 1929, which precipitated and brought to a head the general condition of depression in industry already rendered inevitable by the widespread existence of over-production.

A fall in prices is always accompanied by certain other conditions. Business becomes unprofitable, many existing concerns are forced into liquidation, and the incentive to new business ventures is diminished, or disappears altogether for the time being. This fall in industrial activity causes unemployment. The reduction in profits and in employment entails a widespread reduction in incomes, reducing the spending capacity of the population. Although needs do not become any less " effective," demand, *i.e.*, demand taking the form of both willingness and ability to pay a price, is reduced, and this in turn has a further depressing effect on prices. Thus the original drop in prices engenders a still greater one, and so the depression deepens in what has aptly been described as a " vicious spiral." This process was experienced in the world very markedly after the end of 1929, as was evidenced only too clearly by a progressive fall in trade and production and a progressive rise in the figures of unemployment.

FIGURES THAT TOLD ONLY HALF THE TALE

THE falling off in world production between 1929 and 1930 does not seem very large when given as a general figure, the actual drop being about 3 per cent. This, however, is due to the fact that more than half the goods covered by this figure were agricultural, and the fall in prices had been too recent to have exercised its full effect in restricting crop acreage. The fall in industrial production was very much greater, reaching by 1931 as much as 26 per cent. in the United States. World trade suffered quite to the same extent. It is impossible to find out the precise change in the volume of goods exchanged between nations, since the information obtainable is expressed only in terms of money value, so that a reduced total reflects not only a smaller physical amount of trade but also the fall in the level of prices. Expressed in this way, however, the quantity of international trade done in the first quarter of 1931 was only about 63 per cent. of that done in the first quarter of 1929. On the whole, the decline was in this case more severe in raw materials and foodstuffs than in manufactured goods. As a result, European trade suffered less than that of the world as a whole, the reduction being only about 28 per cent.

Although all countries alike participated in the depression, the effects of it varied according to differences in their economic structure. Unemployment in particular assumed different proportions. In France, for example, where, despite growing industrialisation, a large proportion of the population are still engaged in peasant agriculture, each family farming its own small piece of land and supplying a local market in addition to meeting most of its own needs, unemployment would never become such a serious problem as in an industrial country like Great Britain, where the majority of people are congregated in large towns, and are almost entirely dependent upon their ability to earn wages by working in factories. Again, the actual amount of unemployment in a country must naturally bear some relation to the size of its population. The normal number of unemployed in the United States, for example, would obviously be much in excess of the corresponding figure for a smaller nation. For this reason, a much better picture of general conditions can be obtained by comparing the percentage of unemployment in different countries than by looking only at absolute numbers.

In practically every country unemployment increased steadily and at an alarming pace. By 1932 there were, as far as could be estimated, about 6,127,808 workers unemployed in Germany, representing 33 per cent. of the working population ; in Great Britain, 2,809,103, or 22 per cent. ; in Denmark, 106,464, or 35·1 per cent ; and in the United States the percentage of trade union members registered as unemployed was 23·1, representing something like 12 million workers, although, owing to the absence of any system of unemployment insurance in America, many of those out of work were probably not included in this figure. The one notable exception was Soviet Russia, which reported in 1930 a great increase in industrial activity and a corresponding increase in employment.

The problem of unemployment was affected in a further way by the slump. When employers found their profits disappearing on account of the fall in prices, which they could not prevent, their natural reaction was to look for some means of reducing their costs. The most obvious way of achieving this was to lower wages, and indeed the level of money wages had appreciably fallen in most countries. But to reduce wages, especially when labour is strongly organised, is a slow

	GERMANY	Gᵀ BRITAIN	FRANCE	ITALY	AUSTRALIA	CANADA
NUMBER OF UNEMPLOYED IN THE FIRST QUARTER OF 1929 (THOUSANDS)	2,484	1,204	8·6	309	39	12
NUMBER OF UNEMPLOYED IN THE FIRST QUARTER OF 1932 (THOUSANDS)	6,128	2,809	337	1,174	119	41

WORLD DEPRESSION AND THE WORKER

A comparison between the number of unemployed workers in 1929, the peak year of post-war prosperity, and the figures in 1932, when the economic depression was world-wide.

process, and a dangerous one for the employer, frequently involving disputes, which only hold up production and lower the efficiency of industry.

THE RUTHLESS PROGRESS OF RATIONALISATION

A METHOD which causes less friction is to find more economical methods of production. This incentive to improved methods and greater efficiency is, in fact, one of the points made by those who regard trade depressions as akin to the purging processes of Nature. From 1929 onwards, the invention and introduction of labour-saving machinery became so marked that the new term " rationalisation," which had been coined in Germany some years before, was adopted to describe it. This term was also used to cover the financial re-organisation into which many firms were forced.

The rate at which improvements can be introduced naturally depends upon the rate at which they are invented. Their value to the community, on the other hand, depends upon the rate at which the fruits of the higher productivity can be distributed. At this period, the rate of industrial invention was exceptionally high, and, owing to widespread unemployment, the rate of increase in consumption exceptionally low. The immediate effects of rationalisation, consequently, were to put more men and women out of work. It further induced reckless attempts to recapture dwindling foreign markets by means of price-reduction, leading to a flood of cheap manufactured goods in countries not protected against these imports, with frequent accusations of dumping and unfair competition.

All this served only to intensify the depression. In each country agriculture seemed hopelessly swamped by the fall in world prices, while industry had to face exceptionally intense foreign competition. It was not surprising, therefore, that the belief took hold of people's imagination that, since world recovery seemed to come no nearer, each nation must find its own path to salvation. This outlook led, after 1929, to the beginning of a new raising of tariff walls. Great Britain at first withheld from this policy, clinging to her traditional faith in the benefits of Free Trade, but she, too, succumbed in time.

The introduction of tariffs was encouraged by the belief that the depression proved foreign trade to be an insufficiently firm foundation on which to build up a country's economic system, and that the first duty of its statesmen was to foster and protect from intruders the more reliable field of the home market. But, unfortunately for this policy, home markets are restricted, and do not, even in a large and varied country like the United States, provide sufficient outlets for home industries. Some export trade, therefore, continued to be a necessity.

The result of the growth of this kind of outlook was that most countries were on the one hand raising tariff walls of increasing height, in order to cut down or eliminate their imports, and on the other hand sparing no efforts to increase their exports. The absurdity of this situation, where every one wanted to sell and no one wanted to buy, was not generally apparent at the time, for the substitution of home-produced for foreign goods was very attractive, in view of the overwhelming dimensions of unemployment. The inevitability that if this policy were widely successful exports would also dwindle, causing further unemployment in the industries producing them, was not so attractive, and was, therefore, for the time being conveniently shelved by the politicians.

1931 : THE EDGE OF THE PRECIPICE

DESPITE the efforts made to check the slump, or perhaps because of the lack of wisdom with which they were directed, the depression dragged on, becoming deeper and deeper, and after two years of increasing impoverishment a financial crisis developed. A number of immediate causes precipitated the crisis ; but there can be no doubt that it was really the cumulative result of the years of unsound economic practices to which the world had resorted in the post-war period. A crisis is clearly distinguished by the economist from a trade depression. The term depression applies to the lasting condition of trade and industry. But the term crisis implies only a sudden breakdown in the financial system. This, of course, does affect and is affected by the more general situation of which it is really a special manifestation.

The crisis of 1931 centred round the collapse of the international gold standard, which had been so painfully restored during the period 1925–27. To understand the reason for this collapse it is necessary to distinguish between two different aspects of the financial transactions of any country. First, there are its financial relations with the rest of the world, arising from its foreign trade and foreign lending and borrowing. The significant fact here is the balance of its total receipts and payments. Secondly, there are its internal financial conditions, especially the balance between the revenue and expenditure of the government. A financial crisis is liable to arise when there is a substantial deficit on either or both of these accounts. For, if the balance of international payments shows a heavy deficit, it gives rise to a fear that the country may be unable to meet its foreign payments : while, if governmental expenditure largely exceeds revenue, the fear grows that the government may resort to inflation, *i.e.*, the printing of paper money, as a means of covering the deficit. In 1931, many countries were in a precarious position both internally and internationally.

PAYMENTS THAT WENT ON A CIRCULAR TOUR

THE international situation had grown more and more complicated. It had become increasingly difficult for Germany and the ex-Allies to meet the financial obligations arising from reparations and War Debts. The centre of the trouble was Germany. At no time was Germany able to pay reparations out of a surplus of exports over imports. The payments were made out of money borrowed from abroad. The United States and Great Britain had lent to Germany more than the amounts due as reparation ; Germany paid the reparation annuities to the ex-Allies ; and these, in their turn, had passed the sums back to the United States in the form of war debt instalments. This absurd circle of payments was possible as long as the Unites States and, to a lesser extent, Great Britain, were willing to continue lending to Germany. It is true that the ultimate result would be to place Germany under a crushing burden of debt. But few people looked as far ahead as that. If, however, the stream of loans should cease, Germany would be compelled to meet reparations out of her own resources. Could she bear the sudden strain ?

The test came as early as 1928. In that year, the Wall Street boom in the United States diverted funds from foreign investment to stock speculation at home. When this boom came to an end in 1929, the disastrous slump in the United States made impossible the resumption of foreign loans. Yet the farcical system of payments did not at once collapse. The world depression and the decline in Germany's foreign trade made it impossible for her to bear reparation charges and interest on the debts incurred since the War and at the same time to meet the withdrawals of foreign funds which began with the onset of the slump. For a time British banks and financiers came to the rescue out of a desire to prevent collapse in Germany and to safeguard the large investments which they already had there. But they were unable wholly to fill the gap left by the cessation of American loans. And, in a sense, continued lending only made the final position worse by adding to Germany's debts and postponing a radical readjustment of the situation. By 1931 the whole financial system of Germany was tottering, and threats of political revolution added to the feelings of insecurity.

The imminent crisis became an actual one in the spring of 1931. In May of that year, the *Credit Anstalt*, one of the largest banks in Austria, was declared to be in an insolvent condition. Before the War, the bank had financial connections throughout the Austro-Hungarian Empire. When, by the Peace Treaty, the Empire was dismembered, the bank's transactions were limited to a much smaller and poorer area. Although it managed to survive, it failed to djust itself satisfactorily to the changed circumstances, and, in the spring of 1931, it was announced that its liabilities greatly exceeded its assets. Assistance from abroad enabled it to weather the storm, but the affair caused a shock to the already weakening confidence of Central Europe.

The effects were particularly severe in Germany. The events of 1923 when, as a result of inflation, accumulated savings were rendered worthless, had not been forgotten, and they made the German people incapable of acting with restraint under the suspicion of another financial disaster. The announcement of the difficulties of the *Credit Anstalt* was interpreted in Germany as the first whisper of a crisis and at once a run began on the German banks, which soon caused one of the biggest commercial banks to close its doors. The infection quickly spread abroad ; banks and businesses in France, Belgium, and Switzerland which had balances in Germany began to withdraw them before the domestic panic made withdrawal impossible.

The steady drain of funds from Germany threatened a complete financial collapse there, which was averted only by the arrangement of a " Standstill Agreement " greatly limiting the power of withdrawing money from the country. But the stopping of the German leak did not allay the panic. On the contrary, it tended to increase it. Foreign banks and firms, finding their funds in Germany locked up, turned elsewhere for means of building up their reserves of liquid resources. The only remaining centre from which balances could be withdrawn in any volume was London. So began a steady drain of funds from Great Britain.

THE STORM CENTRE MOVES TO BRITAIN

A FURTHER reason than the desire to secure liquid resources caused holders of foreign balances in London to seek to withdraw them. For some time, doubts and rumours had been spreading concerning internal disorders in England, and these were not without sound basis. The return of Great Britain to gold in 1925 had been accomplished only at the expense of the loss of a considerable part of her export trade, and this had greatly diminished her income from abroad. The depression intensified this loss ; for the dwindling of world trade had reduced the demand for services such as shipping and insurance, in which England had specialised, and which had earned for her a large income.

But Great Britain's foreign expenditure was not reduced by an amount corresponding to the fall in her foreign income It was impossible to cut down imports tremendously, owing to her dependence on imported food and raw materials. Foreign lending, too, was not greatly reduced ; London had, for instance, continued to advance funds to Germany after other financial centres had begun to withdraw their balances. This gap between international payments and income had been developing for some period before the crisis, and had been met by an inflow of foreign credits on an unprecedented scale. For Britain, in pre-war years, had been a centre for lending to other countries rather than borrowing from them. But these foreign credits were mainly held in a highly " liquid " form, being short term credits subject to withdrawal after very short notice.

Thus the slightest trace of suspicion concerning the British financial situation, or the slightest need for immediate resources by her creditors, would lead to the prompt repatriation of the credits. This in turn would lead to a drain of gold from the Bank of England on such a scale that the Bank's stock of gold would speedily be exhausted. There could be no doubt of Great Britain's ultimate solvency. Her foreign investments far exceeded any calls which could possibly be made upon her. There could be, and was, however, doubt of her ability to meet immediately a large drain of liquid balances. In a word, while the long term position was sound, the short term position was very precarious.

A series of circumstances combined in 1931 to shake the confidence of the world in Great Britain's ability to meet a drain of funds and to remain on the gold standard. In the first place, her internal financial affairs were in a very unsatisfactory condition. Unemployment had almost reached the three million mark. Since the insurance scheme had not accumulated any appreciable reserves, the payment of benefit was being made to a large extent out of loans, and there seemed every prospect of the debt increasing by about £40,000,000 a year as long as unemployment remained at its existing figure.

The Budget introduced by the Chancellor of the Exchequer of the Labour Government in 1931 could do nothing to improve the position, the world depression having gone too far.

THE ALARM SOUNDED AT WESTMINSTER

THE political opponents of the Labour administration seized the opportunity of accusing it of thriftlessness, and tended to exaggerate the seriousness of the country's financial position. They seized eagerly upon the publication of the report of the Economy Committee on 31st July. This Committee had been set up in March following a debate on the prospective budgetary position and had been instructed to make recommendations for effecting forthwith all possible reductions in the national expenditure."

In the report the Committee sounded the alarm, stating that it was essential that drastic measures should be taken at once to avert financial disaster. It recommended immediate and extensive reductions in the pay of almost all Government employees, from cabinet ministers to teachers and police, and a substantial cut in the cost of unemployment insurance. This report naturally caused considerable misgivings among the investing class both within the country and abroad. The alarm was not diminished when it became known that the Government was not prepared to act upon the report.

These internal difficulties of Great Britain coincided with a progressive worsening of the situation in Europe. In the early summer, President Hoover had proposed a moratorium on all war debts and reparations until June 1932, with the object of relieving the immediate burdens and of providing a breathing space in which the nations could work for recovery. The proposal was received with delight, and an immediate upward movement of share prices indicated a temporary revival of confidence. But the French Government, anxious for guarantees of the resumption of reparation payments at the conclusion of the moratorium period, delayed acceptance of the plan, and the momentary fillip disappeared. When, after some weeks, the scheme was endorsed, its possibilities for good had been largely destroyed. It did no more than regularise a position which would have arisen in any event.

AN ATTEMPT TO STEM THE EBBING STREAM OF GOLD

BECAUSE of the critical condition of Europe, the withdrawals from Great Britain continued. The Bank of England viewed with alarm the persistent loss of credits and the drain of gold which it evoked, and, in conjunction with the Government, sought to raise new short term credits in France and America in order to cover the withdrawals. Although the

obscurity in which these negotiations are still wrapped mak
it difficult to make any positive assertion, it would seem th
these credits were offered only on conditions. These wer
it is stated, that the British Government should balance i
Budget and cease to borrow further to meet current expend
ture, and that its expenditure be reduced, particularly by
reduction in the cost of unemployment insurance. T
imposition of these conditions gave rise to a political crisi
The Labour Cabinet refused to accept them ; whereupc
the Prime Minister formed a National Government consistir
largely of Conservatives and Liberals and pledged to introdu
emergency measures to deal with the financial situation ar
to " save the pound."

The first act of the National Government was to secu
credits to the sum of £80,000,000 from America with tl
object of meeting the withdrawals from London which we
going on steadily. It then introduced an emergency Budg
modelled on the recommendations of the Economy Committe
Expenditure was drastically reduced by cuts in the pay
Government servants—teachers, police, civil servants, soldie
and sailors, etc.—and by a reduction in unemployme
benefit. At the same time attempts were made to rai
additional revenue by increases in the rates of taxatio
especially of income tax.

These measures which were intended to revive foreig
confidence in the financial stability of Great Britain and
avoid an abandonment of the gold standard proved actuall
to have the reverse effect. For the proposed " cuts " arouse
considerable resentment. In the depressed areas, bitt
hostility to the reductions in unemployment pay were expresse
while the cut in the pay of naval ratings led to a refusal
obey orders at Invergordon. In the foreign press, this unre
was interpreted to be the premonitory rumblings of riot an
revolution.

As a consequence, withdrawals of balances from Gre
Britain took place at an even more rapid rate. After a fe
weeks the Governor of the Bank of England announced tha
if the loss of funds was allowed to proceed unchecked fc
much longer, the Bank would be denuded of gold and Englan
forced off the gold standard by sheer lack of the metal. Thu
on September 17th, the further export of gold was prohibite
The Government which was pledged to protect the poun
itself severed the link between the pound and gold. Hence

forward, the pound was allowed to find its own level in terms of other currencies.

THE "DISASTER" THAT WAS TO SAVE BRITAIN

THIS event, which had been declared only a few weeks earlier to be a disaster and a breach of faith, was now hailed as the salvation of the country. The immediate effect of the abandonment of the gold standard was that the pound fell in value in terms of other currencies which remained on gold. This fall in the external value of sterling gave an advantage to the British export trade, since it enabled exporters to quote lower prices in terms of foreign gold currencies. Hence it tended to stimulate exports, or rather, perhaps, to prevent their further decline. When, later on, the National Government introduced tariffs on a considerable range of goods, imports were checked and the trading position of Great Britain improved for the time being. But she was not left in sole enjoyment of these benefits for long. One by one other countries abandoned the gold standard until, by the beginning of 1936, France alone among the great powers retained an effective gold link.

Thus, in a single year, the international monetary standard, which had been restored so slowly and painfully after the War, was destroyed. Monetary instability, with its resultant hindrances to trade and temptations to competitive currency depreciation, once more prevailed. This turn of events gave added strength to the already powerful forces clamouring for a purely nationalistic control of industry and trade. From now on, by tariffs, quotas, and exchange restrictions, each nation tried to find its own salvation, regardless of the consequences to others. The policy of " each for himself and the devil take the hindmost" became the first principle of statesmanship.

The spread of depression over the world and the steady worsening of conditions after the crisis of 1931 caused men to concentrate upon devising some course of action which would bring the slump to an end. The possibilities of national, and even international, planning of industry, trade, and finance, became a general topic of discussion, following upon the Soviet method of substituting an ordered programme of economic development for the more haphazard organisation of *laissez-faire* capitalism. In the examination of numerous schemes which were put forward for restoring prosperity, one fact stood out : that certain measures which gave promise of

improving the condition of individual nations not onl
would be of no help to the rest of the world, but woul
prove positively injurious to other countries.

Tariffs and quota schemes are of this type. It becam
apparent that the raising of tariff walls or the introduction o
quota restrictions on foreign goods, in so far as they wer
successful in reserving a greater share of the home marke
for domestic industries, necessarily did so at the expense o
the foreign countries whose goods were excluded. An
increase in employment at home, therefore, was offset by
decrease in employment elsewhere, and the world positio
remained unchanged. This method of safeguarding hom
industries has been aptly described as amounting to an expor
of unemployment.

This divergence between national and international interest
soon clarified itself into two distinct and opposed schools o
opinion. At the one extreme were those people who argue
that since this was a world-wide depression due to worl
influences it was capable of solution only by the wholehearte
co-operation of all nations, or at any rate of the chief industria
countries. At the other extreme were those who pointed t
the failure, and occasionally blank refusal of nations to co
operate. Although politicians and economists of all nation
were in general agreement concerning what should be done
there was a great divergence between their pronouncement
and their actions. In view of the practical impossibility o
achieving any common action and of the growing hardship
caused by the depression, it was urged that each nation shoul
take whatever measures were felt necessary to improve its ow
conditions without waiting for any one else, even regardles
of the effects on others.

The absence of international co-operation became a reason
for condemning it. Some attempts at international action
were made, but were almost invariably unsuccessful. The
legacy of ill-feeling left by the War gave the nationalist movements in nearly all countries an opportunity which they did
not fail to grasp, and the tide turned strongly for the time
being against internationalism. Probably no country, with
the possible exception of Great Britain, had ever really
believed in it, and after the panic of 1931 it had little chance
of success. Some few attempts were made to promote international action on specific matters, e.g. the world over-production of wheat, but, for the most part, they were half-

nearted, and were gradually undermined by the conflicting
policies of individual nations.

AMERICA'S POLICY CRIPPLES HER DEBTORS

THE prevalent failure to grasp the true nature of the world's
problems and to make a thoroughgoing attack on them
was seen particularly in the matter of reparations and war
debts. American economic policy in the post-war period had
been directed consistently towards maintaining and increasing
her surplus of exports over imports. Yet this practice of
checking imports made it exceedingly difficult for her foreign
debtors to continue interest payments. The dilemma was
avoided for several years by a large outflow of loans from
America, by which, in effect, she paid herself the amounts
due to her from abroad. When these loans slowed down and
ceased in 1928 and 1929, America still expected payment.
But by retaining, and even raising her tariff walls, she made
payment impossible. Germany soon declared her inability
to continue to pay reparations, and, with the cessation of this
income, the ex-Allies would certainly have announced their
inability to pay war debt annuities due to America. This
situation was postponed for a while by the acceptance of the
Hoover Moratorium in 1931.

When the Moratorium expired in June 1932, it was clear
that some more lasting arrangement must be made if wholesale defaults were to be avoided. Hitherto, most of the ex-
Allied countries, France especially, had been determined for
political and other reasons that Germany must continue to
pay reparations at whatever cost to herself. Now, it was
obvious that to insist upon the complete fulfilment of the
bond would cause monetary collapse in Germany and, consequently, immense loss to those countries with commercial
and financial interests there. A more conciliatory spirit
spread, therefore, and at the Lausanne Conference of July
1932, an agreement was made which virtually marked the end
of reparations. This agreement provided for a complete
moratorium for three years from the date of its signature,
and reduced the capital value of the total sums due from
Germany to one-tenth of their former amount. Germany
was required to deliver to the Bank for International Settlements redeemable bonds to the amount of 3,000 million gold
marks (roughly £150,000,000 at par), bearing interest at 5
per cent. per annum, with a 1 per cent. sinking fund for their

redemption. These bonds were to be issued to the public
by the Bank for International Settlements after the expiry
of the period of three years at a rate not less than 90 per cent.
Any bonds not negotiated at the end of fifteen years from the
date of the agreement were to be cancelled. This agreement
has generally been taken to mean the end of reparations. For
not only did it wipe out the greater part of Germany's previous
liability, but furthermore the unsettled condition of the
country and its poor credit make it unlikely that the full issue
of bonds will be made.

TRYING TO SOLVE THE WAR DEBT MUDDLE

THE Lausanne Agreement referred only to reparations and
left the war debt position unsettled. It was tacitly understood, however, that the signatories should not demand the
payment of debt annuities from one another. But the United
States, the biggest creditor, was not a signatory. Yet there
seemed reason to believe that, having made such a sacrifice
in the interests of world recovery, the signatories would not be
penalised by the United States. In order to clear up the
situation, it was decided at Lausanne to convene a World
Economic Conference to discuss, among other things, the
question of international debts. When, as is described below,
the Conference broke up without coming to any decision, the
matter was thrown back into the melting pot. Each debtor
was left to decide its own policy towards the American debts.

The result was that, when the next payments fell due, only
a very few countries honoured their debts in full. Others,
e.g. France, repudiated their obligations, and yet others, e.g.
Great Britain, recognised the legal obligation but confined
themselves to paying only a considerably reduced " token "
payment until a revision of the debt settlements could be
made. No satisfactory decision was arrived at, however.
The United States accepted the token payments, but did so
" without prejudice " to the resumption of the full annuities
in the future. Repudiation she condemned, and retorted by
refusing financial aid to the countries which had resorted to
this method.

In defence of her failure to follow the reduction of reparations by debt revision she claims that the two subjects are distinct and that she cannot consent to be influenced by decisions
taken quite independently of herself. But while the matter
has remained in this unsatisfactory condition, there can be

little doubt that the end of reparations spells the end of war debts in their old form. The European nations will not resume debt payments on the original scale when their reparation receipts have been so drastically cut.

Despite the growing lack of faith in international action, it was clear that all countries to some extent—and some to a very large extent—stood to lose by a policy of complete isolation. Great Britain was especially threatened by the pursuit of this policy. As a partial check upon it, trade agreements were made with individual countries with the object of maintaining a certain amount of regulated trade with them. Also, an Imperial Economic Conference was held at Ottawa in 1932 with the avowed object of improving trade relations between Great Britain and the Empire.

The Conference was not very successful, for the Dominions made it quite clear that, while they were prepared to give some preference to Britain over foreign countries, they were not willing to allow British competition to endanger their own growing industries. On the other hand, they asked for, and received, several concessions in the British market. Thus, while some agreements were made which secured for Great Britain a certain outlet for her industrial products, the nationalistic attitude of the Dominions prevented the Ottawa Conference from doing much to free the channels of trade.

THE CONFERENCE WHERE NO ONE GAVE WAY

IN the summer of 1933, the second World Economic Conference met in London. The Conference was called to complete the work begun at Lausanne, and to round off the agreement on reparations with agreements concerning debts and world trade and finance. It was thought by some that the essential conditions for the restoration of world prosperity were a freeing of trade and the re-establishment of a stable international basis for currency, preferably by a general return to gold. But, though the Conference was heralded by solemn exhortations and glowing promises of achievement, it proved almost completely abortive. Each country protested the most impeccable principles, but hoped to gain by a breach of them. None would reduce its trade barriers ; none would return to gold as long as there was prospect of gain from the depreciation of its currency. Thus, though the Conference dragged on for weeks, it did nothing save confirm the world in its pursuit of economic nationalism.

The history of the next few years is a record of the mor
intensive pursuit of national paths to economic prosperity
Having failed to agree on common action, the nations turne
more enthusiastically than ever to individual action. So muc
so that it seemed that the advances and ideals of the foregoin
century were to be jettisoned completely. The nineteent
century, with its improvements in transport and its develop
ment of new areas of supply and markets, had gone far t
make the world one economic unit. Now it seemed that th
prevalent belief was that foreign trade was an evil to be cu
down to the smallest possible amount, and even this remnan
to be rigorously controlled and perpetually threatened wit
extinction.

This policy of " economic nationalism " was by no mean
new. In the seventeenth and eighteenth centuries, fo
example, national economic rivalry was pursued in much th
same way as to-day. But the circumstances were differen
Then, each country's main objective was to secure for itse
as large a share as possible in the expanding wealth offered b
the discovery of new lands and new channels of trade. To-da
the aim is to escape from the consequences of over-productio
and trade depression. Modern nationalism is found again
a background of threatened poverty, not of promised wealth
it is the product of despair. Possibly the nations in whic
opinion is comparatively free may eventually realise this an
discarding alike the idea of world conferences and that of
self-contained nationalism, may make agreements with on
another based on mutual concession.

THE HATCHING OF THE " BLUE EAGLE "

THE beginning of a new régime in America in 1933 wa
an event which startled the world. A reputation fo
wealth and prosperity still clung to the United States, ar
other countries had not realised to what an extent she wa
suffering from depression. The American economic syster
which had developed so rapidly during the previous twen
years, was not adapted to dealing with conditions of slum
and unemployment. Yet it was saddled with more than twi
as many unemployed people as any other nation had to de
with, and had no adequate scheme for maintaining or r
employing them. The severity of the climate made th
sufferings in some areas very intense. Moreover, througho

he country the agricultural population, which is an extremely
nfluential section of the community, had been very severely
hit by the catastrophic fall in the world prices of their products.

The United States had never been "internationally-
minded." Of all nations she is perhaps the best equipped
for isolation from the rest of the world. Yet during and after
the War she had developed close trading and financial relations
with many other countries. For this reason, she retained the

THE BLUE EAGLE OF INDUSTRY

*A symbol of the post-war battle against economic depression,
this device was adopted in the U.S.A. to rally manufacturers
to the New Industrial Recovery Act. It was the badge of
recruitment, to be found on many American commodities.*

gold standard after most other nations had abandoned it,
because she felt that her prosperity depended upon its maintenance, and because she had accumulated so large a stock of
gold. When it became clear that these international connections were of no help to her in the revival of her industries,
she willingly—almost gladly—cut adrift from them and concentrated upon her internal problems. The "New Deal"
was a determined effort to set the American house in order
without reference to its effects upon the rest of the world.
The task which President Roosevelt set himself on his in-

auguration in 1933 was to raise the level of prices to that which ruled in 1928, the last year of real prosperity. It was hoped that this would give such a stimulus to business that unemployment would shrink to its usual small proportions, and prosperity be restored. To this end, the National Industrial Recovery Act,[1] which initiated the New Deal to the American people, was passed.

The Act very much increased the amount of control exercised by the central government over industry, and provided for better industrial organisation for the purpose of preventing " over-production " and the inter-state dumping of goods. Wages were raised, in some cases by as much as twenty per cent., while prices were controlled and not allowed to rise to the same extent. It was hoped in this way to increase the purchasing power of the workers and thus to stimulate the demand for goods. In order to ensure the success of these measures, the Government allowed all goods produced by firms co-operating in the scheme to be marked with a Blue Eagle, and it soon became a matter of patriotism to buy only Blue Eagle goods. The Government was also empowered to follow a policy of disguised inflation in the form of heavy expenditure on public works and loans to industrial enterprises at low rates of interest, both intended to help the desired rise in prices. An attempt was made to maintain exports, despite the rise in American prices, by deliberately depressing the external value of the dollar.

WHERE THE "NEW DEAL" AND FASCISM DIFFER

THE American nation was disappointed if it expected an immediate revival to result from these efforts. A considerable drop in unemployment was registered in consequence of the extensive government works. But the recovery of ordinary industry was long delayed.

The outstanding characteristic of the American recovery plan was that it was genuinely an economic experiment and not a political one. Political issues and effects naturally arose from the measures adopted by the government. Roosevelt used his sweeping majority and the popular enthusiasm aroused by his programme to secure practically dictatorial powers. But these powers were terminable by the people, and were not used for the establishment of a personal or party

[1] The Act was declared by the Supreme Court in 1935 to go beyond the powers of legislature conferred on Congress by the Constitution.

despotism. In such respects, the American scheme is sharply distinguished from those movements, mainly found in Europe, which are commonly termed fascist.

These have always been primarily political movements. Nevertheless, the economic policy of the fascist dictatorships is of great significance. It represents an attempt on the part of countries which are, both geographically and economically, closely tied to other nations to become as nearly as possible independent units, no matter at what cost. Such a policy cannot be followed without affecting other countries and increasing political and economic rivalry.

Politically, fascism has meant the appearance of a supreme dictator backed by a militaristic party. Its avowed policy and indeed philosophy, is the unification and aggrandisement of the State, as personified by the dictator and his party. The increase in strength, and especially military strength, of the nation has been sought partly through stimulating the growth of population. Thus in Italy, for instance, many devices, such as marriage bounties, have been used to increase the birth rate, and this when emigration, which used to be very considerable, has been strictly limited by immigration acts. But, in view of the scanty resources of the country, these measures were bound to produce further unemployment and a fall in the standard of living. After ten years of fascist rule, the Italian standards of living were less than one-half those of Great Britain. The low rates of wages implied by these conditions naturally intensified the fear of other countries that their higher wage scales would be endangered by the competition of Italian cheap labour.

THE VICIOUS CIRCLE OF ECONOMIC NATIONALISM

THE increase of national strength has been sought also in the development of the productive power of the community, both manufacturing and agricultural. From a world point of view, these efforts have been worse than useless. They have caused an expansion of industries behind the shelter of tariff walls, although the demand for their products could have been met by more efficient producers. They have caused an increase in the output of agricultural produce at a time when it has been impossible to find profitable outlets for the world's crops. They have helped, therefore, to reduce the already dwindling volume of world trade and to increase the problems of other countries. Nor are the effects of such measures likely to be quickly removed. Industries once established are not readily abandoned; nor are peasants, drawn to the cultivation of more fields and new crops, likely to yield their position without a struggle.

Unfortunately, there is as yet no sign of a desire to relax this extreme policy. Rabid economic nationalism seems to lead to a vicious circle. For the more countries that adopt it, the more are others forced in the same direction out of pure self-defence. Yet this search for economic isolation is bound to involve much waste of productive power and a consequent retardation of material progress. Fascism is a growing obstacle to world co-operation and, therefore, to world prosperity.

Great Britain had before the War earned for herself the reputation of being the most important and beneficent influence in international economic affairs. She followed a policy of foreign investment, by which more backward areas were developed, and not only carried on an extensive foreign trade herself, but, by means of her excellent shipping and financial services, facilitated trade between other countries. The economic supremacy she enjoyed strengthened her considerable political influence in the world. Great Britain's international outlook was not, however, dictated entirely—or even mainly—by philanthropic motives. Her growing greatness and prosperity depended upon the pursuit of such a policy. She could not have developed her rich industrial resources in the nineteenth century without importing large quantities of food to maintain her rapidly-growing town population. Neither could she have found sufficiently wide markets for her manufactured goods except by the creation of new demands through the development of less advanced countries. Thus, Free Trade, the economic symbol of inter-nationalism, came to be adopted as the first article of her industrial faith. Although protectionist movements appeared from time to time, they did not seriously shake this staunch belief.

After the War, it was generally thought in Great Britain that the old relations would quickly be resumed. Even with the growth of economic nationalism abroad, tariffs were advocated here mainly as temporary defensive measures, and were rejected even on these grounds. Great Britain continued her pre-war policy of economic co-operation, and was the moving spirit in numerous international conferences and agreements. After the crisis of 1931, the realisation of two facts caused an abrupt change of attitude. In the first place, it was at last recognised that other countries were not as yet prepared to co-operate. This fact was forced home by the failure of the World Economic Conference of 1933. In the second place, the changed position of Great Britain in the world had to be faced. The expansion of industries in other lands had deprived her of many of her former markets.

The sentiment grew that, in view of her diminished manufacturing importance, she could no longer afford to remain so dependent upon the outside world, but that she should concentrate upon producing more of her needed foodstuffs at home. But the nation was reluctant at first to adopt an extreme policy, and an attractive compromise was sought in the movement for imperial economic unity or Empire Free Trade. But the grave obstacles in the way of such a scheme were made clear by the Ottawa Conference. Great Britain, therefore, felt obliged to take a more independent line, and her policy has become increasingly nationalistic.

THE FIRST MANŒUVRES IN SELF-DEFENCE

THE first step in this new trend was the abandonment of the gold standard in 1931. By thus causing a fall in the external value of the pound, Great Britain eased her difficulties at the expense of foreign creditors who held sterling. This act was in marked contrast to her pre-war policy, in which the preservation of international monetary stability had always been regarded as the prime necessity. Then, early in 1932, the National Government embarked on its tariff measures. These were first introduced as temporary expedients, applying only to a selected list of goods. But they were quickly extended until Great Britain was converted into a protectionist country.

With this change went an alteration in the motives for which tariffs were imposed. From being temporary weapons of economic defence they became permanent instruments for the development of home production, particularly of agricultural goods. Costly quota schemes were introduced, covering wheat, pigs and bacon, milk and other primary products, and subsidies were granted in various forms to a number of industries for expansion and re-organisation. The final effects of these sweeping changes cannot yet be perceived. But it is highly unlikely that they will provide a full solution to Britain's difficulties. The past economic prosperity of Great

Britain has been based upon certain staple industries, *e.g.*, mining, iron and steel, cotton, shipping, all of which found outlets for a large part of their output abroad. No effective supports for these main pillars of our industrial structure have been found. There is, however, this to be said for agricultural protection within limits : it may be partly justified by permanent conditions of national health and the vitality of the stock.

IGNORING THE SIGN-POST TO ECONOMIC PROSPERITY

CONDITIONS in America remained difficult to estimate, but frequent and extensive labour disputes pointed to continued hardships. In practically every country, unemployment was still abnormally heavy in 1934. World industrial activity fell to 68·7 per cent of the 1929 figure in 1932, but had risen to 111·3 by 1936, while by 1937 world trade had attained 98·3 of its 1929 volume. It is open to question whether this recovery was due to economic nationalism or was achieved in spite of it.

It is, indeed, scarcely possible to talk of the development of economic nationalism as an attempt to find a cure for the world depression. In reality, it is a withdrawal from the difficult problem of re-adjusting the economic balance between the nations. This problem must ultimately be attacked. No nation which is not a continent in itself can be a complete economic unit. The rate of economic progress of the world depends upon the use that is made of the special facilities of each country. This, in turn, is dependent upon the willingness of each country to specialise to some extent and to trade freely with other nations.

It has been seen that the depression was characterised by a discrepancy between the world production of certain important commodities and its ability to consume them. By means of restrictions on output and by the cutting down of imports, most countries have in effect shelved the problem by causing a reduction of immediately available supplies. This can only be a temporary solution, however, and does not offer any hope of preventing future crises, while in the meantime it involves a lowering of standards of living by wasting productive power. The encouragement of wheat-growing in England, for example, is wasteful from a world point of view when other countries can already produce more than enough to meet the demand at a lower cost. The British consumer of wheat has to suffer for this waste, either through paying a higher price or, as a taxpayer, through meeting the cost of the necessary subsidies.

The real problem is whether, in order to ensure a high degree of prosperity to the human race as a whole, it will not be necessary to devise some scheme for the world regulation of the production and distribution of goods. This merges into the yet wider question whether such a reorganisation is possible under the existing capitalistic system, or whether it would not be necessary to introduce some form of socialistic control, possibly on an international basis.

EXPERIMENTS IN ADAPTATION : REVOLUTION AND REFORM

by W. E. SALT, M.A., B.Com., Head of the Extra-Mural Department of Bristol University, and R. J. WOODWARD, M.A. (Oxon.), Headmaster of Tetbury Grammar School, Glos.

THE Armistice came to a world which had suffered incalculable losses in life and wealth. If one adds to the number of soldiers killed the number of civilians who lost their lives as the result of disease and privation, the total death-roll hardly falls short of twenty millions. Nor did the signing of the Armistice stop at once the drain of life and vigour. Even the victors required years of recuperation ; men and factories diverted from peaceful pursuits could not immediately be re-directed into their normal channels. For the defeated, the beginnings of recovery were in some instances long postponed. Disorder and revolution continued for years.

These circumstances lay at the root of the later troubles of the world, and especially of Europe, which suffered most from them. The War meant, above all, the slaughter of the young men of Europe. In many countries, the proportion between the generations was drastically altered ; in some, almost all the men between the ages of eighteen and forty disappeared. Their vitality and imagination were absent when most needed. Moreover, the experience of the War left lasting effects. The national hostilities and passions of later years are traceable not only to the tangible effects of the War, but also to its influence on men's minds and actions.

The task of drawing up a treaty of peace was one of colossal magnitude. It involved redrawing the map of the whole of Central Europe ; deciding the disposal of Germany's extensive colonial empire ; and carving new countries out of the old Turkish Empire. Even if entered upon in a purely dispassionate spirit by men who were unaffected by the bitterness created by four years of war, this task would have been appallingly complex, and mistakes would have been made. As it was, the job was undertaken by men who had lived through all the fears and hatreds of the War and now were influenced by the temper of the peoples they represented. The Peace Conference often degenerated, therefore, from an attempt to establish the conditions which would enable men to live in friendly co-operation, to the endeavour to secure for one's own country the greater share of the spoils of war. Whilst in part an honest attempt to make war unnecessary, if not impossible, the Peace Treaty is also in part a document which may make for future wars, unless there is a radical change in the relation of States.

Another factor which helped to make the Treaty an unsatisfactory settlement was the need for haste. The victorious peoples were anxious to make an end of the matter as soon as possible, in order that they might be able to resume their interrupted activities without more delay. The War, to many of them, was an unpleasant task successfully accomplished. "Well, then, let us be done with it without further ado," they said. A much more important circumstance making for haste was the fact that a large part of Europe was in danger of falling into chaos. In Austria-Hungary, Russia, and Turkey, governments and frontiers had ceased to exist, and armies were still on the move. In Germany, the new Republic was only precariously established and feared every moment to find its authority gone. Over whole regions, populations were in distress or in actual want through the destruction of government and industry. It was urgent that some settlement of Europe should be made at once, so that governments could be re-established and set about the reconstruction of social and economic life. So perilous was the condition of Europe immediately after the War that even a bad peace was probably better than a long delayed peace.

In the form in which they were finally ratified, the treaties of peace contained two main groups of provisions : they laid down the price which the vanquished powers must pay for waging war, and they drew new frontiers between States in Europe and elsewhere. In some measure, both sets of provisions had the same aim : to make similar wars impossible by the prolonged, if not permanent, crippling of Germany's military might. At the time, this was regarded as the most important object.

THE PRICE THAT GERMANY PAID FOR DEFEAT

THE price of defeat fell with particular severity upon Germany. In Europe, she was deprived of 12 per cent. of her people and 13 per cent. of her territory, the chief gainer being the new State of Poland. Outside Europe, she lost all her colonies and her concessions in China. Strict military penalties were enforced, including compulsory disarmament. The Allies themselves promised eventually to disarm, and their failure to do so was to prove ultimately a serious menace to European harmony. But the most crushing burden took the form of reparations. The Versailles Treaty stated that Germany should make good the material damage suffered by the civilian population of the Allied countries and should meet the cost of military pensions. No attempt was made to define the total amount payable by Germany. This was left for later decision. Taken together, these provisions were more severe than in any treaty concluded since the beginning of the nineteenth century. For Austria-Hungary and Turkey, the penalties mainly took the form of the dismemberment of their pre-war empires.

The political readjustments necessary were greater and more complex than in any previous modern settlement. The Empire of Austria-Hungary had fallen to pieces, and huge tracts had been severed from Western Russia. These areas, together with the territory taken from Germany, had to be apportioned between many clamorous claimants. As a guide to the solution of this involved problem, the Peace Conference took the principle of nationality. On the whole a sincere attempt was made to draw the new frontiers according to the boundaries between peoples or nations. As a measure of the success of the effort, there are fewer minorities—people living under the control of alien governments—in Europe to-day than in pre-war years. Unfortunately, motives were mixed. The principle of punishment for the defeated was also present and, where no clear-cut division was possible, the decision nearly always proved unfavourable to the ex-enemy powers.

RE-PLANNING THE MAP OF EUROPE

THE main changes in the political structure of Europe can be briefly stated. Germany ceded the provinces of Alsace and Lorraine to France, West Prussia and Posen (the Polish Corridor) to Poland, and part of Silesia, an important industrial area, to Poland and Czecho Slovakia. By these transfers, Germany lost not only eight million people but also one-third of her pre-war coal supplies and three-quarters of her iron fields. Austria-Hungary disappeared as a united empire, and Turkey almost vanished from Europe. Russia lost all the gains she had made in Europe in the preceding two centuries.

Out of the territory thus made available, several new States were created and some old ones considerably enlarged. In Central Europe, Poland and Czecho Slovakia were formed, Serbia was extended and took the name of Jugo-Slavia, and Rumania was doubled in size. In Northern Europe, Finland was declared an independent State, and the three small Baltic republics of Lithuania, Latvia, and Esthonia appeared. Thus was a new Europe created, and the principle of nationality, so prominent during the nineteenth century, given its fullest expression. Events were to show that the triumph was too complete.

Considering the provisions of the Treaty as a whole, it must be confessed that it fell far short of the just and magnanimous peace which the world needed. It was hurriedly drawn up, without sufficient consideration of the possible consequences of some of its terms, and it too often gave expression to revengeful desires. Yet, in many respects, it was better and juster than might have been anticipated, and succeeded in checking the more extreme measures that were often advocated. Also, by establishing the League of Nations, it created the machinery by which the Treaty could be modified in the light of saner counsels and its worst defects removed.

The Treaty left many problems unsolved, notably the amount of the reparation bill to be presented to Germany. Moreover, while the Treaty defined the boundaries between the states of Europe, it could not determine beforehand the relations between them. A new system of states had been created, but no one knew how it would work. The years from 1919 to 1926 represent, therefore, a period of experiment. The nations of Europe tried to adjust themselves to the new conditions, to work out a new mode of living.

During these years, the influence of France was dominant on the Continent and was exercised consistently towards certain definite ends. French policy aimed in this period—and even afterwards—at making Germany pay and at achieving security against future invasion. French losses in the War had been enormous. One and a half million men had been killed, four million acres of her farm land devastated, three-quarters of her machinery and metal foundries destroyed, and half her shipping tonnage sunk. It is not surprising that, in view of these losses and the huge amount of the National Debt, the French were insistent that Germany should pay to the full. This desire was reinforced by another consideration. France had been invaded from the same quarter twice in fifty years, and the fear of another invasion in the future was strong. If, however, German strength could be drained away in the payment of reparations, she could be kept indefinitely in a condition of weakness.

FRANCE WAITS IN VAIN FOR THE SHOWER OF GOLD

THE first step was to fix the amount to be paid by Germany. An Allied Reparation Commission was set up for this purpose and, after many conferences, it decided, in 1921, that Germany should pay 132,000,000,000 gold marks (roughly £6,000,000,000) a sum which many believed to be far beyond Germany's capacity to pay. Such was the financial and industrial unsettlement in Germany, however, that she was unable to meet the instalments demanded, and she was granted a moratorium—a temporary suspension of payments—while she carried out financial reform and industrial reconstruction. This postponement of the expected golden stream caused French public opinion to become restive, with the result that when, in late 1922, German deliveries of telegraph poles were found to be below schedule, M. Poincaré, the French Prime Minister, sent a "mission of control" to the Ruhr, the most important iron and coal area of Germany.

Presumably, M. Poincaré hoped that this gesture would convince Germany of the hopelessness of resistance and stimulate her to renewed payment. The German government declared the "invasion" to be illegal and stopped all reparation payments. Within the Ruhr, the inhabitants resorted to passive resistance and were financed in their idleness by the government. French and Belgian troops were drafted into the area and a state of virtual war developed. But the endeavour to extort payment forcibly was a failure. To Germany, however, it involved a frightful cost.

Even before the Ruhr venture, the internal condition of Germany was unsound. Evidence of this was given in the value of the mark, which stood at approximately 4 to the dollar before the War, but fell to 1·300 to the dollar in September 1922, and as low as 6·800 in December 1922. When, in 1923, the German government undertook to finance passive resistance in the Ruhr, it was unable to raise the necessary funds by taxation, and resorted to the printing of large quantities of paper money. This practice increased doubts of Germany's financial condition, and there began, both internally and abroad, a "flight from the mark." At first, swiftly, and then with catastrophic speed, the value of the German currency fell, until in November 1923, the dollar was valued at the fantastic figure of 4,200,000,000,000 marks. In effect, the mark became worthless, both at home and abroad.

This inflation of the currency caused fearful loss and suffering. People with savings and fixed incomes found themselves penniless, wage-earners were unable to buy enough food to maintain physical health, business almost came to a standstill, and unemployment spread rapidly. To continue resistance in the Ruhr in the face of these sacrifices would have been suicidal. In the autumn of 1923, Herr Stresemann, the German foreign minister, made an unconditional surrender to the French demands. There was no alternative. By her action in the Ruhr, France brought Germany to the verge of collapse and endangered her own financial condition. At the same time, she retarded the economic recovery of Europe which was then slowly beginning, and raised a crop of animosities which have afflicted the world ever since.

THE DAWES PLAN : THE ONE BRIGHT SPOT OF THE RUHR INVASION

THE one good effect of the invasion of the Ruhr was that it stressed the necessity of settling the reparation question as quickly as possible. So long as it remained undecided, Germany's internal recovery would be checked and the relations between the European States unhealthy. Accordingly, the Reparations Commission set up committees at the end of 1923 to inquire into the problem, and, in 1924, the famous Dawes Plan was announced.

Under this scheme, Germany undertook to make stipulated annual payments to the Allies. The fixing of Germany's liability by this Plan assisted greatly in both the political and economic recovery of the country. It was accompanied by an international loan to Germany to help in the financial reconstruction of the country, and paved the way to the evacuation of the Ruhr, which took place in 1925. The only step remaining for the rehabilitation of Germany was to remove the ban which had been placed on her entry into the League of Nations. This was finally accomplished in September 1926.

It thus seemed that the major political difficulties created by the War had been removed. The reparation question had, apparently, been settled, and Germany had been admitted to almost equal status with the great powers of Europe. The course of events was to show, however, that this optimistic view had little foundation. Later developments can be best dealt with by considering in turn the main trends in the chief nations of Europe.

ITALY : THE SUBJECT OF A GREAT AMBITION

THE Revolutions in Italy and Russia were far more complete than the German Revolution of 1918. The latter meant little more than a change from monarchy to republic. The Italian and Russian revolutions led to a radical transformation of social institutions and of political and economic policy.

There is little similarity, however, between the circumstances of Italy and Russia. Italy is a land of very limited economic resources, and is predominantly agricultural, even after a generation of industrialisation. But the amount of fertile land is restricted, since about one-third of her area is unproductive. Thus, although Italy is able to produce most of the food she needs, it is under unfavourable conditions and at a high cost in labour. Her industrial resources, too, are very scanty. She has no oil, practically no coal, and iron is found only in small quantities of poor quality. Yet in this land of limited possibilities, a numerous and rapidly increasing people lives.

THE DOORS CLOSE AGAINST ITALIAN MIGRATION

To prevent an intolerable pressure of population upon the means of maintenance, two courses are open. Numbers may be reduced by emigration ; or, by industrialisation, goods may be produced which will exchange for the needed foreign supplies. Both measures have been tried by Italy. Emigration on a large scale began about 1880, and continued at an increasing pace until the outbreak of War. In the twenty years from 1881 to 1900, 4,700,000 people left the country, and 8,600,000 between 1901 and 1914. Emigration was resumed after the War, but at a lower rate ; only 2,000,000 between 1919 and 1925.

Since 1925 the door into the United States has been practically closed, and the stream has been diverted to France. There are no longer the same opportunities for movement, since immigration restrictions are almost universal. Italy has been driven back upon the second alternative. As a result of her engineering genius, a surprising growth of manufacturing activity has taken place. But the dearth of industrial raw materials casts doubt upon the possibility of its continuance indefinitely. The central problem remains ; that of a rapidly increasing population living in a limited and poor country.

Italy finished the War in a disorganised and almost exhausted condition. Economic distress, which had been kept at a distance by loans from the Allies and the fever of war activity, soon began to make itself felt. Prices and unemployment rose. The precarious state of the national finances caused a long delay in the payment of military pensions and helped to increase the growing misery. In the political field, conditions were hardly less unsettled. The government had no policy for the immediate situation and its unpopularity was increased by disappointment with the Peace Treaty. The gains in territory received by Italy, whilst greater than those promised by the Allies in return for Italian assistance, fell short of its desires. Under the influence of Press propaganda, the people were inclined not only to blame the Allies, but to charge their government with the betrayal of Italy.

Discontent, fed from these varied sources, grew in volume. Food riots occurred in the towns and land raids in the country. Talk of revolution took place openly. But while there was wide agreement in condemning the government, there was no agreement on what should be done. The People's Party was in favour of democratic reforms, but was opposed to violent action. The socialists were hopelessly divided among themselves. The more moderate section deprecated violence and was prepared to co-operate with the People's Party. The extremists, who were growing in numbers, inclined to a revolution on the Russian plan.

A third reform section, the *Fascisti*, was insignificant in size and influence during the early years of peace. This party consisted at first mainly of young ex-service men, who were disgusted with the failure of the " Old Men," and who wanted a revolution to throw out the politicians and restore the lost prestige of Italy. But they were bitterly opposed to the kind of revolution preached by the extreme socialists.

They found their inspiration in the old Roman republic, and from it borrowed their symbols and salute.

MUSSOLINI'S VISIONS OF ITALY'S MIGHT

THE fascist party was led by Benito Mussolini (born 1883). In his youth, Mussolini had been a left-wing socialist and editor of a newspaper of extreme views. On the outbreak of War, before the intervention of Italy, he denounced it as a capitalist ramp. But in September 1914, he changed his attitude and was expelled from the Socialist Party. In reply, he founded another newspaper, *Popolo d'Italia*, and advocated entry into the War on the Allied side. After the Armistice, he founded the *Fascisti*, a party with revolutionary aims but a nebulous programme. Mussolini was then, and still is, a man of very great energy and immense self-confidence. He has not shown himself to be, like his Russian counterpart, Lenin, a philosopher and thinker, elaborating his ideas and plans beforehand. Rather, he is a supreme realist, ready to adapt himself to circumstances if he cannot control them. But behind all the compromises and shifts of policy which his opportunism has caused, there is an essential singleness of purpose—the increase of the might and influence of Italy.

Through 1919 and 1920, social and economic conditions worsened. Strikes followed one another with scarcely a break. Clashes between socialists and fascists became more frequent as the strength of the latter movement grew. Bomb outrages and murder were the normal expressions of this ferment. The turning-point came in September 1920. Over three hundred factories in Piedmont and Lombardy, the chief industrial district of Italy, were seized by the workers, who organised councils to carry on production. It seemed for a moment that the revolution had come. But the government did nothing, and in October the factories were peacefully evacuated after the grant of certain concessions to the workers.

Whilst immediately unimportant, this incident had far-reaching consequences. It caused yet another split in the socialist ranks which reduced the resistance of the party to the growing power of the fascists. It also brought a considerable accession of strength to the fascist party. The persistence of revolutionary propaganda and the continued inactivity of the government gave colour to the fascist claim to be the only saviours of the nation. Clashes between the two extreme parties increased in number and ferocity. Virtual civil war existed during the next two years.

During this period of conflict and growth, fascism developed a more definite organisation and policy. The underlying aim remained : " To give cohesion, authority, prestige to the State," to quote Mussolini. But the earlier republicanism of Mussolini, which had repelled certain sections of the community, was replaced by a support of monarchy. On questions of policy, the only clear statement was that the party aimed at control. Until then it was useless to bind the party to any particular programme.

THE MARCH ON ROME

THE opportunity came in 1922. On 1st July, a general strike, which had been called as a protest against fascist violence, proved a miserable failure. By intensifying the divisions between political parties, however, it produced a practical paralysis of government. Mussolini seized the opportunity, and on 30th October 1922, assumed dictatorial power. The next few years were spent in consolidating the position. Fascists were placed in charge of the most important public offices, opposition newspapers were suppressed and criticism forcibly silenced. By the electoral law of December 1923, the fascists guaranteed themselves a majority in the Chamber.

During these formative years, the originally very nebulous ideas of fascism received more definite shape. The fundamental aim, however, has remained unchanged. This is represented by the symbol of the movement—the *fasces*, the rod-girt axe which was borne before the chief magistrate in the days of ancient Rome. The axe is the symbol of the authority of the State, and the rods express the idea that in unity is strength. Authority and unity are the basic conceptions of fascism. The State is the embodiment of both, since it is the source of authority and embraces and controls all the activities of the individual citizen. Dictatorship is necessary to enforce both ideas because, in the modern world, with its materialism and its worship of individual rights, liberty has been carried to impossible lengths. Democracy and representative methods of government tend to break up society into a series of competitive groups, each so engrossed with its own interests and with its struggle against rival groups that the interest of the community as a whole is neglected. The only way to re-establish the authority of the State and to fit each individual into the social pattern is to assume complete control over government and industry : that is, over the whole of social life.

To the fascist the ideal structure of society is the Corporate or Corporative State. The State, according to this view, is all-embracing. Every activity, whether of individuals or of groups, must come under its control. In economic life, this means that the workers and employers in each industry must be organised into unions. Membership of a union is not compulsory. But any agreement reached by a union is binding upon members and non-members alike. The unions on both sides in each industrial group are linked into corporations, which are the immediate controlling bodies within their field. The activities of the corporations are co-ordinated and supervised by the National Corporations Council. The final step in the establishment of the Corporate State is the abolition of the old parliamentary institutions, with their territorial constituencies, and the basing of government on a semi-occupational franchise instead.

The effect of these developments is to enhance the authority and unity of the State. But this is not an end in itself. There must be some ultimate purpose towards which this organisation is directed. The nature of this purpose is not in doubt. It is the increase of the power and prestige of Italy. Fascism is intensely nationalistic. This is evident from the speeches of Mussolini and his followers, who insist frequently upon the need for an expansion of Italian influence and territory. On this side, inspiration is drawn from the might of the ancient Roman Empire.

ITALY'S AMBITIONS : WHERE WILL THEY LEAD ?

THE curtailment of emigration, the stimulation of the birth-rate and the maintenance of a large army and navy are characteristic of the fascist régime, and disquieting to Italy's neighbours. Her foreign policy in recent years falls into two periods. During the first, ending with the Abyssinian War, which began in October, 1935, she supported the Austrian Government against Nazi designs, and had closer relations with Hungary and Albania. But the imposition of sanctions by some members of the League of Nations caused Italy to leave the League and draw closer to Germany in opposition to France and Britain.

Emboldened by his success in Abyssinia, Mussolini saw in the outbreak of the Spanish Civil War (July, 1936) an opportunity of increasing Italian influence in the Mediter- ranean and also of giving Spanish fascism a helping hand. Italian munitions and "volunteers" assisted materially in the ultimate victory of General Franco in March, 1939. This second phase of Italian policy was based on an under- standing with Germany—the "Rome-Berlin Axis." Italy now gave Germany a free hand in Central Europe, and the two powers co-operated in Spain. As a result, Germany absorbed Austria and the lion's share of Czecho-Slovakia and initiated an economic penetration of Rumania. Italy's gains from the axis policy have been much less, and her annexation in April, 1939, of the neighbouring state of Albania, for many years a dependent ally, appears to have been actuated by the desire to obtain a "make-weight" and to assert the pre- eminence of Italian—possibly over German—interests in the Adriatic. Italy's demands on France are referred to in a later section,* but despite the aggressive tone of some of Mussolini's speeches, and despite the military alliance concluded with Germany in May, 1939, it would seem that Italy is the more cautious partner in the alliance. As a background to this German-Italian alliance there is the anti-Comintern pact of Germany, Italy, Hungary and Japan. Like the Holy Alliance of the post-Napoleonic period its significance is largely ideological, although it expresses common diplomatic interests.

* See p. 433.

GERMANY'S CLAIMS TO THE WORLD'S SYMPATHY

GERMANY, which has become so closely associated with Italy in the public mind because of her adoption of a similar form of social organisation, reached this goal by a very different route. After the financial collapse of 1923, a remark- able economic and political recovery was made. The stoppage of inflation at the end of 1923 and the adoption of the Dawes Plan for reparations in 1924 restored foreign confidence in Germany's future and initiated a stream of foreign loans. With the aid of these sums Germany carried out a policy of reconstruction and rationalisation which brought comparative prosperity again after years of privation. On the political side, the recovery was due mainly to the genius of the Foreign Minister, Gustav Stresemann. The signing of the Locarno Pacts in October 1925, which provided for the peaceful settlement of disputes between Germany and her neighbours, paved the way for Germany's admission to the League of Nations, which took place in September 1926. Thus, from being treated as a criminal and outcast, Germany was admitted as an equal into the counsels of Europe.

But the apparently more settled economic and political condition of Germany in 1925 and 1926 rested upon uncertain foundations. Industrially, her future depended upon the continuance of foreign loans, a very unreliable foundation. Politically, a number of factors threatened to disturb her stability. Hitherto, moderate counsels had prevailed. The social-democratic government of the Republic had pursued a home policy of moderation and had made no radical changes in social and political organisation. Post-war Germany differed from pre-war Germany only in being more democratic. Abroad, the government had tried to win confidence by an honest attempt to fulfil the terms of the Treaty and to honour reparation agreements. This policy had succeeded handsomely, both in gaining the evacuation of the Ruhr and entry to the League and in attracting foreign loans. Yet many unsettled issues remained.

Must Germany accept the Polish Corridor and separation from East Prussia as permanent facts? Was she to submit to the " war guilt " clauses of the Treaty and to a one-sided compulsory disarmament? Could she continue to bear the heavy annual drain of reparation payments? These issues acted as constant irritants in the political life of Germany and formed the political capital of the opposition parties. Should the moderate government fail to make progress towards the satisfactory solution of these problems, or should temporary prosperity give place to depression, a swing to the extreme was certain.

SPONSOR OF SIXTY-FIVE MILLION SOULS : ADOLF HITLER

ON the left wing were the communists, who inclined to welcome distress and discontent as means of impelling the masses towards the social revolution. On the right wing were the national socialists, the nazis, the creation of Adolf Hitler. Hitler was an Austrian workman who joined the German army soon after the outbreak of War. After demobilisation, he came into contact with a small group of malcontents in Munich and early became its leader. They used to meet in a beer cellar. In 1921, he ejected the original members and transformed the organisation into the National Socialist Party. Little headway was made for some time. But, in 1923, he joined with Ludendorff, the ex-Chief of the Imperial General Staff, in a march on Berlin to overthrow the government. The crusaders travelled only a few hundred yards before dispersal, and Hitler was condemned to a period of . imprisonment. He spent this time in writing *Mein Kampf* (My Struggle), an account of his life and ideas.

Hitler himself is a master of propaganda and popular oratory. But he lacks constructive capacity. From the outset it has fallen to his lieutenants to give form and meaning to his hazy ideas, and even they have been only partially successful. For, in the early days of the movement at any rate, national socialism was not a political creed but a collection of hatreds and prejudices, knit together by emotionalism. Foremost came the anti-Jewish campaign and the gospel of nordic superiority. The Jews are said by the nazis to be an inferior people, devoid of honour and patriotism, parasites upon the community they settle in. The nordics are the master breed, destined to superiority. The regeneration of Germany demanded, therefore, the establishment of nordic supremacy and the extermination of the Jewish menace.

GERMANY'S REIGN OF TERROR

CLOSE in popularity to this race hatred was their condemnation of the Peace Treaty. Responsibility for Germany's condition was charged to the "traitors of 1918," the "November criminals" who accepted the humiliating Armistice and the still more damaging treaty. The nazis had no constructive substitute ; but propaganda does not concern itself too closely with facts. The economic policy of the party was almost incomprehensible. It promised all things to all men. The worker and the capitalist, the farmer and the manufacturer, the small employer and the combine, all were to find their heaven in the national socialist State.

So long as reasonable prosperity held in Germany, Hitler and the nazis could not hope for power. Their numbers grew, since discontent was never absent, especially among the middle classes who had lost so much during the 1922-23 inflation.

But their political influence remained limited. The industrial tide turned in 1928 and 1929, however, when the stream of foreign loans ebbed and finally ceased to flow. Very soon Germany was in difficulties, hard pressed to find the means to pay interest on borrowed money and to continue reparation instalments. As depression spread over the world, Germany's export markets fell away and unemployment grew. Dr. Brüning, the Chancellor, tried to meet the situation by reducing wages and prices and by increasing taxation. But the only effect was to increase discontent. The Allies came to Germany's aid, first by adopting the Hoover Moratorium, 1931, which granted a year's freedom from debt and reparation payments, and then, in 1932, by the Lausanne Agreement, which virtually wiped out reparations. But these measures failed to improve the situation. By then depression had too firm a grip of Germany and the world.[1]

At once the threatened swing to the nazis occurred. Dr. Brüning could offer only continued sacrifices. Hitler offered hope of immediate improvement. Herr von Papen and General von Schleicher, who succeeded Brüning as chancellors, failed to stay the growing clamour, and, in January 1933, President von Hindenburg offered the chancellorship to Herr Hitler. Instantly a reign of terror began. Jews, communists, and social democrats were ruthlessly persecuted. The trade union movement was destroyed and its funds confiscated. Officials unsympathetic to the nazi régime were weeded out, and opposition newspapers suppressed. Even the former allies of the nazi party were absorbed or dispersed and religion brought under its tutelage. The new government set out to establish the totalitarian state which had been founded in fascist Italy, and, by terrorism and violence, quickly achieved its end.

When its power was consolidated, the government turned its attention to economic affairs. Two characteristics mark nazi economic policy : the desire to reduce unemployment and to share out work, and to establish as complete a system of autarchy—economic self-dependence—as possible. The successs of the first endeavour is difficult to estimate, since there is no means of distinguishing between reliable statistics and propaganda. Several laws have been passed aiming at the creation of work. Credits have been granted to assist public works and to finance the scrapping of redundant plant.

[1] See p. 317.

With the object of withdrawing women from industry and stimulating the furniture and allied trades, assistance is given to young people wishing to marry. Peasant farming is being fostered in a variety of ways.

By all these and many other devices the government has sought to increase employment and reduce distress. At the best, however, its success has been limited. German trade and industry continue in a depressed condition, and far-reaching revival will come only with world improvement. There are signs that the government is beginning to realise this dependence on world conditions and to relax its policy of extreme economic nationalism.

In the organisation of industry, a system similar to the Italian corporation scheme has been adopted. German industry and commerce are divided into twelve groups, each with its " leader," the object being to preserve individual management as far as possible, while bringing industry into line with government policy. Workers are organised under the supervision of the State, and are subject to the new Labour Code, which is a substitute for the lost power of collective bargaining. No radical change in industrial control and relations has taken place, however. There seems little doubt that in National Socialism the stress is not placed on the second word.

ACHIEVEMENTS OF THE GERMAN CULTURAL PURGE

THE Nazi Revolution has succeeded in establishing a totalitarian state in Germany, a society in which the government is regarded as the source of all power and the dictator over the lives and activities of its subjects. Certain directions in which this power will be used are already apparent. The nazi state is anti-cultural. Not only by its expulsion and persecution of Jews and socialists has it impoverished the cultural life of Germany, since a continuous attack is being waged upon intellect, justice, and the freedom of the human spirit. The purging of schools and universities of people of liberal outlook, the public burning in the University Square in Berlin of books by Freud, Remarque, Marx, and others, and the introduction of the " quota " on admissions to the universities are expressions of this policy. The low valuation of education and mind and the yet lower valuation of women suggest a level of civilisation which we had hoped Europe had outgrown.

Another feature of the nazi régime is its militarism. Its

insistence upon the supreme value of power necessarily implies a glorification of war and preparedness for war. Against whom this military preparation is directed is unknown, since Germany is under a variety of pledges, most of them voluntary, not to use force against her neighbours. In the absence of certain knowledge, suspicion holds the field and taints European relations.

It is idle, however, to condemn the nazi revolution without attempting to understand the causes which gave rise to it. It is unbelievable that millions of Germans would have rallied to Hitler if he did not express some fundamental need or discontent. It is essential for the outside world to realise the nature of these discontents. By the Peace Treaty, a people sixty millions in number was placed in a position of inferiority and subjected to heavy losses and burdens. Germany was made to feel that she was thought responsible for the War, and attempts were made to arraign several individuals as " war criminals." She was excluded from original membership of the League, and was compelled to reduce her armed forces to a bare minimum, while the Allies contented themselves with an expression of their pious intention ultimately to bring about general disarmament.

GERMANY'S GRIEVANCES AGAINST THE ALLIES

BY such means, the Germans were made to feel themselves the outcasts of the world. They considered, too, that whilst some loss of territory and the payment of an indemnity were inseparable from defeat, the Allies took advantage of the weakness and divisions of post-revolution Germany to put unjust and excessive burdens upon her. Was it really necessary to cut through eastern Germany in order to give Poland access to the sea ? Was it just to hand over to Poland towns and industrial districts in Upper Silesia which were German in foundation and population ? Above all, did the Allies, in fixing the amount of reparations, pay enough attention to Germany's capacity to pay ? Was not the ill-disguised object to cripple Germany ?

Suspicions and animosities of this kind rankled in the minds of Germans throughout the post-war period. If the moderate parties had succeeded in obtaining modification of the Treaty, probably bitter feeling would have died down gradually. But whilst, particularly under the leadership of Stresemann, some improvement was gained, concessions were

anted by the Allies grudgingly and after long delay. The
oover Moratorium, for instance, was postponed until it lost
uch of its good effect. The Lausanne Agreement, also,
ould probably have checked the growth of extreme opinion
it had been reached a year earlier. These delays made it
ossible for the extreme parties to assert that the policy of
oderation would never be successful, and enabled the Nazi
arty to carry through the Revolution of 1933.

The foreign policy of the German government since that
ate has undoubtedly received the support of large numbers
f the people. The withdrawal from the League was ap-
lauded as a vigorous protest against international insincerity.
he later withdrawal from the Disarmament Conference was
lso approved as an exposure of the hollowness of the Allies'
romise to follow the example compulsorily set by Germany.
Even anti-Nazis welcomed the calling of the Allied bluff.
)n the other hand to meet all Germany's claims would
ianifestly be impossible, and even if they were granted,
othing could check the vaulting ambition of Hitler. Never-
heless, some of these ambitions have already been realised
-the purge of the communists and Jews, the ceding to Ger-
nany by plebiscite of the Saar district, conscription in
iolation of the Versailles Treaty, the remilitarisation of the
Rhineland, the reunion with Austria, the absorption into the
Reich of Sudetenland and Memel, and the occupation of
Bohemia-Moravia. Other strong ambitions remain—the
ecovery of the German colonies, of Danzig, with its large
German population, and of the Polish Corridor.

FRANCE: A PREY TO THE FEARS OF INSECURITY

IN the years since the War, France has become politically
and economically a power of the first order. The founda-
ions of her present industrial strength were laid by the
Treaty, which gave to her the rich coal deposits and iron ore
ields of Alsace and Lorraine. For a considerable period,
iowever, there was no remarkable growth of industrial
.ctivity. The devastation in north-east France had to be
nade good, and there was a shortage of labour owing to the
ailure of the low birth-rate to compensate for the huge war
osses. Development was held back, too, by the reluctance
of successive governments to face the post-war financial

situation. Not until Poincaré's re-organisation of Fren
finances in 1926 was the fall in the value of the franc stopp
and business credit restored. From that time forwar
France became one of the strongest industrial and financi
nations in the world. To her flourishing small industri
and prosperous agriculture was added an extensive large-sca
manufacture. So stable was this structure that France wit
stood the world depression better than most other countries

The economic advance of post-war France assisted tl
growth of her military and political power. Ever since tl
War, France has been dominant in the European politic
field, and her military strength is greater than that of al
other Continental nation, with the possible exception
Russia. Yet she has never felt secure. Her policy h
throughout been dictated by fear of Germany.

The French cannot forget that the Germans are half
numerous again as themselves, and they have tried by eve
possible means—increased military expenditure, treaties
guarantee against aggression, defensive alliances—to gua
against the eventuality of another German invasion. O
aspect of this policy has already been touched upon. At tl
Peace Conference, certain French representatives tried
dismember Germany or to annex the Rhineland with tl
object of making her permanently weak. The invasion
the Ruhr in 1923 was a later expression of the same polic
The tardiness in granting a modification of reparation oblig
tions in 1931 and 1932 is a more recent instance.

FRANCE RIVETS HER CHAIN OF ALLIES

BUT France did not rely solely upon attempts to weake
Germany. She turned also to the time-honoured poli
of alliances. She sought to bind to herself other natio
whose interests were similar. Immediately after the Wa
France hoped to establish a firm understanding with Gre
Britain and the United States, and an agreement was ma
between the three countries in 1919 to guarantee the Pea
Treaty. But when the United States government refused
ratify the Treaty, this agreement fell to the ground. Tl
hopes of a close Anglo-French association were dashed by
violent dispute between the two countries at the Washingto
Naval Conference, 1921, over submarine policy. Lat
approaches were met by the invincible British reluctance
accept any responsibility for events in Europe. Great Brita

desired peace, but was not prepared to run the risk that, in guaranteeing peace, she might be involved in war. France, on the other hand, wanted something more than a promise of moral support. She was compelled to look elsewhere, therefore, for the needed allies.

These she found in the new States of Central and South-Eastern Europe. Most of these countries had either been carved entirely out of ex-enemy territory or had received large areas from Germany or Austria-Hungary. Their fears and desires were accordingly similar to those of France. They feared the revival of a strong and prosperous Germany which might jeopardise their ownership of the new lands. They wanted the means to establish firm government and to build up defence forces. France could not only provide them with armed support but could also give them financial aid for carrying through reconstruction. Gradually, France drew these states into her orbit, until she had built up a circle of alliances and armaments around the ex-enemy countries. An understanding with Belgium was easily reached, and a defensive alliance was signed in 1920.

It was natural that France and Poland should move together without much delay. Poland was a somewhat artificial creation, containing many alien groups and without natural frontiers. But she occupied a strategic position as a buffer state between Germany and Russia, and offered to France a substitute for the lost Russian alliance. So a political and military agreement was made in 1921, and cemented by a French loan. Understandings were shortly afterwards arrived at with Czecho-Slovakia, Rumania, and Jugo-Slavia, and were similarly reinforced by French credits.

With the rising military might of Germany since the accession to power of Hitler, and especially since the declaration of German conscription, Poland's position changed. She tended to abandon her relations with France, who had proved disappointing, and, on condition that Germany would cease agitating for the return of the Corridor, to look with a less unfriendly eye on Hitler's plans elsewhere. France then turned to Soviet Russia, with whom she concluded a military pact.

Even in France, however, criticism of the policy of alliances began to grow. Were these States allies or liabilities? Their military strength was more apparent than real, and they involved France in more risks than they guarded her against.

12

The loans which usually accompanied the alliances wer
doubtful assets, likely to prove disguised gifts. And th
alliances tended to provoke counter-alliances and rapproche
ments, as witness the neutrality agreement between Germany
and Russia in 1926, the Italian understandings with Albania
Hungary, and Austria, and the growing friendly feelin
between Great Britain and Germany before the nazi revolu
tion. Such criticisms made the French governments realis
the inadequacy of their policy, and they resorted to anothe
expedient, keeping in mind always the ultimate end of security
There began a movement to strengthen the League, to mak
it a really effective instrument for preserving peace—and th
Peace. French representatives urged the formation of ar
international army under the control of the League to ac
against any nation guilty of aggression. Later, Briand tabled
a scheme for the formation of a United States of Europe.

But the League became weaker instead of stronger, particularly when it failed to restrain Italy's attack on Abyssinia in
1935. French foreign policy became uncertain. It vacillated
in its estimate of the relative value of collective security
obtained through the League of Nations and that offered by
the " Stresa front " with Italy. Consequently France was
unable to obtain either. Thus the way was paved for Hitler's
remilitarisation of the Rhineland, for his incorporation of
Austria, the Sudetenland and Memel, and for his assumption
of a protectorate over Bohemia-Moravia.

Thus France, confronted by a re-armed Germany, is in the
unhappy position of seeing her carefully devised system o
collective security crumbling about her. Nor is the story o
France's troubles confined to her international position. In
February, 1934, the country was rocked to its foundations by
rioting in Paris caused by the suspicion that the Governmen
was involved in the Staviski swindles. There was bloodshed,
and for the moment it seemed that the extremists of eithe
the Right or Left might prevail. But the storm passed, having
wrecked the Daladier ministry. However, the various governments which succeeded it failed either to balance the budget,
despite severe " cuts," or to keep down the cost of living,
while in foreign policy they were equally unsuccessful.

When the Popular Front (i.e., socialists and radicals, with
communist support) took over the government in June, 1936,
they attempted to solve these problems by introducing a forty-
hour week, devaluing the franc, reforming the administration

f the Banque de France and dissolving the fascist organisa-
ions. The reversal of this policy by the Daladier government,
n November, 1938, led to an abortive general strike. Since
hen the dangerous international situation and the threat to her
African possessions has rallied most Frenchmen in support of
he government's firmer foreign policy.

THE TANGLED SKEIN IN CENTRAL EUROPE

SOME reference should be made to the states of Central
Europe which were created or greatly enlarged by the

THE LOST EMPIRE OF THE HABSBURGS

*The shaded areas show the territory taken from Austria-
Hungary after the World War. It will be seen that Hungary
became an independent state. Five neighbouring countries
received important additions to their territory.*

Treaty. It has been said that the War, which was fought
to Europeanise the Balkans, ended by Balkanising Europe.
Whilst this statement is only partly true, it does emphasise
one disturbing feature of post-war Europe—the appearance
of new frontiers and states and the development of trade and

political animosities between them. Nowhere is this characteristic more marked than in the area which was formerly Austria-Hungary.

Pre-war Austria-Hungary was a medley of peoples held in subjection by the German-Austrians in the west and the Hungarians (Magyars) in the east, and seething with nationalist discontent. At the same time, it was one of the largest free-trade areas in the world. Transport, trade, manufacture, finance, were all organised on the basis of a united Empire and were centred on Vienna. When the Emperor abdicated on 11th November 1918, practically every nationality asserted its independence. From an empire, Austria-Hungary became a welter of squabbling peoples, who have continued to quarrel ever since. These divisions are not only a source of weakness to the peoples themselves, but a grave cause of disquiet to Europe.

AUSTRIA LOSES HER INDEPENDENCE

THE situation of Austria became particularly acute. By the Treaty of St. Germain, the country was reduced from 116,000 square miles and 29,000,000 people to 32,000 square miles and 6,500,000 people. The denial of the right to unite with Germany confronted Austria with problems impossible of solution. Vienna, a city of two million inhabitants, had fallen from being the capital of an empire, to being that of a small group of Alpine provinces. Political and tariff barriers cut it off from its former commercial connections. How could the city survive ? For years after the War, Austria was practically maintained by international relief loans. But no solution was found.

Internal dissensions aggravated the difficulties. Bitter political divisions existed between socialist Vienna and the conservative provinces, which culminated in 1934 in the forcible suppression of the socialist organisations. A strong Nazi movement grew up, which advocated union with Hitlerite Germany and used terrorism as its normal political weapon. The murder of Chancellor Dollfuss in 1934 by the Austrian Nazis brought Europe to the verge of war. After this, strong measures were taken against the Nazis, but proved in the end unavailing. In March, 1938, Hitler brought an army to their rescue. Austrian officers were ordered to offer no resistance, Schuschnigg resigned, yielding, as he said, to force, and Austria was united to Germany.

EUROPE ON THE BRINK OF WAR

THE incorporation of Austria into the Reich was the immediate prelude to the German threat to Czecho-Slovakia.
This country, carved by the peace treaties out of the old
Hapsburg empire, although rich in industry, free from any
crushing debt, and comparatively prosperous in the post-war
years, contained minorities of Poles, Ruthenians, Magyars
and, most important of all, three million Germans. In March
and April, 1938, the latter, inhabiting chiefly the Sudeten
region nearest to Germany and Austria, under their leader,
Henlein, demanded self-government and the right to profess
German (i.e. Nazi) political philosophy, and were supported
by Germany. The governments of France and Britain
attempted mediation, which broke down because of the un-
compromising attitude of both sides. The German army's
summer manœuvres were on an unusually large scale. When
it was seen that Germany wanted the cession of the Sudeten
lands, the situation rapidly deteriorated until the danger of a
general war overshadowed the European sky.

EVENTS LEADING TO THE MUNICH AGREEMENT

ON September 14th, 1938, the British Premier took the unprecedented step of flying to Germany to see Herr Hitler
at Berchtesgaden. They discussed a plan of settlement which,
with the concurrence of France, was submitted to the Czech
government and accepted by it. Chamberlain and Hitler met
again a week later at Godesberg on the Rhine when, to
Chamberlain's chagrin, he found that Hitler had increased his
demands. War now seemed imminent, French reservists were
called up, trenches dug in the London parks, and many
children evacuated from London.

Then came a dramatic movement. On the afternoon of
September 28th a packed and tense House of Commons heard
the Prime Minister's account of his visit to Godesberg. He
was relating how he had " bitterly reproached " the Führer,
and was describing how he was still desperately trying to
preserve peace in Europe, when a message arrived. It was to
the effect that, at the instance of Signor Mussolini, whose intervention had been invoked both by President Roosevelt and
Chamberlain himself, Hitler had agreed to a conference of
Britain, Germany, France and Italy. The conference was held
at Munich two days later, and an agreement was reached. War

was averted—but Czecho-Slovakia paid the price. She had to cede 12,000 square miles of territory—some of her most valuable industrial areas and her only defensible frontier, with three million inhabitants, to Germany. President Benes, who had offered a stout resistance to Germany's demands, resigned and soon a compliant government was in office in Prague. Czecho-Slovakia had entered the Nazi orbit.

AFTER MUNICH

THE relief of all the peoples of Europe at the removal of the threat of war was heartfelt. Chamberlain's return to London from the airport was a triumphal progress. Yet the voices of critics of the Munich agreement were soon heard. They alleged that Britain and France had not only abandoned Czecho-Slovakia, but had given way unnecessarily. There would be no satisfying Germany now, they said. There was no immediate improvement in Anglo-German relations, and Britain's rearmament continued.

On the continent, it became immediately apparent that the post-war French system of alliances had broken down, and that the " Rome-Berlin axis " was in the ascendant. Hungary and Poland eagerly seized the opportunity to press upon Czecho-Slovakia the cession of territories containing Magyar and Polish minorities. This was the opportunity which Hungary had awaited so long. Ever since the Treaty of Trianon (June, 1920) had stripped away the large alien minorities of pre-war Hungary and transferred a large number of Magyars to foreign rule, a campaign of protest and propaganda had been maintained. The Little Entente of Czecho-Slovakia, Jugo-Slavia and Rumania, backed by France, had existed to checkmate Hungarian hopes of treaty revision. Now, with the absorption of Austria and the Sudeten land into the Reich, with Czecho-Slovakia abandoned by the very powers who might have been expected to support her, the situation had completely changed.

HUNGARY AND POLAND TAKE THEIR SHARE

AN understanding with Germany paved the way for the Hungarian demand, made immediately after the Munich Agreement, for the cession of territory from Czecho-Slovakia and, as a result of the " arbitration " of Germany and Italy, Hungary received 4,630 square miles of territory and over million inhabitants, about 600,000 of whom were Magyars.

Poland also gained territory from Czecho-Slovakia—770 square miles and 240,000 inhabitants—and for a few months the object of her policy was a " common frontier " with Hungary, sharing Ruthenia with her and shutting off Czecho-Slovakia from Rumania. But the whole situation was changed for Poland by the events of March, 1939, when Germany, disregarding the Munich agreement, made friction between the Czech Government and the Slovaks a pretext to march into Prague. The Czech President, Dr. Hacha, who had been invited to Berlin, was compelled, under the threat that Prague would be bombed, to sign a document placing the fate of the Czech people " in the hands of the Reichsführer." A week later Lithuania, similarly threatened, was forced to cede Memel to Germany, while Rumania deemed it politic to agree to Germany's request for a commercial treaty making great concessions.

POLAND'S DIPLOMATIC DILEMMA

IT is therefore not surprising that Poland became apprehensive. Her possession of the Corridor, her commercial interests in the " free city " of Danzig, her Ukrainian minority, all made her the object of a possible German attack, for Germany appeared to be encouraging Ukrainian nationalism and her press adopted a violently anti-Polish tone. She proposed that Poland should join the anti-Comintern pact, cede Danzig to Germany, and allow her to construct a road across the Corridor.

BRITAIN STEPS IN

IT was at this point that Britain took a hand. The policy of " appeasement " was abandoned, and guarantees were offered to Poland and, later, to Rumania and Greece. The closest co-operation was maintained with France, a defensive agreement was concluded with Turkey, and overtures for an alliance were made to Russia. As an earnest of her intentions Britain introduced a measure of conscription—all men between 20 and 21 were to undergo six months' military training—and budgeted for the expenditure of over 600 million pounds on rearmament.

Germany's reply was to renounce her non-aggression pact with Poland and the Anglo-German Naval Treaty, and to conclude a military alliance with Italy.

Besides Poland, both Rumania and Jugo-Slavia have had reason to fear German aggression. Both were left diplomatically " in the air " by the break-up of the Little Entente. Rumania possesses oil-wells which Germany covets, she has been embarrassed by internal political dissensions and knows that her neighbour, Bulgaria, desires treaty revision. Rumania's position, however, is a little different for it has been strengthened by her inclusion, with Greece and Poland, in the British guarantees offered to those countries. Jugo-Slavia is a conglomerate state of 12 million Serbs, Croats and Slovenes, formed by the addition to pre-War Serbia of Montenegro and parts of the Hapsburg Empire. It is scarcely surprising that both of these countries have adopted a temporising policy towards Germany and Italy.

Thus, the events of March and September, 1938, and March, 1939, have completely transformed the European situation. Poland has abandoned her policy of " sitting on the fence " between Germany and Russia and made a " declaration of friendship " with the latter country. Britain has inaugurated a new foreign policy, which she describes as one of resistance to aggression, but which is denounced by Germany as one of encirclement.

RUSSIA'S MIGHTY ENTERPRISE

RUSSIA is an immense country, in size, population, and resources. It is immense also in its variety. Every type of climate, from the tropical to the arctic, is to be found within its borders, and almost every stage of civilisation is represented there.

But this huge country, covering one-sixth of the land surface of the globe, has always been comparatively weak. Before the War, its great natural resources were practically unused. Some modern factories had been established in and near the large towns, but the bulk of Russia's limited industrial production was still organised on a domestic basis. Poor transport facilities retarded industrial advance. Outside the big towns, metalled roads were rare, and the railroad and canal systems were probably the least developed of any in Europe. Russia's natural resources, therefore, were of little use to her, since they could not be transported. Even agriculture, upon which more than four-fifths of the people depended, was organised in an exceedingly crude manner.

he primitive open-field system prevailed, the wooden ox lough was everywhere used, and sowing, reaping, and areshing were all done by hand. This feeble economic rganisation was yet further hampered by an inefficient and orrupt political system and by a backward social structure. .ussia was a land of immense potentialities, but remained, a the words of Dr. Nansen, " a world still unborn."

Long before the War, discontent with political corruption, ocial inequality, and economic distress found expression in variety of ways. The most significant movement in the ght of later happenings was the development of a number f revolutionary groups conducting underground propaganda a the larger towns. Some were mildly socialistic and hoped o secure social reform by peaceful means. Others were ommunistic, advocating the overthrow of Tsardom by orce and the seizure of power in the name of the workers.

Extreme Bolshevik views gained little ground before the Var. But Russia's terrific losses (nearly four million asualties in the first ten months of fighting), spreading isease and distress, and a realisation of the extent to which aese sacrifices were due to the incompetence and corruption f the government, led to a growth of unrest. The March .evolution, 1917, was an almost bloodless and spontaneous utbreak of strikes and food-riots. The Kerensky govern- aent of moderate socialists and liberals which followed did othing to reduce war losses and increase food-supplies. oviets (councils) of workers, peasants, and soldiers were ormed all over Russia under the influence of the Bolsheviks nd raised the cry of " All power to the Soviets." The Jovember Revolution, with very little fighting, placed the olsheviks in power.

There followed a period known as that of War Communism, uring which the new government sought to consolidate its ontrol over the country and to repel invaders and counter- volutionaries. This was an attempt to establish com- nunism speedily and by force, and was killed by the cramping ffect of over-centralisation and the drought of 1920–21, vhich led to a disastrous famine.

THE SOVIET FINDS A USE FOR CAPITALISM

WITH the intention of relieving the immediate situation and preparing more slowly and surely for the initiation f the communist state, Lenin declared in 1921 his New

Economic Policy. The idea of conducting economic lif
without money and private trade was abandoned. Man
of the characteristics of private enterprise, such as freedo
to choose one's occupation and to enter into business, wer
restored. It was not a complete relinquishment of Stat
control ; rather, it was a kind of State capitalism.

On the surface, this was a retreat from the communist
ideal. But it was a strategic retreat, determined by th
necessity of gaining control over agriculture and convertin
the peasant to the Revolution, and of preparing a coherer
scheme for the re-organisation of industry and financ
A new personnel had to be trained as workers, foremen, an
managers for the new factories. Means had to be devise
for overcoming the reluctance of the peasant to adopt socialist
methods of farming. Above all, time was needed for th
collection of information and the elaboration of schemes f
the planned reconstruction of industry. By 1928, the tim
judged favourable for the introduction of the Planned Econom

Why was it considered necessary to resort to a Five-Yea
Plan ? Of the many reasons suggested, two call for speci
comment : the desire to consolidate the revolution and
achieve self-sufficiency in the quickest possible time.
the revolution was to be permanent, not only must th
common people receive tangible proof of its benefits in th
form of higher standards of living, but also the course
future development must be laid down. For both reaso
the planning of industrial growth was necessary. It w
further thought necessary to accelerate the pace of industria
isation to the utmost possible limit in order to make Russ
secure against threats of foreign invasion or boycott. Th
motive is still evident in the military phraseology in whi
industrial developments are described.

A PLAN TO TRANSFORM SIX MILLION SQUARE MILES

THE first Five-Year Plan was not conceived as an end
itself. It was intended as the first of a long series
planned advances, each stage following upon the earli
ones and providing the materials for the later steps. T
first ten years may, however, be regarded as the crucial peric
of this planned structure. For the first two Five-Year Pla
aimed at carrying through an economic revolution in
decade. Russia and Siberia, with their six million squa
miles and 160,000,000 people, were treated as one hu

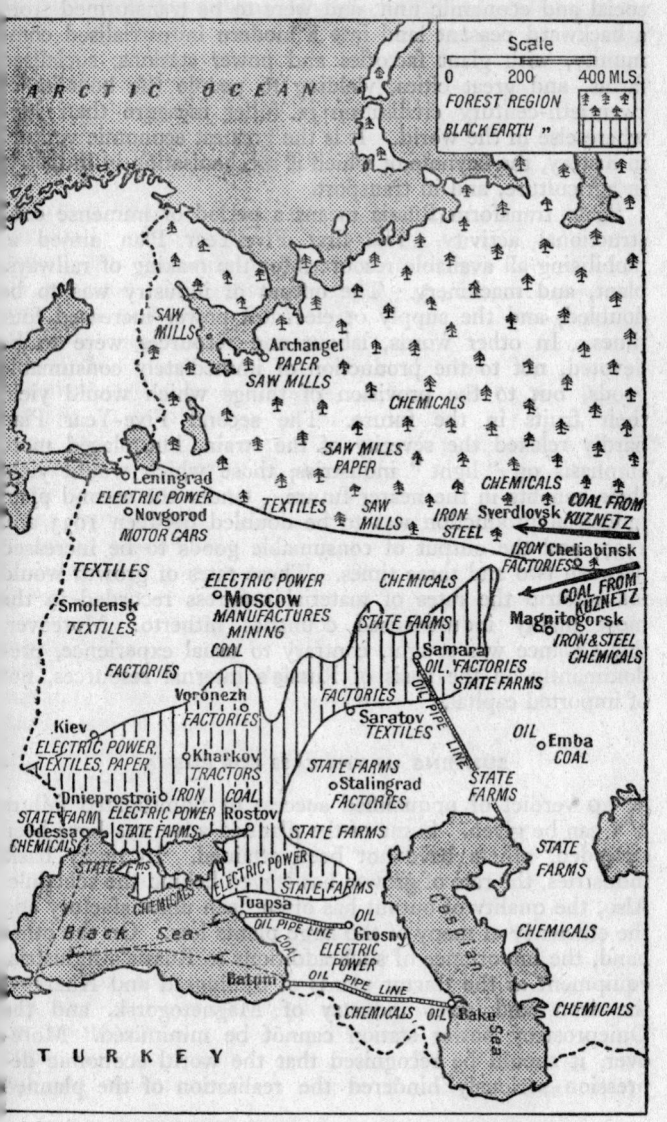

SOVIET EXPANSION UNDER THE FIVE-YEAR PLAN

social and economic unit, and were to be transformed from a backward peasant land into a modern industrialised community, with giant factories and power stations, socialised farms, and great cities, yielding to people the benefits of twentieth-century civilisation in fuller measure than anywhere else in the world.   It is the greatest economic venture in history, the keynote of which is mechanisation in industry, in agriculture, and in transport.

So to transform Russia means a period of immense constructional activity.   The first Five-Year Plan aimed at mobilising all available resources for the making of railways, plant, and machinery.   The output of industry was to be doubled, and the supply of electrical power increased four times.   In other words, labour and resources were to be devoted, not to the production of immediately consumable goods, but to the provision of things which would yield their fruits in the future.   The second Five-Year Plan hardly relaxed the severity of the strain, but placed more emphasis on " light " industries, those which would yield their benefits in the nearer future.   Under the second plan industrial production was to be doubled between 1933 and 1937, and the output of consumable goods to be increased between two and three times.   These rates of growth would far outstrip the rates of material progress recorded in the most highly industrialised countries hitherto.   Moreover, this advance was sought, contrary to usual experience, predominantly on the basis of Russia's internal resources, not of imported capital.

SUMMING UP THE CASE FOR RUSSIA

No verdict of unqualified success or unmitigated failure can be given.   Some of the planned advances have been exceeded, others have not been attained.   In many basic industries, the rate of growth has lagged behind the schedule. Also, the quality of output has often been unsatisfactory and the efficiency of many of the large plants low.   On the other hand, the importance of such additions to Russia's industrial equipment as the tractor plants of Stalingrad and Kharkov, the iron and steel industry of Magnetogorsk, and the Dnieprostroy power station cannot be minimised.   Moreover, it should be recognised that the world economic depression seriously hindered the realisation of the planned outputs. The prices of Russia's exports of food and raw materials fell so much more severely than the prices of the manufactured goods she needed to import that the original constructional plans were undermined.

But it would be false to assume that all the hindrances are external. With Russia there exist several "narrow places" which must be removed before advance can proceed swiftly and securely. Transport is a grave difficulty. Although the railway mileage has been increased by about one-third, the volume of traffic has increased still more rapidly, with consequent congestion and delay. The whole transport system of Russia—rail, road, canal, river—is inadequate to the needs of an industrial country. Further, it has not yet been possible to create a labour force of sufficient numbers and skill to handle effectively the vast new equipment which has been provided.

Probably agriculture has proved the biggest obstacle. All the grandiose industrial schemes have an agricultural basis. Increased output from the land is needed to feed the growing industrial population, to provide raw materials for manufacturing industry, and to provide exports to exchange for foreign machinery. The Plan contemplated the collectivisation of agriculture, *i.e.* the establishment of large communal farms on which the newest machinery and farming methods could be applied. But the peasant did not take kindly to the loss of his fields and liberty of action, and a great campaign of propaganda and coercion was necessary before the collective farm became the dominant agricultural unit. Even now the result is uncertain. Possibly it will be necessary to wait for the appearance of a new generation bred to the revolutionary ideal before a satisfactory solution of the land problem can be assured.

RUSSIA'S CHALLENGE TO THE WORLD

THE most significant aspects of the Russian experiment to the outside world are the new conception of social relations embodied in the Soviet system and the attempt to plan in advance the development of the social and economic structure. Democracy in the Western sense does not exist in Russia. Freedom cannot mean the same thing in a collectivist as in an individualist society. The Russian is denied the right to choose his employer, since there is ultimately only one—the State. Rights of property and choice of occupation are severely restricted. In the political field the individual cannot participate in the determination of industrial or foreign policy, nor can he form an opposition party.

But the communist would assert that the forms of liberty in a capitalistic state are very different from the realities. Moreover, while parliamentary democracy does not exist in Russia, considerable power of criticism is allowed, and the administration of industry and local affairs is subject to more direct popular control than in other countries. An attempt is made to submit to the decision of the common man the things on which he is competent by his experience to express a valuable opinion, and to withhold from him matters which are beyond his horizon. As it has been expressed, " In Russia, opportunity is stressed in place of rights."

The idea of Planning has become a commonplace of political discussion. The boldness of the Russian experiment has fired the imagination of the world, and everywhere the effects are visible. The possibilities of planning the organisation and direction of industrial and financial systems are not merely being discussed but tried, notably in the United States. The importance of planning the growth of towns and of co-ordinating transport systems is generally recognised. Russian methods will need and will receive drastic modification in their application to other countries. But the Russian experiment has provided a powerful stimulus to the spread of these ideas.

The challenge of Russia to the world is not—immediately, at any rate—a military one. Nor is it a trade menace. Russia is unlikely for many years to come to be a powerful competitor with the leading commercial countries. The challenge is one of ideas. Two systems of ideas confront one another. Communism throws down to the old world the challenge of new moral values (the chief being the complete submersion of the individual in the community), new conceptions of industrial and social organisation and of political relationships. Will the world retort with the counterblast of fascism ? Or will it eventually embrace the new faith in its entirety ? Or will it select certain features of the Russian system and absorb them into the existing structure without violent upheaval ?

DEMOCRACY RETREATING BEFORE THE DESPOTS?

ONE of the most striking, and certainly one of the most important, features of post-war Europe has been the widespread reaction against democracy.[1] In state after state, representative methods of government have been superseded by dictatorship in one form or another. This is

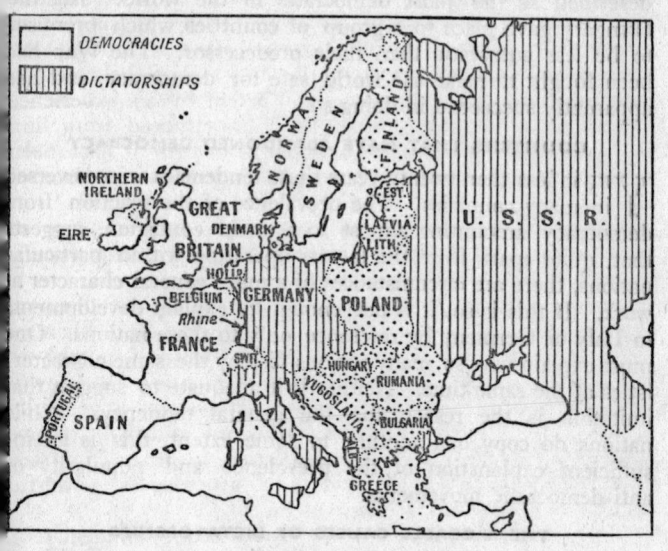

EAST OF THE RHINE : SOUTH OF THE BALTIC

Rise of dictatorships in Europe. The dotted-in states are those that possess a parliamentary system, but cannot be described as democracies in the Western sense.

all the more remarkable because, during the nineteenth and early twentieth centuries, there was an almost unchecked development of parliamentary government. In Great Britain, the franchise was extended by successive steps until the right to vote was enjoyed by all adults. In Germany,

[1] Widespread, but not general. It has occurred in the area east of the Rhine and south of the Baltic.

France and Italy, similar, though not so complete, change took place. Even Imperial Russia made some concession to the popular demand for representation.

The War itself was proclaimed as a struggle of the western democracies against the more autocratic powers of Central Europe. When it ended it seemed for a time that the day of dynasties and despots was done. Germany became a democratic republic, and the Weimar Constitution has been described as the most democratic in the world. Austria-Hungary gave place to a group of countries which promised to be less autocratic than their predecessor. The War had been fought to make the world safe for democracy, and had apparently succeeded in doing so.

COUNTRIES THAT HAVE ABANDONED DEMOCRACY

YET in less than twenty years these tendencies were reversed in many countries. The prevalence of the reaction from democracy, amounting almost to a world contagion, suggests that, quite apart from the factors operating within particular nations, there are circumstances of a more general character at work. If this is so, it is not enough to explain developments in Italy or Germany by reference only to these nations. One must explain why so many nations display the same characteristics at the same time. Neither is it adequate to suggest that imitation is the reason for the general tendency. While nations do copy one another to some extent, this is an insufficient explanation of the prevalence and popularity of anti-democratic movements.

THE PROBABLE CAUSES OF DICTATORSHIPS

A RAPID survey of the course of events in Germany and Italy may help to make clear whether or no there are certain tendencies which are not confined to a particular country and which encourage the resort to dictatorial methods. In Italy, economic distress resulting from the War and other causes was accentuated by the incapacity of the government. In these circumstances, the revolutionary elements in the community, both left and right wing, flourished. Both preached the need for a curtailment of individual liberty in order to deal effectively with the condition of the nation. The Fascist party was able to make use of a fortunate combination of circumstances and its superior financial strength to seize power for itself. But, in the absence of a fascist revolution, there would seem to have been danger of a red revolution.

A somewhat similar state of affairs is apparent in Germany. After the War, acute economic distress prevailed, and seemed to be beyond the control of the political authority. The consequent unrest fed the revolutionary parties. The communists advocated the seizure of power by the workers. The Nazis cast their net wider, enlisting the discontents of the middle and upper classes who had lost so heavily by inflation and resented the humiliation of Germany, and of the young people for whom there appeared to be no place in the post-war world. As conditions improved, however, the strength of both parties declined. But when the spread of world depression brought more and more privation, revolution regained its popularity.

The existing government could hold out little hope of speedy improvement. All it could suggest was the prosaic and uncomfortable process of cutting Germany's coat according to the available cloth. By this time, however, divisions in the left wing ranks had weakened their force. The Nazis, on the other hand, were much stronger. By a skilful adaptation of their programme and by the financial attractions of membership of the " Brown Army "—made possible by large contributions from German industrialists—they were able to harness a considerable part of the working-class discontent, and to gain sufficient strength to carry through the revolution of 1933.

It will be evident from this sketch, or from a fuller examination of developments in modern Europe, that discontent is a necessary prelude to the successful overthrow of democratic institutions. The discontent may be of an economic or political nature. But more usually, the dissatisfaction will be with economic conditions, political issues serving to intensify the rebellion against economic circumstances. Thus, as long as reasonable prosperity prevailed in Germany, the Nazi movement did little more than provide the comic relief to German political life. Again, the swing towards dictatorship noticeably increased in strength with the spread of the world depression. For this tendency to turn to despotic rule as a remedy for discontent, two general explanations find wide acceptance.

The first stresses the inability of the average man to grasp the drift of the modern world. Politically and economically the world has been in an unsettled condition ever since the War. Changes take place with a bewildering rapidity; problems become ever more numerous and complex; and the difficulties and uncertainties of ordinary life seem to increase. These tendencies are apparent in England. How much more distracting are they in some of the countries of Central and Eastern Europe! People do not relish continual uncertainty. There has been a general tendency, therefore, to seek a more simple and sure basis of life. Democracy, unfortunately, does not offer this. All it offers is responsibility. For, in giving individuals the right to participate in government, it places upon them the duty of equipping themselves to exercise this right; of thinking out problems and making decisions. But so complicated are our post-war problems that most people are too lazy or too diffident to undertake this duty. They prefer to leave the fatigue and responsibility to some one else. And ultimately this leads to dictatorship.

Again, another cause of dictatorship is the class war engendered by modern industrialism. Communists aim at a dictatorship of the proletariat, while fascists believe in a dictatorship of their own party—which stands for a preservation of the capitalist structure of society subordinated, however, to the nationalistic and militaristic policy of the state. It is obvious that if one section of society seeks to deprive another of its economic or political privileges there will be a struggle, possibly a violent and bloody one. This happened, indeed, in the early stages of the Russian Revolution and during the Spanish Civil War.

SPAIN TORN BY THE BITTERNESS OF CIVIL WAR

THE history of Spain, the character of the Spanish people, acute economic, political and religious disputes, all contributed towards bringing about the Spanish Civil War, which broke out in July, 1936. For several generations Spain had been regarded as a picturesque backwater, whose disturbances had little effect upon the broad stream of European affairs. Soon this was all changed, and Spain became front-page news, a diplomatic focus, and a battleground of rival ideologies.

After a brief period of greatness in the sixteenth and seventeenth centuries, during which the *conquistadores* established her enormous empire in South and Central America, Spain entered upon a period of decline. During the eighteenth

entury she came under the rule of a branch of the Bourbons,
he French royal family, and was practically a satellite of
France until the French Revolution. When Napoleon
attempted to put his brother on the Spanish throne the
people revolted and evinced a genius for guerrilla warfare.
After the Napoleonic Wars the Bourbons were restored.
With French help they survived a revolt against their wretched
rule in Spain, but lost their American empire. From 1833
here was a miserable period of dynastic strife known as the
Carlist Wars, ending, after a short-lived republic, in the accession of Alfonso XII. Plunged in her own troubles, Spain
lagged far behind the rest of Western Europe. The masses
were poor and illiterate; there was a small, but very rich and
intensely-proud land-owning aristocracy; and the Church,
which was reactionary and believed in the absolute authority
of the Pope, possessed enormous wealth and influence.

CAUSES OF THE GROWING DISCONTENT

THESE facts, coupled with dissatisfaction at maladministration, the loss of Cuba and, in the ensuing war with the
U.S.A. (1898), the loss of the Philippines, led to discontent,
expressing itself in the growth of Republicanism, Socialism
and Anarchism. A series of wars in Morocco, not often very
successful, had the double effect of adding to the dissatisfaction
and at the same time making the army a permanent factor in
the Spanish political situation. The officers formed a sort of
political clique, which always took the reactionary side, and
after the unsuccessful Moroccan War of 1921, General Primo
de Rivera, Governor of Catalonia, rebelled against the government. Alfonso XIII. accepted the coup d'etat, and Primo
de Rivera governed Spain until 1930, when the economic
depression, and a quarrel with the army, weakened him to such
an extent that the king was only too glad to save himself by
sacrificing his minister. Alfonso's wiliness was unavailing,
however, for the overwhelming victory of the Republicans in
the 1931 elections resulted in his flight, and the end of the
Spanish monarchy.

THE STRUGGLE BEGINS IN EARNEST

THE new Republican government initiated a sweeping policy
of social reform. The religious orders were dissolved, the
estates of the Jesuits confiscated, twenty-five million pounds
worth of grandees' estates confiscated, and the franchise was

granted to women. Such enormous changes produced economic dislocation. There were many strikes as well as rioting
accompanied by attacks on churches. Nor must the existence
of strong separatist movements in Viscaya and Catalonia be
overlooked. Declining trade resulted in a reaction, and in
1934 a right-wing government was returned to power. It was
faced with insurrections in Barcelona, the capital of Catalonia,
and in Asturias (the two " reddest " parts of Spain). These
were ruthlessly suppressed with the aid of Moorish troops—too
ruthlessly, for the pendulum swung violently to the left again
in February, 1936, when the Popular Front (Liberals, Socialists and Anarchists in alliance) won the elections. Again the
army took a hand for, in July, General Franco headed a
military revolt against the Government in Morocco. Risings
followed in Spain, and the Spanish Civil War had begun.

The policy of the League of Nations, and of its two most
powerful supporters, France and Britain, was to isolate the
conflict. But partisanship of the conflicting theories of socialism and fascism was too strong in some countries
for them to accept the doctrine of non-intervention.
Italian and German help resulted in victory for Franco.
What price, if any, will be exacted for this help remains
to be seen.

THE EMPIRE'S COMING OF AGE

JUST as the War altered the relations and importance of
states in Europe, so it caused many disturbances within the
British Empire. Old problems were intensified and new ones
created. Moreover, with the development of closer trade connections and more rapid communications in modern times,
the Empire has become a more sensitive organism, unrest or
distress in one part being quickly reflected in the others. And
unrest has been, unfortunately, only too prominent a characteristic of the post-war Empire. The ferment of race relations
has created particularly acute problems. Not only in India,
but in places as dissimilar as South Africa, Egypt, Kenya and
Cyprus, friction between races has been a serious difficulty.
This issue is probably the most important of all contemporary
Imperial questions.

The British Empire includes roughly one-quarter of the
land surface of the globe and one-quarter of its population.
The diversity of its people is remarkable. Of the total

population of nearly five hundred millions in 1931, only seventy millions were white. Of the rest, 360 millions were natives of India and Ceylon, 40 millions were negroes, six millions Arabs, six millions Malays, and one million Chinese. There was a similar variety of religious beliefs ; 210 millions were Hindus, 100 millions Mohammedans, 80 millions Christians, and 12 millions Buddhists. These figures make it apparent that the Empire is a unique experiment in linking different lands and peoples in a world society.

THE EVER-CHANGING EMPIRE

In forms of government there is an almost equal variety. There are four distinct sections of the Empire. First, the United Kingdom, the centre of the whole structure. Next, the self-governing Dominions, which, as their name implies, are politically independent of the Mother Country. These Dominions are populated mainly by people of British stock and speech, and are ruled by democratically elected governments. Thirdly, there is the Indian Empire, containing nearly three-quarters of the population of the Empire. Lastly, the Crown Colonies and Dependencies. These form the Colonial or Dependent Empire, and consist of a great variety of territories, climates, and peoples. Thus the Empire is a conglomeration of peoples, religions, and forms of government. It is not a completed structure, with settled relations between its different parts. Indeed, it cannot be said that there is any constitution for the Empire at all. A continuous process of change goes on, and shows no sign of cessation.

This was particularly true during the War and has been so since. The Dominions have been given much more responsibility and power, and a new dominion—the Irish Free State —has been created. To symbolise the changed relations a new name has been coined—the British Commonwealth of Nations. In India, the right to ultimate self-government has been conceded, and the beginnings of this development made. Already her relations with the Mother Country are being modified. By the invention of the Mandatory System under which the ex-German colonies are ruled, not only has the Empire been extended, but new conceptions of the duties to the Colonies have appeared.

That mandated territories can be a burdensome responsibility is shown by events in Palestine. Both Jews and Arabs claim that Britain promised them the country. Outrages throughout 1937 and 1938 involved the sending of British troops and the appointment of the Peel Commission, which recommended partition. The British Government at first accepted this recommendation and then, because of vigorous Arab resistance to increased Jewish immigration caused by German anti-Semitism, reversed its policy and, in May, 1939, proposed to restrict Jewish immigration for five years, give Palestine self-government in ten, and so end the mandate.

THE GROWN-UP CHILDREN DEMAND THEIR FREEDOM

IN the early days of imperial expansion, the customary view was that colonies were mere plantations, to be cultivated for the benefit of the home country. The settlers were denied any voice in determining colonial policy and were even excluded from full control over their local affairs. The loss of the American colonies and troubles in Canada taught the British government that, if the Empire was to be preserved from dissolution, this dictatorial attitude must be dropped. The Colonies must no longer be regarded as sources of profit to the Mother Country. Their economic development must be determined, not by the dictation of the central power, but by the decisions of the colonists themselves. If they decided to industrialise, they should be free to do so, even if it meant that their industries would come into competition with those of Britain. It was realised also that, even in the political field, the Colonies must be given equality ; that is, they must be free not only to control their own local affairs but also to decide the nature of their relations with Great Britain. Thus, by 1914, there were five Dominions, each with its own government and sense of nationality, but all members of a wider association.

But the process of evolution was not completed. The principle of partnership between free and equal associates had not yet been admitted to the full. While the Dominions controlled their own overseas trade relations and defence, they left the guidance of imperial foreign affairs to the central government in London. They had probably refrained from invading this field because they had been fully occupied in developing their own lands and had not much time or interest to devote to outside affairs. They may, too, have felt it wiser to leave the conduct of foreign negotiations to the trained diplomats of the old country. With this single exception, the Dominions were on a practically equal footing with Great Britain. To the foreign critic it seemed that the unity of the Empire had gone in all but name. There was no central imperial government. Every attempt to establish imperial federation or close economic co-operation had failed. Another war, we were told, would complete the destruction of the Empire.

Yet during the Great War, a million men from the Dominions took part in the fighting. This participation of the Dominions in the War had far-reaching effects, quite apart from the proof it gave of the survival of a bond of Empire. The Dominion forces were organised as separate units. This gave them a stronger sense of nationality. They felt that they had been placed on the same footing as the other Allied nations. It also caused them to realise what leaving the determination of foreign policy to the British government meant. While this state of affairs persisted, the Dominions might at any time be involved in a war in which they had little interest or sympathy. They determined, therefore, to extend their power to the one field so far denied to them—foreign policy.

THE DOMINIONS BECOME MASTERS OF THEIR DESTINY

THE first step in this direction was taken during the War. In 1917, at the invitation of the British government, the Dominion Prime Ministers formed with the British Cabinet an Imperial War Cabinet. The powers of this body were vague, but it gave the Dominions a new status. Also, a resolution was passed endorsing the recognition of the Dominions as independent self-governing nations within an Imperial Commonwealth, and recognising their right to a full voice in deciding foreign policy. This verbal acknowledgment of the new relation was confirmed when the Dominions were admitted to the League of Nations as separate members ; and when it was agreed that they should have their own ambassadors if they so desired, and that they should not only be free to negotiate with foreign states, but also to make separate treaties. As the Imperial Conference of 1926 declared, each Dominion " is now the master of its destiny. In fact, if not always in form, it is subject to no compulsion whatever." Thus the freedom and powers of the Dominions were made as wide as those of Great Britain.

Governors-General were now recognised to be representatives of the King alone, and it was made clear that in Dominion affairs the King acts on the advice of his Dominion ministers. The Statute of Westminster, 1931, declared the authority of all the parliaments of the Empire to be equal. The essential provisions of the Statute are (1) that after 1931 no law passed by a Dominion Parliament shall be void or inoperative merely because it conflicts with a British law or Act of Parliament: (2) that the parliaments of the Dominions shall have power to make laws having extra-territorial effect.

It is obvious that the Statue of Westminster increases the importance of the monarchy as a link between the Dominions, and the enthusiasm evoked in all parts of the Empire by George V.'s Silver Jubilee showed how influential such a personal tie could be. His death in January, 1936, brought to the throne Edward VIII., a monarch who seemed ideally suited for the part he had to play in the new conditions. Yet, by the end of the year, his subjects had seen him abdicate and pass into exile, leaving the throne to his brother. The question whether Edward VIII. could be permitted to contract the marriage he desired affected the Dominions as well as England, and was accordingly put, not only to the British Cabinet, but (in accordance with the Statute of Westminster) to the Premiers of the Dominions as well. The permission was not forthcoming, but the king was resolved on marriage, and bred, as he said, in the constitutional tradition of his father, he was unwilling to form a " king's party " and accordingly abdicated. It was left to King George and Queen Elizabeth, by their visit to Canada and the U.S.A., in May, 1939, when they were received with genuine enthusiasm, to aid the cause of Empire unity and friendship with America in a way that no previous British sovereign had done before.

IRELAND'S TROUBLED STORY

THE new conception of Dominion status which was adopted after the War was felt at the time to offer the means of solving the age-old Irish question. Just before the War, it seemed that Home Rule would be granted. But the opposition of Ulster and the outbreak of hostilities prevented the enactment of the measure. As a result, the Sinn Fein party, standing for complete independence from Great Britain, increased in strength, and resorted to rebellion at Easter in 1916. At the

December, 1918, election, 73 of the 105 Irish constituencies returned Sinn Feiners, and these declared an Irish Republic in 1919.

For two years a murderous guerrilla warfare was waged between the Irish Republican Army and the British forces. It was brought to an end by the signature in December 1921, of a treaty which gave to Ireland " the same constitutional status in the community of nations known as the British Empire as the Dominion of Canada, etc." This agreement was clearly a compromise and did not satisfy de Valera, the leader of the Sinn Fein party. For two more years he maintained resistance against the forces of the newly constituted Irish Free State. But, in 1923, he and his followers abandoned armed resistance, and took their seats in the Dail, as the lower house of the Free State Parliament is called.

The Cosgrave government, which was in power during the early years of the Free State, pursued a policy of cordial co-operation with the British government. But when de Valera became Prime Minister in February, 1932, he changed the whole direction of Irish policy. In his view, the Treaty of 1921 was imposed by force and could not, therefore, be regarded as binding. Friction quickly developed between Ireland and Great Britain. The oath of allegiance to the British Crown was abolished without previous negotiation with the British government. Then the Irish Land Annuities —interest on money advanced by English investors to enable Irish peasants to purchase their holdings—were withheld by the Free State government. In retaliation, Great Britain levied special tariffs on Irish goods with the object of recouping the lost annuities. Ireland retorted, and a tariff war developed, which greatly reduced the trade between the two countries.

A truce was called to this economic warfare by a trade agreement in 1935. De Valera's next move was to promulgate, in 1937, a constitution, which renamed the Free State " Eire," gave her a President, assumed her sovereignty over Northern Ireland, and made no reference to the king, Great Britain, or Eire's position in the British Empire. Whatever the British government thought of this gesture was not allowed to impede the conversations which led up to the signature of a new Anglo-Irish treaty in April, 1938. By this a trade agreement was made, harbour defences were handed over to the government of Eire, and Britain renounced the Land Annuities in return for a final payment of £10 millions.

CAN TRADE HOLD THE EMPIRE TOGETHER ?

THE course of events in Ireland since the establishmen of the Free State illustrates the most serious problem o the Empire. In modern times, the self-governing Empir has taken on a new form. The unity arising from control b a central government has disappeared. The Dominion have become completely autonomous, bound by no lega obligation, unless voluntarily accepted, either to the Mothe Country or to one another. The new conception is that o a partnership between free and equal states. But if thi partnership is to rest on no more solid ties than the bonds o sentiment, will the Empire endure ? It is almost certai that the relations between the members would ultimately b indistinguishable from those between foreign states, and th Empire would become nothing more than a memory and a name. It is essential for the permanence of the Empire tha the old bonds should be replaced by new ones.

On the surface, there seems to be no reason why clos economic ties should not be developed. Both the Unitec Kingdom and the Dominions would gain from imperia economic co-operation. The prevalent drift towards nationa self-sufficiency has seriously diminished the foreign trade o Great Britain. If this tendency continued, it would be disastrous for the country, for its large population and prosperity are dependent on expanding overseas trade. I would be hardly less disastrous for the Dominions, witl their enormous undeveloped resources. Without a growing export trade, their future material progress would be greatly slowed down. If, as seems likely, the ideal of world fre trade is unattainable, could not a partial substitute be founc in close economic relations within the Empire ? The manu-facturing industries of Great Britain could provide the materials for the exploitation of the undeveloped resources of the Empire, while the Dominions could find a market for their produce in the home country.

It is not suggested that the Empire could become a self-contained economic unit. Any attempt to make the Empire into an exclusive system would conflict with the major interests of both Great Britain and the Dominions. The economic organisation of Great Britain has been founded on world trade, and it would be highly dangerous to relinquish foreign sources of supply and markets in favour of still undeveloped

Imperial ones. On the other hand, the Dominions for the last quarter of a century have fostered the growth of manufacturing industries behind tariff walls. It is improbable that they would forego these in order to give freer entry to British goods. Moreover, they have trade relations which they are unprepared to sacrifice. The bulk of Canada's timber exports go to the United States, while Great Britain meets her requirements from Scandinavia. To try to divert this trade into Imperial channels might do more harm than good. Is there, then, any reasonable prospect of creating close commercial relations within the Empire ?

THE ROAD TO OTTAWA

SOME guidance to the answer to this question will be gained from an examination of the efforts which have been made since the War. In 1923, following upon the Imperial Economic Conference, the Baldwin Government made an offer of tariff preferences to the Dominions, but the defeat of the Ministry caused the scheme to be dropped. The indirect outcome was the formation of the Empire Marketing Board for the purpose of promoting British consumption of imperial produce. For several years afterwards, no further step was taken. The Imperial Conference of 1930 discussed the feasibility of Imperial Preference, but without coming to a decision. As long as Great Britain retained free trade, preference could be given to colonial produce only by imposing new taxes on foreign goods, a proposal which was not very popular.

After 1931 events moved swiftly. The financial crisis of that year led to the introduction of tariffs to check " abnormal imports," and these soon developed into a system of all-round Protection. Thus the opportunity was created for the fostering of Empire trade. The new British tariffs could be adjusted so as to give preference to Dominion goods. In order to negotiate a series of trade agreements between the countries of the Empire, the Ottawa Conference was called in July 1932. The desire to reach agreement was strong, because success would not only promote co-operation within the Empire, but would also, it was hoped, lead to a general reduction of tariff barriers and a freeing of world trade.

There were serious obstacles to success, however, arising from the differences in economic conditions and attitude between Great Britain and the Dominions. The industries of the Dominions were no longer complementary to those of the United Kingdom, but competitive. Who should be the first to make concessions ? More important was the difference in attitude. Great Britain was still free trade at heart, and believed the prime purpose of the conference to be, in Baldwin's words, " to clear out the channels of trade among ourselves." The British delegation, therefore, sought to secure imperial preference by reducing tariffs within the Empire while leaving the tariffs on foreign goods unchanged. This method would have resulted in some freeing of trade. The Dominions, on the contrary, being traditionally protectionist, wanted to retain the existing tariffs on British goods while increasing those on foreign goods. This difference in attitude went far to nullify the efforts to achieve agreement.

It is probably too early to pass final judgment on the outcome of the Conference. But the general effect seems to have been to benefit the Dominions more than Great Britain. British tariffs on foreign goods were raised in order to give a preference to imperial products. But there has been no substantial reduction of Dominion tariffs in favour of Great Britain. What improvement there may have been in imperial trade has probably been secured by diverting trade from the rest of the world. Moreover, as an essay in imperial unity, Ottawa has not proved highly successful. Ill-feeling has been aroused between the participants by charges of failure to honour the spirit of the agreements. The almost inescapable conclusion is that the prospects of knitting the Empire into a close economic association are as yet very remote.

Are we to resign ourselves, therefore, to a slow weakening of imperial ties and an eventual dissolution of the Empire ? Many issues remain on which conflicting interests do not clash with the same force that they do in matters of trade. Within these fields the possibilities of co-operation are considerable. For example, a combined attack upon disease and plant pests would benefit all parties. Co-operation in research to improve the quality of imperial products and processes of manufacture would be fruitful. By agreement, industrial standards may be fixed for the whole Empire. In several such directions co-operation is possible. It would be much more profitable to explore these practicable fields than to enter upon grandiose and ill-considered schemes which may do more to jeopardise imperial unity than to promote it.

INDIA : A PROBLEM OF UNPARALLELED COMPLEXITY

THE clash of colour within the British Empire takes its most acute form in India. Here, unfortunately, the problem is one of peculiar complexity because of the special characteristics of the country. In size and population, India is one of the major divisions of the globe. Its area is as great as that of Europe, excluding Russia, and its people form one-fifth of the population of the world. Within this vast territory there is no sort of unity. In other regions, there has been a tendency for races living in contact with one another to fuse together. This has not been so in India. The social system has tended to keep the different races distinct in status, beliefs, and ways of life. As a result, the differences of blood, tradition, religion, language, and level of civilisation are enormous. The problem of developing a wider measure of self-government within the Indian Empire must be viewed in the light of this unparalleled social complexity.

Needless to say, there is as yet no fully developed sense of nationality in India. By herself, India never developed political unity. But with the spread of British rule in the nineteenth century and the penetration of Western political ideas, there began to emerge for the first time a sense of a common Indian nationality. Originally, it was confined to the small educated section of the people, and was combined with a belief in the necessity of retaining British control. But at the end of the century, there appeared the demand for more and more self-government, expressed at times in a violent form. Under the pressure of these claims, some reforms were introduced, notably the admission of an elected element into the legislative councils of the provinces. Far from appeasing the nationalists, these concessions made them more vocal, for their representatives were denied any responsibility for the conduct of government.

The Great War quieted the agitation for a while. The fundamental loyalty of the Indian Empire was shown by the participation of a million Indians in the struggle. But it meant also a considerable strengthening of the nationalist movement. India was admitted as a colleague with the self-governing Dominions to the Imperial War Cabinet, the Peace Conference, and the League of Nations. This recognition of responsibility made difficult the permanent denial of equal rights. Furthermore, Indians imbibed the ideals for which ostensibly the War was fought. It was natural that they should claim the same liberties as the Dominions and should look to the ultimate establishment of complete home rule. In 1917, the British government had conceded the reasonableness of this attitude by announcing that its policy would be the progressive development of self-governing institutions leading finally to autonomy within the Empire. This declaration of policy was embodied in the *Government of India Act* of 1919. Responsibility for the determination of the time and manner of each advance was retained by the British government.

The first step was taken by the Act of 1919 which established the system of provincial dyarchy. Under this arrangement certain responsibilities were passed to Indians, and others—the more important—retained by the British government. Broadly speaking, the control of finance and the maintenance of order and peace were " reserved " to the Crown, and other functions transferred to the Indian legislatures. Since, however, practically no action can be undertaken without raising financial issues, the degree of responsible government granted to the Indians was more apparent than real. It was laid down that the scheme should be reviewed every ten years and, if it worked satisfactorily, the sphere of self-government would be steadily enlarged.

GANDHI AND "NON-VIOLENT NON-CO-OPERATION"

THE scheme of dyarchy did not work too well, however, since it whetted appetites without satisfying them. The majority of the India nationalists refused to co-operate, and a continuous and violent agitation was waged for increased powers. A leader for the discontented elements appeared in Gandhi, an Indian lawyer. He was inclined to regard Western civilisation as an evil thing in itself, and dreamed of leading India back to the reputed simplicity and spirituality of former ages. The best way of combating the materialism of the West was to strike at its roots—trade. So Gandhi devised the plan of " non-violent non-co-operation," which involved a boycott of British goods, especially textiles. Amid the excitements of the time, however, a peaceful policy of this kind was impossible. Gandhi's followers were fre

ently drawn into violence, and for several years a dangerous
unrest developed, punctuated by sharp counter-measures, as
Amritsar.

These years were instructive, nevertheless, in that they
made evident the terrific complexity of the situation. Large
minorities existed who viewed with dread the prospect of
self-government in India. The Moslems feared that it
might mean the supremacy of the Hindu, who would use the

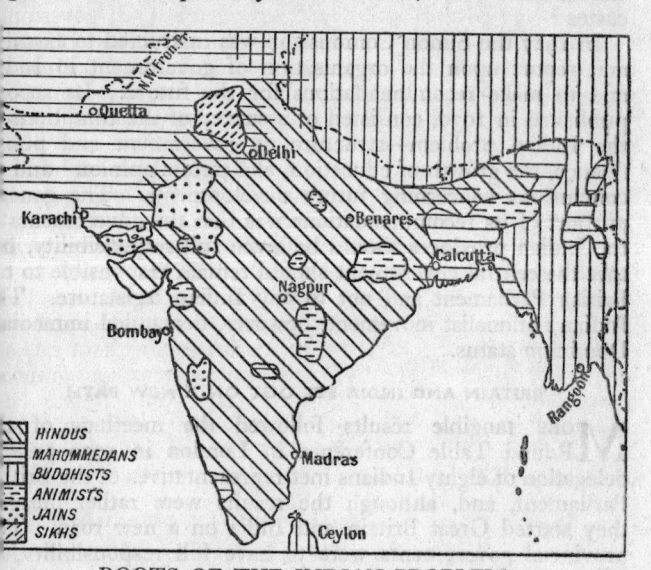

HINDUS
MAHOMMEDANS
BUDDHISTS
ANIMISTS
JAINS
SIKHS

ROOTS OF THE INDIAN PROBLEM

*The distribution of conflicting religions that have been
instrumental in preventing Indian national unity.*

opportunity to retaliate upon his hereditary religious and
military foe. The native princes, who govern one-third of
the area and a quarter of the population, feared that they
would be subordinated to a government controlled by half-
educated and socialist lawyers and politicians. Moreover,
the disturbances of these years emphasised the lessons of the
past. The appalling differences of race, caste, and religion
were bound to make the establishment of any government
based on discussion and agreement exceedingly difficult. It

was felt—and is still—that only the presence of British pow
restrained the forces of disorder, and saved India fro
complete anarchy.   Moreover, the conceptions of nationali
and democracy imply a certain common outlook and purpo
and a degree of equality, if only in a legal sense.   How cou
these ideas be successfully grafted on to a community, one-fif
of whose people are " untouchable," without rights or soci
status, their very shadows defiling members of the high
castes ?

In 1927 the Simon Commission was instructed to exami
and report upon the organisation of government in Indi
and to make recommendations for the future.   Its repo
published in 1930, consisted of a survey of the conditions
the Indian problem—structure of government and publ
finance, the growth of education, and public opinion—and i
conclusions concerning future developments.   The gener
purport of its recommendations was that the governments
the Indian provinces should be given full responsibility, b
that the central government should remain responsible to tl
British Parliament and not to any Indian legislature.   Tl
Indian nationalist movement, however, demanded immedia
Dominion status.

BRITAIN AND INDIA SET OUT ON A NEW PATH

MORE tangible results followed the meetings of tl
Round Table Conference in London in 1930–31.
delegation of eighty Indians met representatives of the Britis
Parliament, and, although the results were rather meagr
they started Great Britain and India on a new road.   Tl
provincial governments were to have full responsibility, ;
recommended by the Simon Commission, and approval w;
given to a federation between British India and the nativ
Indian States.   But the Conference suggested that the ne
central government should be organised on the basis of th
dyarchy which had proved so unsatisfactory.   Defenc
foreign affairs, and the position of minorities were to b
reserved to the Viceroy, other subjects being in the hands
ministers of the Indian federal legislature, which would n
longer be responsible to Parliament.   Two further meeting
of the Round Table Conference followed, and in 1933 th
British government published a White Paper containing it
proposals for Indian constitutional reform.

The provisions of this document followed very closely th

cheme outlined by the first Round Table Conference. It laid
own that the new constitution of India should be based on
he three principles of " federation, responsibility, and safe-
uards." The Indian States and the British Provinces were
o be joined in an Indian federation with a federal Parliament.
The Federal Government would have control over all matters
vith the exception of the army and foreign affairs, for which
he Viceroy would be responsible to the British govern-
nent. The Provinces were to have full responsible govern-
nent, subject to the power of the Governors to intervene
n order to safeguard financial stability and credit and to
rotect the interests of minorities. Conservative opposition
o these recommendations fell away when international tension
ncreased over German re-armament in 1935. In the same
ear the New India Act was passed.

These concessions have been sharply criticised both in India
nd Great Britain. Indians complain that they give too little,
ince immediate Dominion status is withheld. Many British
pokesmen assert that they give too much, and will spell the
eginning of the end of British rule in India. To this it
nay be retorted that the British government is bound by
olemn pledges to move towards self-government in India,
nd undue delay in honouring these pledges would amount
o a breach of them. Further, it is fantastic to suppose that
 vast population can be held indefinitely in subjection by a
andful of foreign troops and administrators. Great Britain is
nder the compulsion both of promises and circumstances to
ursue the policy of granting more and more responsible
overnment to India until the Indian Empire becomes a free
nd equal member of the British Commonwealth of Nations.

THE STRUGGLE IN THE FAR EAST

IN the last ten years of the nineteenth century, the ascendancy of Western civilisation over the world seemed un-
uestioned. Its military and naval strength were unrivalled.
ts products were everywhere used. Its culture and in-
titutions were the recognised models. And it was in pos-
ession of the greater part of the world's surface. But this
scendancy received setbacks early in the twentieth century.
The Boxer Rebellion in 1900 was a protest against the partition
f China by the Western Powers. And the Anglo-Japanese
Alliance, 1902, was the first recognition of a coloured people

13

on equal terms. Then, in the Russo-Japanese War, 190
one of the great European Powers was decisively beaten b
an Asiatic nation. This victory had a profound effect.
broke the spell of European supremacy and gave birth to
claim by the coloured peoples for equality. The Great Wa
strengthened this claim by weakening European prestig
yet further. Nowhere has the demand for new relation
between the Western Powers and the rest of the world bee
more insistent than in the Far East, from China and Japan
The situation there has created problems and difficultie
which are likely to occupy the world for many decades.

Nowhere is the clash of races more violent than in the Fa
East. There, two great peoples contest for mastery and fo
equality with the White nations. One is huge in numbers–
about 400,000,000—but in a chaotic condition. The othe
makes up for its comparative lack of numbers by an extra
ordinary sense of national unity and by its ready adaptabilit
to new conditions. The rest of the world cannot stand asid
from a struggle which involves a quarter of the populatio
of the globe.

THE AWAKENING OF CHINA

CHINA embraces from one-fifth to one quarter of th
human race. This vast people was highly civilise
before Europe entered the Iron Age. The superiority
their civilisation over that of their neighbours and the la
of contact with the developing Western Culture led the Chines
to despise all foreigners as barbarians, and to hold aloof fro
them. But this isolation was broken down early in th
nineteenth century. The West was drawn to China by th
desire for tea, and stayed to trade. By the last decade of th
century, all the Great Powers had forcibly acquired co
cessions and spheres of influence. Thus, China was broug
unwillingly into contact with Western ideas and ways. Th
West showed the Chinese how to build and operate railwa
and machines. Western merchants taught them to organi
machines. Western merchants taught them to organi
business and industry on Western lines. Missionary colleg
taught them chemistry, physics, and medicine.

What the West failed to teach China was how to organi
human society on a stable basis. The new ideas and metho
undermined the old ways of life and thought. Moder
factory production cannot readily be reconciled with th
Chinese family system. Unfortunately, too, during the peric

increasing contact with the West, the Manchu dynasty was
decline.   China, therefore, suffered the impact of a new
orld when lacking vigorous leadership.   The troubled years
the twentieth century represent a confused attempt to adapt
e ancient Chinese civilisation to the new conditions.   It is
a age of revolution for China—political, social, economic, and
tellectual.

CHINESE DEMOCRACY FINDS A LEADER

N 1911, impatient of the reactionary policy of the Manchus,
the Chinese reformers declared a Republic.   It was not a
mplete break with the past.   The first President, Yuan
hih-kai, welcomed the Republic as the end of a useless
ynasty, but looked to the eventual establishment of a new
ynasty, preferably by himself.   To this end he organised
ilitary schools for the training of his future lieutenants.   On
s death in 1916, his pupils seized control of the provinces
China, extorting from the peasants and merchants the
eans to pay for their armies.   Chaos ensued.   As the War
ords—Wu Pei Fu, Chang Tso Lin, Feng Hu Siang, and
any others—defeated or betrayed one another, they estab-
shed themselves or their nominees as rulers in Peking.   To
rovide revenues, they fostered the national vice, opium
noking.

During this " Government of the Major-Generals " in the
orth, attempts were made to establish ordered government
the South.   The inspirer of these efforts was Dr. Sun Yat
en (1867–1925).   Born of a Christian father and educated
a doctor in Hong Kong, he early became a revolutionary.
e saw that Western ideas had destroyed the foundations of
onarchy in China and believed that the only lasting alter-
ative lay in popular government.   To guide the transition
om despotism to democracy, he organised the *Kuomintang*
ationalist party) which was to head the revolution.   The
ationalist party would create a government and educate
e people in the tasks of self-government.   After a period
tutelage, a democratic united government of China would
introduced.

In April 1921, Dr. Sun was elected President of the Chinese
epublic by the southern government in Canton.   To achieve
s first task of extending control over the whole of China,
reign help and advice were needed.   This help he sought
vain from Great Britain and the United States.   When,

therefore, he was offered aid by Soviet Russia in 1923,
accepted it, and a Soviet mission was sent to Canton. I
Sun realised that Russia would use China as an instrume
to further world revolution, and that communism was fun
mentally opposed to his own ideas of democracy. But
took the risk since there was no alternative.

Unhappily for China, Sun Yat Sen died in March 19
At the time of his death, China was still in complete cha
In the North, a group of adventurers were in contin
conflict with one another. In the South, the *Kuominta*
seemed split into factions. The party was agreed, howev
that China must develop on Western lines and, to this er
a united government resting on the consent of the peo
must be established.

The ultimate victory of the nationalist party of the Sou
was due to the military training and political re-organisati
carried out under the guidance of the Russians, and to t
leadership of Chiang Kai Shek, the southern general w
assumed the mantle of Dr. Sun. His military success
enabled him in 1928 to dispense with Russian assistance a
to establish a central government in Nanking.

The formation of this government did not, howev
imply the immediate unification of China. Its power h
still to be extended to the remote provinces, and it had
try to convert anarchy into order and to provide the mea
of living to starving millions. This work of reconstructi
was slow in starting, and its future outcome remains in dou
For while the group of moderates is working with so
small success to unify and re-organise China, it is depende
on the militarists, who have not entirely abandoned t
tendency to set up as local War Lords. Moreover, there
a grave discrepancy between the admirable plans for reco
struction which have been drawn up and the vigour w
which they are pursued. China still suffers from its anci
tradition of slovenly and corrupt administration.

JAPAN TRANSFORMED WITH STARTLING SUDDENNESS

ONE of the most serious obstacles to China's recovery h
been the bitter conflict with her nearest neighbour. Jap
offers a striking contrast to China. Until 1853, Japan h
been for several centuries completely cut off from cont
with outside people. The arrival of an American fleet
that year heralded the most startling transformation

istory.   From a feudal society, Japan became in fifty years
first-class power.   Although Japan came in touch with
he West many years after China, she soon gained a position
f respect and authority still denied to her neighbour.   She
von her place by the establishment of ordered government
nd by the adoption of Western industrial and commercial
nethods.   The proof of her skill in the use of Western
veapons afforded by the victories over China and Russia
nhanced her political strength.

The Great War provided an opportunity of consolidating
ier industrial position.   Japanese trade spread throughout
he East and as far afield as Australia and New Zealand.
Politically, also, the War was a blessing to Japan.   She
aptured the German concessions in China and took advantage
f the pre-occupation of the world to present to the Chinese
;overnment the notorious Twenty-One Demands (1916),
vhich, if accepted, would have established a virtual Japanese
·rotectorate.   At the Washington Conference (1921) she was
ompelled to withdraw these demands, but succeeded, never-
heless, in retaining extensive powers in the Shantung province
nd elsewhere.   Since that time, Japan has steadily pursued
ier industrial and commercial expansion and has become
iot merely a mature industrial power, but a serious trade
nenace to the Western nations.

JAPAN'S SHARE IN WORLD TRADE

THE amazing growth in Japanese trade since the Great
War, and especially since 1930, has caused serious mis-
;ivings to the older industrial countries of the West.   Many
actors have combined to give her an advantage in some of
he most important markets of the world.   She is nearer
han Europe or the United States to the great markets of
China and the East Indies.   This proximity gives her the
enefit of lower costs of transport, and enables her to maintain
nore intimate contact with buyers.   She has at her disposal
t large supply of cheap labour.   Long hours of work and low
·ates of pay have played an important part in the development of Japanese trade.   And, contrary to the usual experi-
!nce, cheap labour does not here mean poor labour.   The
Japanese worker reaches a very high level of efficiency.
Further, this skilled labour is provided with the best equipment.   Many foreign investigators have testified to the
excellence of the organisation of Japanese industry, and to

the rapidity with which mechanical improvements ar
adopted.

Another circumstance which, since 1932, has been of grea
assistance to Japan in building up a large export trade is th
depreciation of the *yen*. In December 1931 Japan abandone
the gold standard, and the value of the unit of money—th
yen—quickly fell from two shillings to less than one shillin
and threepence. This meant that the Japanese exporte
could reduce his price in English money for a piece of clot
by approximately one-third and still cover his costs. Thi
ability to export goods at very low prices enabled the Japanes
to invade new markets and to enter on the production of ne
commodities. So intense has become the competition fror
this quarter that the industrial countries of the West, wit
their higher wages and more rigid industrial conditions
are feeling its pressure very keenly.

But there is one disquieting skeleton in the Japanese cup
board. In 1870 the population of the country was abou
thirty millions. From the 'nineties, with the developmen
of modern industry, population began to increase quickly
and by 1930 exceeded sixty millions. At present rates c
growth, it will be eighty millions in 1947. Yet Japan is
very poorly endowed country. Much of the land is moun
tainous and unusable. That which remains is so intensivel
cultivated as to offer little prospect of considerable increase
in the domestic supply of food. Mineral resources, too, ar
strictly limited.

Japan's pressing problem, therefore, now, as for man
years past, is how to provide for her increasing million
Emigration does not offer any solution of the problen
Less than one year's increase live abroad. The strengt
of home ties and the inability of the Japanese to adap
themselves to extremes of climate restrain them fro
venturing overseas in large numbers. Also, the stringer
immigration regulations of the United States and Australi
exclude them from these desirable countries. Japan ha
been forced, therefore, to try to secure the necessary supplie
by developing her foreign trade. In this she has achieve
a phenomenal success. But can she rely upon the expansio
of trade keeping pace with the growth of population ? Th
pivot of her trading system is the cotton industry, whic
depends upon foreign raw material and foreign markets
Should a war impede the supply of raw cotton or should

ycott cut off the most important markets, the whole system
trade would be thrown out of gear, and millions of Japanese
uld be threatened with starvation. Again, there is a ten-
ncy in the modern world to move towards national self-
fficiency, which implies the exclusion or restriction of foreign
ports. Can Japan face this possibility with equanimity?
Japan recognises the seriousness of this prospect, and there
s long existed a body of opinion which advocates drastic
tion to provide against the contingency of declining foreign
de. If Japan depends upon foreign supplies and markets,
uld not her position be made more secure by gaining
rect control over them? As a supplement to, if not a
bstitute for, trade expansion, this group urges the need
r territorial expansion. But throughout the Pacific there
no vacant land. Territorial expansion, therefore, can only
secured by the invasion of already occupied country.
hat place could be more suitable in the light of this con-
eration than China? The forcible occupation of almost
y other Pacific land would involve war with a major power.
ina, on the other hand, is easy prey. Rent by internal
ssensions, and weakened by civil war and famine, she could
fer little resistance. The concessionary Powers, jealous
d suspicious of one another, could be relied upon to remain
active. So Japanese eyes turned to the Asiatic mainland,
d did not fail to find adequate pretext for action against
e Chinese.

JAPAN AND CHINA STRUGGLING FOR MASTERY

RELATIONS between China and Japan have been acrimonious
ever since the Great War. The Chinese rightly inter-
eted the Twenty-One Demands as an attempt to establish
panese overlordship, and hailed with delight the annulment
these demands by the Washington Treaty. Japan, on the
ntrary, accepted this rebuff resentfully, and, although as
ignatory to the Treaty she undertook to " provide the fullest
d most unembarrassed opportunity to China to develop
d maintain for herself an effective and stable government,"
e could not but feel that this outcome would be directly
posed to Japan's interests. Later events increased the
nsion between the two countries.
China contested the validity of certain concessions to Japan
South Manchuria and sought by various means—sometimes
doubtful honesty—to evade them. Japanese dissatisfaction

with these attempts was not allayed by the development of threats to Japan's economic penetration of Manchuria Japanese capital had been spent on the building of railway in the province and in the development of agriculture. Japan was now faced with the construction by the Chinese [1] of a parallel railway to compete with the Japanese South Manchurian Railway, and with a very rapid immigration of Chinese into Manchuria, which threatened to endanger the dominant position of the Japanese merchant and financier Negotiations were conducted in a resentful spirit and proved of course, unsuccessful.

Then began a general Chinese boycott of Japanese good This exasperated the Japanese beyond endurance. The serious effects upon their foreign trade, combined with the check to their expansionist plans in Manchuria, provided the military party in Japan with ample excuse for taking action

THE SPARK THAT SET THE FIRE ALIGHT

THE spark was fired on 18th September 1931, when part of the track of the South Manchurian Railway was blown up near Mukden and a Japanese railway patrol was fired on Immediately, Japanese reinforcements were dispatched and Mukden captured. By a series of swift strokes the Chinese armies were either driven out or dispersed into groups roving bandits, and, in February 1932, Manchuria was declared an independent State and renamed Manchukuo The smoothness with which the Japanese operations were carried out suggests long preliminary preparation, a view which was endorsed by the Lytton Commission.

Meanwhile, developments had been taking place Shanghai. Japanese aggression in Manchuria had naturally aroused the hostility of the Chinese. Owing to their military weakness, the Chinese could only reply by intensifying the boycott of Japanese goods which had been carried on intermittently for many years. The boycott centred in Shanghai which was the chief port for Japanese trade and where Chinese national feeling was strong. The tension increased da and was fed by the dispatch of Japanese warships to the Yangtse River. Finally, the Japanese government seized the occasion of riots in Shanghai to launch a military a

[1] The Soviet capital invested in this railway was the cause of much friction with the U.S.S.R. until the sale of Soviet interests to Japan was effected.

naval attack upon the city. Despite the unexpectedly stout resistance of the Chinese army, the result was a foregone conclusion. China had to cease hostilities, and to accept terms which included the withdrawal of official approval of the boycott. The setting-up of the new state of Manchukuo and the attitude of the League of Nations towards this act are dealt with in a later section.

In Japan, the Press and vocal political opinion, heralded the success of the Manchurian venture as a great gain. By the foundation of the puppet state of Manchukuo, Japan brought under her control a large country, equal in extent to France and Germany combined, which has a growing agricultural industry and considerable possibilities as a mining and manufacturing area. In addition to acquiring such extensive sources of supply, Japan secured in the large and increasing population of Manchukuo an important market for her products.

These gains have involved a heavy cost, however, for the success of the invasion of Manchuria has confirmed the power of the military party in Japan. The aggressive militaristic policy of this party runs counter to the important commercial and financial interests of the country, which depend for their prosperity on smooth relations with foreign states. Financially, also, the burden has been heavy. One must include not only the direct cost of the campaign but also that of pacifying Manchukuo, ridding it of bandits, and maintaining an army there. Further, the militarists have insisted upon increasing the efficiency of the instrument which has, in their opinion, served Japan so well, with the result that military expenditure accounts for one-half of the annual budget.

It is doubtful, too, whether the gain has proved so great as might be supposed. The Japanese have never been strongly attracted to life in Manchuria, and it seems problematic whether it will become an important outlet for the excessive home population. Moreover, proposals to build factories in Manchukuo and develop local industrial possibilities have not been welcomed by Japanese mill-owners and operatives. These difficulties are not insuperable, but they imply that, while the cost to Japan is immediate, the gain is likely to be long postponed.

When the League of Nations failed to restrain Japan there was no lack of prophets to assert that Japan was only at the beginning of her encroachments in China. That they spoke truly, subsequent events have shown. For several years the

Nanking Government kept on friendly terms with Japan, despite the bitter anti-Japanese feeling in many parts of China, and even accepted Japanese assistance to suppress a revolt in Fukien province. In December, 1935, General Chiang Kai-Shek, Commander-in-Chief of the National Revolutionary Army, became Prime Minister at Nanking. He had had much to do with enforcing the authority of the Nanking Government and driving the Communists out of Kiangsi across China to Shensi. Meanwhile, friction had been increasing between Japanese and Chinese in the northern provinces (whose "independence" Japan advocated). A curious episode during this period, when exasperation was mounting on both sides, was the seizure of Chiang Kai-Shek by one of his generals, Chang Hseuh-Liang (son of the war-lord, Chang Tso-Lin) who demanded a cessation of the anti-Communist campaign and a stiffer attitude towards Japan on the part of the Nanking Government. He was prevailed upon to release the Premier, and a good deal of face-saving on both sides followed.

Meanwhile the Japanese complained of various alleged anti-Japanese outrages in China, and as early as September, 1936, landed marines at Shanghai. The relations between the two countries became strained to breaking point. Hostilities began when Chinese and Japanese troops clashed near Peking in July, 1937. Soon the two countries were at grips in Northern China, from Shanghai along the Yangtze, and around Canton.

A DISTRACTED WORLD GIVES JAPAN HER CHANCE

IF, as is generally thought in Britain, Japan eagerly seized the pretext for beginning a war with China, we may ask what her motives were, and why she chose the summer of 1937 as the appropriate moment for doing so. It is generally thought that the military party in Japan forced the pace, possibly encouraged by the impotence of the League of Nations to save Abyssinia from Italy, as well as actuated by a desire to distract attention from deteriorating economic conditions at home. Britain, a power with important interests in the far East, was absorbed in European affairs and keeping a watchful eye on the Mediterranean, while the United States was wedded to her policy of isolation and still suffering from the depression. But, above all, Russia seemed for the time being to be out of the reckoning.

The triumph of Stalin over Trotsky had resulted in the latter's exile to Norway and afterwards to Mexico, but the murder of Kirov, one of Stalin's chief lieutenants, in December, 1934, had led to allegations that a vast Trotskyist conspiracy existed in the U.S.S.R. Subsequent investigations and spectacular state trials, where the accused seemed to vie with one another in protesting their guilt, resulted in the execution of such members of the Bolshevik Old Guard as Zinoviev, Kamenev and (in 1938) Bukharin. Purges went on all over the Soviet Union, and numerous generals and commissars, as well as minor functionaries, were transferred from their offices to prison on charges of conspiracy and sabotage. Even if Russia had been willing to take action against Japan in China she was too embarrassed with her own difficulties to do so.

China naturally appealed to the League of Nations, although the League could do nothing but pass a resolution of moral support. There was a good deal of genuine moral indignation in many countries, not only at Japan's aggression, but also at the particularly ruthless way in which she was conducting the war ; and President Roosevelt caused something of a sensation by declaring that " the people of the United States must give thought to the rest of the world " and referring to " the present reign of terror and international lawlessness." The people of Britain were almost unanimous in their condemnation of Japan, although British commercial interests were far from unmindful of the 250 million pounds worth of British investments there. Of the Great Powers, Italy and Germany alone signified approval of Japan's actions.

JAPAN'S ANSWER TO THE CHARGE OF AGGRESSION

CAN anything be said in justification of Japan ? Of her methods, no ; but any condemnation should take into consideration the dilemma in which she finds herself. Japan is a small country with scanty material resources, taxed to the utmost by a rapidly-growing population. China is near at hand, and affords both the opportunity and the pretext for an ambitious and needy neighbour to take advantage of her unsettled state. Her million and a half square miles support four hundred million inhabitants, but Japan thinks there is room for more.

There are, of course, attractive lands in the Pacific, such as Australia, whose population does not exceed that of

London, and which contains large tropical regions in the North unsuitable for white colonisation. This area would be admirable for the Japanese; yet they are rigorously excluded. It is small wonder, therefore, if the Japanese retort to the charge of aggression that the Whites, by monopolising the most desirable parts of the world, have left them no alternative. No solution of the Sino-Japanese problem is possible unless Japan's need for room to expand is given sympathetic consideration by those nations who are in a position to help her.

THE UNITED STATES : A NATION STANDING ALOOF FROM THE WORLD

FUTURE American historians will probably describe the Great War as a turning-point in the development of the American nation. For, although the United States did not enter the War until 1917, and hardly participated directly until 1918, the effects upon her were of fundamental importance. A great economic transformation took place. In 1914 America was comparatively young and dependent in an economic sense. During the War she was able so to develop her industries and foreign trade and investment that in 1918 she was industrially mature. Politically, too, her world importance was enormously enhanced. By her intervention in the vital years of 1917 and 1918 and by the prestige of President Wilson, she gained the right to a deciding voice in the making of peace.

Immediately after the War, her influence grew, for she was the only State to whom the European nations could look for financial assistance. This prestige and power have not been lost since. The United States remains the wealthiest nation in the world and potentially the most influential. No doubt the growth in stature would have taken place in any event. But it is equally certain that the War had the effect of bringing the United States to economic and political maturity many years before this development would otherwise have occurred.

The chief contribution of the United States to the modern world has been of an economic character. Her goods and methods of manufacture have set the standards of modern times. Her prosperity was the means of helping other nations to recovery, and her disastrous slump accentuated their troubles. Her schemes for regaining her lost estate are the subject of general study. Any account of her post-war history must, therefore, pay particular attention to economic developments.

AMERICA FINDS IT PAYS TO ADVERTISE

AFTER 1919, the War orders, on which the great economic expansion since 1914 had been based, ceased. If industry was to find full use for the new machines and plant which had been built, it must create new demands. Since the " Wild West " was by now occupied, the old demands for the goods needed in opening up new territory—rails, wire, ploughs, building materials—could not be relied upon. Consumers' industries had, therefore, to be brought into greater prominence. From this time dates the resort to seductive advertisement and " high pressure salesmanship " for the purpose of stimulating new wants.

The motor-car trade was the most revolutionary of these new industries, in that it produced a far-reaching social change and gave rise to many subsidiary industries. By a fortunate chance, this need for the expansion of consumers' industries came at a time when the liquor trade was suffering a serious set-back. As a result of Prohibition, millions of dollars were transferred from the saloon to the drug-store and the movies, although many of them returned when the bootlegging industry became more highly organised.

The systematic development of the instalment plan also contributed substantially to the expansion of demand. It is noteworthy that this method was applied to foreign trade as well. By granting loans to potential overseas customers, America greatly extended her foreign trade. From 1924 to 1929 her excess of exports over imports averaged over $700,000,000 (£140,000,000). Although this policy proved ultimately to be more misguided than the financing of home consumption, it provided large outlets for her factories during the boom period.

BRIGHT LIGHTS AND DARK SHADOWS : THE BOOM YEARS

THUS the rapid industrial advance which had been stimulated by the European demand for munitions continued after the War almost without interruption. Year by year, the totals of output, exports, and foreign investments soared. The United States was not merely the greatest manufacturing country in the world ; in many industries, pig-iron and steel, for example, her output exceeded that of the rest of the world put together. These developments were reflected in standards of living. In some trades, though by no means in all, wages doubled in the post-War years. An official report stated in 1926 : " The highest standard of living ever attained in the history of the world was reached last year by the American people." At the higher end of the income scale, fortunes of a fabulous size were accumulated. The United States was truly the wealthiest country in the world.

What were the characteristics of the United States in prosperity ? A high standard of living can be accompanied by glaring social inequalities and defects. In the United States, the successful pursuit of wealth diverted the attention from many acute social problems. In the first place, the great riches which were accumulating were very unequally distributed and were often wastefully and even injuriously used. The boasted policy of high wages was not everywhere applied. While some skilled workers, e. g. railway engineers, enjoyed the highest standard in the world, there were millions of poorly-paid workers, quite apart from the negroes.

In the southern Atlantic states, to which the cotton industry was moving, no trade unions existed. There was neither any compensation law for industrial injuries nor satisfactory regulation of the hours of work for children. Wages were low, hours of work were long, and employment very irregular. In the household coal industry similar conditions prevailed. The absence of trade unions and of any machinery for negotiation meant that strikes, which were frequent, were fought with the ferocity of wars. These conditions are in great contrast to the statement that the Mellon family made $300,000,000 in a single year.

UP LIKE A ROCKET, DOWN LIKE A STICK

OF the misuse of wealth, only one aspect need be touched upon. The belief that prosperity was to be permanent not only gave rise to a general scramble to share in the flesh pots, but created a conviction that even the wildest schemes were bound to prove profitable, eventually if not immediately. Thus were fostered those speculative manias which frequently spread through wide areas and even, at times, infected the whole nation, and caused a colossal waste of wealth. The Florida Land Boom of 1925–26 is a case in point. Florida was an attractive winter resort, which increased in popularity as the number of well-to-do people grew. Land values naturally increased as the towns extended. Suddenly, a craze for the purchase of land in Florida arose, and was fed by skilful advertisement until it reached the pitch of a mass mania. A plot of land in Miami which had been sold in 1914 for $1500 was sold in 1926 for $1,500,000. Hurricanes in 1926 cause a disastrous collapse in the boom and a swift exodus from the state. Buildings were left unfinished and others became derelict. Millions of dollars were lost without hope of recovery.

An even more noteworthy and calamitous example of the unwise use of wealth is provided by the Wall Street boom of 1928–29. Again, the underlying cause is to be found in the belief that the United States had discovered the secret of perpetual prosperity. People of all classes, anxious to have a stake in the golden future, began to buy the shares of industrial companies, convinced that whatever price they might pay, their investments would ultimately return a handsome profit. Incomes, houses, farms, personal belongings were all mortgaged in order to secure the means to pay the first instalment on a purchase of stock. The prices of industrial securities rose to fantastic levels, quite out of contact with the realities of the situation. When the first whisper of doubt was heard, these prices fell with a crash, involving hundreds of thousands of people in ruin and heavy loss. Nor were the effects confined to the United States. The flow of loans from America to Europe, which had been going on since shortly after the War, was brought to an abrupt stop, and the collapse of prices and the other financial disorders which were already afflicting the rest of the world were seriously aggravated.

POLITICS NEGLECTED IN THE RACE FOR WEALTH

ANOTHER way in which the sedulous pursuit of wealth reacted adversely upon the life of the community is to be seen in politics and social life. Americans were so busy accumulating wealth that they had no time or interest left for local and national affairs. The result was that they tolerated gross evils in their public administration, and even found in their contemplation a pleasant relaxation from the rigours of their business activities. This, however, was merely an exaggerated form of a long-standing American problem. There is no uniformity of law in the United States, such as exists in most European countries. The powers of the Federal Government are strictly defined by the written constitution drawn up in 1787. Amendments to the constitution require a two-thirds vote in each House of Congress and ratification by three-fourths of the State governments. Thus changes are very difficult to make, especially changes which would limit the power of the State legislatures. The separate States which form the Union have complete control over all those matters which are not specifically reserved to the Federal Government. Since each State can, within prescribed but wide limits, pass whatever laws it pleases, and since it can determine the nature of county and municipal government, there is, to say the least, very great diversity.

One result of these conditions is that there is a multiplicity of laws and law-making bodies. It has been said that over twenty thousand statutes were passed in one year concerning railways alone. Moreover, the laws vary, frequently conflicting violently with one another, and deal at times with the most trivial matters. It is inevitable in such circumstances that a disregard of law, amounting almost to contempt for it, has grown up, and militates strongly against the recognition of law observance as a fundamental civic virtue. The unreality of American political life serves to exaggerate this tendency. To the outsider, there is no distinguishable difference between the Democrats and Republicans, and even the American is unable to perceive in their election programmes any clear policy on national or international affairs. They have become mainly organisations for the control of elections and the distribution of patronage. The lack of a healthy civic and political life is the consequence of the prevalent obsession with business and money-making, and is a hindrance to social improvement.

THE COMPLEX PROBLEM OF A PATCHWORK POPULATION

IN considering the failure of the United States to deal with some of her more obvious social and industrial problems, it should be remembered that the composition of her people presents difficulties of extraordinary complexity. The race problem of the United States has two quite distinct aspects, the immigration question and the negro problem. It is a country peopled by immigrants, who have flocked from overseas in a succession of waves. Until about 1880 the bulk of the newcomers hailed from North Europe, and were of a type that could easily be absorbed into the social system. From 1880 there was a great flood of immigrants, mainly Latins and Slavs, the vast majority of whom came from Southern Europe. These immigrants were very different from their predecessors. They were not pioneers and farmers, but city dwellers and factory workers. They had not the same social traditions or religion, their standards of culture and living were lower. They were, therefore, much more difficult to assimilate.

Many Americans perceived the dangers of this new type of immigration. If it were allowed to continue unchecked, the quality of life in the United States would be entirely changed in a single generation. They advocated a stringent control over entry into the country. When, therefore, the inflow recommenced after the War, action was taken. By the law of 1921, a quota system was applied. As a result, the number of Italian immigrants fell from a quarter of a million in 1921 to 42,000 in 1922. At the same time, the effect was to reduce total immigration to about one-third of its former volume. Even more strict regulations were introduced in 1924 and 1929.

While these measures dealt with the inflow of new people, they left untouched the problem of how to deal with the alien elements already living in the country. About half of the American families are of Anglo-Saxon stock. Some others are of similar characteristics. But there remain one-third who are of other races. These constitute the problem. Can they be assimilated into the social organism ? It is not an impossible task, but it will be a slow one. In the meantime, difficult problems will exist. Many large cities have been so populated by Latins, Slavs, and Jews, people who tend to live together and to retain their own language, religion, and habits, that they have ceased to be American.

Whole industries, such as mining, tend to be swamped by low-paid immigrants. And there is a tendency to a stratification of occupations, the new arrivals taking over the most arduous and poorly-paid jobs. The native-born white American, for instance, rarely enters domestic service. Such a division of occupations is not entirely healthy and does not conduce to social solidarity. The presence of so many language groups also makes trade union organisation difficult, and tends, in many trades, to hold back improvements in standards of living. In political life, the existence of a number of distinct foreign-born groups in the cities and industrial areas, easily swayed by ward bosses and place seekers, is a factor making for the perpetuation of corruption in municipal affairs.

It is hoped, by concentrating on the Americanisation of the children of immigrants, gradually to remove this source of weakness in the community. But even this process has its dangers. There is the risk that, though the old traditions and controls may be removed, no adequate substitute will be provided : the newly-found freedom of America may be interpreted as licence. It is notorious that large numbers of " gangsters " are recruited from the foreign elements.

THE CEASELESS FEUD BETWEEN BLACK AND WHITE

THE negro problem is even more difficult, although to the southerner the question appears simple—the negro is an inferior, to be tolerated only as long as he is kept in subjection. In the South, the negro, by a variety of laws and customs, is denied political rights, social equality, and reasonable facilities for education and life. In the northern states the negro long enjoyed better conditions. But, during the World War, there was a considerable migration of negroes to the northern industrial centres, partly in order to escape the galling discriminations of the South. The cessation of foreign immigration in the War years created a demand for cheap black labour. The restriction of immigration after the War continued this demand. This northward trend had a double effect. It tested the tolerance of the northern white and found it wanting. It almost seems that racial tolerance cannot survive racial contact. In the second place, it increased negro unrest under the traditional suppression.

What the ultimate outcome will be cannot yet be judged. It may be that the marked drift of negroes to the cities will provide a solution. For, congregated in the poorest and most congested quarters, they quickly fall victims to urban diseases. In the towns, the death rate among negroes exceeds their birth rate. It seems a terrible way of escape. Black and White seem to be incapable of learning to live amicably side by side.

THE STORM BREAKS OVER AMERICA

THIS is not the place for a detailed account of the passing of the great boom. But some brief reference to the circumstances is necessary as a prelude to the discussion of later events. While the tide of prosperity was flowing ever higher during 1926, 1927, and 1928, the first threatening clouds were gathering. American farmers found it difficult to pay their way because of a fall in agricultural prices. In the oil industry, the opening up of new fields led to excessive production despite the vastly increased demand. The coal industry suffered from the competition of oil and electricity, and the rivalry of road transport caused a heavy loss of traffic to the railways.

This unhealthy condition of many of the most important departments of economic life made some recession from the boom inevitable. But so great was the activity in the consumers' industries, that the shadows went unheeded, with the result that the unavoidable depression was transformed into a collapse. Speculation in shares continued in 1929 with increasing fervour. This was obviously not based on any reasonable forecast of the future, for current conditions pointed to an early relapse of industrial activity. In the event, it destroyed itself by diverting money from the purchase of goods to the purchase of shares and by pushing the prices of the latter to preposterous heights. When the true position was realised in October 1929, there was a panic and a crash. The average price of ordinary shares, taking 1924 as 100, fell from 309 in September to 207 in November 1929. (It was to fall to 77 at the end of 1931.)

The sudden fall in share values was a disaster to people of small means, many of whom had bought shares with borrowed money, or had bought " on margin," *i.e.* gambled on a rise in the price of a particular stock. Thousands were unable to meet their liabilities, and were forced to sell out at any price they could obtain, thus depressing share prices still more. Others were compelled to economise in their ordinary expenditure, thus causing a further decline in the demand for goods. The boom was at an end. The prosperity of the United States was based on the consumption industries. When the demand for these goods fell, prosperity ceased.

By the summer of 1930 there were five million unemployed people and the steel industry was working at only half capacity.

It was thought that the depth of the slump was reached. But
as unemployment grew, home demand continued to fal
The spread of depression over the world caused a seriou
decline in foreign demands. At the end of 1930, nin
million people were out of work, and the steel industry wa
running at only 41 per cent. of capacity. Nor was this th
end. Unemployment steadily grew until it was betwee
twelve and fifteen millions. In 1932, only one quarter c
the capacity of the steel industry was occupied.

The swiftness and intensity of the slump caused reper
cussions in every department of life. The disastrous fall i
prices which accompanied the depression increased th
burden of debts of all kinds. Farmers owed in mortgage
amounts which were out of proportion to the value of thei
farms and crops. Banks which had lent to farmers an
business men on the security of land and plant and ha
bought shares on their own account, found the value of thei
assets dwindle, sometimes to nothing. Banks closed thei
doors by the thousand, and, early in 1933, the whole bankin
system threatened to collapse.

PRESIDENT ROOSEVELT TAKES OVER A GIGANTIC TASK

THROUGHOUT the rapidly worsening condition of th
country, the Hoover government had no policy fc
stemming the tide. This is not remarkable. The causes c
the slump lay in the mistakes of the past, and no politic
action could undo them or succeed in doing more tha
mitigate their consequences. But people suffering the miser
of unemployment are not prepared to listen to such explana
tions. They wanted immediate action, and they saw tha
none was taken. President Hoover stressed the fundament
soundness of the nation, and his government tried to " bally
hoo its way back to prosperity." But prosperity did no
come ; the downward slide continued. In their despair an
anxiety for strong action, the people gave Franklin Rooseve
an overwhelming mandate, and in March 1933, he wa
inaugurated President.

Swift measures were needed. The banking system wa
tottering, farmers everywhere were in a state of bankruptc
and industrial unemployment had reached undreamt-of height
Roosevelt was convinced that the traditional methods
dealing with depression were inappropriate to this crisis. Bu
he did not assume office with an already prepared plan. H

was an opportunist : " If we cannot do it this way, we will do it another. Do it we will." His first steps were emergency ones. Immediately on taking the oath, he declared a national bank holiday, with the double object of preventing more bank crashes and of giving time to prepare relief measures. The next step was to abandon the gold standard. This was intended both to contribute directly to recovery by stimulating a rise in prices, and to free America from world financial conditions which might hamper her in working out some new policy. The decisive step was taken on 17th May 1933, by the introduction of the National Industrial Recovery Bill.

A full discussion of the " New Deal " which was initiated by the Bill would be out of place in this section. But some reference to it is necessary because of its possible effects upon the future development of the United States. Two main aims run through the many measures which were passed during 1933 and 1934. The first was to create the conditions necessary for recovery. By a vast expenditure on public works and relief schemes the necessary stimulus to industrial revival was to be given. This process was described as " priming the pump " and was intended to be purely temporary. The second aim was to introduce permanent reforms, to give a " New Deal " to the American worker. The ultimate end of these reforms was never precisely stated, being described vaguely as " the re-distribution of wealth in the interests of social justice." But they included the recognition of trade unions and the legal regulation of wages, hours, and other conditions of work.

THE SIGNIFICANCE OF THE AMERICAN EFFORT

WHAT the outcome of these efforts will be can only be guessed. The industrial recovery of the United States is certain : her enormous resources ensure that. But the consequences of the attempts at permanent reform are more problematical. American industrial law and relations have hitherto been based on the principle of freedom of contract. The " open shop," *i.e.* a workshop refusing to employ members of trade unions, has been the typical feature ; and legal control over conditions of work and compulsory insurance against unemployment have been resisted as foreign to American traditions. It was not surprising, therefore that in May 1935, N.I.R.A. was declared outside the U.S.A.

Constitution by the Supreme Court. But it is hardly likely that the opposition will be able to stem the tide altogether. The New Deal may not amount to an attempt to carry through a consistently planned reorganisation of industry ; but it is a sign that the old order is being called in question. For this reason alone, and apart from the success of the individual measures, the experiment is of immense significance to the world.

THE STRUGGLE OF THE UNITED STATES FOR " SPLENDID ISOLATION "

UNTIL the War, the United States had little close or permanent relation with the political affairs of the world, which means, of course, the political affairs of Europe. During the greater part of the nineteenth century nearly all her energies were devoted to the development of her own land. She had neither time nor need to bother about international relations. Also, by the tradition established by the Monroe Doctrine of 1823, she held aloof from European affairs so long as Europe refrained from interference in the American continent. In time, the practical consequence of these circumstances became crystallised into a doctrine. Isolation became the guiding principle of American foreign policy, and is still regarded as the ideal.

But the World War thrust her suddenly into the heart of world affairs. Industrially and politically, she quickly became a great power. Probably too quickly, for she was not prepared either for the problems or responsibilities which such a position entails. Ever since, with certain exceptions, she has struggled to avoid the consequence of her new power.

Another factor to be taken into account when considering the post-War relations of the United States with the rest of the world is the size of the country and the diversity of its population. The country is so vast that it is a little world in itself. The inhabitants cannot feel the same interest in foreign affairs as the people of Great Britain, whose lives are largely determined by events and conditions abroad. The origins of the American people, too, are so varied that in a foreign crisis they speak in a confusion of tongues. At the outbreak of the World War, for instance, hundreds of thousands of people suddenly resumed their British, French, or German enthusiasms, or even nationality. The result of these circumstances is that there has not been in the United

States any evolution of an international outlook or set of ideas corresponding to that which is visible in many European countries. The American is still at heart an isolationist.

The first great American internationalist was President Wilson. After the outbreak of War, but before his country's entry, he conceived of her influence being used to promote peace and to secure justice for the vanquished. When the United States was drawn into the struggle, Wilson refused to regard it as a war for gain. In his Fourteen Points, issued in January 1918, he expressed his ideals which he hoped would be translated into practice on the conclusion of peace. These ideals were not war aims in the traditional sense, but an assertion of the need for disarmament, open diplomacy, and freedom of trade and intercourse between peoples. At the time, these aims were applauded by Americans to whose idealism they appealed.

WHERE WILSON AND AMERICA WERE AT VARIANCE

BUT a split between Wilson and the American people began shortly after the Armistice. To Wilson, the end of the War was merely the beginning of the task of world reconstruction. In this task the United States was to take a prominent and permanent part. But to the average American the end of the War was an end of the whole matter. Wilson's ideals were excellent in themselves, but the American people were not prepared to accept the responsibilites and entanglements involved. Their reluctance was increased when the terms of the Peace Treaty were published. It was clear to them that the Treaty was vindictive, and created a states system in Europe which obviously could not work. The only one of Wilson's ideals which was embodied in the Treaty was the Covenant of the League of Nations. This was inserted so that, in accepting the Treaty, the American government would be unable to avoid all responsibility for the future.

Feeling grew among Americans, however, that they were being exploited for selfish ends in which they were not interested. They suspected, too, that Wilson had been duped by the more astute and unscrupulous European politicians. Had not Clemenceau cynically remarked that Wilson required Fourteen Points when God had been content with Ten ? Also, there was much distrust of the departure from the policy of isolation. These doubts combined with domestic political friction to create strong opposition to Wilson.

At the presidential elections of 1920, Wilson and the democrats were heavily defeated, and power was assumed by Harding with his policy of " normalcy." Harding's programme of sound common sense with no frills concealed a distrust of Wilsonian idealism and internationalism. When a violent " Red " scare broke out shortly after the elections, it was easy to foster the belief that the revolutionary influences came from abroad. The ultimate outcome was that the Treaty was rejected and the United States refrained from becoming a member of the League.

The three Presidents who followed Wilson were true to the isolationist tradition. Judging from their pronounce-ments on European affairs, that continent was inhabited exclusively by militarists and ruled by untrustworthy poli-ticians. But complete aloofness from European concerns was impossible. The United States was lending large sums to Germany and doing a growing foreign trade. Therefore, political contacts were maintained primarily through the agency of " unofficial observers."

SIXTY NATIONS IN ALLIANCE AGAINST WAR

IN another direction the United States was forced into the international field. America and Great Britain were the greatest naval powers in the world. Because of her long association with the sea, Britain had the larger fleet. The United States was not prepared to submit to a position of inferiority indefinitely, and yet she did not want to enter into a naval race. At the same time, relations in the Pacific were becoming strained. Three great naval powers met as rivals in Chinese waters—Great Britain, the United States, and Japan.[1] Two of these—Britain and Japan—were in alliance. This situation added to the American desire to come to some agreement on naval strengths. At the Washing-ton Naval Conference of 1921, the United States secured her chief aims. The Anglo-Japanese Alliance was terminated

---

[1] The possessions of the United States in the Pacific, including the Philippines, which were granted Home Rule (Nov. 15, 1935) impinging as they do on the Japanese sphere of influence, make it increasingly difficult for the United States to remain aloof from world affairs. The conflicting world interestes in the Pacific, indeed have led some to suppose that the centre of gravity, politically speak-ing, is shifting to the Pacific.

and the United States was accorded parity in capital ships with Great Britain.

This result did not completely satisfy the American government, however, since the agreement on capital ships did not extend to cruisers and submarines. Accordingly, President Coolidge called another conference at Geneva in 1927. He invited the three Powers to complete the limitation of naval armaments begun at Washington. The United States asked that the ratios for capital ships agreed at Washington should be extended to all categories of war vessels, and that a limit be set on total tonnage. Great Britain admitted the strength of the American claim, but determined not to grant it, and the conference finally broke up a complete failure.

It had served one useful purpose, however, in clearing the way for a further attempt. This time more careful preparation was made. In August 1928 the Pact of Paris, usually known as the Kellogg Pact, after its initiator, was signed by the leading nations of the world. This was a general treaty for the renunciation of war, its signatories agreeing not to make use of war as an instrument of national policy. In quite a short period it was subscribed to by over sixty nations. The intention of Kellogg was by this means to prepare the way for a further attack on armaments, and to re-open the question of the relation of the United States to the whole problem of world peace.

The prospects of success for his scheme were enhanced by the election of Hoover to the presidency in 1928. Great hopes were raised by this appointment, for Hoover had considerable knowledge of European conditions gained from his experience with American relief missions during and after the War. Hoover himself increased these hopes by announcing his intention to abandon the policy of isolation and to intervene actively in world affairs. But the good intentions were doomed to frustration. Hoover shared with his predecessors—not excluding Wilson—a profound misunderstanding of the European situation. To him, the problem of peace in Europe was entirely a question of armaments. If these could be limited by agreement, future peace would be assured. He did not realise that his country's repudiation of the Treaty and refusal to join the League were largely responsible for the position.

In the absence of the help of the United States in the building of a system of world peace, such European nations as were able had increased their arms as a guarantee against forcible revision of the Treaty. Hoover now asked them to give up the assurance provided by their superior armaments, without offering any pledge of American responsibility in return. These defects—failure to grasp the true nature of the European situation, and a readiness to interfere without being prepared to accept the consequences of intervention—vitiated Hoover's foreign policy. The London Conference of 1930, the Hoover Moratorium of 1931, and his message to the Disarmament Conference in 1932, were all brought to nothing or robbed of much of their force by this lack of insight.

This temporary abandonment of isolation was, therefore, ineffective. The U.S.A. was too absorbed in domestic affairs to take much interest in foreign affairs. In general, American opinion was strongly opposed to foreign entanglements, an attitude expressed in the Neutrality Act forbidding the sale of munitions to foreign belligerents. As early as July, 1937, however, the President declared that the U.S.A. must take a more active interest in preserving the world's peace. In the European crisis of September, 1938, he intervened by asking Signor Mussolini to mediate between Germany and Britain. In March, 1939, the U.S.A. sent a Note to Germany protesting against the annexation of Bohemia-Moravia, and imposed a tariff of 25 per cent. on German imports. After the invasion of Albania by Italy, the President even sent a message to Hitler and Mussolini asking for a guarantee of non-aggression against a number of countries. However, American opinion remains sharply divided on the question of isolation.

WHAT THE EXPERTS HAVE WRITTEN ABOUT THE WORLD CHAOS

THE foregoing sections have indicated the vital questions of our age in the economic and political fields. Further discussion of these by one of the most acute and informed minds of to-day will be found in Cole's *Intelligent Man's Guide through World Chaos* (Gollancz). Economic and political problems are here related to one another. A scientifically economic view of the case is given in *World Economic Crisis* (Macmillan), by Einzig. For an interesting aspect of our own national problem one should go to *England's Crisis* (Cape), by the French economist, André Siegfried

For an array of good hard facts to fill in the framework provided by these sections, two publications of the League of Nations are very useful : *The Course and Phases of the World Economic Depression* (Allen and Unwin) and *World Economic Survey*, 1931-32, published by the same firm. There is a number of good books describing the political field, among them Ramsay Muir's *Political Consequences of the Great War* (Home University Library, Thornton Butterworth Limited), Gibb's *Since Then* (Heinemann), and *A Short History of the World*, 1918-28 (Gollancz), by Delisle Burns. John Gunther's *Inside Europe* (Hamish Hamilton) gives a clear and interesting picture of modern trends on the Continent.

German history during this period naturally falls into two phases. The first one corresponding with the rise of democracy in post-war Germany is covered very accurately by a close observer in Daniels' *The Rise of the German Republic* (Nisbet). The second phase, beginning with the accession to power of Hitler, is described by Vernon Bartlett in *Nazi Germany Explained* (Gollancz), and Roll, *Spotlight on Germany* (Faber). Two good books on the other great adventure in dictatorship are *The Fascist Experiment* (Faber), by Villari, and Barnes' *Fascism* (Home University Library, Thornton Butterworth Limited).

From the many books on Soviet Russia one might pick out the books of the Americanised Russian, Maurice Hindus, all published by Cape—*Humanity Uprooted*, *Red Bread*, and *The Great Offensive*. Fine impressionistic sketches of scenes and characters in Lenin's and Stalin's new world have been made by Malcolm Muggeridge in *Winter in Moscow* (Eyre and Spottiswoode). Portraits of another kind, adding light to a scene which many have found gloomy enough, have been made by the cartoonist, Low, in his *Russian Sketchbook*. A brief examination is to be found in *Soviet Russia and the World*, by Maurice Dobb (Sidgwick and Jackson).

So much for Europe. The importance to the West of modern developments in the East can be read about in Curtis's *Capital Questions of China* (Allen and Unwin), and in Allen's *Modern Japan* (Allen and Unwin).

Great as have been the economic and political upheavals and reforms in Europe and the Far East, America's fortunes since the War have probably been more varied than those of any other country. The America of to-day can be read about in Adams's *Searchlight on America* (Routledge),

Siegfried's *America Comes of Age* (Cape), and Benn's *Prosperity* (Hopkinson).

Last but not least, there is the British Empire which, together with the rest of the world, has undergone rapid development since the War. The change in Empire status is described in a book by Hall, *The British Commonwealth of Nations* (Methuen), and in Zimmern's *The Third British Empire* (Oxford University Press), while a good general introduction to Empire problems is to be found in Somervall's *The British Empire* (Christophers).

GENEVA : THE STORY OF THE FIGHT FOR PEACE

by R. T. CLARK, B.A.(Oxon), M.A.(Glasgow)

THE practical experience of the World War drove home into men's minds two lessons : first, the advantage of unity and the single command, and secondly, the disadvantages of war as a means of settling international disputes. The sense of living among great events quickened the perception of ordinary people. The conviction in the Allied countries—a conviction heightened by revolutions and popular movements for political independence—that the War was actually fought for democracy, created a powerful, if rarely formulated, demand for a new international order, which would ensure the freedom at once of the individual and of the nation, and from the world community banish the spectre of war. It is one of the curious results of a deadly struggle that it should inspire a new vision of unity, but the mind of man invariably seeks compensation for the destruction which his errors have caused. To the colossal blunder of world slaughter there could only be that reaction which, expressed popularly in the phrase "never again," sought compensation in the elaboration of a new social order.

The idea of a world alliance of nations in some form or another is not a new one. Many statesmen had toyed with it for their own ends ; many idealists had worked it out ; and more than once behind this or that scheme there had been an impetus, as in revolutionary France, to base it on the triumph of a principle. During the War many politicians and thinkers had considered a league of nations as a possible means of maintaining world peace, but it was left to President Wilson, liberal, democrat, and idealist, and by virtue of his position as head of a nation which was not merely geographically remote from the quarrels of Europe, but was likely to be at the end of the War the most powerful nation in the world, to interpret politically the vague aspirations of the common run of men.

As early as January 1918, he had declared in the last of the famous Fourteen Points that, as a result of the Allied victory, " a general association of nations must be formed under specific covenants for the purpose of affording mutual

guarantees of political independence and territorial integrity
to great and small states alike " ; and twelve months later
nothing was more certain than that a peace settlement must
if it were to satisfy world opinion, contain such a covenant
No other task of the Peace Conference of Paris was so great
as this, and no other of its achievements so approved. That
it was a great achievement is undoubted, for it was carried
through in the teeth of a good deal of opposition, and after
long negotiations between rival interests and rival conceptions

THE NATIONS JOIN IN THE SEARCH FOR FREEDOM

ITS importance lies in the fact that it was an attempt to
express the principles necessary for the maintenance of
a peaceful and productive world in terms of contractual
obligation. It is the fashion nowadays to describe the League
Covenant as a document to be interpreted. This is true
but to insist overmuch upon it is to forget the truth that the
Covenant is a definite treaty the violation of which ought
to meet with the condemnation of civilised opinion and the
retributory action of the other members. If there is to be
an interpretation, such as any Treaty needs, then it must
be progressive interpretation and not such interpretation as
leads one back to the state of things which its signature was
intended to make for ever out of date ; there must be evolutionary interpretation to widen its scope and to increase its
power.

The Covenant itself is a compromise between many conflicting views, and the result of prolonged public and private
discussion. In many respects the lessons learnt before and
during the War determined its provisions more than did
aspiration for the future, but it remains, and always must
remain, a tribute to the force of an idealism which rose
alike above prejudice and that least wise of all wisdoms that
goes by the name of " safety first." It was indeed that
latter wisdom which insisted on its being needlessly indeter-
minate, and which perpetually raised the issue of sovereignty

Two main issues remained unsettled, or rather were settled
in a manner which at once weakened the Covenant and laid
down lines of amendment which, if followed, were not
calculated to strengthen it. The first is a forgotten controversy which yet in one form or another continually recurs
with usually disastrous effect—the issue of equality, an issue
very difficult to define. The problem before the conference

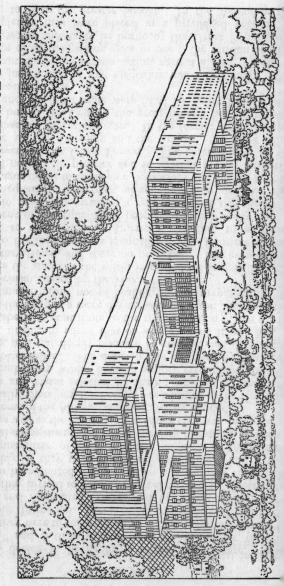

TEMPLE TO INTERNATIONAL UNDERSTANDING: NEW LEAGUE BUILDINGS, GENEVA
A new building was decided on in 1926. 10,000 plans were submitted. 500 workmen were employed for two years. The Secretariat alone holds 400 offices. Cost of construction was 13 million pounds.

was to decide if, in Kipling's phrase, there were " less
breeds " and, if these were to come within the law, on wh
terms they were to come within it.   The second was settled b
invidious distinction.   Membership was to be confined to th
Allied and Associated Powers and to certain neutral stat
which they invited to become original members.   Other stat
were to be admitted if approved by a two-thirds vote of th
Assembly, if they were " fully self-governing," and if the
gave guarantees of their intention to observe their inte
national engagements.   Thus at the very beginning ex-enem
states as well as the Soviet Union, where civil war, participate
in by some of the Allies, was raging, were excluded.

Initially, therefore, the League was a league of the victorio
powers and states selected by them ;   any other candidat
for membership would have to supply credentials and ri
being blackballed.   The decision was criticised by Europe
liberals, and was deeply resented by the German democrac
which, unable to admit that on any grounds it was less
than Liberia to contribute to the reconstruction of the worl
saw in the League a mere device to enforce the Treaty sett
ment, and a means not of healing, but of perpetuating, th
great schism caused by the War.

Thus the states of the world were divided at once into th
elect, the elected, and those on probation.   But even amo
the two former there was inequality.   The Japanese in va
sought to overcome the American objection to a form
statement of the equality of peoples, and eventually had
agree to what was virtually a restatement of the theory
race inequality.   Moreover, although Wilson declared th
the League ought to establish a democracy and not an aristo
racy of nations, in practice and in precept greater authori
was given to the Great Powers.   The chief organs of t
League are the Assembly and the Council, the latter bei
in a sense the executive organ.   In the former all states we
equal, but in the Council the great powers had permane
seats, and the other seats were filled by ballot from amo
all the other states.

The justification of that inequality was very simple.   T
Covenant envisaged certain action against a state which,
defiance of its obligations, goes to war ;   the burden of su
action would inevitably be borne by the Great Powers, a
consequently they were placed in a privileged position
having to bear the greater burden.   In the Assembly t

gal equality of all states was recognised ; in the Council
e natural inequality of states received equal recognition.
he greater states received greater power, simply because
ey were greater in size and importance and were entitled
 a position of superiority because their responsibility was
eater. The Covenant admitted the old distinction between
eater and lesser states as politically valid, an admission
hich, if not strictly in accordance with democratic theories
 equality, none the less corresponded to the realities of
e situation. But it also declared the equality of states by
aking them all subject to the same restrictions, and thereby
ft it to the greater states to justify the superiority attributed
 them by establishing that moral supremacy which makes
e claim to political supremacy tolerable even to a democrat.

THE LEAGUE BECOMING MAID-OF-ALL-WORK

HE object of the League is laid down in the preamble
to the Covenant as " the promotion of international co-
peration and the achievement of international peace and
curity." In the phrase " international co-operation " there
 at once a tremendous opportunity and a tremendously wide
eld of activity. In a world where geographical distance is
eing reduced in time almost daily, in which remote lands
e so knit together that the effects of a catastrophe in Japan
e felt in the London stock markets as soon as the telegraph
in flash the news, there are any number of tasks, necessary
sks, which can be performed only by an international
rganisation. That was recognised even before the War,
nd the establishment of a permanent international organisa-
on had become necessary, if only to co-ordinate the work
hich was being done, and which could not but develop to
n extent that only the visionaries could adequately prophesy.
The accumulation of these tasks upon the shoulders of the
eague was at once a measure of efficiency and a guarantee
f League stability, for, if it became the centre of international
lations in the technical, social, intellectual, and other
elds, it would acquire a prestige and importance that would
 far to make it the centre of international relations in the
ost difficult field of all, the political one.
It was, moreover, a convenient organisation for the Allied
owers, busily seeking to effect the post-War settlement ;
nd to the League were handed over for settlement or for
ontrol many of the important issues which the Powers felt
14

were too difficult for them, or would be better settled by a
international organisation. Thus, the peace settlemer
entrusted to the League a variety of duties. It was, fe
instance, charged with the safeguarding and improvemer
of labour conditions on an international basis, and for th
purpose it set up the autonomous International Labour Offic

Under the leadership of the Frenchman, Albert Thoma
as Secretary (succeeded since his death by H. B. Butler, a
Englishman), the friendly co-operation of all the worker
organisations in the work of the International Labour Offic
has been secured. The annual conferences of this boc
consist of representatives of the governments, employer
organisations, and trade unions of nearly all the countries
the world, each group having equal voting powers. Th
subjects discussed include wages and conditions of wor
affecting the maritime trades, mining, and indeed ever
industry which is of more than national importance. Thu
the work of the International Labour Office has far-reachir
effects on the markets of the world, which are so great
affected by costs of production in the first place, and con
suming power in the second. For example, no other organisa
tion can frame and secure agreement on regulations whic
will make it possible for the comparatively well-paid worke
of the West to compete with the practices of child-labou
and the totally different standard of life which obtain in Japa
and the Far East.

The League was also charged with the duty of receiving an
examining the reports on their stewardship of those Powe
which had received German colonies as mandated territor
Many small tasks were also given it, and, as time went or
this aspect of its work became increasingly important. A
one time, indeed, it looked as if the League would becom
the maid-of-all-work to the world as a whole and as a collectio
of states.

This type of work, which appears to many to be the tru
as well as the most important function of the League, is no
enormous in its extent, and League commissions have dor
a vast amount of social, charitable, financial, technical, an
intellectual work which could not have been done by an
other organisation, and whose literary monument is th
formidable array of League reports, a library in itself. Th
abundant value of an international organisation upon whic
all work of this kind naturally devolves has now been prove

yond shadow of doubt ; and in this proof that inter-
tionalism is a practical policy lies an achievement of
eat significance.

WHY WAR COULD NOT BE ENTIRELY RENOUNCED

THE achievement here has been almost too great, for it has
tended to obscure in many people's minds the fact that
must always be secondary to the true function of the League
the preservation of the peace of the world. A good deal
the criticism of the League is criticism of the stupider
ealist type which would criticise something for not being
mething else. The League is not a super-state. Its
tion in preserving peace is strictly defined ; it is not united. There is, for instance, in the Covenant no positive
nunciation of war, and it may be believed that the omission
es credit to the realism of its drafters. There could be
1919 no enunciation of a doctrine of non-resistance (for
at is what a positive renunciation of war implies), as may
seen from the elaborate explanations given by the framers
the later Kellogg Pact. Although war is there formally
nounced as an instrument of national policy, the right of
sistance to aggression is retained.

In 1919 the world was not prepared to accept the extreme
ctrines of a logical pacifism, and very wisely the drafters
the Covenant did not try to do any more than to make the
claration and waging of war an international legal offence
less a delaying procedure was duly observed. A member
ate agrees " to respect and preserve as against external
gression the territorial integrity and the existing political
dependence of all members." That, if it means anything,
eans the renunciation of *imperialist* war.

Further, it agrees to admit the right of any member " to
ing before the League any circumstance whatever affecting
ternational relations which threatens to disturb international
ace." That, if it means anything, means that it admits
e right of other states to intervene by this method in its
nduct of policy. It then agrees that if there arises any
spute which it " recognises to be suitable for submission
arbitration [1] or judicial settlement, and which cannot be
tisfactorily settled by diplomacy, it will submit the whole

[1] The League set up the Permanent Court of International Justice
a League arbitral tribunal to give " counsel's opinion " to League
gans or League members when desired.

subject-matter either to arbitration or judicial settlement.
Any dispute about a treaty is declared to be so submittabl
If the dispute goes to arbitration, the disputants agree i
advance to accept the award.

If the dispute is, in the opinion of a member state, n
suitable for submission to arbitration, then it *must* be sul
mitted to the Council. The Council reports after full di
cussion and investigation, during which it can itself receive
judicial report, and its findings may be rejected or accepte
But a state concerned in the dispute cannot go to war unt
three months after the Council has reported. All repor
and arbitration must be delivered within six months. Th
matter is finally summed up by the obligation on all membe
to treat any member which resorts to war in defiance of i
obligations as having committed an act of war against a
other members of the League, and in general to obey th
Council's recommendations as to the appropriate action to I
taken.[1]

To the ordinary man the position here is perfectly clea
The sovereign rights of a nation to defend its interests by w
are maintained, and it is left the sole judge of the wisdom c
righteousness of warlike action, but it must observe a
accepted procedure. Whatever happens, no matter ho
much in the right it feels itself to be, no state can proceed
war until nine months have elapsed since, by following th
procedure laid down, it publicly indicated that there was
danger of war. It is hardly too much to say that any Leagu
member which duly fulfils its obligations is extremely unlike
ever to go to war, and that if it does so, contrary to its oblig
tions, it automatically—and this without any Council decisic
—is in a state of hostility with every other member state.

THE FUTILITY OF RULES THAT NO ONE WOULD KEEP

THE criticism of these provisions took and still tak
odd forms. The extreme pacifist complained, ar

[1] What the League may recommend are the famous sanction
" Sanction " in law is defined as " the specific penalty enacted
enforce obedience to a law." In the Covenant it is laid down th
if a state be declared by its colleagues to have violated its internation
obligations, as laid down in that document, by resorting to war
defiance of them, " specific penalties " are enacted to enforce respe
of these obligations. These take various forms—diplomatic relatio
are to be broken off, financial transactions stopped, trade relatio
ruptured, and ultimately force may be employed.

me of the lesser states with powerful neighbours appar-
tly eyeing them greedily on the farther side of an un-
efended frontier asserted, that the right to make war had
ceived further consecration. That is simply to raise legal
uibbling to the level of principle. The right to go to war
oes not depend on the presence or absence of a legal text ; it
epends solely on individual conscience, and it is stupid to
y to evade the fact that there may be times when a thoroughly
legal act is the highest righteousness. Nothing, therefore,
as to be gained by refusing to look facts in the face, and
y adding an obligation which no nation could guarantee that
would in all circumstances fulfil. The obligations under the
ovenant, modest as they are, have not been fulfilled uni-
rsally, and the framers of the Covenant were right when
ey refused to put too great a strain initially on member
ates, preferring to heroic measures such steps as would
adually accustom nations to a new dispensation. They
dged recourse to war with legal restrictions which had
thing to do with conscience but were simply restrictions
y procedure.

It is perhaps important to stress this, and to repeat the
sson of history that no nation will permit any one else to
e the keeper of its conscience, but will retain the right of
aking the last decision when existence is at stake until the
y—and sometimes, as history shows, long after that—
hen it is merged in a larger unity. No legal document
n make war impossible, any more than the severest or
blest of penal codes can make crimes impossible. Instead
criticism of the Covenant for not making war impossible
ere should have been only congratulation that it had made
ar very unlikely. This " gap " in the Covenant is not
ally a gap ; it represents a stage in an evolutionary process
which the unlikely ought to lead to the impossible.

Another and more serious criticism was directed against
e lack of means to make the Covenant effective. The
ench, with their sense of reality, and thinking only in
rms of the German menace, asked pertinently enough
hen the Covenant was being drafted what was the true
lue of the guarantees of mutual aid. If the aggressor
tion, they pointed out, was determined not to pay any
tention to its obligations it might, by a swift act of aggression,
erwhelm a neighbour before the Council could organise
l or even agree on the means of supplying it. They

pleaded, therefore, for the creation of a League force—the
suggested a general staff initially, but not necessarily
League army—capable of being set in motion on a Counc
decision. The suggestion was rejected at the time, and right
rejected. The possession of a force and the power grante
to the Council to use it would, in fact, have made the Leagu
a kind of super-state ; and it had already been agreed tha
whatever else the League might be, it certainly was not tha
In vain the French pointed out that, although the preamb
mentions " security " in addition to " peace," no security ha
in fact, been attained. It was the absence of " security
in the sense of instant combined action, that did cause
" gap " in the Covenant, and was to cause endless troub
later on.

The idealist criticised the Covenant for not being suffic
ently idealistic, not bold enough, in its treatment of tl
problem of war ; the realist objected to its being too idealist
and trustful of the noble nature of man. Of the two, tl
latter criticism alone is valid, and the history of the League
an instrument for preserving peace shows that it was al
just. But it is really irrelevant criticism for, like the forme
it does not go deep enough. The League has no power
its own ; it can do nothing apart from its members. Tl
justification of the Covenant, as of all legislation, lay in tl
fact that there existed so great a demand for it that it w
likely to be obeyed. In 1919 that demand did exist, and
the war-weariness of humanity there did seem a guarant
that, when the War flickered out finally, the Covenant wou
be respected.

The Covenant was much more than a treaty betwee
governments ; it was a peoples' charter and it was for tl
peoples to watch over it. If it failed, statesmen, politician
and publicists might have conspired malevolently against
but the blame for failure would rest on the democracies
the world. The person finally responsible for the succe
and failure of the League in the matter of war is the perso
in the garden suburb and the mean street, the frequenter
the " Proms " or the devotee of the " dogs." The criticis
that governments never fulfil their obligations and that
sane legislator should ever have expected that they woul
unless the penalty of non-fulfilment were inevitable, is unfai
The League was founded not because the statesmen wante
it—how few of them really did !—but because the peopl

d, and in a democracy the peoples are responsible for their governments.

THE THREE-CORNERED FRAMEWORK OF THE LEAGUE

THE organisation of the League is a curious mixture of the framework of an international association, of international parliamentary discussion and of an *ad hoc* committee. It works through an Assembly, a Council, and a secretariat. The Assembly meets each year. It consists of not more than three representatives of each member state, each state having one vote ; and it is the deliberative assembly controlling the League budget and the admission of new members. It can discuss anything, but it has no law-making power. The Council consists of permanent members—the great powers—and non-permanent members.[1] It normally meets four times each year, but can be summoned to meet at any time in extraordinary session. It is, though not specifically stated to be, the League's executive organ and it is its duty to formulate all plans for preserving peace or defending the interests of member states, either on instruction from the Assembly or on its own initiative.

The duties of neither body were definitely fixed, because it was impossible to say what duties might fall to them. Actually the Council has tended to acquire a power which is likely to weaken the authority of the Assembly. But the impressive nature of an Assembly decision remains, and in the Assembly the smaller states, if they will, have an opportunity hitherto denied them of making their views audible—and even painfully audible. Both the Assembly and the Council work very largely through commissions, some of which are permanent, others temporary ; and to the number of such commissions there is no limit. The commissions are clothed with all the majesty appropriate to the agent of an international Areopagus, and may have assigned to them the rôle of drafters of legislation, reporters on this or that issue, special investigators, and the like ; they are expected to suggest a solution of a difficulty, or to recommend action.

[1] Originally five (Japan, Britain, U.S.A.—which did not ratify the treaty—France, Italy) permanent, and four non-permanent ; in 1926 Germany was added to the permanent members. The number of non-permanent members rose in 1922 to six, in 1926 to nine. By 1939, the permanent members had sunk to four, Britain, France, Italy and Russia, and Italy had given notice of withdrawal.

The report goes to the appropriate body and is accepted (
rejected by it.

THE FOLLY OF BLAMING THE LEAGUE

ACCEPTANCE by the delegates to Assembly or Council
equivalent to the acceptance of the recommendatio
by their governments, but not necessarily to the acceptan
by their parliaments. Thus, delegates of a country m
collaborate in commission on the drafting of a treaty ar
may accept it in the Assembly, and yet the nation is boun
by it only when its own legislative organs have freely accepte
it and instructed its executive to carry it out.

The position is, of course, simplified by the fact that while
theory the *nations* are represented, in practice *governments* ar
Thus, if a British representative in the Council or Assemb
accepts a recommendation on behalf of his government,
theory he commits his government to nothing, but in practi
his acceptance means that he has been instructed by h
government to accept it, and it becomes, therefore, part
the policy of the British government of the day. That
to say, at Geneva no decisions are taken except formall
they are taken beforehand in the chancelleries of the Powers-
taken, therefore, in a very real sense by the democracies
those countries where governments are still popularly electe
Wrath against the League at this or that decision is misplace
the decision was not the work of the League, but the resu
of opinion in the various countries.[1]

In the Secretariat a new organ was created which is perha
the most important of all. Here, extra-national if not supe
national, is a permanent body with legal existence whi
besides the individual loyalties of its officials to their countri
has a collective super-loyalty to the League. The chi
positions in it are held by nationals of the Great Powers, b
they are not expected to hold these posts to serve natior
interests. They are servants of the League, and they co
stitute the League's civil service. The duties of tl

---

[1] The reservation of the right of decision is clearly seen in t
history of the famous " Protocol " (1924–25) for mutual assistar
in case of war. It was in part the work of British delegates ; it w
accepted as the policy of the British Government of the day by
British Prime Minister ; but after a change of government in Brit
it was rejected by the new government. The decision here w
clearly not a *Geneva* decision, but a national and a popular decision
Britain.

ecretariat are on the whole formal, but, like all civil services, tends to encroach on the province of the legislature and the executive, and in it there lies the embryo of a forthcoming uper-national organisation.

THE LEAGUE SURVIVES AMERICA'S OSTRACISM

ALTHOUGH in its early days the League suffered a tremendous blow in the refusal of the United States to accept the Covenant and even the idea of the League, as constituting an infringement of national sovereignty, it very rapidly grew both in prestige and importance. There was in the minds of men of goodwill a general assumption that was a more important body than it was. For in its initial stages it was virtually an instrument of the Allied Powers who, weary of settling issues, found it convenient to place the onus of dealing with difficult but not vital problems on a body which they controlled, but in which, at the same time, neutrals were so active as to give it a real impartiality, such as would commend its decision even to those who disagreed with it.

Thus to the League was left the settlement of the Aaland Islands dispute between Finland and Sweden in October 1921 ; the drawing of the Turco-Iraq frontier ; the control of the Saar territory and other questions arising out of the Treaty settlement. Even awkward questions like the partition of Upper Silesia between Poland and Germany, which threatened to disturb inter-Allied relations, were left to it ; and in addition it had to deal with a series of disputes which involved the danger of war.

It was the latter which revealed at once the strength and weakness of the League, and the results went far to justify the cynical verdict that the only danger of war comes from the Great Powers. In effect it was seen that, if the Great Powers were united, no one would be allowed to go to war ; but where the Great Powers were not united, injustice would be done and the chances of war increased. Thus, when Jugo-Slavia threatened the integrity of Albania in 1921, the mere hint of League blockade after a League investigation ended the latter ; when, after the death of a Greek officer in an incident on the Bulgarian frontier, a Greek corps conducted a regular invasion of Bulgaria in October 1925, the invasion was stopped dead by an energetic League intervention, and

Greece agreed to pay compensation. In each case the Gre
Powers were united.

On the other hand, when, in defiance of the League vet
the Poles seized Vilna, the Lithuanian capital, in 192
France's support of Poland paralysed League action ; a
when in August 1923, to avenge the murder of an Itali
officer engaged on delimiting the Greco-Albanian fronti
Mussolini, without waiting for any investigation, sent
ultimatum to Greece and, mobilising the fleet, bombard
and seized Corfu, the League, despite the general indi
nation in civilised countries, was unable to achieve anythin;

The accusation that the League was for the Great Powe
only an instrument of national policy was not quite fair, b
it was abundantly clear that the Great Powers would n
recommend, much less take, action against what they co
ceived to be their national interests, and that League intere;
would not be regarded as something so definite as to dema
armed defence. The crux of the Polish-Lithuanian dispu
was the method of enforcing a League decision ; the feeli
that British boys should not be sent " at the decision of
South American State " to die for something that seem
to have no conceivable relation to British interests betra
a lamentable lack of knowledge and sense in those who f
it. But it accurately represented a feeling prevailing amo
the majority of British people in the absence of a lead fro
their government, which dared not explain that in a questi
relating to French interests France, and neither the Leag
nor that abstract justice of which the League is the custodia
was allowed to have the decisive vote. It was more importa
to maintain the Entente than to preserve League prestige 1
making its decisions respected.

The two incidents were startling evidence that the pow
of the League was strictly limited. Had the troublous tim
continued, the League would either have had its politic
work reduced to a minimum, or public opinion would ha
been so awakened as to force the Powers to consolidate tl
League so as to let it dispose of force in the swift handling
disputes.

ACHIEVEMENTS THAT WON OVER THE STERNEST CRITICS

BUT the troublous times passed, and between 1924 a
1930, except for storms in the Far East, there was
period of reconstruction and pacification, particularly

urope. Problems were not indeed always solved, but at
ie worst they were postponed for amicable later settlement.
he admission in 1926 of the German democracy healed the
reat schism and broke up the dead weight of Allied control
the League.   It was a control that was already negative, for
rance and Britain had been for some time in opposition,
ld that opposition was in itself sufficient to render the League
eble.   But after 1926 a new harmony seemed to have been
tained, and in spite of divisions and disputes League prestige
se steadily—the desire of Germany to enter is proof of it
-as its fruitful tasks multiplied.   To it and to its organs was
ft much of the reconstruction of Europe, and through it
ungary, Austria, and other lands received that financial
ipport which they would not otherwise have obtained.   So
reat was the prestige of the League, so obvious the value of
ie work it was doing, that its two most serious critics, Russia
ld the United States, co-operated more and more in its
ork.

It was this success, more even than the great economic
isis, that was its relative undoing.   The original con-
eption of the League was that it should be left free to develop,
ld in the years of reconstruction the evolution of the League
ore and more tended towards its internal consolidation
ld its supremacy as a whole over its parts.   Inevitably the
reat Powers took alarm.   The prestige of the League was
high that a majority condemnation even of a Great Power
uld not be ignored, and the tendency therefore arose for
ie Great Powers more and more to assert themselves by
rivate agreements, which they then presented to the League.
Vhat were formally Council discussions became in essence
rivate consultations of the Great Powers and from these dis-
ussions there often emerged a decision which, though it
ecame a League decision, took into account little more than
ie interests of the consultants.

THE FAILURES OF THE LEAGUE

THE economic crisis had an immediate salutary effect in
inducing the realisation that at such a time international
nity was essential, and thus appeared such deceptively
icouraging symptoms as the arms truce, the tariff truce,
oth framed in 1931, the Hoover Moratorium in June 1931,
nd the like.   But the desire to make constructive capital
ut of the crisis was absent ; behind that appearance of unity

differences were coming to a head. The rise of nationalism
in Italy and Germany made the revision of the Versailles
settlement a burning issue again ; it broke up the unity of
the Great Powers and once again divided them into two camps
into which were attracted many of the minor states.

More and more the limitations of the League were insisted
upon, and the right of national self-interest upheld. The
machinery of the League was left unimpaired, but it was less
and less used, and there was at once a return, partly due to
the personal conceit of the statesmen of the day and partly
to the desire to secure national gains, to the system of conferences such as had obtained immediately after the War
and there was a great extension of the system of regional
pacts and local groupings. States no longer came to Geneva
with an open mind ; they came having privately settled on
their course of action and advocated the interest of a group
The most notorious case was Signor Mussolini's ingenuous
attempt to revive the Concert of Europe by the Four-Power
Pact, which virtually created a league of the four Great
Powers inside the League, and the history of which revealed
to the world the depths and dangers of the rift between the
Powers concerned. It was, in fact, a profession of the
Italian belief that not only was the League impotent to
perform its primary object, but that it was unlikely to prove
an obstacle to selfish policies ; a belief which was at once
justified and strengthened by the failure of the League to
defend an important member from aggression.

For some years the relations between China and Japan
had steadily worsened, until, in 1933, there broke out between
the two countries a war with biggish battles and heavy
casualties. With true Oriental guile the Japanese, who were
pursuing that policy of expansion which they conceived was
forced upon them by their geographical position and their
increase in population, had substituted the phrase " state of
war " for the Covenant's expression " act of war." They
claimed that all the fighting was done simply to protect
legitimate interests and that such defence did not constitute
an " act of war." There were battles in fact, but in law
peace.

While their armies were engaged in mutual slaughter
neither side violated the Covenant by declaring war, but
China appealed to the League against an act of war. The
League argued ; the statesmen were eloquent ; com-

nissions were appointed ; and meantime the fighting went
·n. The Powers were divided, not on the legal merits of the
ase, but on the political action to be taken, and the affair
ragged on until the Japanese, confident that there would
·e no serious intervention, proceeded to detach from China
n entire province with 70,000,000 inhabitants and make it
nto an independent state under what was virtually a Japanese
·rotectorate. This was too much for public opinion, and the
Great Powers finally agreed in March 1933 to permit the
League to recommend its members not to recognise the new
tate and to condemn the Japanese action. Japan at once
notified her withdrawal from the League.

THE LEAGUE AS SCAPE-GOAT

To the realist the whole development of the Far Eastern
situation was inevitable, but the fact remained that,
or whatever reason, the League had conspicuously failed to
·reserve the territorial integrity of one of its members
·ecause the Great Powers had seen no gain in doing so, but
·ad taken advantage of the pacifism that was so widespread
o declare that all the League could, or ought to do, was to
·rotest. It was argued at the time that the use of force
vas impossible, partly as a result of the political developments
n Europe, partly because of the economic crisis ; so that,
ven if force had been available, public opinion in the
European countries would have been against its use, and even
he application of an economic boycott was impossible.

The League came in for severe criticism, but it was helpless, and for the first time the idealists began to realise the
ruth that realists have tried to din into them for years, that
he League is not so much a living organism as an instrument, and that the efficacy of an instrument depends not
nly on the instrument itself, but on the user. The efficacy
f the League depends entirely on its members, and the
·rdour of the members is in direct ratio to the pressure of
·ublic opinion. The failure to defend China lay in the fact
hat there was no great public feeling for China and that
he statesmen carefully refrained from putting the case for
League action before the peoples.[1]

[1] Still less was public opinion worked up over the Gran Chaca
var between Bolivia and Paraguay, which raged for years (officially
rom 1932–34) without any effective League action whatsoever,
hough many attempts were made to stop it.

Perversely enough, however, opinion, instead of blaming
the members, that is to say, its own governments, drew the
conclusion that the instrument was useless. It is not too
much to say that the failure in the Far East helped to confirm
the nations in a gradually-growing belief that national security
depended not on an international organisation, but on their
own political and military efforts.

THE GERMAN UPHEAVAL : A JOLT FOR THE LEAGUE

THE access to power in Germany in January 1933 of the
old militarist régime under the guise of a National
Socialist revolution completely upset European relations.
The record of the new rulers of Germany was suspect and
their future policy still more so. The German agreement
with Poland, and still more the entente with Italy, flung France
back on the defensive in the matter of maintaining the Treaty
settlement to which, as affording her a measure of security,
she attaches tremendous importance. Her diplomacy succeeded in robbing the Four Power Pact of its character as
a new concert of Europe in which she might find herself in a
minority of one, and the reaction of Great Britain to the
repressive measures of Hitlerism caused a revulsion of feeling
which did more to restore the popular bases of the Entente
than all the diplomatic work of past years had done to restore
its political bases. Once again Europe was aligning herself
before a German menace, just as in the years prior to 1914.
In these circumstances the League could not function.

Failing to get its demands for equality of armaments met
at once, the Hitler government dramatically left the League
of Nations altogether, a step which, however logical, did, in
fact, strike a blow at the whole League conception, for it
virtually claimed what the Covenant denies, that resignation
can free a state from its obligations. The failure of the
League to emphasise the loss caused by resignation to the
revolting state completed the blow to League prestige, and
latterly the League was more and more ignored. When,
with the suspected connivance of the German Government,
the Austrian National Socialists risked a rising and murdered
the Austrian Chancellor, Dr. Dollfuss, the League was not
invoked by any party.

When, in September, 1934, the Soviet Union joined the
League, it appeared that the League had once again become
what its critics said it was in 1919—an instrument against

Germany; but a powerful bloc of anti-League states was created by Italy's conquest of Abyssinia in defiance of the League, and her annexation of Albania; Franco's victory in Spain; the Sino-Japanese War; Germany's annexation of Austria, the Sudetenland and Memel, and her assumption of a protectorate over Bohemia-Moravia.

ITALY SUCCESSFULLY DEFIES THE LEAGUE: SANCTIONS FAIL

WHEN, in September, 1935, the clash between Italy and Abyssinia was brought before the League, idealists feared that it would do little but provide another example of the League's lack of strength and courage. Instead, they were treated to the spectacle of a revivified League. Sensitive to public opinion in the country, as manifested, for example, in the Peace Ballot, the British Government took the lead in pressing the League to face the issue. All the League members, except those which were virtually client states of Italy, branded her as guilty of a breach of her Covenant obligations. Not merely so, but under British leadership, 52 of the 56 member states proceeded to put into force those measures which the Covenant declares should be taken to restrain the aggressor.

But the only "sanction" that might have ended the war was an embargo on oil. This, a number of League states feared to impose; and, in any case, the U.S.A. was not willing to co-operate. Probably foreseeing the outcome of the Italo-Abyssinian dispute and of the League's attempts to settle it, the French minister, Laval, and the British Foreign Secretary, Sir Samuel Hoare, agreed in Paris on a peace plan that seemed at the time unfair to Abyssinia, and appeared to be a plain case of the League's giving in to might. Public opinion in Britain killed the plan, however, and Hoare was sacrificed to save the Government's face.

Sanctions failed, and Mussolini's mechanised forces conquered Abyssinia. The results of this were far-reaching. The "Stresa front" formed between Britain, France and Italy after the announcement of German conscription, was disrupted. Italy was particularly incensed against Britain, both as the leader of the sanctionist movement, and also, as an obstacle to Mussolini's Mediterranean ambitions. During the period of tension produced by sanctions the British Government became convinced that the country's defences had been unduly weakened, and in March, 1936, a White Paper heralded a great programme of re-armament with the words, " taking risks for peace has not removed the dangers of war." Mean while in February, 1936, Germany had taken the opportunity of re-militarising the Rhineland, offering the Franco-Soviet pact of May, 1935, as her excuse. The net result was therefore a weakening of the League ; the estrangement of Italy from the League in general, and from Britain and France in particular ; and a general loss of faith in the ideas of disarmament and collective security.

THE NYON CONFERENCE OPENS A FRESH CHAPTER

WHEN the Spanish Civil War broke out in July, 1936, the Spanish Government protested to the League of Nations that German and Italian troops were being used by the insurgents. Spain and Italy were both members of the League and bound therefore to obey League decisions. But the League was impotent to do anything. A so-called Non-Intervention Committee did what it could for months, thwarted in its efforts by the non-co-operative attitude of Germany, Italy and Portugal, until submarine and air attacks on shipping in the Mediterranean rendered it imperative that something should be done. What was done is instructive. Britain and France, acting independently of the League, convoked the Nyon Conference on " piracy " in the Mediterranean. Germany, Italy and the latter's client state, Albania, refused to attend, but when Britain and France showed that they were prepared to go forward with a scheme for an " anti-piracy patrol " without Italy, if necessary, and, further, withdrew from the abortive " Non-Intervention patrol," Italy changed her mind and said she would come in after all, if she was given an equal share of the patrol with Britain and France.

Before the League had had time to recuperate from its previous set-backs the Sino-Japanese conflict burst upon the world. Japan had left Geneva in a huff after the Lytton Report, but China was still a member and appealed to the League. The Assembly passed one resolution morally supporting China and another condemning Japanese bombing of Chinese open towns; then ruefully handed the matter over to the Sino-Japanese committee set up in 1933. The outcome of this was that a Far Eastern Conference met at Brussels but as Japan refused mediation and was supported in her refusal by Italy and Germany, little could be done. It came as no surprise when, in December, 1937, Italy left the League after joining Japan and Germany in the " anti-Comintern " pact

The Czech crisis and the Munich agreement profoundly affected the European situation. Not only had Europe returned to the " old " diplomacy of pre-war days as contrasted with " League " diplomacy, but the anti-League powers had gained considerable diplomatic triumphs, and seemed in the ascendant. In November, 1938, the Anglo-Italian agreement was signed, and Britain recognised the Italian conquest of Abyssinia. Next, France and Germany concluded an agreement, stating, among other points, that they both acknowledged the frontiers between them as definite. Unfortunately this coincided with a severe set-back in the relations of France and Italy, as the latter began to make new claims on France. In the following spring Germany's seizure of Bohemia-Moravia destroyed the Munich agreement and brought about a reversal of Chamberlain's " appeasement " policy.

ARMS AND THE NATIONS: TEST OF THE LEAGUE'S SUCCESS

To many people, and certainly to most champions of the League of Nations, the test question of the efficiency of an international political association is its success in dealing with the question of disarmament. In the fact that at the present moment the movement towards disarmament has given place to what promises to be a new and disastrous race in re-armament they see what, from the formal point of view, is the failure of the League, and, from the point of view alike of idealism and realism, is the treachery or incompetence of the statesmen of the Great Powers.

The question is one that requires very clear and conscientious thinking. Many of what pass for logical sober views are, in fact, distortions caused by keen personal feeling and special pleading, and take so little account of reality that, whatever credit they may be to the hearts of those who hold them, they do very little credit to their heads. There is, for example, as a case of special pleading, the German contention that the introduction to the disarmament clauses of the Treaty of Versailles constitutes a *legal* obligation on Germany's ex-enemies to cut down drastically their own armaments. The words in question are: " In order to render possible the initiation of a general limitation of the armaments of all nations Germany undertakes . . ." This, in a well-known and useful work of reference, is described as a " specific promise."

Anything less like a specific promise it would be difficult to find. The signatories could not speak for all nations then, and the number of nations for which they could speak later dwindled steadily.

All that the Allies are pledged to do is to " recognise that the maintenance of peace requires the reduction of national armaments *to the lowest point consistent with national safety* " (Covenant : Art. viii), which is merely the pious recognition of a by no means universally admitted thesis and commits no one to anything. Nothing but confusion has been caused by the unjustified assertion that in the reduction of armaments, forced on Germany for military and political reasons as the result of a lost war, there is something in the nature of a legal obligation, or even a binding moral obligation upon any individual nation to disarm itself to the same extent.

THE BUSINESS OF MAKING WEAPONS GOES ON

ARGUMENTS that expenditure on armaments may injure or benefit trade, that the money would be better employed in other ways, or that increased armaments impose too heavy a strain on national finances, are all alike irrelevant to the main issue. The question of the private manufacture of, and trade in, arms is a vast and complex one. In the present writer's view the permission of such trade is incompatible with any peace professions and contrary to the whole spirit alike of the League Covenant and of the peace pact system. The revelations of private war-mongering made at a United States Senate inquiry are significant, but much more significant is the fact that in 1928–32 according to the " Statistical Year Book of the Trade in Arms and Ammunitions," published by the League of Nations, the international trade in munitions of war amounted to a total at par value of £51,000,000. Apart from the minor fact that a considerable proportion of the exports may quite conceivably be used against the exporting nation, the disservice to the cause of peace is obvious, not to say glaring. The only questions that must be answered in any introduction to the disarmament controversy are (i) Does disarmament make for peace ? (ii) What is the meaning of national security ?

There is so far no authority to answer the second question acceptably ; and the first question can only be answered by history. From history it would be very difficult to prove that armaments cause war, or that a frantic desire for armaments is anything more than a symptom of profound unrest and uneasiness in the body politic. At the most, his own possession of arms inspires the war-monger with confidence, and the possession of arms by his neighbour inspires him with caution. The argument in both cases is purely academic ; it is not based on impartial investigation of the facts, an investigation which would have shown that from the facts no such conclusions can be drawn. So long as it is regarded as legitimate in any sense to go to war to defend national interests, so long will the nations insist on the possession of such arms as will enable them to win the wars on which they embark.

But when the nations admitted, and embodied the admission in a legal document, that war was not permissible except in defence of national interests, new issues were raised. Was it, for instance, consistent with that obligation to possess weapons of offence ? Was it consistent to possess more arms than were necessary for defence ? The armament question thus merely becomes part of the question of the legitimate organisation of national defence, and of the legitimacy of choosing any and every method of making it secure.

THE UNIVERSAL RIGHT TO SELF-DEFENCE

AN analogy—although no more perfect than any other analogy drawn from ordinary civil life—may help to make the position clearer. No British citizen may possess lethal weapons of a particularly deadly type without a licence. The duty of guarding himself and his property is taken from him, and entrusted to the forces of the law. But, in the event of aggression, the right of the citizen within his own house to use even illegally-maintained weapons to defend himself is recognised. Here and here alone the use of force, even lethal force, is recognised, but the user is required in law to justify himself before the courts. The admission is made by the law that it is powerless to prevent crime being conceived, that it may be powerless to prevent crime being committed, and that therefore the individual, in the possible absence of legal protection, may protect himself as he will. But he may incur no penalty in these circumstances for his possession of means of defence, which might equally be means of aggression.

If we apply the analogy we may say that international law admits that it cannot eradicate war, any more than a penal code can eradicate crime, and that the eradication of crime in the moral sense is not the business of law. But what it can do is to control the possession of war-weapons, and restrict their use and their number. Clearly the validity of its claim to this right depends entirely on the success of the law in defending the innocent, that is to say, on its possession of a force which the criminal fears. The analogy between the police of a nation and an international police force, between the possession of force by law inside the boundaries of a nation, and its possession by international law, strikes many people as perfect, and therefore many plans for a League army or for an international police force have been suggested. But the authors of all these plans seem to forget that in the former case, a single acknowledged authority controls the force available and that, in the international sphere, there is as yet no such authority. A League army is, in fact, impossible until the League becomes a federal state.

After peace had been legally restored there was, as compared with the war-years, a colossal amount of disarmament in the sense of the scrapping of weapons and the reduction of armies, for the double reason that their maintenance at the 1919 level was unnecessary and expensive. Disarmament beyond that was an academic issue because there was no security.

"Security" in the political vocabulary of post-War years has come to mean almost invariably *French* security, but Security is, in fact, the keynote of the policies of all the powers. It was felt that disarmament, however desirable in itself, could take place only when a nation was convinced that security could be obtained by means other than by powerful armaments. In 1919–20 there was still a state of war in many parts of the world; the United States had declined to throw her weight into the balance on the side of peace and security, and there was already growing up in many quarters a decided hostility to the peace settlement. The air was filled with high explosive, and in the circumstances no disarmament could be expected beyond the routine disarmament brought about by the cessation of the World War.

A LOGICAL DEMAND THAT WAS NEVER MET

THE attitude of the French was perfectly simple, and, as usual, logical. They said in effect: "Germany is bound to try some day to reverse the result of the War; she may do so by war. If she does, we shall be saved only if we ourselves are in a state of superiority of armament, for we cannot within the time anticipated be in a state of superiority in resources of men or material. We must, therefore, refuse to surrender our superiority in armament unless it can be made good by alliances or treaties." That is to say, they demanded as a pre-condition of any disarmament a guarantee of security, either by the formal alliance of Great Powers, or by the strengthening of the League in such a way as would enable it to use force. Actually, they could obtain neither.

The first part of the history of the disarmament controversy is thus the history of the security controversy, and we shall have very briefly to trace that history to make the sequel intelligible. The position in 1920-21 was that the world was threatened with a possible " crime wave " of war, and, in the absence of an international force whose concern was the prevention or punishment of such crime, each nation took its own individual measures, with the net result that in 1924 Europe was probably better armed, though not better prepared, for war than in 1914, and in each individual case solely on the grounds of self-defence.

It was because of the inevitability of such a development that the framers of the peace settlement had tried to create collective security by the League of Nations. League members were bound to defend their fellows from aggression, but nothing was laid down as to the methods whereby such defence was to be made. The Council indeed could suggest a course of action, but there was no formal compulsion on the individual states to adopt it. The French, therefore, asked that this pledge of support should be particularised and made definite. The result was the famous Geneva Protocol or Treaty of Mutual Assistance, which was intended to lay down the rules for bringing immediate help to a state which was the victim of attack. The Assembly agreed to it unanimously, but national feeling took alarm. It was declared to be an instrument of war, the net effect of which would be to involve states persistently in wars in which they had no national interest. Largely owing to the opposition of the British government, the Protocol was abandoned.[1]

The substitute for it (for it was recognised that one must be found) was created in the Locarno treaties which form in

[1] The rejections by the governments of a treaty which national delegates had accepted was a grave blow to League prestige.

essence a limited treaty of mutual assistance, with specific reference to France and Germany. Britain and Italy promised to give armed aid to either if it were made the victim of aggression by the other, but there mutual assistance stopped. There was nothing said about aid to Britain if she were attacked by Germany. But the Locarno treaty cleared the air immensely by creating a new spirit between the Western powers, by getting Germany into the League and by enabling a beginning to be made with the removal of the last visible sign of war, the occupation of the Rhineland by Allied troops. What was not so clarifying was that it set a fashion in pacts, which now multiplied alarmingly—pacts of arbitration, friendship, non-aggression, neutrality, and the like—culminating in the famous Kellogg Pact, by which the nations solemnly renounced the use of war as an instrument of national policy.

PEACE PACTS FAIL TO CONQUER FEAR

To the ordinary person, security could hardly be made more secure, for it was now practically impossible for any nation to make war on any other nation without breaking at least two solemn treaties and convicting itself of an insincerity that would call down universal condemnation. In point of fact, nothing is less secure than a treaty system of security. The weakness of such a system does not consist in the resolve of a signatory to use it as a cloak for future violation, but in the fears of each signatory that some one of the others may be contemplating violation. The notion of the sanctity of treaties is no more a popular notion than is the sanctity of an income-tax assessment form. The majority of people fill the latter up honestly, but they do not feel inclined to ostracise the man convicted of dishonest filling-up, and they are rather inclined enviously to admire the man who, in the popular phrase, " gets away with it."

Although most people would agree that treaties ought to be observed, they are not prepared to attach deep moral stigma to a violator, unless they themselves are the victims. The difference between the reaction to the German violation of Belgium in 1914 and the reaction to the Japanese violation of China nearly twenty years later was typical and betrayed not merely a decline in the general respect for treaties but even a sense of contempt for treaties as a result of their rapid multiplication.

Whatever the idealists asserted, the governments and most people believed that in a treaty system there was no security, and that in the last resort the defence of the nation depended on arms. With such beliefs prevailing, it was not likely that any nation would willingly consent to be deprived of weapons.

The history of the disarmament controversy which runs parallel with that of the quest for security, is the history of the discovery of reasons and yet more reasons for not disarming; and it is very difficult, given the state of mind existing in Europe, to deny that they are valid. In the early years it was obvious to the war-weary that war on a large scale was unlikely, and that the existing state of armaments was excessive for defensive purposes. It was that spirit and a cool sense of reality that made possible the achievements of the Washington treaty of 1922, which, if not as far-reaching as it might have been, enabled Britain, the United States, and Japan to effect a real limitation in naval armaments by their acceptance of a ratio of 5-5-3 for certain classes of ships. The Washington success encouraged the League to attempt a general disarmament scheme, and its advisory commission on armaments worked out a ratio plan. But disarmament on land raised political issues which were absent from the Washington discussions, and the draft convention was silently dropped after various governments had pronounced their hostility to it.

THE FIRST MOVES TOWARDS DISARMAMENT

THEREAFTER came the great security discussion and the burst of pacts and alliances, and after Locarno the peace atmosphere was so strong that it was impossible for the governments to hold out any longer against what was becoming an insistent demand for disarmament. There were two trends of thought in every country. There was what may be called the reactionary side, which distrusted the foreigner and felt that disarmament was dangerous because one never knew what would happen, and what may be called the progressive side, which trusted the foreigner and felt that disarmament was a financial and social necessity; the risk was underrated in order that it should be taken. Behind the demand for disarmament was the whole strength of the international pacifist movement, which was very great between 1925 and 1927. Under pressure from this influence and, to do the governments justice, because they honestly felt the need for

relief from armament expenditure, and put no small degree
of sincerity into their pacific professions, the League began
to move.

The Preparatory Conference for a Disarmament Conference
had already been established, and was now commissioned to
prepare a draft convention which would serve as a basis of
discussion for the full Conference. It first formally met to
begin its drafting work on 18th May 1926, that is, after
Locarno, but before Germany had become a member of the
League. The Conference, possibly wisely, was not asked to
formulate a philosophy of disarmament. It was to take for
granted that disarmament was desirable and to make concrete
proposals, a course which actually meant handing the question
over to experts, of all people in the modern world possibly
the most dangerous in providing obstacles to enlightened
thought.

The real difficulty before the Conference was not the
reconciliation of views, which are the less reconcilable the
more " expert " they are, but the discovery of a way to secure
simultaneous and equivalent disarmament. A small nation
like Denmark can and does make a unilateral gesture, without
arguing about it with other nations, but, obviously Great
Powers, and particularly those with overseas commitments,
cannot. The tendency is to wait for one's neighbour, and, if
possible, let him precede oneself. There is no tendency less
likely to make progress possible.

The terms of reference of the Conference asked it to suggest
definite reductions in men and material. To the uninitiated
the issue is perfectly simple ; one simply reduces either by
a universal flat rate or by ratio. One needs no experts at all
except arithmeticians. But assume that national defence is
not a right but a duty, and one is bound to take into consideration the views of the expert on defence. He would not
be an expert if he did not view the disarmament issue as one
of limiting his own disarmament as much as possible ; and,
to the astonishment of the politician and the angry dismay
of those to whom disarmament was a cause, he raised issue
after issue on which only he himself could give an opinion.

PROBLEMS THAT HARASS THE MEN AT GENEVA

To enable the reader to appreciate the intricacies of the
problem, it may be worth while to give just a few examples
of the type of issue raised, even at the risk of being tedious.

Let us assume that it has been suggested that every country should reduce the number of its machine-guns by ten per month. But that might mean, A having 400 guns and B 120, that in twelve months A would have 280 and B none. Very well, reduce by a certain percentage, say twenty-five per cent. In six months. A will then have 300 guns to B's 90. But that is a far more serious disproportion than 400 guns to 100. Very well, reduce by ratio. Let the proportion be, for A and B, as 5 to 3, because A is the bigger country with more to defend. B points out that the only frontier on which A can use machine-guns is the A-B frontier, so that he can concentrate all of his there, while B, having two frontiers, can spare possibly only one-third of his. "Very well," says the exasperated non-expert, "abolish machine-guns altogether." A admits the possibility; B declares that he needs them against C. Then why not have universal abolition in the manner suggested by Litvinov? But the expert only smiles blandly and says, "No machine-guns, no national defence"; and immediately nation A begins to clamour that it will be left defenceless, because every one knows that B and C will not destroy all their machine-guns, that they have been making new ones secretly, and that, if they are needed, more can be turned out at the rate of one hundred a week by a plant that is now producing motor-cars. In the end, the politician, exhausted, simply says that the discussion about machine-guns had better be postponed.

Unlike much of the eloquence and ingenuity wasted on trying to define "the aggressor," that is not legal quibbling. It is a genuine technical issue, and cannot be settled save by halting compromise until the mind of man recovers its freedom, and rises above all technical issues. The records of the Conference are full of such disputes, some even more trifling, others raising vital issues. For instance, let us take the discussion of naval disarmament as viewed by Italy and France.

ITALY AND FRANCE AT LOGGERHEADS

HERE the issue was the ratio of disarmament. Italy claimed "parity" on grounds of prestige, and as affording her a reasonable chance of success in war. As these Powers were in different political camps at the time and were tied up in alliances the objects of which were certainly not peace, the chances of war, Covenant or no Covenant, could not be overlooked. France rejected parity for sound technical

reasons, contending that in the event of war in Europe he
success would depend on the rapid and safe transport by se
of troops from Africa and that " parity " for her must mea:
parity *plus* provision for that particular defensive need, an
parity, not with the Italian fleet, but with that fleet *plus* tha
of any likely ally. Her experts would hold that to be saf
she must be protected either by trustworthy alliances or b
naval construction sufficient to make her the equal of an
combination brought against her in the Western Mediter
ranean. " Parity," therefore, would really be inequality i
favour of Italy. That is, in brief, the French thesis, and it i
unanswerable. The only solution here is not a technical bu
a political one. Opposition to nazi Germany may end th
problem by bringing France and Italy together and securin
a new definition of " parity " satisfactory to each.

Again, in calculating the size of standing armies, to use th
old term, ought one to include the number of trained reserv
ists ? If one reckons them in for purposes of reductio
France is in a position of inferiority ; if not, she is in a positio
of superiority, thanks to the speed with which she can mobilis
them. To talk here of parity is to bring up a whole string
technical details on the definition of a trained reservist, o
the value of a trained reservist and the like, details whic
must be considered, but on which rival experts will neve
agree.

The expert having by now disgusted the unfortunat
politician with " parity " and " ratio," on which no agre
ment can be obtained, indicates a way out. We are, he say
in effect, agreed that national defence is sacred, and tha
national aggression is vile and illegal. Obviously, then, or
should scrap all offensive weapons. This is a promising lir
of approach until one discovers that what looked like
definition is not a definition at all. When Britain, with he
sea-borne trade and her war-time experiences, advocated th
abolition of submarines as being in all senses of the wor
offensive weapons, it was at once replied that to the small
naval powers they constitute the defensive weapon *par e:
cellence*. Both statements were true. The whole gamut
armaments was run through, but no weapon was found whic
was universally admitted to be suitable only for defensiv
purposes. Even the positioned guns of a fortress can be u
rooted at will and placed at the service of invading armies.

Nothing could be more instructive to the technical stude

an the discussions of the Conference, but its practical results ere almost negligible. It eventually produced an extra-rdinary draft convention, based on a British draft and a rench draft, which, on points where agreement could not be ached, printed both versions. It showed perfectly plainly nat no progress had been made towards arriving at principles f disarmament and that, in the minds of the experts, dismament, except on their own countries' terms, was incompatible with national security.

THE EXPERTS TANGLE UP A CONFERENCE

HE draft convention was allowed to simmer for three years. During that time, as new forces increased the nse of insecurity, the multiplication of security pacts proeded apace. But by 1929 even the most nervous felt that nough paper had been signed to still their fears, and the way as paved for the Kellogg Pact, which, by its negative uarantee against aggression, in turn led to a further step wards the solution of the armaments problem. The ellogg Pact marks the last triumph of the post-War peace irit, and the atmosphere of success was therefore favourable r another effort. In the interim between the first draft and e second, however, there had been several incidents the utcome of which was not without significance for the future.

In 1927 the United States government had taken the itiative in calling a naval disarmament conference to suppleent the work of that of 1920–22, and to discover a means of miting vessels in those classes which were not covered by e earlier agreement. The invitation was refused by France nd Italy. The United States was willing once again to accept e ratio 5-5-3 for the classes to be discussed with Britain nd Japan, which did not admit the attitude of France and aly that disarmament should be discussed only as a hole.

A three-power conference was then held at Geneva, and as an unqualified failure, because the spirit that had preailed at Washington was absent. There was no one able or illing to restrain the experts, and the official British view ctually summed the matter up thus : " We could not find formula to equate ships carrying 8-in. guns with ships ounting 6-in. guns ; although we agreed on equality we ould not find a formula." The fact was that at the moment e political spirit was too feeble to force an agreement as it

had been forced in 1922, when the experts had raged no les
furiously. In the absence of that spirit the feeling that eac
side was trying to steal a march on the other easily prevailec
The result was that a conference intended to promote friendli
ness ended in a noticeable tension in relations which, if the
had not been very cordial, had been so far unstrained.

BRITAIN BUNGLES THE NAVAL PROBLEM

BRITAIN, at any rate, now knew the American standpoin
and, in spite of that knowledge, attempted to ease th
deadlock which had arisen between herself and France o
the draft convention by reaching a compromise with her o
the naval issues. There is no reason to doubt the honesty c
the effort, but it was hopelessly bungled. The basis wa
precisely that which the United States had declared it coul
not accept. It was originally represented as a purely nav
basis, whereas actually, in return for French naval com
placence, Britain had agreed to what she had so far steadi
resisted in the Preparatory Conference—the exclusion fro
" effective military strength " of trained reservists.   Th
storm of indignation that arose, particularly from the Oppos
tion parties in Britain itself, and the rejection point blank c
the suggested naval " compromise " by the United States le
to the dropping of the whole agreement, and to what man
people felt to be an Anglo-American crisis.

The sixth session of the Commission therefore met in Apr
1929, under the ægis of the Kellogg Pact, but also under th
shadow of failure and difficulty. The inclination was to dela
further any consideration of the draft convention, bu
Germany, then girding her loins for her final reparatior
battle at the Hague, insisted on proceeding with it. Ver
early in the discussions the American representative made
dramatic gesture of reconciliation by declaring that his goverr
ment would accept any thesis as a basis of discussion fc
immediate naval limitation. He connected his declaratio
with the Kellogg Pact, as though that precious instrumer
had really brought about " a change of attitude towards th
use of force in the settlement of international disputes." H
was on surer ground when he said that " parity " and kindre
conceptions were based on the idea of conflict, when wha
was wanted was a formula based on the idea that " we wei
all going to be friends." That was coming very close to th
truth, i.e. the supremacy of the political issue.

The response to this eminently sane but rather novel idea as not very ready ; but there was response, and the experts ere listened to somewhat less. The response became more ordial when the Labour Party returned to office in Great ritain, and Lord Robert Cecil, who had resigned over the ascos of 1927, returned again to Geneva as British delegate. Ie at once expressed disapproval of what he described as ae dropping of any proposal to which any one objected. He emanded clear-cut progressive recommendations. The atter ended for the moment in pious resolutions, but the eague Assembly was assured that the Conference would ow proceed to draw up a final draft convention, embodying ae progress that would be made, and thus make definite a rst step towards real disarmament.

That convention was not produced until October 1930, ad during that time the whole political situation had changed or the worse ; the world was drifting into the trough of the eat economic depression ; nationalism of the peculiar quasi-volutionary post-War type was in the ascendant; in Europe oth the economic and political systems seemed to be breaking own. In comparison with these facts the conclusion of a hree-Power naval agreement in London, although hailed as a iumph, was really an event of very little significance. istory generally was passing into a new epoch. The new ignments of the Great Powers and their satellites, the fears at the economic crisis might end in revolution, and the mergence of the spectre of alliances thrust the League more d more into the background, and the disarmament question itered upon a new phase. Nations which have refused to sarm when surrounded by doubtful friends are not likely show greater willingness when to the doubtful friend cceeds the potential enemy.

The curious circumstance is that when the changes in the litical situation were revealing the increasing difficulties nfronting those who sincerely wished to see armaments duced, and even when these changes made reduction of maments fundamentally impossible, the statesmen never avered in their public professions that a disarmament nvention must, could, and would be reached and be success-ly applied. Whether they believed what they said is certain. It is at any rate difficult to decide which is the ore pitiable—the small group who did believe or the great ajority who did not.

1932 : NATIONALISM RESULTS IN HOPELESS CONFUSION

ABOVE the League problem, above the disarmament problem there loomed the greater problem of the new nationalism The Preliminary Conference succeeded with great difficul in getting a draft convention together ; the nations agree on 1st November 1931 to an arms truce for a year and th full Disarmament Conference was summoned for Februar 1932, with Arthur Henderson as chairman. It duly opene on 2nd February, and began with an effort to abolish aggre sive weapons. The experts wrangled fruitlessly until th American delegate tried to bring reality into the proceedin by tabling the so-called " Hoover plan " which proposed reduce at once by one-third, tanks, large guns, gas, a bombing aircraft. Sixty-four states were represented at th conference, and only Italy was prepared to accept the pla as it stood.

Alternative proposals were being discussed, when German dropped her bombshell by demanding equality in armamen a demand equivalent to the abolition of the disarmame clauses of the Treaty of Versailles. The demand w political, an endeavour to strengthen by an impressi foreign political success, the presidential " régime " whi had succeeded the parliamentary system in Germany. Priva negotiations between the Great Powers went on in the ho of finding a compromise, but the Germans were adama and only when on 11th December they obtained the sign admission of " equality " would they return to the co ference. A few weeks later the advent to power of Hitleris a recrudescence of the old militarist Prussianism under t guise of a pseudo-revolutionary movement, threw the wh conference into confusion. Disarmament was now impossil in face of the German menace. The statesmen tried in va to soothe the experts who were now, for the first time, findi a rising popular opinion behind them. When the conferen re-assembled in February 1933, the experts were in f control, befogging themselves and every one else. It w apparent to everybody, with one or two exceptions, includi Henderson, who, as chairman, clung to optimism with praiseworthy obstinacy, that no disarmament agreeme was possible.

On 16th March MacDonald appeared in person to ma an impressive appeal and to table the " British plan,"

odel draft convention which he hoped would serve as a
asis for fruitful discussion. It was much too late. The
rench would have none of it ; they were already beginning
re-arm, and a section of British opinion was beginning to
ress for government action to strengthen British defences.
June the Conference adjourned until October, and that
riod was filled with private negotiations, including a round
ip by Henderson to the European capitals.

On 14th October the bureau of the conference met and
iscussed the proposal to place all the continental armies
pon a short service basis. Germany saw in the proposal an
tempt to get rid of the *Reichswehr*, the best-trained force in
urope, and, failing to get any satisfaction, the Hitler govern-
ent took the bit between its teeth, and ostentatiously left
th the Conference and the League of Nations. The
onference decided not to dissolve, but adjourned *sine die*.
he first phase of the disarmament effort was over. The
litical situation was now more tense than it had been since
14, and, under the pressure of events, there came instead
disarmament a formidable increase in the re-armament
ans of nearly every nation.

PEACE DEFEATED BY THE NEW MILITARISM

T has already been pointed out that the establishment of
dictatorships with a frenzied nationalist policy rendered
e League impotent. It is quite impossible to kill democracy
home and then to make international democracy work.
he abrogation of democracy in Russia, in Italy, in Germany,
d elsewhere entails theoretically the complete dominance
the state, whether the state is conceived as an instrument
class, nation, or race, and, in practice, the absolute rule
an oligarchy determined to maintain itself in power. To
so, to whip nationalist feeling to its height, any dictatorship
es the language of militarism. Germany, Italy and Russia
to-day the three most highly militarised countries in
rope. In the two former, military training begins in
cradle and the nation's man-power is thought of only in
ms of war ; that war is masked under the phrase " national
fence " makes no difference. The appeal at home and
road is not to law, but to force. It must be noticed, how-
er, that in Soviet Russia's case militarism may be more
ictly defensive, for no definite warlike aim, as distinct from
evolutionary aim, has been proclaimed by the Soviets.

It is idle to talk of formal disarmament in the sense
reducing the uniformed forces to a low level, if every abl
bodied male is receiving military training.　War has change
the old year-in, year-out training is unnecessary.　T
technician can be trained through peace-time work ; muniti
plants can operate as harmless producers of peace-time goo
until they are needed for war.　The mere existence of t
active spirit of militarism in one country is enough to evo
in others the counter-feeling of national insecurity, perha
nowadays the strongest of all national feelings, a feeling
strong as to convince a nation of the necessity of armi
to the teeth against an imaginary enemy.　After all the pa
and plans by which war has been renounced we are aga
living in a war atmosphere ; and from one end of the ear
to the other the nations are taking " precautions."

THE FAILURE OF HALF-MEASURES

THOSE who advocate disarmament have now to face tw
alternatives.　There is, on one hand, total disarmamer
as was contained in the Litvinov proposal, which has
chance of being accepted.　On the other, there is the recog
tion of what even President Wilson recognised—that
nation will disarm beyond that point at which it feels secur
is menaced—and of what President Wilson did *not* recogn
—that what a nation feels on this matter is purely irration
and may, as in Russia and Germany, become a phobia carefu
maintained at a dangerous height by unscrupulous politicia
The alternatives are really total disarmament or no d
armament.

It is hardly possible that any serious student of the politi
situation believes the former to be possible ; it is less cert
that such a student realises the full implications of no d
armament at all.　The mere admission that the natic
cannot now disarm implies the end of any effective int
national co-operation, for it is an admission that war is n
very well within the bounds of possibility.

THE MODERN STATE CAN MOBILISE OVERNIGHT

IN the palmy days of democratic international co-operati
when the pre-War generation was still producing statesm
the problem was merely that of fitting armaments to pe
pacts, that is to say, taking measures to eliminate the co
ventional weapons used in aggression.　That elimination,

e have seen, failed because there is, in fact, no distinction
etween an aggressive and a defensive weapon and, even if
 had not failed, the new developments in technical science
ould have rendered success insignificant. The innocent
emicals used in industry can be transformed into the
eadliest of all weapons ; innocent passenger and cargo
rcraft can be transformed in a matter of hours, not indeed
to fighting 'planes, but into bomb carriers ; the population
 regimented ; industry is organised on the basis of self-
ufficiency, the ideal of the beleaguered fortress, completely
compatible with any form of international intercourse.
he state-organised machine, embracing every citizen, can
vernight be transformed into a fighting machine. What is
orse, transforming a population from a co-operative organisa-
on of independent sentient beings into a machine controlled
y the irresponsible, wipes out at once the distinction between
ldier and civilian. In the dragooned countries there are
ow no civilians, although there may still be a few people
ft who have ordinary shirts. In these circumstances it is
le to talk of disarmament.

AN EFFECTIVE LEAGUE OR AN ARMAMENTS RACE?

HE state of things at the present time does not alter these
facts. The Italian aggression and the obvious incredulity
d dismay of the Italians at the reaction to it indicates how
en's minds had grown accustomed once again to treat war
 an instrument of national policy. In the section on the
eague it was stated that side by side with loyalty to the
eague principles there existed a conflict of interests. No-
here is it better seen than in relation to disarmament. The
-armament of Germany and the acquiescence to it by her
eighbours, put that question in many minds as a new basis.
he Italian aggression was to many a vicarious " try-out "
r a future German aggression. The resistance of the
eague to the former aggression and the defiance of Italy led
ill more to fear that lack of armaments encouraged an
gressor and conferred the halo of respectability on re-arma-
ent. Before every nation to-day of political importance
ere lies a re-armament programme such as was not thought
 some years ago. Such re-armament makes war probable,
d we are faced with the paradox that while the statesmen
e on the whole honestly seeking to establish the reign of
w and peace at Geneva, they are seeking to help on the cause

15

by a programme which must end in the disruption of wh
law and order there may be.

Why such a paradox ? There are many answers, but
the present writer it seems that one answer, and that not t
least, is the existence of schism in Europe. There are to-d
nations whose whole structure is based on war. They are n
actually mobilised for war, and the assertion that such mobilis
tion is intended for defence has no meaning when it is ma
by an irresponsible chief of state or committee whose avow
aim is the aggrandisement of the people he rules. "Have
nations and "have-not" nations is a subtle distinctio
there is no subtlety in the distinction between mobilised a
non-mobilised nations, and the action of Italy in giving t
lie to the pacific assertions of dictators, has revealed the g
before Europe.

The case is plain. There is in Europe to-day no uni
of thought, no unity of purpose such as existed in embryo
1919, and was given a supreme chance of developme
between 1926 and 1928. Instead, there is intellectual a
moral division of a much more formidable kind than exist
in 1914, because it is one that divides not governments b
peoples. There is in nearly every country to-day a feeli
that individually and collectively the nation and what
stands for is menaced. It is perhaps difficult to discov
whence the menace comes, but it is absurdly easy to discov
whence it should not. It should not come anywhere from
democratically-governed state, and, for the democratic sta
now particularly menaced, there can be no security, apa
from the creation of a larger unity.

DEMOCRACY OR DICTATORSHIP, WHICH IS IT TO BE ?

IN the section on the League of Nations it was said th
if democracy went down, the League went down, and w
would be upon us. It is idle to talk of disarmament wh
what is at stake is no less than the future of Western civilis
tion. That is what one hopes Baldwin meant when he sa
that Britain's frontier was on the Rhine—at which for t
moment (except for the Dutch-Scandinavian-Baltic fring
Western civilisation stops.[1] But equally there is nothi

[1] For beyond the Rhine there is no great State which does n
reject decisively those rights of man which were Western civilisatior
supreme political discovery, whose successful assertion was its suprem
political achievement, and on whose maintenance it in the fulle
sense depends.

re idle for the democracies than to abandon themselves
solation to what looks like the alternative to a new organisa-
1—an armaments race.   Such a race makes war inevitable.
ere is no need to dwell on the horrors of a future war, in
ich no distinction will be drawn between combatant and
1-combatant, and no consideration will be shown to age
sex ; they have been amply described in a score of books.
great war to-day means a universal war, and a universal
r means the end of Western civilisation as we know it.
The reality before us is that for the first time since 1919
re exist persons, factions, and states which are *willing war*.
is is the reality that dispersed *sine die* the Disarmament
nference and reduced the League of Nations to a pale
dow of the State to which one hopes it may be raised.
:ore either can function usefully, the political issue now
ore us must be settled.   It may be settled in peace if
 democracies can find a method of united action ;   it
y be settled in war.   If it is settled by a victory for the
ces of dictatorship and militarism, then those of us who
ieve in democracy will have run our race, and, if we
vive, may cease to interest ourselves in disarmament,
in every other political issue.   If it is settled by the defeat
those forces, then political unity will be attained, politics
 become the interest, the vital interest, of every one,
 in a new organisation of the nations disarmament will be
lised in a form that will satisfy the most sanguine.

SOME ARMOURIES OF FACTS ABOUT
THE LEAGUE

OR all those who read daily accounts of the doings or the
 misdoings of the League of Nations, scoff or sigh and turn
another page of their newspapers, how many are there who
lly know the scope of the League's activities ?   Very few.
mittedly there is much to criticise in the League ;   faults of
ission there have been, and farces of commission.   But
ch the League might have done circumstances have made
possible ;   much, again, that it has done has been neglected :
 results in checking the white slave and drug traffics, for
:ance, and the creation of the International Labour Office.
'o get at the truth and for an independent judgment upon
ss reports, the reader is advised to study the authentic
uments appertaining to the League.   There is an *Official*

Journal, published monthly by Allen and Unwin, 40 Museu
Street, London, W.C.1, which gives a full record of what t
League is doing. The debates in the Disarmament Conferen
are printed separately by the same firm, which are the age
for all League publications. A veritable armoury of facts
accessible to any one who cares to send up for the annu
Armaments Year Book, where the armaments of all nations
fully set forth.

On the origin of the League, the best book is Dr. Hun
Miller's two-volume *The Drafting of the League Coven*
(Putnam), with a full appendix of texts. A smaller and ve
useful book is Miss Florence Wilson's *The Origins of*
League Covenant (Hogarth). C. Howard Ellis carries t
student one step farther in *The Origin, Structure, and Work*
of the League of Nations (Allen and Unwin).

The vexed question of disarmament has found an assiduc
expounder in Wheeler Bennett, who has written th
very informative books, all published by Allen and Unwi
Information on the Problem of Security, 1917–26 (192
Information on the Reductions of Armaments (1926), a
Information on Disarmament and Security, 1927–31 (193
The League of Nations Union and the various peace societ
publish useful pamphlets, but the reader will be well advi
to neglect the pamphlet and, as far as possible, to study
larger books, particularly the publications of the Leag
itself. A full catalogue of these can be obtained from
agents, Allen and Unwin.

For study of some triumphs of the League which are
sufficiently appreciated, one should obtain the reports of
International Labour Conference Draft Conventions, publisl
by H.M. Stationery Office, or the *Annual Reports of Gove*
ments on Opium Traffic (Allen and Unwin).

THE GREAT HUMAN PROBLEMS OF OUR TIME

y W. E. SALT, M.A., B.Com., Head of the Extra-Mural Dept. of Bristol University, and E. J. PROPERT, M.A.

THE post-War period has been one of great contrasts. It has seen a remarkable expansion in productive power and a great increase in the amenities of life. Wireless, road transport, and cinemas are only a few of the more outstanding examples of this change. But this period has seen also unemployment on an unparalled scale throughout the world, dire poverty and sometimes starvation, and the desolation of idle factories, mines, shipyards, and other normal centres of production. Privation and food shortage in some parts of the world have existed at the very time when over-abundant and unsaleable crops were being destroyed elsewhere. This has truly been described as an age of " poverty in the midst of plenty." But before these anomalies and hardships can be removed there are many problems to be faced.

The real significance of the social problems which exist becomes clear only when we define the underlying aim towards which society is consciously or unconsciously directing its efforts. Unfortunately, this is rarely discussed except as a matter of academic interest, and is far from the minds of most people, who become absorbed in the details of daily life. Idealistic and unpractical aims are held by many to be desirable, but society as a whole can only work within the fabric of its existing resources. It is probably best to assume that society should have as its object the " optimum " well-being of its members—that is, the greatest degree of material and mental well-being, taking into consideration the limitations of our environment, the imperfections of human beings in planning and carrying out their schemes, and the physical difficulties imposed by space, time, and the limitation of material resources. Even this is a very vague conception, capable of a number of interpretations. For example, the greatest total of prosperity, even supposing this were capable of measurement, may or may not be arrived at by an equal distribution of wealth. This is one of the many problems upon which society has as yet failed to pronounce, but which must ultimately be faced.

Again, " prosperity " itself is a very unsatisfactory word. It implies mainly the possession of material things. But the well-being of society depends quite as much on the happiness obtained from other sources, which can neither be measured nor adequately controlled. For example, the growth of mass production has greatly increased the supply of many material things, but against this must be weighed the greater mental and physical strain of more intensive factory work and the loss of happiness caused by it. Again, the accidents caused by motoring, and the cost and trouble of traffic control must be taken into consideration in thinking of the gains from the increased use of automobiles.

Thus, society, as at present constituted, is bound to manage its affairs in a somewhat " rule of thumb " manner, concentrating its attention upon specific problems as they arise rather than following any detailed plan of progress. In this rather haphazard search for greater prosperity many difficulties are encountered, some of which, like unemployment at the present time, can be compared to a cancer in society, and must be removed if progress is to be maintained. At the present time, the factors preventing society from making the best use of its resources may be divided into two classes. There are first certain permanent obstacles which limit our powers, and secondly, certain features peculiar to the post-War world, giving rise to serious problems.

THE PRICE WE PAY FOR NATURE'S " GIFTS "

THE prosperity of mankind is affected by the limitation of the resources at its disposal. Economists in the last century debated the question whether Nature is generous and kindly, or whether she is niggardly. She is generous in supplying us with the means of life, but niggardly in that these are limited and frequently require great cost in effort before they are available for consumption. To increase the production of raw materials often requires a more than proportionate increase in effort. The deeper a mine is sunk for example, the higher will be the cost of extracting the coal and the more intensively land is cultivated, the greater is the unit cost of its products. Again, natural resources are rarely found in the place where they are most wanted. It was accidental that Great Britain's coalfields were found near to her other natural resources, giving her such an advantage in the last century. Generally, a considerable cost is incurred in transport before raw materials can be utilised. The coal and iron fields of the United States, for instance, are widely separated.

This intractability of Nature places limits to the increase of material wealth at any time, and is a fundamental limitation to human prosperity. In recent years, particularly, scientific research has enabled us, temporarily at any rate, to reduce its seriousness. Agricultural research has made it possible to grow two blades of grass where only one grew before, while improvements in transport have made distant resources very much more attainable. But there are other obstacles as well. These arise mainly from the fact that all production must necessarily be carried on in advance of demand, so that discrepancies, causing waste of materials and effort, cannot be avoided. Every producer of goods has to estimate beforehand the quantity he is likely to sell, and if he makes an error of judgment, waste is caused, or some demand goes unsatisfied. In either case, from the point of view of society, the resources at its disposal have not been used to the greatest advantage.

But such occurrences cannot be avoided. Apart from the imperfections of human judgment, it is impossible completely to forecast demand, which may change suddenly as a result of unforeseen circumstances. The death of a king, for instance, tends to reduce the demands for coloured cloth and increases that for black. The introduction of short hair for women threw many thousands of Chinese makers of hair-nets out of work. Every such change, or transfer of demand, while creating new wants and new occupations, renders some already produced goods useless and some occupations unnecessary.

But supply, as well as demand, is not subject to complete regulation. This is found particularly in agricultural industries, where the vagaries of climate produce uncertain results. Thus a quantity of seed and an amount of effort one year may produce a rich harvest of wheat, causing glut and wastage, while the next year the same expenditure of seed and labour may bring an exceptionally poor yield and

the threat of famine. The uncertainty involved renders
impossible to make the fullest possible use of the actua
fruits of production, and reduces the well-being of th
community.

THE CHILD OF NECESSITY ALSO THE PARENT OF PROBLEMS

OTHER things being equal, the rate of economic progres
of any society depends upon the rate at which im
proved methods of production can be discovered and intro
duced. This factor, the rate of invention, has come to h
of very great importance in modern society, and is the sourc
of some serious problems. Of these, the most important
the tendency for better methods of production to make un
necessary the skill of many workers, and sometimes to reduc
considerably the demand for labour. This will be dealt wit
more fully when the whole problem of unemployment
discussed.

There are two other important consequences of inventio
In the first place, any change in methods of production, o
the introduction of any new commodity, is bound to caus
a certain amount of dislocation. Thus, the use of ne
sources of power in industry has adversely affected coa
mining, causing hardship to all those whose living depende
upon it, while the introduction of artificial silk has similar.
reacted upon the other textile industries.

In the second place, the purpose of invention in pr
duction is generally expected to be the reduction of unit cos
This provides the incentive to producers to adopt the ne
methods. But this end is sometimes defeated. When
new machine is installed, part of the income earned by it h
to be set aside as a depreciation fund, so that by the tim
it is worn out the capital value has been recovered. If th
rate of invention is very high, that is to say, if new machin
are constantly being invented, producers will often have
scrap their machinery before it is worn out. This mea
that the rate of depreciation becomes very high, and r
presents a heavier cost to be balanced against the great
efficiency of the new machine. For producers are boun
to keep their methods up-to-date in order to compete wit
others, so that a high rate of invention, while apparent
advantageous, may actually tend to increase rather tha
reduce cost of production.

These limitations to the success of man's efforts at pro-
ding for his own well-being are unavoidable. They may
: reduced and modified at times, but they are permanent
)stacles to a completely satisfactory condition of society.
is important to realise that whatever the organisation of
·ciety such difficulties are bound to be met with, and must
: allowed for.

MODERN MAN AS THE THRALL OF HIS OWN CREATION

)NE of the most striking features of the post-War world
has been the tremendous advance in the mechanisation
production. Man's power to produce has grown with
nazing speed and in many directions. In industry the
plication of new and improved sources of power, the
troduction of more efficient machines and the intensifica-
·n of mass production have resulted in a considerable
owth in actual output, and have increased potential pro-
·ctive capacity still more. In agriculture the develop-
·ents have been if anything even more startling. The
owth of large-scale farming, the enormous increase in the
·e of tractors and electrical appliances, and the results of
opting scientific methods have transformed the old fears
a possible food shortage into anxiety concerning the
arket for crops.

The rapidity with which these changes have taken place
:alls the Industrial Revolution of the eighteenth and nine-
·nth centuries. And there appears no reason to believe
at the pace of change need slacken in the coming years.
ientific study of methods of manufacture and farming
ntinues to yield new knowledge and to offer prospects of
·l greater outputs. The lurking fear of scarcity which
·cupied men's minds before the War has gone, and in its
·ce has come a desire to make the most of the resources
·ich are at hand, but which have not yet brought greater
·osperity.

It is, on the other hand, easy to exaggerate the growth of
·oductive power. A visit to a modern factory suggests
·t we can produce to an almost unlimited extent. But
·must not be forgotten that the production and upkeep of
·chinery absorb a good deal of skilled labour, and represent

an important item in the cost of production. The organis
tion of large factories has also become increasingly comp
cated and costly. These factors must be set against the grea
output of the factory in arriving at the actual advance whi
has been made.

It is not, of course, possible to estimate exactly the incre
of potential production. Actual production received a s
back in the depression which began in 1929. But so long
unemployment exists on a large scale, it can be assum
that the community is not enjoying the maximum of
power to produce goods and services. The problem is
direct production into those channels where it can best
absorbed.

TROUBLES CAUSED BY THE FICKLE SHOPPER

THE normal difficulty of producing a supply of goc
just suited to the demands of consumers has be
made much more serious in recent times by two factors.
the one hand, for various reasons, demand has become m
capricious ; while, on the other hand, modern methods
production are on such a large scale that a big and sta
market is required if they are to be utilised to the full
possible extent. The increasing fickleness of demand
become more and more noticeable since the War. In m
countries, incomes are somewhat higher than before 19
and generally speaking people have a larger margin of inco
left over to spend on luxuries after buying the necessaries
life. Saving seems to be a virtue of the past, for with
coming of all kinds of insurance and old age pensions, it
no longer so essential to make provision for the future or
contingencies.

The essence of the enjoyment of luxuries is variety, so t
a considerable part of the demand of nearly every one is
this fickle nature. Pianos give way to gramophones, a
gramophones to wireless sets. The fashion for motor-c
makes coaches and carriages practically useless. And
only does the nature of demands change in this way, bu
is swayed also by small details. A new model of motor-
or wireless set diverts demand from the model of the y
before. Every advance of education tends to cause chan
of taste and to make people's wants more capricious t
before.

This is a problem which causes much difficulty to mod

dustry. Nor is it a problem which can easily be dealt with
der existing conditions. Indeed, producers, impelled by
e force of competition to try to secure for themselves as
ge a share in the market as possible, instead of deterring
nsumers from being troublesome and particular about
tails in buying, encourage them. The modern tendency in
vertisement is to draw the attention of the potential con-
mer to some new but minor characteristic in the commodity
ich gives it a special attraction. The apparent ease with
ich demand can be stimulated by these methods has led
anufacturers to concentrate on novelties, which have a
ort vogue and then frequently disappear for ever. This
a wasteful tendency, for the knowledge that at any moment
mand may drop off, generally forces the producer to charge
r the commodity a higher price than is really justified by its
tual cost of production. Thus society does not really get
e full benefit of its productive capacity, while producers
e subject to intensive competition, and are in constant
nger of losing their markets. More important still, every
ange in demand brings the threat or reality of unemploy-
nt.

The tendency towards a constant shifting of demand comes
o conflict with an equally marked tendency for the con-
ions of supply to become more rigid. The development
the use of machinery in industry, and the standardisa-
n which is inevitable if the more efficient methods of mass
oduction are to be made full use of, are profitable only
en large outputs are possible and when no radical altera-
n in the product is likely to occur for some time to
me.

The modern factory is equipped with complicated machines
rough which the commodity passes in the course of its
oduction, and which must therefore be working in complete
rmony. Even a small change in the character of the
mmodity may so upset the chain of processes as to cause
nsiderable cost and interruption of production. The over-
ad charges of the modern factory are so high that the
achines, unless they are allowed to run steadily over a long
riod, producing a large output, are very costly. Thus,
e constant changes and readjustments necessary to cater
a varying demand represent a considerable addition to
st. Industry therefore is in need of stable markets to meet
e more rigid conditions of supply.

THE DILEMMA OF MODERN INDUSTRY

How can these two opposing tendencies be reconciled
The problem is further complicated by the fact tha
within industry itself the demand for the instruments (
production has also undergone revolutionary changes. Th
growth of road transport has reacted upon the railway.
which have huge amounts of capital sunk in plant that canne
be diverted to other uses. Again, the increasing use of o
and electricity for power in factories, and the introduction (
more economical ways of using coal, have injured the minin
industry and have rendered useless many millions of pound
of capital, leaving many thousands of miners idle.

The conclusion seems to be that a very rapid rate of chang
in consumers' wants, or in industrial methods, creates tl
need for far-reaching re-adjustments in production ; an
that, as industry is organised to-day, these adjustments ca
only be made slowly and at a very great cost, both human an
financial. If industry is to be made more elastic and adjus
able to changing conditions, we must be prepared to sacrifi
some of the advantages of mass production. If we a
reluctant to pay this price, then some limitation of the freedo
of choice of consumers is unavoidable.

All these imperfections in our productive organisatio
cause the community to be less well-off than it might othe
wise be. In order to get over the difficulties involve
responsibility for production has been delegated to o
section of the community who enjoy in the form of profi
the reward for successfully estimating and providing for t
wants of consumers. This system has resulted in a ve
unequal distribution of wealth. Although productive pow
has increased at a great rate, the problems of poverty a
unemployment have also grown, and the condition of t
modern world is such that much dissatisfaction is felt amo
the majority of people. Three important features of socie
are felt to be unsatisfactory : (1) Modern conditions
work ; (2) the unequal distribution of wealth ; and (3) t
way in which industry is controlled.

The first of these will next be discussed. The second c
best be dealt with in two parts—the special problem of th(
who are unable to earn any income, the unemployed, an(
general survey of the way in which wealth is divided in *

community. The third involves a discussion of the future of capitalist society, and the possibility of alterations or alternatives.

SCIENCE THAT MAKES WORK DULL

THE conditions under which the majority of people have to work nowadays are far from ideal. It is recognised that the introduction of machinery, and particularly of mass production methods, has made a great alteration in the position of the worker. Much attention has been paid to the changed condition of the manual worker, but it is sometimes forgotten that the black-coated worker has also suffered from the altered structure of industry. The growth of large-scale business has made mechanisation and greater specialisation essential in this branch also, and the life of many clerks has become very much a matter of dull routine and mechanical repetition. In so far as these changes cause dissatisfaction, they bring unhappiness and loss of well-being, if nothing more serious, and they must be recognised as problems of twentieth century society.

Perhaps the most striking feature of present-day industry as compared with that of the last century is the decline in the need of skilled work. Where mass production has been introduced, very little employment can be offered other than machine-tending of some kind, and this is almost always a semi-skilled or unskilled job. The worker has been affected by this change in two ways—his status has altered, and his environment is different from what it used to be.

The status of the worker has declined, first in that he no longer has very much value as an individual. His work requires comparatively little training, and he can be easily replaced. When less mechanical methods of production were used, the artisan, having completed his seven years or so apprenticeship, had a high personal value in the exercise of his skill. He had also a good deal of responsibility, and the quality and design of the work he produced were partially within his control. To-day, the factory worker sees only one small part of the process of production of the commodity. He himself creates nothing, and is responsible for nothing but the performance of a mechanical task. This change has not, of course, been absolutely sweeping, and some skilled occupations remain. In the printing industry, for example, the full apprenticeship is still necessary in many branches of work, for no machine can remove the need for accuracy and personal skill in some operations. But here, as in practically every other industry, the proportion of skilled to unskilled workers is declining.

Secondly, it is generally agreed that chances of promotion are considerably fewer than they used to be. The increase of specialisation has narrowed the scope of individual ability, and the worker in a large factory has little chance of standing out. There seems also to be an increasing tendency to put in positions of control men who have received a special training at a university or elsewhere, rather than to promote employees who are " working their way up."

Thirdly, security of employment has become much more doubtful. Generally speaking, the skilled artisan still retains a scarcity value of his own, and it has always been to the advantage of employers to keep their trained workers in employment if possible even in times of bad trade, since they could not easily be replaced. But to-day it is perfectly easy for the employer, when business is slack, to dismiss or " stand off " his men, for not only are they provided for when unemployed, but, if any of them find alternative employment their places can readily be filled. The position of the worker therefore, tends to be less dignified and less secure.

THE WORKER MENACED BY STRAIN AND DISEASE

THE changes which have taken place in environment have been in some ways advantageous. Government intervention in industry, making compulsory a certain standard of cleanliness, ventilation, and sanitation, and the growth of interest in welfare, have made the modern factory an increasingly pleasant place. But, on the other hand, factory work itself is sometimes far from pleasant. It is sometimes extremely monotonous and uninteresting, calling for little thought or ingenuity, yet requiring the constant attention of the operator. Neither is modern industry particularly healthy. For not only are bad accidents sometimes unavoidable, but in many occupations there is a grave risk of disease. Tuberculosis is still a very serious problem, while in some industries the materials used are found to cause poisoning.

Another menace to the well-being of the worker has been the tendency to speeding up. In their desire to increase productive efficiency in order to compete more effectively, employers have in some cases introduced what is known as scientific management. This implies an attempt to carry specialisation to its extreme limits, and to increase output by more intensive work.

This tendency has been much more strongly marked in American than in British industry. By means of studying the motions of workers in each process, specialists in industrial psychology have thought out simplified movements which each worker is required to follow, in order to economise effort. While in some cases the workers may benefit from this, the development tends still further to destroy the freedom of the individual and to increase the strain under which he works, and it is looked on with disfavour, especially in Great Britain. It is claimed that workers who are employed in factories organised in this way generally become " played out " at an exceptionally early age, on account of the exhausting nature of the work.

The discontent caused by these changes in industry has frequently found expression in disputes between workers and employers. The trade unions have studied conditions of employment and have worked to prevent the lowering of the standards of their members. Sometimes they have been unduly suspicious of innovation perhaps, but their growth has helped to replace the falling status of the individual worker by the strength of the organised body of men.

Moreover interest in the affairs of his union has to some extent provided scope for the more ambitious worker who finds a diminishing outlet for his powers in his daily occupation. Nevertheless, the dullness of much work to-day has led people to seek excitement rather than interest in their leisure time. Educational facilities, although generously provided, attract only a small minority. There is a danger that many who are no longer required to think in their daily work may cease thinking almost entirely, and adopt instead mass opinions and mass sentiments. This may prove a social problem of great importance to the future of democracy, for it is obvious that if this danger were realised the masses would insensibly become the prey of dictatorial methods of government ; they would cease to assert any rights of criticism, and apathetically consent to whatever they were told.

VICTIMS OF THE MODERN JUGGERNAUT :
THE UNEMPLOYED

UNEMPLOYMENT is undoubtedly the outstanding industrial and social problem of this age. However unpleasant the conditions of work may be, the absence of work is even more unpleasant when livelihood depends on it. But unemployment implies something much more than the mere absence of work. In any society the full enjoyment of the rights of citizenship normally goes hand in hand with the performance of some share in producing the wealth by which the community lives. In a capitalist society this share may be active, in the form of work by hand or brain, or passive in the form of the loan of capital or land. The man who does not share in this responsibility has at present no real place in society, and is made to feel himself under a stigma.

Yet society has failed to provide all its members with a place in production, and through no fault of their own they are forced to subsist precariously on what is allowed them from the wealth that others have produced. In most civilised countries it is now recognised, however grudgingly, that the responsibility belongs to the community, since unemployment can only to a very small degree be attributed to personal defects. Even if every work-shy were transformed into a model of efficiency it would not be possible to give him unfailing scope for the exercise of his powers. Unemployment is almost entirely a problem of industry, and one toward which numerous factors contribute.

It is commonly supposed to-day that, since so many of our troubles seem to have been caused directly or indirectly by the War, the pre-War world must have been an almost ideal place. In connection with unemployment particularly this notion is popular. But actually, although the problem has altered in aspect during recent years, it is one which has been present since industrialisation began. If people wanted always exactly the same things in exactly the same quantity, and if methods of production did not alter, it would be possible to organise industry so minutely that only those incapable of working need be unemployed. But changes in demand and in methods of production are constantly taking place, and these result in dislocation, which in turn produce unemployment. Whenever one commodity loses popularity

nd another takes its place some unemployment is caused.
'he growth of the cinema, and of " canned " music, while it
as provided employment of a new kind, has thrown many
ctors and professional musicians out of work.

The majority of people are trained only in narrow occupa-
ons, and cannot adapt themselves readily to others. One of
ne most tragic and difficult aspects of unemployment among
ne miners in South Wales is that many of them are too old
 be moved to other occupations, and, in any case, lack the
nowledge and the means of moving to other places where
ney might have a better chance of finding work. This
roblem of the immobility of labour is one which tends to be
emedied with each new generation, who can be brought up
 flourishing occupations, but fresh changes or transfers of
emand constantly renew the difficulty. This is a problem
hich is bound to arise under any organisation of industry,
hether capitalist or socialist, and must be regarded as one of
e penalties of progress.

THE TRADE CYCLE : A MYSTERY THAT NO ONE CAN SOLVE

UNEMPLOYMENT of a different kind is caused when the total
demand for goods declines. Total demand, that is, the
tal amount spent on goods of all kinds by the community,
 at present a factor beyond the control of society. But
r more than a hundred years the phenomenon has been
bserved that even when the long-period trend of prosperity
emed to be upwards, there came periodically a fall in
mand. This was accompanied by a fall in industrial
tivity on the same scale, and unemployment of an abnormal
nount was experienced. Thus, over a long period of time,
e figures of unemployment rose and fell. In the year
eceding the War, the highest percentage of workers in
gistered trades who were unemployed in Great Britain
 any year was 12 per cent., and the lowest 2 per cent. The
erage amount of unemployment at all times was between
 and 5 per cent. Since the War this average increased—
en before the depression of 1929—to about 8·5 per cent.,
 figure which represented over a million workers. This
ernation of periods of good trade and extensive employ-
nt with periods of bad trade and high unemployment,
hich forms what is known as the Trade Cycle, has as yet
fied a satisfactory explanation or cure. It is claimed by
me to be an inevitable flaw of the present system, while

others regard it as even more fundamental. That it is
serious deterrent to satisfactory conditions of employmer
has been emphasised only too clearly by the depression.

Changes in methods of production also frequently resu
in unemployment. Improvements in machinery general
enable the same number of workers to produce a larg
quantity of goods, and, unless demand similarly expanc
unemployment is inevitable. In the last century the increa
in the productive capacity of industry was accompanied
a steadily growing population at home and steadily growin
markets abroad. Thus, increased production could
absorbed, and more machinery seemed to mean more good
more demand, and more employment. But in this centu
conditions are radically different. Methods of producti
have improved even more rapidly than before, but populatio
at home is nearly stationary, and foreign markets ha
dwindled. Demand, therefore, has lagged behind potent
supply, or rather productive capacity has temporarily oversh
demand, causing unemployment on a large scale.

This, however, does not mean that the mechanisation
industry is in itself an undesirable thing. But unless socie
is organised so that the output of industry can be dispose
of, unemployment cannot be avoided. The ability to abso
the rapidly increasing output of the nineteenth century w
created mainly by accidental circumstances. These are n
absent. The question is therefore forced upon us wheth
such an important matter should be left to chance, or wheth
production and distribution should not be submitted
" planning "—a term greatly in vogue since the beginning
the Russian Five-Year Plan.

HOW THE ELEMENTS PLAY TRICKS WITH TRADE

ANOTHER factor which contributes to the severity of uner
ployment at all times is the existence of casual occupatior
Building, for example, is dependent on the weather, and
the winter workers in this trade frequently find themselv
unemployed. Conditions in the docking industry are simil
Here employment for the majority of the workers is n
certain for more than two or three days at a time, and depen
on the vagaries of weather and tide, as well as on the gene
state of trade at any time. It is necessary to the employ
to have sufficient men available to meet the needs of t
busiest days. Yet such days come only at intervals.

Attempts have been made in recent years to minimise this
oblem by rigidly limiting the number of men in the
dustry, and by trying to ensure that despite irregular
ployment their incomes always reach a certain level. But
e evils of casual labour cannot entirely be avoided. Blind
ey occupations are also a serious industrial problem, the
ly solution of which appears to lie in more thorough
ganisation and control ; and possibly also in removing the
cessity of earning an immediate income, which confronts
many juveniles on leaving school.

The figures of unemployment which are published every six
onths in Great Britain include all those who normally belong
insurable trades and are registered at the Labour Exchange.
is of course does not cover the whole working population.
t in other countries available information is often still less
mplete. In the United States, for example, the only
ures of unemployment to be obtained are those got from
de unions and institutions such as municipalities and
arities which are concerned with the relief of poverty. Until
e Unemployment Insurance Acts of 1935 and 1936 several
portant categories of workers were not included either in
e unemployment insurance schemes or the published un-
ployment figures in Great Britain. The two most important
sses to whom this applied were agricultural and " black-
ted " workers. The latter were affected not only by trade
oression, but through the amalgamation of businesses and
ationalisation." No doubt these people would frequently
dergo hardship rather than submit to what their traditions
ke them consider the indignity of claiming public assistance.
e 1935 and 1936 Acts, however, admitted to the scheme the
n-manual worker earning less than £250 a year, and the
icultural worker, the latter paying a lower subscription and
oying a lower rate of benefit.

According to statistics compiled by the International
bour Office, there were during the depression as many as 29
lions unemployed in the world, and in 1934 the number was
l as much as 22 millions. But these figures, as has been
lained, are probably much below the actual total. The
intries most affected were Great Britain, Germany, the
S.A. and Italy. In Great Britain the figures exceeded 3
lions in the worst period, in Germany they reached at least
millions, in Italy over a million, while the maximum un-
ployment in America, while it cannot be told accurately,

must have been at least 12 millions. By the spring of 193
however, there had been a considerable reduction of u
employment in all countries except Canada, Denmark, Polan
Bulgaria and Jugo-Slavia.

THE TRAGEDY OF YOUTH LEFT IDLE

THERE are certain aspects of the unemployment proble
which must be taken into account before its true seriou
ness can be appreciated. There is first the question
juvenile unemployment. The number of juveniles, th
is those between the ages of 14 and 18 in Great Britai
who were registered as unemployed in June 1934, was
little below 80,000, and the fall in numbers during the pr
ceding period was considerably less than in unemployme
as a whole. This was partly due to the abnormally hig
birth rate in the years immediately following the War, b
it must not become a permanent feature of unemploymer
Some of these juveniles have never had any work at a
A large number leaving school are unable to obtain ar
employment, and consequently grow up without any industr
or other training. Blind-alley occupations are little bette
and the possibility of these children becoming useful citize
is very small.

Important features of modern unemployment are its pe
manence and the stagnation attached to it in many instance
Before the War, the unemployed, apart from those who we
quite incapable of working, were in and out of a job ; althoug
the numbers might remain fairly constant over a period, t
personnel was all the time changing. The majority we
only out of work for comparatively short periods. B
to-day, many of those who are unemployed have not work
for years, and some have little prospect of ever worki
again. This is largely due to the fact that so many former
important trades and occupations have now suffered a se
back through the permanent decline of industries, such
cotton and coal-mining, and to the superseding of skill l
machinery.

This lengthening of the average period of unemployme
has greatly increased the seriousness of its effects on physiq
and morale. In both these ways enforced idleness is bou
to cause deterioration. The unemployed have no marg
of income to spend on hobbies, and can have few intere
of an uplifting kind. Time is bound to hang heavy

them, causing them to feel depressed and dissatisfied. Suicide is becoming more prevalent among those who have no work. Hanging about at street corners is unavoidable in the majority of cases, and the aimless life is likely to make them unfit for a return to the strenuous routine of industrial work, should the opportunity present itself.

The effects on physique are likely to be even more serious. The allowance which is made to unemployed workers and their families is found to be almost always inadequate for their maintenance over a long period. After other necessary expenses have been met, the amount left over for food is insufficient, and malnutrition may result, injuring the health not only of the adults, but, worse still, of the younger members of the family.

ATTEMPTS TO FOB OFF UNEMPLOYMENT : STATE AID

BEFORE 1911 the only assistance which was available to unemployed workers in Great Britain was obtained either in the form of benefits from the trade unions or friendly societies to which they belonged, or through the ordinary mechanism of the Poor Law. In this year, however, an Act was passed which applied an entirely new principle to the problem—the principle of Insurance. This was first applied over a limited section of industry, but was extended after the War to cover nearly the whole field, with certain important exceptions, which have already been mentioned. According to this scheme, a fund was instituted into which was paid weekly a compulsory contribution by each employer and each worker, and an additional contribution by the State. From his fund, a weekly benefit was to be available to any unemployed worker having contributed for at least a stipulated period, the benefit being only paid for a limited number of weeks.

Such a scheme was probably suitable for dealing with the problem on its limited pre-War scale. But after the War it was found to be quite inadequate, partly because the total demands on the fund were considerably greater than the total contributions, and partly because the average period of unemployment became much longer, so that the limited benefit period was too short. Some additional provision for the unemployed had therefore to be made. Consideration was given to a proposal to continue the insurance principle in the case of all those workers who had had sufficiently regular employment to make this possible, and to make alternative provision for the remainder. But before this was done a Labour Government adopted the device of giving " uncovenanted benefit." Under this scheme the old qualifications concerning the number of contributions paid in and the restricted period during which relief might be obtained were suspended, and any unemployed worker became eligible for benefit. This scheme, while much was to be said in its favour, proved very costly, and was later modified by the National Government, who introduced the Means Test.

According to this, every applicant for relief beyond the covenanted benefit had to show that he had first exhausted every alternative source, including his own savings and the incomes of other members of the family. While being more economical from a national point of view, this regulation caused much hardship and injustice, and still further increased the poverty of those who were unemployed for long periods. This was naturally resented by those who suffered under it ; but even more unrest was caused by the introduction into Parliament in November 1933, of a new Unemployment Bill which became law in 1934. This Bill made a clear distinction between the two classes of unemployed—those still eligible for insurance benefit, and those whose claims were exhausted. It made provision for a self-supporting insurance fund for the former. The latter were to come under the control of a new national body, to be known as the Unemployment Assistance Board, which would work through its local officers, and in conjunction with the local authorities. Unemployment relief would be given, still subject to a Means Test, but recipients might now be required to undergo a course of physical training or to work for the local authorities. Special provision was made for the training of juveniles.

This Bill had many good points, but the continuance of the Means Test and resentment at being forced to any work demanded of them immediately alienated the feelings of those whom it affected. There was a fear, too, that this method of obtaining labour for municipal work might be the beginning of an attack on wages. One very strong expression of feeling, however, was shown in the hunger march of 1934. Unemployed from all parts of the country marched to London to take part in a mass demonstration in which an indictment of the new Bill was prominent. But this did not have much effect. The modern world, indeed, seems so accustomed to spectacular scenes that efforts of this kind are soon forgotten.

BRINGING THE MAN AND THE JOB TOGETHER

UNEMPLOYMENT schemes in Great Britain do not stop short at the provision of relief. An attempt was made before the War to minimise the problem by assisting workers to find the kinds of occupation to which they were suited. One of the difficulties which confronts an unemployed worker seeking a new job is ignorance of what vacancies exist and consequent failure to be where he is needed at the right moment. It was thought that the establishment of labour exchanges, to which employers could apply when in need of new hands, and at which the unemployed were forced to make regular attendance in order to qualify for relief, would help to overcome this problem of immobility. The success of this scheme was limited because of the rapid change in conditions. It could not be expected to be of very great use when unemployment grew to such a size that every vacancy called forth a flood of applications. The labour exchanges have, however, proved a very useful organisation, as a means of administering insurance and collecting information. Anything which they could achieve, however, while useful and necessary, was only a palliative, and in no way an attempt to get to the root of the problem other than by granting relief to the unemployed.

There are two ways of looking at unemployment. Some people regard it as an evil which has developed in society and must be removed as speedily as possible at any cost, while others accept its presence, do not inquire into its fundamental causes, and are content as long as the troubles caused by it are alleviated in the most economical way. The first of these views is the more important, but the second is also extremely vital because of the immediacy of the problem, although without a long-period policy it is likely to be more wasteful in the end. It must be admitted, however, that existing legislation concentrates on alleviation, while little effort has been made towards a radical cure. Many remedies have been suggested, ranging from a complete reorganisation of society to wholesale emigration. But capitalist nations tend to lack the courage and foresight necessary to carry through extensive schemes of this kind, preferring to accept as inevitable the waste and hardship of trade depression and to wait for an automatic revival. The United States has in recent years made a determined effort to overcome the slump and its attendant evils, but its lead has not been followed, and only the future can determine whether the courage of its leaders has taken them far enough for success.

THE CITIZEN'S WELL-BEING : TEST OF A NATION'S GREATNESS

AT times in the history of civilisation political domination and military power have been accepted as the outstanding features of national greatness. Such beliefs are held by many people to-day. But greatness of this kind does not necessarily lead to the prosperity of the individuals who comprise the nation. In some of the relatively small countries such as Sweden, there is little real poverty, while in the big industrial countries poverty is generally a marked feature of national life. Yet it is true to say that scientific invention and industrial advance can have no real value unless they in some way add to the total of human well-being, which is best judged by the conditions of life of the majority.

The standard of life indicates the state of society. Like prosperity, it cannot be exactly measured. It is made up of two parts ; the economic part, covering food, clothes, shelter, and other material amenities, and what may be called the psychological part—the capacity to enjoy environment. The first is dependent on the possession of income, while the second is derived mainly from individual characteristics and can therefore hardly be regarded as the responsibility of society. For all practical purposes the standards of living can be supposed to be measured by money income, taking into consideration the level of prices, and by such services as are provided by the state. This standard of living varies widely within any one country, from the very rich to the very poor. The actual value of a given money income also varies from place to place ; for instance, an income of £500 a year provides a higher standard of living in the Provinces than in London because prices are higher in London. On the other hand, the town dweller has the advantages of sanitation, free libraries, and other services which the country dweller is often denied. Thus no readily definable standard exists

t in so far as a rough measurement can be made, it is found
at the standard of living of the majority of inhabitants of
country falls within fairly narrow limits.

It is still more difficult to generalise concerning the com-
rative standards in different countries. The South Sea
ander, while lacking the conventional comforts of Western
e, is richly endowed with sunshine, natural beauty, and
od, and is able to live a very pleasant existence. He gets
:isfaction from simpler things than the average Englishman,
t he is just as happy and healthy, if not more so. Even
vague comparison of standards is impossible in this case,
ere environment and mode of living are completely different.
ain, a comparison between England and Japan is unsatis-
:tory, for although wages are much lower in Japan, the
rker there is so used to living mainly on rice that he may
t be very much worse off from his own point of view than
e Englishman on his more varied diet. It would only
possible to compare standards of life in different places
assuming that the inhabitants shared the same tastes.
us a comparison between England and America could
fairly accurately made, for ideas of culture and comfort
much the same in the two countries.

HOW POVERTY PERSISTS THOUGH WANT IS KEPT AT BAY

LTHOUGH society's productive power has grown so largely
in modern times, it has not resulted in providing adequate
ndards for all people. Poverty still exists in Western
intries on a serious scale. The amount of poverty which
sts can only be ascertained through a detailed study such
is possible only in a limited area. In Great Britain a
mber of such investigations has been made, yielding
newhat varying results, but all showing that in all parts
the country poverty remains an outstanding feature.
ere is no universally accepted definition of poverty. The
thod which has usually been adopted by investigators is
determine a standard of living which is just adequate and
discover how many people are receiving an income in-
ficient to obtain this. This basic standard is known as
" poverty line."

n a recent survey the standard used was arrived at in the
owing way. The minimum nourishment, expressed in
ries, upon which men, women, and children can subsist,
been estimated by scientists, making it possible to decide

the lowest possible diet and expenditure by which this c
be obtained. To this was added the cost of a minimum
light, clothing, heat, rent, and compulsory insurance. T
income which will just purchase these was taken as t
poverty line, its amount varying, of course, with the size
the family. This attempt at a scientific definition, wh
very useful in an investigation of poverty, does not give
completely accurate picture. For instance, the majority
people have certain fixed habits of expenditure and have r
sufficient knowledge to lay out their income to the great
advantage. Beer, trade union subscriptions, tobacco, a
newspapers are some of the modern " luxuries " which ha
come to be almost essential, but which were not allowed
in this investigation. According to modern standar
therefore, some of those whose incomes came actually abc
the chosen line were probably living on an inadequate scal

Before any estimates of the amount of poverty are discuss
it must be emphasised that the abnormal degree of unemplo
ment during recent years is responsible for a great deal.
the last century the problem of poverty was chiefly a probl
of low wages. This has now to a great extent been remedi
for, owing to the better organisation of labour, inadequ
wages are found only in a small section of industry. Inde
it is argued by some people that the insistence of trade uni
on the comparatively high post-War wage rates in Engla
is partially responsible for her loss of world markets, a
therefore, indirectly for a good deal of unemployment.
this is so, then it seems that despite the growth of product
power we have not yet learnt to overcome poverty, and m
suffer it either in the form of insufficient wages or of unempl
ment. This view, however, appears to be unnecessar
pessimistic, for there can be little doubt that under a bet
organisation modern industry could provide an adequ
living for all.

There has been a marked tendency for poverty to incre
since the War, although actual want is probably much
than in pre-War times. In 1924, in a survey of five selec
towns it was estimated that about 4 per cent. of worki
class families were living below the poverty line, compa
with 11 per cent. in 1913. But in Southampton in 193
survey disclosed 20 per cent. below the line, the effects
the depression having been severe. In the Merseys
Social Survey of 1929-30, as many as 17·3 per cent. w

und to be in poverty, this area having been particularly
ected by the slump in shipping. In London, poverty is
obably less severe, on account of the variety of occupations ;
: it is found that most hardship has been experienced during
e years of depression in areas almost entirely dependent
one industry, as South Wales is on coal-mining. Between
91 and 1903 Charles Booth published the results of an
vestigation into conditions in London. Using the same
ndards of poverty as he adopted, it was estimated in 1929
fore the worst of the depression had taken effect) that the
oportion of the population of London then below his poverty
e was only one-third its former size.

A comparison of this apparent improvement with the
ures already quoted for other towns would suggest that
: minimum standard of living which is considered necessary
considerably higher to-day than it was forty years ago.
iis is, of course, a natural development in view of the
ater resources of to-day. Indeed, total wealth is so much
ater that, while the absolute degree of poverty has
ninished, relative poverty has not, and the gap between
h and poor is as wide as ever. It is sometimes argued,
: without grounds, that this gap is widening, since the
evalence of unemployment and the exhaustion of savings
ong the unemployed caused by the operation of the Means
st are reducing to the propertyless class a large number
working people of the type which in earlier years would
ve enjoyed steady earnings and some limited possessions.

SOCIAL SERVICES : THE STATE AS FAIRY GODMOTHER

NOTHER and even more urgent aspect of poverty is the
necessity of providing for the poor. In Great Britain,
rt from the unemployed and their families, who are kept
inly by unemployment benefit and, when this is inadequate,
forced back on the Poor Relief, the rest of those who
ve to be maintained have generally been reduced to poverty
the sickness or death of the breadwinner, by inadequate
ges, or by old age. In March 1934, it was announced by
Ministry of Labour that, in spite of improving economic
ditions, the number of people in receipt of Poor Relief
s not diminishing. The total number of people receiving
ef was then 1,409,089. In some districts at this time
re than 10 per cent. of the population were obtaining
r Relief, and in 1930 it had been estimated that about

one-sixth of the total population of the country was dependi
on some form of state assistance, either Pension (Old Age
Widows'), Unemployment Benefit, or Poor Relief.

The actual cost of Poor Relief to the community is a lit
difficult to calculate, since it is almost entirely in the har
of local authorities, who meet it from local rates. But t
amount paid out in this form in 1929 came to a total of abc
£41,000,000, while the total cost to the State of Old A
Pensions, War Pensions, Widows' and Orphans' Pensio
Unemployment Benefit, and Poor Law Relief, reached t
sum of approximately £163,000,000. The problem
poverty is not, however, overcome when these payme
have been made. Pensions and Poor Relief provide th
recipients with just sufficient to live on, and leave nothi
over for contingencies, for which the community m
further be responsible.

The two main contingencies for which allowance has
be made are personal disability and the provision of hous
Personal disabilities include old age, which is provided
by small pensions obtainable by insured persons at the a
of sixty-five and by others at seventy, and sickness. H
again insured persons can obtain treatment on a spec
system, the panel, but there are also costly national servi
such as public health, hospitals, and mental homes. Si
a certain standard of training and culture is also conside
essential, provision has also to be made for the educat
of those whose parents are unable to meet this additio
cost. The total cost which the nation has to bear for all th
services was in 1929 just over one million pounds per day

HOW THE HOUSING PROBLEM BEGAN

EVER since industrialisation developed in England th
has been a housing problem. This was for a long ti
regarded mainly as a problem of overcrowding. T
population increased rapidly, being nearly quadrupled in
last century, and house-building could not keep pace. Hou
of a very poor type, crowded together and often built b
to back, and with no gardens, were hurriedly put up to m
the immediate needs of the big industrial areas as t
developed. Possibly the houses were intended only
temporary dwellings, to be replaced before long, but
pressure for more building continued, and people had to
on living in these insanitary and unhealthy dwellings.

Before transport had reached its present efficiency, it was
even more important than it is now that the workers should
live near the place where they were employed, and the owners
of these houses were frequently able to collect very lucrative
rents. There was no incentive to a sufficient expansion of
building, for the poor were not in a position to provide
anything towards obtaining accommodation of their own.

THE CITY OF TO-MORROW

*One of Sir Ebenezer Howard's plans. It resulted in 1903
in the building of Letchworth Garden City.*

middle-class families it is usual for sufficient saving to
be made to purchase a house, but the poorer classes, receiving
wages barely sufficient to live on from day to day, could
never hope to accumulate enough money for this. Their
landlords, the owners of existing property, had no incentive
to encourage building on the necessary scale, since they
benefited by the shortage of accommodation which allowed
them to obtain high rents.

Thus the increase in housing accommodation failed t keep pace with the needs of the rapidly growing population and in the towns large areas of poor houses, badly over crowded and very unhealthy, were formed. This was th origin of our twentieth century slum problem. It is no confined to industrial areas, for the agricultural workers ar also in the main badly housed. Their cottages are frequentl very old and insanitary, and unsuited to the requirement of family life.

IN SEARCH OF HEALTHY HOMES FOR THE PEOPLE

SINCE the War, the problem has grown even more acut During the years 1914 to 1918, building was practicall at a standstill, with the result that a shortage even of middl class houses was felt, while the slum problem increase The difficulty experienced by people with moderate incom in finding suitable houses in the years following the W; has since almost entirely gone, owing partly to the conversio of large dwelling-houses into flats, and partly to the boo in the building of medium-sized houses. Private builde can profitably produce houses to be sold at anything ov £500, or to be rented at a minimum of about twelve shillin; a week. But this expansion of building has been of litt help to poor families. These are, as a rule, unable to p; more than ten shillings a week in rent, and private enterpri; has not succeeded in producing at this rent houses whic meet modern requirements. The housing of the poor i healthy dwellings is not within the scope of private busines The community has therefore once again to shoulder th responsibility.

There are several ways in which this might be carried ou In the years immediately succeeding the War, the governme; had its hands full with re-organisation schemes of all kind and therefore adopted the quickest method in dealing wit housing. Subsidies were given to private builders, wh were then able to let their houses to poor tenants at le than the rent necessary to cover the cost of building. Thi however, was a temporary measure, in view of the urgen of the problem, and, like all subsidy schemes, it was foun to be expensive. Recent tendencies in housing have been in the direction of the acceptance of greater dire responsibility by the government and by local authoritie The post-War years have seen the growth of extensiv

nicipal housing estates on the outskirts of towns. But
e housing problem is by no means solved. The first
ficulty is that of building sufficiently fast to meet not only
e growing demand for houses, but also to tackle the inherited
oblem of slums and overcrowding. The second difficulty
to meet the needs of the very poor, the people for whom
is most essential to cater.

Most new building necessarily takes place on the outskirts
a city, which involves a high expenditure on transport
the occupants. Again, most municipalities have tended
put up houses at rents above the ten shilling maximum

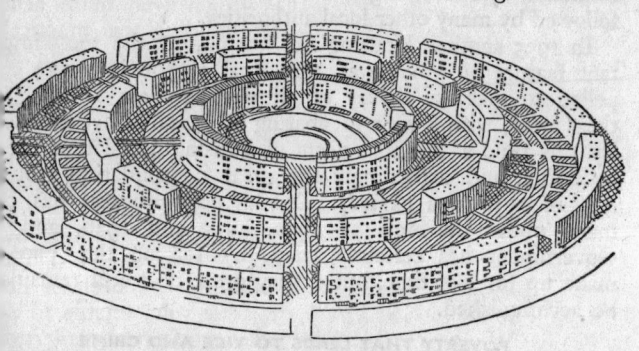

A MODERN WAY WITH THE HOUSING PROBLEM

*Space, light, comfort mark this workers' settlement in Leipzig.
The lawns and central garden are enjoyed in common by the
workers' families. There are similar buildings in Berlin.*

ich is required, and in their anxiety to obtain good tenants
ve often let them to people who really have no right to
e in houses subsidised by public money. This has tended
hold back the rate of slum clearance, and the necessity
still further control has been made apparent. In the
months ending March 1934, for instance, the total
mber of middle and lower class houses built was 153,290.
these, about 30,000 were built by local authorities, while
assisted private enterprise produced 120,781, of which,
wever, only 45,000 were working class. Only a proportion
these 45,000 will have been let at rents within the reach
the poor.

This mediocre achievement was partly due to the remnants

of the economy campaign of 1931, which had held back a determined effort at dealing with the housing problem. As the economic situation improved, the Government pressure on local authorities to implement the Housing Act 1930, and clear away slums without any compensation to the owners. The Leeds Corporation led the way with a five-year scheme to demolish 30,000 dwellings considered unfit habitation, and to re-house their occupants at a cost of twelve million pounds. They vindicated in the courts their right charge lower rents to their poorer tenants, who obtained reduction by submitting to a Means Test. This example followed by many other local authorities.

In 1935 another Housing Act was passed, the most important feature of which was that local authorities were compelled to make a survey of all working-class dwellings their areas, with a view to abating all cases of overcrowding. By this time a hundred years of housing legislation needed codifying, and accordingly the great consolidating Housing Act of 1936 was passed. Considerable progress has been made under the Acts of 1930, 1935 and 1936, and Government has certainly tried, by forcing the pace, make up for lost time, but a very great deal still remains be accomplished.

POVERTY THAT LEADS TO VICE AND CRIME

ALTHOUGH a variety of circumstances combine to produce the forms of vice from which society suffers, it can be denied that poverty has been the breeding ground many of them. Drunkenness more often than not results from a desire to escape from the drabness of a miserable existence such as poverty causes. Crime has similar influences, and frequently arises from a consciousness of injustice of poverty in a world well supplied with wealth. Perhaps, indeed, it would not be unfair to add to the national cost of poverty the upkeep of an extensive prison system. Even in the best regulated society these evils would no doubt exist in some degree, but the unpleasantness of life for a not inconsiderable proportion of the community is certainly responsible for the greater part.

The main problems of to-day, therefore, are still those which centre round poverty. This suggests a question of vital importance. Does poverty arise from an inadequacy of the total resources of the community, or is too great

roportion of the national wealth diverted to some sections
f the community, leaving too little for others ? No dog-
atic answer can be given to this question as yet, for knowledge
 to the composition and origin of the national income is still
ery imperfect. But from such data as are available it is
ossible to form a tentative judgment. In a book on the
ational Income, Colin Clark estimates that the total income
f Great Britain in 1931 was £3499 millions. Of this, wages
nd salaries accounted for 65·5 per cent., covering over three-
uarters of the population. He then goes on to calculate
at if this income were divided equally it would provide an
verage family income of £270 per annum, as well as maintain
e present rate of investment. This conclusion does not,
owever, receive universal agreement. But it seems clear
at in an industrialised community such as Great Britain or
e United States, wealth is produced in sufficient volume to
rovide an adequate standard for all, given more equal
istribution.

IN SEARCH OF ANTIDOTES

THERE has long been substantial agreement among
students of economics and social organisation concern-
g the nature of our modern social problems and the need for
emoving them. Unemployment, poverty, industrial war-
re, monotonous and degrading work, are all evils which
ause considerable material waste and enormous loss of
uman happiness and vigour. Such agreement has not
ways existed. Early in the nineteenth century, it was
enerally held that, in so far as social problems were not the
esult of personal defects, they represented the growing-pains
f the new industrial system. The best policy to adopt,
erefore, was to leave the new industry to develop along its
wn lines, confident that in time its less pleasant consequences
ould remedy themselves.

Experience has shown that this complacent view is un-
enable. Time has elapsed and the scale and fruitfulness of
e productive system have become ever more vast. But
e old problems remain and have even become more acute.
 is now widely recognised that only by deliberate and
oncerted attack can these problems be removed. Un-
ortunately at this point agreement ceases. The origins of
e problems are the subject of controversy, and fundamental
16

differences of opinion exist concerning the best means o
dealing with them.

One school of thought insists upon the need for gradua
change and feels that the complexity of the economic syster
and the conflicting interests of men make it advisable t
introduce reforms slowly, each new step waiting upon th
success of earlier advances. Other thinkers agree with th
need for caution, but stress the advisability of having som
coherent plan of social development into which each individu
change could be fitted. Only by this means, they asser
can we ensure that each step is closely related to the othe
and that all make steadily towards the preconceived goa
A third and more extreme school denies the possibility o
slow and peaceful change. Every successive reform wi
encroach more and more on the preserves of the possessir
class. Sooner or later, this class will offer resistance—t
force of arms, if necessary—to further advance, and a clas
will be unavoidable. Better to recognise the inevitability o
conflict and organise from the outset with that end in view

Thus it will be seen that there are different views abou
what constitutes social progress, and radical differences o
opinion concerning the most appropriate means of securir
it. In the following pages, an attempt will be made to outlir
the character and contributions of these conflicting schoo
of thought.

PATCHING UP THE SYSTEM

PROBABLY the majority of people who give any attentic
at all to social problems may be described as soci
reformers. They realise the desirability of improvemer
but hold that it should be sought by gradual stages. Th
best policy is to concentrate upon specific evils and to wor
for their removal. Thus, step by step, society will be tran
formed. The social reformer is opposed to socialisr
whether of the peaceful or the militant order. For, in h
view, it is not merely unnecessary, it is strongly inadvisab
to lay down in the beginning a detailed plan of socialisatio
Such a procedure smacks of arrogance and of the desire to di
tate to unborn generations. Moreover, economic and soci
change take place so rapidly in modern times that the co
ditions of the problem alter from decade to decade. It wou
be folly, therefore, to tie one's hands by a scheme which
obsolescent from birth. One step at a time is sufficient f

social reformer ; the distant scene may safely be left for
ming generations to fill in.

He is equally critical of the policy of social revolution.
y attempt to overthrow the existing order by violence is,
his opinion, foredoomed to failure. It may call up
ccessful resistance, and destroy the hopes for which it
ght. Even if temporarily victorious, revolution would
volve such a heavy cost in life and material as to hold back
ther advance for many years. Further, revolution implies
attempt to establish a new order by force, even against
wishes of the majority. Such a policy is repugnant to
social reformer, who relies upon the peaceful use of the
linary democratic machinery.

In short, then, social reform aims at the piecemeal removal
particular abuses and does not seek to lay down an elaborate
n of radical social reconstruction. This does not mean that
social reformer works entirely at haphazard. He may
k ahead for many years. The British Poor Law Com-
ssion of 1909, for instance, drew up a scheme of social legis-
ion which required years to be put into execution. But
social reformer does refrain from trying to conceive the
imate destination of society. This is a problem future
nerations alone can decide.

SOME ACHIEVEMENTS OF SOCIAL REFORM

HE record of achievement of the policy of social reform
since the War is an impressively large one. In Great
itain there was an outburst of social legislation which
ntinued almost without a check until the coming of the
pression. By a series of measures, more adequate provision
s made for those who, as a result of unemployment, old
or bereavement, had lost their chief means of livelihood.
e Unemployment Insurance Act of 1921 extended com-
lsory insurance against unemployment, which had been
roduced before the War, to the majority of wage workers.
e thrift disqualification was removed from the old age
nsions, and widows' pensions were introduced. The
tem of statutory poor relief was reformed and placed
der the control of newly constituted Public Assistance
mmittees. In public health and housing considerable
vances were made. The establishment of the Ministry
Health in 1918 made possible unified control of the public
lth services, and led to a substantial development of them.

It also greatly facilitated an attack upon the housing probler Builders were stimulated by the offer of financial aid fro: the central government and by the activity of local authoritie and nearly two million houses altogether—not all of then unfortunately, of the best type or built in the most economic manner—had been erected by the end of 1933.

In the more purely industrial field, many changes too place. Before the War, it had generally been held undesi: able and unnecessary for the State to intervene in the deter mination of the wages of adult men. One important ex ception to this general rule was made in 1909 by the passir of the Trade Boards Act, which established wages board whose decisions had the force of law, in the most " sweated trades. After the War this method was extended to a trades in which no efficient machinery for the regulation of wages existed, and ultimately about one and a quarter millic people enjoyed the benefits of statutory control of their rat of pay. Similarly, under the Agricultural Wages Act, near 700,000 agricultural workers were brought under the shelt of wages boards.

BETTERING THE WORKER'S LOT ABROAD

ABROAD, similar, though less spectacular and extensi developments in social legislation took place. Cor pulsory insurance against unemployment was adopted l more and more nations, the United States providing notable exception. Health insurance, compensation agair industrial accidents, and statutory regulation of wages ar hours of work became increasingly common, and gover ments assumed more responsibility for the housing and soc amenities of their people. Perhaps the most striking chan in social policy took place in America under Preside Roosevelt's New Deal. This included not merely a recove programme, but also an attempt, by legal recognition of tra unions and the right of collective bargaining and by t assumption of government responsibility for wages and hou to assert the need for central control over industrial co ditions. The changed attitude has not been welcomed who heartedly by the American industrialist. But it is unlik that he will be able to secure a complete return to t individualistic philosophy of earlier times.

Changes such as those outlined have frequently be described as socialistic. In one sense they are, in that th

volve greater social control over conditions of life and work.
t it would be untrue to suggest that they are aimed at
: ultimate establishment of a socialist commonwealth.
r the most part, their authors regard them as ends in them-
ves, not as steps to a clearly envisaged future goal. Rather,
:y should be viewed as expressions of a newly aroused social
nscience which seeks to remedy the worst evils of social
: but is content to go one step at a time.

THE SYSTEM ATTACKED FROM LEFT AND RIGHT

THE policy of social reform—if one may use a term
which implies a greater degree of foresight and coherence
un is ordinarily present—receives some shrewd blows from
> groups of critics. The more conservative and orthodox
nomist suggests that a social conscience, while an admirable
ng in its place, may prove a very unreliable guide to wise
aviour. It is sometimes asserted that, in attempting to
tect the weaker members against the hard knocks and
ustices of our economic system, the social reformer has
ually increased their burdens. For instance, the intro-
ction of a general scheme of insurance against unemploy-
nt made more difficult the scaling down of wages which
lining prosperity might be held to demand. In this
1 other ways social reform has increased the rigidity of
economic organisation, and by thus diminishing its
ibility has increased the risk of unemployment.
On the other side is the socialist, who is critical of the
ory which underlies social reform and, therefore, ex-
mely sceptical concerning its possibilities. His view is
t by concentrating upon particular problems, the social
ormer foredooms himself to slow advance and often to
lity. Social problems are not independent phenomena
ich can be dealt with in isolation. They are the results
he operation of one social and industrial system. There-
e, by tackling one thing at a time, the social reformer
rely pushes the balloon in at one point and causes it to
ge at another. To provide houses the rents of which
beyond the means of the average worker is not to relieve
housing shortage, but to increase discontent. Or again,
nemployment insurance leads to the discharge of juvenile
kers when they reach insurable age, insurance is of
btful advantage to them. Social legislation which deals

with one specific issue without relation to its cognate proble is bound to have unforeseen effects.

Moreover, the socialist avers that while one evil is bei tackled and removed others are arising. Industrial a social change are so continuous and rapid that the soc reformer is always a little behind the times. Events mar too quickly for him. His labours are like those of Sisyph never ending and never completely successful. This is certain result of any policy which does not forestall and cont developments. Finally, the socialist criticises the reform for accepting almost without question the fundamen features of the existing economic system.

The aim of social legislation such as we have known duri the past century has been to bring improvement within framework of the present order. To the socialist, this is impossible aim, for it is the economic system which is very root of the evils and the obstacle to their remov The socialist is convinced that piecemeal reforms mer avoid and confuse the central issue by glossing over so evils. The problem is not one of slums or poverty or temperance ; it is one of the system as a whole. Rem this, substitute for it a more just and reasonable struct of society, and the problems which vex the social refor will disappear. Anything less than this will merely skim surface.

A TWOFOLD CHARGE AGAINST CAPITALISM

THE charge brought by the socialist against the capita order of society is a twofold one. On the human s it denies to the mass of people adequate opportunities the development of self and for the achievement of a sa factory way of life. On the material side, it is a wast system which fails to do the job it sets out to do. In the the existing order is highly individualistic, offering n freedom to the individual than is afforded by any other kn system. Each person is free to choose his own occupat subject to certain minimum restrictions by the State. his leisure he is again free to follow whatever pursuit pleases. It provides a continuous stimulus to pers vigour through the incentive to acquire wealth for one's enjoyment.

In practice, however, these freedoms are illusory for n people. For society to-day is riddled with inequal

ich nullify legal liberties. The chief source of these in-
alities is to be found in the present distribution of income
wealth. For a variety of reasons the division of property
income is so unequal that some persons enjoy an over-
elming advantage in the pursuit of wealth, while others,
majority, have not a dog's chance. It follows from this
qual division of possessions that very great inequality of
ortunity exists also. Effective freedom of choice of
upation depends to a considerable extent upon the wealth
social status of one's parents. If they are well-to-do,
ir child receives advantages of education and training
ch substantially enlarge his range of choice. If they are
r, the child is denied these opportunities [1] and is, for the
st part, condemned to manual or semi-skilled clerical
loyment.

gain, the son of a miner or an agricultural worker finds
ery difficult to escape from his father's occupation, since
e is so little alternative employment in the mining village
ural area. For most women the range of choice is even
e restricted than it is for men. Thus the inequalities
the present system involve great injustice and loss of
dom for the majority of people. The only true freedom
yed by most individuals to-day is the power to grumble
ut their circumstances ; and the wise man will exercise
liberty with discretion even in Great Britain.

apitalist society stands condemned in the eyes of the
alist not only for its injustice but also for its gross in-
iency. The world depression is a glaring manifesta-
of the shortcomings of the existing economic order. We
not call an organisation efficient which permits millions
vorkers and vast productive resources to remain unused.
the charge does not rest solely upon such a spectacular
ikdown. The socialist asserts that inefficiency is the
nal feature of capitalism. It is the essence of the system
it is not subject to any central control and direction. In
ain industries, the growth of large combines has brought
nsive areas of production under unified control. But

It is true that the State does provide facilities for exceptionally
d children of poor parents. And such facilities are increasing :
e are scholarships and grants from local education authorities.
it remains true that the professions, owing to the length of
ing required to qualify for them, are still largely the preserve of
children of the well-to-do.

the system as a whole is not subject to any central co-ordi
tion. The various operations of producers, traders, financi
are knit together by the price system. Movements of pr
serve as an indicator to producers, helping them to de
what things to produce and in what quantities. They
determine how much consumers will buy. On the wh
the guide of price works with considerable success. Bu
is subject to grave defects.

In the first place, producers may fail to interpret the p
indicator correctly. A fall in the price of motor-cars,
example, indicates to the producers that a more exten
and profitable market for motor-cars is available. Bu
does not give any precise suggestion of the actual numbe
additional cars for which a market may be expected. '
result is that the producer is prone to err in two directic
first, in his estimate of the increase in total sales ; secon
in his estimate of the share of this increase which he
secure for himself. Since each manufacturer is apt te
optimistic concerning the quality of his own product and
business acumen, the probability is that each will increase
output to an extent unwarranted by the expansion of
market and that over-production in the industry will en
causing a period of idleness for factories and men.

In the second place, the price indicator itself is not ar
fallible guide. It may be falsified by the operation of m
polistic combines. Or monetary disturbances may c
fluctuations in the general level of prices and in relative pr
with serious reactions upon industry. These faults, fin
their expression in human privation and misery which at t
reach an appalling scale, are inseparable, in the opinion o'
socialist, from an economic system which, like capitalis
essentially unco-ordinated and unplanned. The only
remedy, he believes, is to establish an organisation from w
the element of chance has been banished ; one in which
duction, consumption, investment, all economic activitie
fact, are brought within the framework of a grand econ
plan.

By this means alone, the socialist thinks, can we remov
great material and human wastes of the present system, and
the productive forces of mankind, whose vast potentialitie
are only now beginning to realise. The introduction of
a system of social planning would also make possible
abolition of the injustices of the present order. From t

e victim of blind economic forces over which he has no con-
rol, the individual would become a participator in the opera-
ion and guidance of a social plan and a sharer in its more
avish fruits.

ACHIEVING THE IDEAL BY PEACEFUL MEANS

THUS far, practically all socialists are agreed. Differences
of opinion exist, of course, concerning the precise con-
ent of the plan and its ultimate destination. But there is
unanimity on the need for the substitution of plan for chaos.
Concerning the methods by which the goal of social planning
s to be reached there is acute controversy. Probably the
majority of socialists hope to secure their end by peaceful
means, by gradual development from existing conditions.
Others, a minority, but a very vigorous one, ridicule the idea
that such a radical transformation of society can be attained
by peaceful methods. They urge the importance of recognis-
ng that the use of force is inevitable and of organising for the
social revolution.

The first group have much in common with the social
reformer. Indeed, their criticism of social reform is directed
not so much against its methods as against its fundamental
aimlessness. They are at one concerning the desirability of
peaceful development. The hopeful line of advance is not to
knock the present structure of society to pieces and then to
rebuild according to some pre-arranged plan. It is rather to
start from the circumstances of to-day and gradually to rebuild them until a planned organisation of the community
emerges. One of the first steps would be to secure control
over the financial machinery of the country. In Great
Britain, the Bank of England and the five big joint-stock banks
would be nationalised, and thus control over the issue of credit
facilities secured. Command over financial resources, thus
gained, would be of immense assistance in initiating the other
elements of the plan. In industry, a start could be made by
establishing social control over certain trades of fundamental
importance. The socialisation of the mining industry, the
iron and steel trades and the railways would provide a very
powerful lever in the extension of planning to other
services.

It is unnecessary to detail the various steps by which socialist
planning could be introduced. It is sufficient to say that
peaceful socialists insist upon the use of none but constitutional

methods in the establishment of their ideal society. Socialis
planning is not merely a matter of thinking out a more satis
factory organisation of industry and society and then trans
ferring the plan from paper to practice. Any scheme must b
run by men and women. If they do not understand the prin
ciples and aims of the plan or if they disagree with them, thei
ignorance and hostility could wreck the whole project. It i
necessary to begin, therefore, by making the average individua
more alive to the need for order in our economic affairs, an
by arousing him to demand change. This process of educa
tion is likely to be a long one ; but it is the only secure one
And it is essentially a peaceful process. Violent revolutio
may seem swifter. But it is much more costly, and far les
certain in its final outcome.

THE COMMUNIST MARCH FROM CONFLICT TO CONFLICT

THE more militant socialists, generally distinguished b
the name communist, are extremely impatient of th
ideas just outlined. They contend that this complacen
belief in the possibility of peaceful progress is based on a pro
found misunderstanding of the true nature and causes o
social change. They themselves rest their theory of soci
development on the Marxian dialectic. Put in its simple
form, this is a theory which explains social progress in tern
of conflict. They conceive the whole of the universe as bein
in an unceasing condition of change, of development from on
stage to another. The force which produces this change an
which determines its direction is conflict. Every thing an
every creature is in a state of perpetual conflict with i
opposite : cold wars against heat, riches against povert
This contradiction or opposition eventually produces a ne
condition of things, a new synthesis, by which the conflict
resolved. The process of conflict does not cease at each ne
stage, but begins again, although its terms have been change
    The progress of communism is envisaged by the Marxia
and the follower of Lenin as a movement towards a highe
stage of communism that can be attained only after wor
revolution and the complete extinction of classes. The fir
objective of the communist, they hold, should be the contr
of means of production, and at first the state machinery wou
be taken over by the representatives of the workers. The
would eventually be a classless society, and the phase of th

Dictatorship of the Proletariat would be over. The "conflicts" that would succeed this state are not specified.

Karl Marx (1818–83) did not originate this line of thought, but borrowed it from the German philosopher, Hegel. Marx's contribution was to apply the dialectical process to social development. In his view it was possible to explain the transition of society from one stage of culture to another in terms of social conflict and in terms of nothing else. Social change is not a mystical process, the result of the incalculable appearance of "great men." It is something purely material, the product of the contradictions which exist within society itself. The fundamentally important human activity, upon which all others depend, is that of getting a livelihood, of production. Each stage of human culture has its appropriate means and methods of production, or economic organisation. The means of production of each age will determine the social structure of that age, its customs, laws, morality, etc. As new means of production are developed, new forms of social structure will develop also, more adapted than the old to the changed economic system. This must be so. The laws which are appropriate to an agricultural society would not be serviceable in an industrial community, and the morality of a primitive group of hunters would be inconvenient in a large modern nation. Thus changes in the means and methods of production are the driving force of social change.

There still remains the question : How do changes in economic organisation bring about an alteration in social structure ? The answer is to be found in the class struggle. Each stage of economic development produces its own arrangement of social classes, adapted to the existing organisation of production. In the agricultural stage one sees a few large landowners and a mass of peasants. In the industrial stage, the essential division is between the comparatively small number of capitalists, who own and control the means of production, and the millions of propertyless wage workers. Between these social classes conflict is inevitable, and out of the conflict new social groupings and new ways of life develop. Here is the key to social change. The whole of history is the story of social struggles. Even the uprising of the Israelites against their Egyptian taskmasters is explained this way.

REVOLUTION : THE COMMUNIST KEY TO A NEW SOCIAL ORDER

APPLYING this theory of social development to the problem of guiding future social change, the communist conclude that only by violent revolution can the introduction o a socialist state be secured. It follows from the fact tha society is divided into classes corresponding to the economi organisation of the time, and that the dominant class wil secure social control. They will dominate the government and through it control the police and armed forces of th community. The state is in reality nothing more than weapon of class dictatorship. It is true that in many moderi nations the forms of political democracy have been intro duced. But this is only a subtle device for disarming dis content. For, in practice, most of those who are electe represent the interests of the ruling class ; and those who d not are impotent. Changes in the political labels of goverr ments do not amount to anything. All governments are alik and all capitalistic, says the communist.

In these circumstances it is crass stupidity to expect sut stantial social improvement to take place peacefully. Sop will be handed out occasionally in order to keep the peopl quiet. But the ruling class is hardly likely to decree its ow spoliation. The workers must organise, use the injustices c the present system to increase discontent, and ultimatel seize power by force. In the process, bloodshed and destru tion will probably occur. But that is an unfortunate necessit which must be faced. New worlds are not born witho pangs. Having gained power, the workers must not on take away the privileges of the existing ruling class ; the must sweep away all the forms of democracy. Democrac implies the right of all to a voice in determining the polic of the government. But members of the old privileged cla must have no part in the creation of the new society. Durir the transition from the old order to the new, therefore, rigid dictatorship of the proletariat must rule. This dictato ship will re-model society, eliminating the old injustices ar inefficiences of capitalism, and prepare the way for the intr duction of the ideal classless state.

WHERE SOCIALISM DIFFERS FROM COMMUNISM

APPLYING these ideas to the conditions of the present da the communist asserts that capitalism in its old form the last ditch. Its wastes and injustices have grown to an tolerable degree, and class hostilities have nearly reached eaking-point. This does not imply that capitalism is effete, d that it is merely a matter of waiting until the system llapses under its own rottenness. Rather than see a comete disappearance of their privileges and possessions, the opertied class will support and organise movements which ll sidetrack the discontent of the workers.

The propertied class may have to make concessions. It at least there will be a prospect of retaining some of eir present wealth and power. To the communist, the scist movements of the post-War world are an expression this latest stage of capitalism. Their grandiose proammes of national regeneration, their appeals to patriotism d racial fervour, and their lavish promises of prosperity e merely the cloak under cover of which the " old gang " e consolidating their position. Mussolini, it is said, a socialist who was bought by the enemy ; Hitler is in e pocket of the big German industrialists. Far from ing a movement with a new philosophy, fascism is only e latest expression of the old antagonism. But it makes e nature of the conflict more clear. Fascism was established violence and can only be overthrown by violence. In the ne way, violent methods are necessary for the overthrow capitalism.

Thus among those who seek an improvement in the ganisation of society and a more wide dispersion of the hes which our modern productive forces could afford, ere is grave difference of opinion concerning the path ng which these goals should be sought. But in one respect y are all agreed. The social reformer is content to take w and cautious steps. But he looks to the time when a re ordered and equitable system of industry will be ablished. The constitutional socialist differs from this int of view largely in matters of degree. He would desire ifter change and a programme of social reconstruction ided by a carefully thought-out policy. The communist's al aim is very similar to that of the socialist, but his methods re ruthless and direct. All of them, however, have as their ject the introduction of a planned order of society, one in ich the decisions that are now left to the operation of the ce system shall be brought under deliberate central direc-n. It is necessary, therefore, for us to examine the nature

and problems of the planned society which is the comm
goal of such diverse groups.

LIMITING INITIATIVE FOR THE COMMON GOOD : PLANNING

IT should be realised, in the first place, that not all th
who desire an extension of the principle of planning ag
on the meaning of the term. Some envisage merely a par
reconstruction of the existing system, one which wor
remove some of the more obvious defects but which wor
leave the general character of the system unchanged. Oth
contemplate a root and branch destruction of the old or
and the building of an entirely new structure. Sir Ba
Blackett may be taken as representative of the first sche
In his book, *Planned Money*, he defined planning as " a nec
sary corrective of the major wastes and frustrations aris
from the unregulated impact of one economic activity up
another ; or again as the conscious and deliberate provis
by human forethought of means for regulating production
relation to demand." These definitions bring out the cen
element of all schemes of planning, which is that the econo
activities of human beings shall not be controlled solely
the operation of economic forces but shall be brought un
conscious regulation. It is further pointed out that any p
should be nation-wide in its scope. Any smaller unit wo
be inadequate, while a larger one would be impractical
International planning may be a dream of the future ;
it is not an immediate possibility.

Sir Basil Blackett then made it clear that his conception
planning was narrower than that of Soviet Russia. " In Gr
Britain, planning must leave the consumer's choice free.
will leave prices to be determined by demand and will
seek to regulate the relative prices of particular commoditie
He also expressly dissociated planning from socialis
" Planning as here conceived is a policy poles asunder fr
state socialism with nationalised industries, nationalised la
a state medical service, and a thorough-going regimentat
of every phase of the citizen's life. Planning has no de
to enshrine equalitarian doctrines or to eliminate from busir
the motive of personal reward." We should have, not a v
development of government control over industry, bu
series of " functional bodies covering all the major econo
activities of the nation, and the devolution to these bodies
the government of powers, responsibilities, and duties

ich present political and economic machinery provides
ner inadequately or not at all." These extracts make it
in that planning, as here defined, does not imply a radical
nsformation of society but merely the removal of some of
more glaring illogicalities and wastes of the present day.
e most important innovation contemplated is the intro-
ction of new methods of monetary control.

WHAT THE RUSSIAN PLAN MEANS TO THE CITIZEN

R BASIL BLACKETT'S ideas are in striking contrast to those
which have found expression in Soviet Russia. There an
empt has been made to formulate a plan which shall guide
activities and development of the whole social and indus-
ıl organisation. The Central Planning Commission, acting
the information received from factories and large industrial
ts, prepares a programme of industrial development. This
gramme lays down what goods shall be produced and in
at quantities, and fixes the prices at which they shall be
d. The prices are not determined by the same considera-
ns which operate in a capitalist community. Subsidies,
example, may be granted to enterprises which are deemed
be of exceptional importance. The main purpose of
cing seems to be that of serving as a means of estimating
efficiency of each unit.

The planning of production is supplemented by strict
trol over the distribution of incomes and consumption.
e principle of equal incomes has not yet been adopted in
ssia, although it is regarded by many as the ultimate ideal.
t the inequalities of income are very much less than those
be found elsewhere. Even those inequalities which exist
minimised by the charging of differential prices. There
n operation a system of rationing by cards which permits
ividuals to buy stated quantities of goods at fixed prices
m the co-operative and state shops. Additional supplies
only be bought in the open market at very much enhanced
ces.

The essential difference between planning as conceived by
Basil Blackett and as applied in Russia is that, whereas
former would have limited individual freedom and initia-
e as little as possible, in the latter there is no place for
edom of enterprise. The industrial system of Russia is
huge state concern. The central government owns the
tories and banks and controls practically the whole of the

trade of the community. It is the sole employer of labor and it regulates the people's consumption of goods. N economic activity of any moment can take place in Russ without the authority of the state. If planning meant Sir Basil " a process of gradual development," in Russia means working to an elaborate blue-print.

These, then, are the aspirants to the succession of *laisse. faire*. What should be our choice ? The decision must I made. It is abundantly clear that to rely upon the unregulate clash of economic interests and forces involves the persisten of existing inequalities and material loss. Should we the choose the Russian method of complete dictatorial contro or the less extreme method of trying to develop a plan whi is reconcilable with the retention of the old traditions individual liberty ? No final decision can be given he This is a matter which each individual must decide for hir self after an examination of the alternatives. Some general r marks on the possibilities of planning may be offered, howev

A FIVE-YEAR PLAN IN ENGLAND : HOW WOULD IT WORK ?

IT is frequently stated that a rigid planning scheme like t Russian is unnecessary in an advanced industrial nati such as Great Britain or France. Pre-War Russia was ov whelmingly agricultural. Now, thorough-going socialis principles cannot readily be grafted on to an agrarian co munity. The conservatism and individualism of farmers a peasants would present an almost insuperable obstac Moreover, the wealth and power of an agricultural state bound to be limited in the modern industrialised wor Thus it was necessary, both for the consolidation of t revolution and for the increase of Russia's might, to ind trialise. The Plan represents an attempt to achieve t object within the shortest possible time. Most West nations, on the other hand, already possess a complete a reasonably efficient industrial structure. There is not, the fore, the same need to impose stringent sacrifices and limi tions upon the people. Planning, in these cases, may star a later stage and concern itself, not so much with creating industrial equipment, as with introducing that measure conscious control which will secure to the people at larg completer enjoyment of the fruits of industry and a gre degree of liberty of action than they have hitherto possess

This measure of control may be highly desirable. T

ransference of workers under a deliberate plan may be a
much less painful process than the resort to unemployment
nd wage cuts. But it obviously involves further restrictions
n the nominal liberty of action of the individual. It is quite
ntrue to suggest that planning is possible without some check
pon the freedom of the consumer, the worker, and the in-
estor. Unless individuals can be compelled to adapt them-
elves to the requirements of the plan, it ceases to be a plan
t all. We must decide, therefore, whether we prefer the
berty which an unco-ordinated system offers, with all its
mplications of poverty, unemployment, and waste, or would
hoose the restrictions of a planned organisation, in the hope
that we should reap compensating benefits.

A further problem of planning is less capable of satisfactory
ecision. As has been explained earlier in this section, the
ate at which new inventions are introduced varies consider-
bly from one period to another. During the post-War period,
he rate of invention has been high, and there seems no reason
o believe that it is likely to slacken in the near future. Indeed,
cientific advance and discovery are promised in even more
oundant measure. Now the application of any new invention
nvolves some alteration in the methods and organisation of
roduction, some inventions calling for considerable change
n industrial processes. It also involves some change in the
olume or quality of the output, otherwise the invention would
ot be adopted.

THE PROBLEM OF WHAT TO PLAN FOR

N a planned economy, therefore, the introduction of a new
invention will alter the terms of the plan. The adoption
f a labour-saving device, for example, will mean either a
eduction in the number of workers originally allotted to this
articular process or an increase in output beyond the sched-
ed limit. In either event the plan will be upset. In some
ases, the effect will be so small as to be negligible. But one
n conceive of innovations which would revolutionise
ndustrial processes and organisation in a comparatively short
ace of time. The spread of the petrol engine in the post-
'ar years is a case in point. It called forth new industries—
otor manufacture and repairs, garages and road building;
nd severely injured old ones—mining and rail transport.
What should be the attitude of a planning commission
wards the adoption of some such revolutionary change ? If

they do not introduce it, they will be guilty of retarding industrial progress and of depriving the community of the benefit of more goods and services or of increased leisure. If they do introduce it, they destroy their original plan. In other words, either the plan is adhered to in its entirety which means static industrial conditions, or else perpetual change converts the plan into an aspiration which is never realised. The problem has here been outlined in a very clear-cut form : but it is apparent that it would present serious difficulty to any planning authority.

Another problem of planning is, to what end should the plan be directed ? An industrial plan is not an end in itself. It is merely the means to some further end. What should this end be ? In Russia, the decision has been comparatively simple. It was deemed necessary to concentrate first upon industrialisation, and this provided a clear goal towards which the plan could be directed. The matter is much more complicated in Western nations, however, where a reasonably complete industrial equipment already exists (and will become increasingly difficult for Russia as the present scheme materialise). Here the element of choice enters. Should the plan aim at an increase in the volume of goods available for consumption, or should it seek an increase of leisure at some sacrifice of other satisfactions ? If the first aim is chosen, there is still the problem of deciding which goods shall be produced in greater abundance. One can readily perceive that these are decisions which would cause the planning authority considerable difficulty. And it is certain that whatever they might be, they would cause widespread dissatisfaction.

SOME BOOKS ON OUR SOCIAL PROBLEMS

THIS is an age of specialisation, and no one man can arrogate to himself the many spheres to which a general overhaul must extend. Realising this, President Roosevelt created his Brain Trust. There are economists in England to-day who might put our financial affairs in a healthier condition than they are now, were they given a free hand and could they co-operate. The same could be said of social affairs.

Prominent among experts is G. D. H. Cole, who has written a number of books about possibilities of economic olitical, and social reform. His *Intelligent Man's Review of urope To-day* (Gollancz) covers a wide field and raises many iteresting points, and contains, too, a useful bibliography.

To take the issues one by one, the crying evil of our times, nemployment, is treated in Davison's *The Unemployed* ongmans) and Bowley and Hogg's *Has Poverty Diminished?* . S. King). A more detailed discussion of the problem is ven in Beveridge's *Unemployment* (Longmans). Other of .e issues raised in the foregoing article are dealt with more lly in *The New Industrial Revolution* (Gollancz), by Meakin, he *Problem of Industrial Relations*, by Clay (Macmillan), and Clark's *The National Income* (Macmillan). Theories of construction are to be found in Robertson's *The Control of dustry* (Cambridge Economic Handbooks, vol. iv.), in ootton's *Plan or No Plan?* (a brilliant comparison of pitalism with the Russian model), and in a symposium lume by various authors published by Macmillan, *A ve-Year Plan in England : What would it be?* Webb's *The ecay of Capitalist Civilisation* (Allen and Unwin) is a search-g criticism of the present order, while Blackett's *Planned oney* (Constable) provides constructive suggestions as well criticism. Laski, in *Communism* (Home University Library, hornton Butterworth Limited), and Macmurray in *Philo-hy of Communism* (Faber and Faber) treat of Communist eory, while Laski's *Democracy in Crisis* (Allen and Unwin) amines the possibilities of securing reconstruction without e resort to violence.

CONCLUSION: WHITHER HUMANITY

by R. J. WOODWARD, M.A.(Oxon)

THOSE who have read this book have done so becaus
they are interested in the world in which they liv
because they find the spectacle of the human dram
an absorbing one. This interest, however, cannot be merel
academic, for the modern world described and analysed in th
second part of this book is one in which we ourselves have t
live, to play a part, to suffer or rejoice. We know only too we
that when mankind makes a mistake or takes the wrong pat
that we shall feel the consequences, and we are all therefor
passionately concerned that the human race shall master th
problems that beset it ; and this concern is not only for ou
selves, but for posterity, for our children and our children
children. We are not merely concerned with the questio
Where stands the world to-day ? We want to know what t
future holds in store for it, and what we can deduce from o
study of the trend of the forces which make up the moder
world.

MODERN MAN : THE HEIR OF ALL THE AGES

As he stands on the uttermost verge of time, Western Ma
appears to us as the heir to the past—to all its legacy, bo
of good things and evil. His upright posture and his comma
of fire and tools he owes to those unknown and great
innovators who lived in the childhood of the race. His spee
and writing have filtered down from the distant past. T
philosophy and culture of the Greeks ; the empire and wid
spread justice of Rome ; the teachings of Christianity and t
august Church it bequeathed to the world ; feudalism, wi
all its existing social vestiges ; the intellectual re-awakeni
of the Renaissance and the religious upheaval of the Refo
mation ; the Europeanisation of the world, beginning in t
sixteenth century ; industrialism ; the political and soc
ideals of the last hundred years ; these are the forces that ha
made him what he is, and that are working in him and abc
him, however obscure, simple-minded or poor, howev
powerful, intellectual or wealthy he may be.

Our attention has to be concentrated on Western Man, r

erely because we are interested in him more than in the rest
mankind and can understand him better, but because his
vilisation is, for better or for worse, the dominant civilisation
the world to-day. It has contacts with others, but, ever
ice the Turks—the last wave of the Eastern invaders—
:re rolled back from Vienna late in the seventeenth century,
actically all of its contacts have been either physical or
:ellectual conquests, although it is by no means certain that
is generalisation will always continue to hold true in the
:ure. The East may simply hit back at the West in the
rely physical sense; it may, on the other hand, swallow
, digest and make part of itself all that the West has given it
forced upon it. The relations of the East and West, indeed,
ord one of the great problems of the future; and not the
st interesting thing about Russia to-day is that it extends
m the bounds of the culture of the West to those of the
lture of the East. At present, Russia belongs to neither of
ese worlds. Will it ever do so? Will it ever provide a
idge of thought, as it does now a transcontinental railway,
tween the two?

Russia is a centre of interest, too, as the scene of the com-
nist experiment about which civilised opinion is still at
riance. This question of communism or capitalism is
other of the major issues with which Western Man is
nfronted to-day. Communists and socialists differ in their
ilosophical background and in the means by which they
pe to seek the Promised Land rather than in their hopes of
at that land will be like. Pragmatically, it seems possible
at the difference between communism and the state-con-
lled capitalism of the future, which seems to be well on its
y, will not be much greater.

WILL MAN LIVE IN AN ANT-LIKE SOCIETY?

VHATEVER may happen ultimately, the tendency of society
seems to be in the direction of an ant-like existence for
: mass of humanity—one in which there will be very little of
it jollity and rich extravagance of character and behaviour
ich the British associate with the comic creations of their
at writers, Chaucer, Shakespeare, Dickens. If the society
the future is to escape monotony and sterility it will have to
ange for the wise distribution of leisure, that all-important
-product of modern industrialism. The machine is rapidly
ing man from the necessity of hard work, but it is also

robbing him of his craftsmanship. It is producing wealth
unexampled profusion, but reducing the numbers of consume
by throwing men out of work. Leisure, which is a boon wh
rightly distributed throughout the community, becomes
curse when, accompanied by privation, it is forced upon sor
sections of it. These are some of the paradoxes before t
world to-day, and there is little sign at present of th
solution, especially as international co-operation, an essent
preliminary, seems far distant.

A move has been made in France to reduce hours witho
lowering wages, but it remains to be seen whether oth
nations will follow suit. In the matter of tariffs and tra
restrictions an impasse exists and seems more likely to co
tinue. As long as it does so, however, " recovery " ca
never be a world-wide reality. Unless some cataclys
upsets prophecy, it seems possible that the nations w
gradually feel their way towards the creation of groups
states with common economic interests, linked up by mea:
of trade agreements. Another great war would be such
cataclysm ; and it must remain a terrifying possibility
view of the present state of international non-co-operatio
uneasiness, and tension. It is not surprising if, in the atm
sphere of an international skin-game, the players keep the
guns within reach. Armaments are increasing and wa
talk is in the air. The struggle between pacifist and militar:
grows sharper, and the latter seems to be winning.

On the surface, the problems of the modern world wou
appear to be mainly economic ; actually, however, it wou
be true to say that, although they are generally economic
form, they are nevertheless all aspects of one fundamen
question—how to attain here on earth the Good Life of whi
Aristotle speaks. Mankind to-day is beset with grave dange
These can be overcome, and will only be overcome, if
resolve that man, whether fallen from before the throne
God, or risen from the slime of one of His outer courts, sh
not be thrall to a machine, shall not be bondsman to a desp
shall not blunder into self-destruction. We may be su
that, even if our difficulties are great, they may be surmount
by clear thinking, stout hearts, and firm wills.

INDEX AND PRONOUNCING GLOSSARY

Compiled by L. M. MONT-CLAR

How to use this index.—In order to facilitate immediate refer-
e to the principal entry on a particular subject, the page number
this entry is set in italics, thus: *258*. Subsidiary references to
subject which occur elsewhere in the book are indicated by
nerals in roman type, thus: 387. References to illustrations
indicated by numerals in roman type surrounded by square
ckets, thus: [156]. Cross references given in the index refer
y to the index pages.

The pronouncing glossary.—Where the pronunciation of
per names and technical terms is not immediately understood
n the spelling, or where the spelling may be misleading, a separate
nunciation is given after the first index entry. In simple cases a
t may be considered sufficient; in all doubtful cases a complete
netic re-spelling is given. The word is broken into syllables
t is spoken and an accent mark (′) follows the syllable on which
stress is placed. The notation used for the phonetic re-spelling
s follows:

ā	*mate*	a	*pat*	ė	*there*	th	*thin*
ē	*mete*	e	*pet*	å	*father*	TH	*thine*
ī	*mite*	i	*pit*	ẹ	*her*	zh	*leisure*
ō	*mote*	o	*pot*	aw	*awl*	ch	*church*
ū	*mute*	u	*nut*	oi	*oil*	g	*get*
ōō	*boot*	oo	*foot*	ow	*owl*	j	*jam*

The French nasalised *n* is denoted by italicising the vowel and
nasal concerned, thus: *un*, *bon*, *vin*. The German modified ö
the similar French sounds are denoted by *oe*, the German soft
nd g by *ch*, and the guttural ch (as in Scots " loch ") by CH. The
nch *u* and the German modified *ü* are indicated by ü.